THE BRAGANZAS

DYNASTIES

A series of substantial narrative histories that look at the genesis of dynasties, their dynamics and the derivation of power, demonstrating that history can be seen and reflected through the dynastic process and who or what ruling dynasties believed themselves to be. It seeks to put dynasties under discussion and reflection.

Already published:

The Braganzas: The Rise and Fall of the Ruling Dynasties of Portugal and Brazil, 1640–1910
MALYN NEWITT

Forthcoming:

The Borjigids: The Dynasty of Chinggis Khan
TIMOTHY MAY

The Mauryan Dynasty and Ashoka the Great
COLLEEN TAYLOR SEN

THE BRAGANZAS

The Rise and Fall of the Ruling Dynasties of Portugal and Brazil, 1640–1910

MALYN NEWITT

REAKTION BOOKS

Published by
Reaktion Books Ltd
Unit 32, Waterside
44–48 Wharf Road
London N1 7UX, UK

www.reaktionbooks.co.uk

First published 2019
Copyright © Malyn Newitt 2019

Printed and bound in China by 1010 Printing International Ltd

A catalogue record for this book is available from the British Library

ISBN 978 1 78914 125 2

Contents

Preface

Writing the history of a dynasty presents an unavoidable dilemma – how to write about kings, emperors and queens without writing a history of the countries where they reigned. The choices that have had to be made in order to make this book manageable will be only too obvious. The key factors of the history of Portugal and Brazil, especially the economic and social developments, if not exactly ignored, have been given only a supporting role. If this book is largely about royal families, this does not mean that I consider them to have been the principal movers of history. In fact, it is only too obvious that monarchs like D. João VI and D. Maria II were never in control of events and had to confine their activities to trying to stay afloat in very stormy political waters.

There have been very few books in English about members of the Portuguese Braganza dynasty, the exception being Catarina of Braganza who has been, and continues to be, the subject of numerous biographies and fictional writing. These apart, Francis Gribble's *The Royal House of Portugal* (1915) has some witty turns of phrase but is now largely forgotten. Marcus Cheke's *Carlota Joaquina, Queen of Portugal* (1947) provides a detailed account not only of the queen but of the whole reign of her husband D. João VI. It is very readable, but long out of print. More recently there is only Jenifer Roberts's excellent *The Madness of Queen Maria* (2009). Malcolm Howe's *The Braganza Story* (1999), published by the British Historical Society of Portugal, is a somewhat eccentric book, full of fascinating information and particularly notable for the author's collection of photographs of the Braganzas, a large number of which are reproduced in the book. The emperors of Brazil have been better served. There are two recent biographies of D. Pedro I:

Sergio Correa da Costa's *Every Inch a King* (1950) has, perhaps, been superseded by Neill Macaulay, *Dom Pedro: The Struggle for Liberty in Brazil and Portugal, 1798–1834* (1986). There are two outstanding biographies of D. Pedro II: Lilia Moritz Schwarcz's *The Emperor's Beard* (1999), translated from the Portuguese, and Roderick Barman's *Citizen Emperor: Pedro II and the Making of Brazil, 1825–9* (1999) and his companion study of the Princess Imperial, *Princess Isabel of Brazil* (2002).

Writing about royal families, their marriages and networks of family relations can be very confusing. In Portugal the title 'Dom' or 'Dona' (often abbreviated to 'D.') was always used as a prefix to the names of the kings and queens, but this title was also used by noblemen and women and by other people of high rank. However, I have adopted the convention of using the title only for reigning monarchs and I have abbreviated it thus: D. Maria I, D. Pedro II to refer to Queen Dona Maria I and King Dom Pedro II. This, I hope, will make a clear distinction between the monarchs and other people who may have had the same name. I have also used Portuguese versions of names (except in some quotations), so D. José, *not* King Joseph, and Catarina, *not* Catherine. However, it has been decided to use the anglicized 'Braganza' rather than the Portuguese 'Bragança' for the name of the dynasty.

It is a quaint custom in Portugal to give each sovereign a descriptive title: D. Manuel the Fortunate, D. Afonso the Victorious and so on. These popular titles have been included in the list of the monarchs at the start of Chapter Three.

1

The Idea of Monarchy and the Rise and Fall of the Dynastic State

The Braganza dynasty came to the throne of Portugal in 1640 as the result of a *coup d'état* carried out by a small group of minor nobility. There was general acquiescence by the population in the change of dynasty and no serious attempt by the armed forces to oppose the coup. In 1910 the monarchy fell as the result of a *coup d'état* carried out by a small group of republican politicians, generally supported by the population of Lisbon, with most of the armed forces standing by and not intervening. A moralist might conclude that those who rise through a *coup d'état* are fated to fall by a *coup d'état*, an interpretation that seems to fit with an understanding of Portuguese history as being marked by 'the organic mode of thinking in terms of growth and decay', to use Alan Freeland's phrase.[1] The Braganza dynasty reigned in Portugal from 1640 to 1910 (and in Brazil until 1889) and its story is the story of the rise, flowering, turmoil, decline and eventual demise of European monarchy itself. After the events of 1640 it took nearly thirty years before the Braganzas were fully accepted throughout Europe as the legitimate ruling dynasty of Portugal. Throughout the succeeding two centuries the fortunes of the dynasty were inextricably linked to Brazil, which provided the wealth that ensured Portugal's survival as an independent state and its continued existence during the French revolutionary era. In the nineteenth century the Braganzas, in both Portugal and Brazil, tried to reinvent themselves as bourgeois constitutional monarchs, but in the end they failed and were deposed by republican revolutionaries. This chapter looks at some of the issues that surround the history of the institution of monarchy in Europe and the underlying contradictions that were to lead to its failure.

The monarchical tradition weaves together two distinct and often conflicting strands of thought and imagination. On the one hand, there is the idea of the warrior king who is strong enough to defend his kingdom, defeat his enemies and provide security for his subjects. On the other is the belief that the king's authority is ordained by God and that he rules in order to fulfil God's purposes. Quite early in human history it was believed that rulers possessed divine powers received from the gods or were themselves divine beings. These ideas extended authority beyond the exercise of force and protection and provided monarchical power with a supernatural legitimacy. For the ruled, this gave the security of feeling that they were governed by someone able to bring prosperity and supernatural protection. However, it was self-evident that this protection could be provided only by a competent ruler, and from this grew the idea that the welfare of the community depended on the health and strength of the monarch, the concept of the 'divine king' famously described by Fraser. If the king began to fail through impotence, old age or illness, the people as a whole would suffer. In those circumstances it would be legitimate to remove the king and replace him with someone more vigorous and more able to protect the kingdom. According to Lilia Schwarcz in her remarkable study of Brazil's emperors, Emperor D. Pedro II 'mediated these two forces: the political and institutional monarchy on the one hand, and the mythic figure in the popular imagination on the other'.[2]

As kingship developed in western Europe there was always an interplay between the idea that monarchy was somehow an institution through which divine authority was exercised and the assumption that the king needed to be able to perform the functions of a ruler and provide protection, justice and a guarantee for the lives and welfare of his subjects. A king, it was believed, should also hold the balance between competing forces within society. He should be a 'moderating' influence as the idea was developed in the two Braganza monarchies of the nineteenth century. Struggles between different regions or elite factions, or even between the elites and the mass of the people, could, in theory, be mediated by the king, while loyalty to the throne could provide a bond, countering forces that were otherwise centrifugal and might lead to disintegration and chaos. Nowhere was this idea of kingship better illustrated than in the remarkable career of Emperor Pedro II in Brazil.

It was with these considerations in mind that the Aristotelian concept of 'the just king' gained acceptance. The dangers of tyranny and oligarchy, when the state was captured by narrow sectional interests, were best avoided through rule by a king whose legitimacy was manifest through acting justly and enforcing the law. In this formulation the 'law' was the absolute authority and the king, to some extent, its servant. The law was enshrined in legal codes, like the Justinian Code or, in Portugal, the Manueline Code, which was elaborated in the early sixteenth century. It was not accepted that the king could change the law at will. This was what tyrants did.[3]

In early modern Europe the authority of the monarch was severely circumscribed by his need to respect the interests of the most powerful noble dynasties which often became alternative centres of influence and patronage.

> Rather than being a centralised institution in which power 'radiated' from the person of the prince . . . influence and, in some cases, formal authority as well, emanated at court from a variety of subsidiary sources: entrenched office-holders, noble magnates, senior prelates, major army commanders . . . the carapace of autocracy concealed a diversity of partly complementary, partly competing, 'foyers of power'.[4]

The hereditary principle was supposed to give monarchy some stability, but always came with the risk that a weak or incompetent heir or a minor might succeed. Occasionally a situation presented itself where a number of possible heirs disputed the Crown and the normal rules of succession seemed difficult to apply. Such was the situation in Portugal in 1580 on the death of Cardinal Henrique, the last king of the Avis dynasty. Moreover, the problem of females succeeding to power was never fully resolved and attempts automatically to exclude women did not always succeed when confronted by the logic of the hereditary principle.

The hereditary principle contained within it other dangers. In societies, for instance in Africa, where multiple marriages were the norm, the king could use marriage as a way of binding different sections of society to the Crown, but this made the succession difficult to determine as the children of different wives competed for the prize. In Christian Europe, monogamy made it difficult for the king to bond in this way with the society over which he ruled. A monogamous royal marriage with a subject would be highly divisive and could upset the balance within society. As a result, royal marriages were usually contracted with the royalty of other states, a practice which had the added purpose of cementing alliances and providing additional security against external threats. In Portugal, for example, the marriage in 1386 of D. João I to Philippa of Lancaster, granddaughter of Edward III of England, was an essential element in strengthening the foundations of the famous Anglo-Portuguese alliance.

One way of preserving the inheritance of a dynasty, which might be lost through an injudicious marriage, was for kings to marry a close relative within their own families. In Europe first cousin marriages were a frequent occurrence and the marriages of uncles to nieces or nephews to aunts were also commonplace, especially in the Portuguese and Spanish royal families. An anthropologist, taking the long view, might see in this practice a survival of the incestuous brother to sister marriages of pharaonic royalty, a practice also known in parts of sub-Saharan Africa.

One bizarre consequence of the tradition of marrying royalty from other countries was that royal families were often foreigners in the countries they ruled. Sometimes they could not even speak the language, like George I of Britain who could not speak any English. The Braganza dynasty in Portugal was no exception. Only one of the Braganzas married someone who was Portuguese: D. Maria I married her uncle D. Pedro III. Marriages were made either with Spanish or with German princesses (except for D. Pedro II, whose first marriage was with a French princess, and D. Carlos, who also married a French princess). After D. João VI most of the Portuguese Braganzas married Germans and by the time the monarchy came to an end the royal family had become unmistakably blonde-haired and Teutonic.

The idea that kingship was hereditary, and that its mystical as well as its secular authority was passed down within a single family, led to the emergence of royal dynasties. Marriages between members of these dynastic families created an intricate pattern of family ties that made the ruling houses of Europe nodes in a vast network that stretched across western and even, to some extent, eastern Europe. Each dynastic marriage was the result of often prolonged negotiations and in this world of dynastic diplomacy princesses as well as princes became a highly marketable commodity. Almost as much care was taken over their marriages as over those of the rulers themselves and each marriage constituted a treaty aimed at securing friendship, peace and cooperation.

For most of the ruling families of Europe, the interests of the dynasty stood high in their order of priorities. There was an endless quest to extend the power and prestige of the dynasty through magnificent dowries, new inheritances, the acquisition of new lands. A consequence, not always intended, was the creation of large dynastic states whose parts might have little cultural or even geographical affinity. One can immediately think of the Angevin 'empire' of the twelfth century or the Habsburg empire of Charles V in the sixteenth. The dynastic state was multi-lingual and multi-ethnic, held together through allegiance to the sovereign, not by any idea of national identity. The renown and power of the dynasty was often seen as separate from the interests of the nation or the state and was deemed to take precedence over it. The gradual emergence of the Habsburg and Hohenzollern dynasties, with hereditary lands scattered throughout Germany and the rest of Europe, is the clearest example. By the eighteenth century it was becoming increasingly common for territories where a dynastic title was held to be bargained, and transferred from one ruling house to another, almost in the same way that maritime powers bargained, swapped and traded colonial territories. Although the Peace of Westphalia in 1648 is supposed to have established the modern world order of sovereign nation states, it took a long time for this idea to influence the dynastic pre-occupations of Habsburgs and Bourbons in Italy and the Netherlands, let alone the ambitions and behaviour of the German princes within the empire.

The common interests of the dynasty remained strong even when the family split into different branches, as occurred with the Habsburgs in the sixteenth, the Bourbons in the eighteenth and the Braganzas in the nineteenth centuries. The family ties between the different branches of the Habsburg family were a central factor in European politics until the Habsburg dynasty in Spain died out at the end of the seventeenth century, while the 'family compacts' that linked the various branches of the Bourbon dynasty, which ruled in Spain and Naples as well as France, dominated eighteenth-century politics.

Throughout the nineteenth century the web being woven by dynastic marriages became ever more intricate. If Queen Victoria's daughters tied most of the royal families of Europe more or less closely to the old matriarch, in other dynasties sons could play a similar role and the princes of the Saxe-Coburg and the Orléans families provided husbands for European royalty and added their interests to the dynastic web. However, the growing power of the militarized nation state gradually put an end to the old idea of a multinational dynastic state and with it to the old dance of dynastic diplomacy.

Hereditary kingship was not universal in Europe. Poland–Lithuania had an elective monarchy, as did the Holy Roman Empire, and in other states there were vestiges of the elective, or at any rate the selective, principle. In Portugal, for example, the right to succeed to the throne needed the consent of the Cortes and a new king was formally acclaimed at a ceremony with reciprocal oath-taking, a practice that contained within it vestiges of the idea of elective kingship and a social contract. Nor was monarchy itself universally adopted. Venice, until the seventeenth century one of the great powers of Europe, was a republic, not very democratic to be sure, but definitely not a hereditary monarchy, and the fifteenth century saw the emergence of the Swiss Confederation, also briefly a European power of consequence, and one that was firmly republican and which in some cantons retained remnants of primitive direct democracy. Most of the Imperial Cities were also republics, as were provinces like those that broke away in the 1570s to form the United Netherlands. The republican principle was, therefore, well understood and accepted in parts of Europe, though elected heads of state, like the Doge of Venice, the Stadholder of the Netherlands and the Pope, tended to approximate their style of rule to that of neighbouring monarchies.

By the sixteenth century two ideas predominated: that kingship was ordained by God and was passed through hereditary succession, and that the king was bound to rule according to the law and to provide security and protection for the people. Did this mean, however, that the king who ruled by divine right was above the law? Or did it mean that even divinely sanctioned rulers could be replaced if their rule was not deemed just? What was the origin of the state, philosophers had begun to ask. Did the state originate with the family and the natural authority of parents over children, or was it a defensive mechanism with individuals pooling their freedoms for the sake of security and the cooperation needed for survival? If the latter, could the authority freely given by the people be just as freely reclaimed? If so, wherein lay the divine element in the royal authority? Here lay contradictions and the interplay of these ideas formed the tapestry of much of European history. When they came into conflict, as they did with increasing frequency, the result could be profoundly disruptive.

There were other contradictions as well. The idea that monarchs in some way embodied the national identity gradually took hold but had to coexist with the idea that monarchy transcended mere national differences and constituted the unifying principle in multinational states like those of the Habsburgs or Great Britain, with its three kingdoms and three separate parliaments, or even Portugal where the royal title, King of Portugal and the Algarves, kept alive the fiction that Portugal was made up of more than one kingdom.

Moreover, not far below the surface of European culture lay the idea that monarchy was an inherently absurd and ultimately unjust institution. In the early seventeenth century the follies and waste of rulers faced mounting criticism and these perceptions were sometimes articulated as a strain of republicanism. In France, the authority of the Crown was profoundly challenged when the Protestant Henry of Navarre succeeded to the throne of a Catholic kingdom. In Bohemia in 1618 the Protestant nobility tried to install their own king rather than follow the strict line of hereditary succession and in England the Civil War led to the declaration of a republic in 1649, though one that soon assumed a curious semi-monarchical form. In Portugal, the idea of declaring a republic, as an alternative to continued rule from Madrid, was apparently seriously discussed. So, when the duke of Braganza was acclaimed as king of Portugal in 1640, it was at a time when the whole idea of monarchy was in a state of flux.

To this crisis of authority, the ruling dynasties of Europe responded with a strong reassertion of absolute power and divine authority. As the critique of monarchy and traditional authority increased, so the counter-claims of royal absolutism became ever more extreme. The more hereditary right was criticized, the more emphatically it was defended. However, for absolutism to be a reality the ruling dynasties had to have the financial and bureaucratic resources, as well as the military capacity, to enforce the king's will in all parts of the kingdom and over all elements in society. The military revolution of the seventeenth century gave rise to the standing armies that underpinned absolutism and the ideas of the Cameralists paved the way for an expansion of the state's administrative capacity. In Portugal, however, these changes were slow to take root and the newly installed Braganza dynasty had to struggle to assert its authority. It was not until the discovery of gold in Brazil at the very end of the seventeenth century gifted the Crown with substantial financial resources that the absolutism of the dynasty became established.

The exotic rituals that were observed in royal courts in the seventeenth and eighteenth centuries were not the perpetuation of ancient custom so much as examples of the invention of tradition. The rituals that surrounded the French king in Versailles were largely invented by Louis XIV and, though they were supposed to enhance the dignity of the throne and stifle opposition and dissent, under his successors they became empty ceremonies that merely encouraged the groundswell of criticism of the king and the contempt in which the court was held. As the subterranean swell of opposition to royalty grew, so the absurdities of court ceremonial became ever more divorced from the realities of the everyday life of the people. At the Braganza court in Portugal, for example, no one was allowed to sit in the royal presence and courtiers had to stand or kneel, even when playing cards, though women were sometimes allowed to sit cross-legged on the floor.

The propaganda that supported monarchical absolutism became ever more elaborate. Celebrations of royal births, baptisms, betrothals and marriages became occasions for demonstrating royal power and authority before the public. As Ana Pereira puts it, 'the whole spectacle was supported by a collection of symbols where abounded allusions to the virtues of princes: Fame, Justice, Prudence, Magnanimity, Sovereignty, Love and Truth . . . In a society impregnated with religiosity the spectacle of monarchy employed, to a great extent, the ecclesiastical ceremonial.'[5] These elaborate public displays were designed as a visual representation of royal power in societies where the majority of the population was still illiterate, though they were more often aimed at impressing other rulers and establishing a monarch's place in the wider hierarchy of European royalty. This display found its most extreme expression in the royal palaces themselves. While the constitutional kings of Great Britain were content with the modest and somewhat antiquated quarters of Hampton Court and Kew Palace, the absolute monarchs of continental Europe vied with each other to imitate and eventually to outdo Versailles. It was the eighteenth century that saw the strong intellectual challenge to the idea of monarchy, but this was also the century that saw the building of Mafra in Portugal and Caserta in Naples. In Portugal, ancient practices continued whereby a narrow group of noble families received pensions from the Crown, even when they were not performing any public duties, and benefited from the antiquated forms of land tenure – the *morgados*, *prazos* and *capelas* – by which they defined and maintained their status. However, these became ever more removed from the economic realities of the time and from the experience of the population of the country.

The excesses of monarchy, however, were never just propaganda posturing imposed from above, but were to some extent called into being by the people. The strange rituals of the French and British monarchies, whereby those suffering from scrofula could seek relief by being touched by the monarch, represented a longing, even a demand, by the common people for divine intervention in their lives.

Royal courts were bastions of class privilege and places to which those seeking offices, honours and appointments had to come but they were also centres of cultural patronage, as was demonstrated during the reign of D. Manuel 'the Fortunate' in Portugal or in the Habsburg and Bourbon courts of the sixteenth and seventeenth centuries. When the Crown of Portugal passed to the Spanish king in 1580, there was no longer a royal court in Lisbon from which patronage could be dispensed and this, over time, became a source of grievance for the Portuguese and contributed to the cultural barrenness of the period.

While the political philosophers of the eighteenth century openly speculated about the idea of a social contract and a republic without a king, monarchists had to find a response that went beyond merely re-asserting their absolutism. After the 1688 'Glorious Revolution' the British crown had managed to combine monarchical and republican ideas to produce a hybrid system of constitutional monarchy. Elsewhere in Europe, the defenders of monarchical power sought to shore up their authority by modernizing their states and co-opting the interests of classes below the traditional elites. Various systems of service nobility allowed members of the middle classes to invade the preserves of the elite, whose exclusiveness had hitherto been protected by the Crown. Nowhere was this attempt to co-opt middle-class interests more apparent than in the measures taken, in the Habsburg lands and in Portugal, for the emancipation of the Jews.

By the nineteenth century the absurdities of absolute monarchy were only too apparent. The pantomime rituals, performed in the elaborate fancy dress of court costume, became increasingly divorced from real life with the actors seeming ever more like stage characters in drag. The divorce between rational, liberal thought, social progress and the institution of monarchy inexorably widened. Hans Christian Andersen's famous story 'The Emperor's New Clothes', first published in April 1837, was a scarcely disguised commentary on monarchy in the

mid-nineteenth century. Even so, monarchy as an idea and as an institution continually tried to reinvent itself. One device was for kings to
turn themselves into emperors in spite of, or perhaps because of, the
Napoleonic associations. In the nineteenth century the British monarchy refurbished its image with the assumption of imperial splendour in
India. In Germany, the Kaiser tried to become the symbol of a national
unity that had only been achieved by force of arms, and in far-off Brazil
the Braganzas ceased to be kings and became emperors displaying a
bewildering array of invented symbols and traditions, borrowed from
Europe or invented by enthusiastic local artists. For nearly seventy
years the emperors successfully prevented the fragmentation of the vast
territory over which they ruled. Nothing, however, could prevent the
intellectual challenge to the hereditary principle of power that finally
died after the First World War.

The story of any ruling dynasty, therefore, is the story of the
struggle of the monarchical principle not only with the competing forces
within society that ultimately found expression in republicanism, but
with the inherent absurdities and internal contradictions that continually threatened to undermine and weaken the monarchy from within.
As Amy Jenkins wrote in *The Guardian*, 'the whole fantasy of royalty
is a construct, an illusion. A "king" is an invented idea. As invented as
unicorns' – and inevitably, as people grow up, they no longer believe
in unicorns.[6]

2

The Early History of the Portuguese Monarchy

Τhis chapter will look at the two dynasties that came before the Braganzas. The Avis dynasty that reigned in Portugal from 1385 to 1580 witnessed the great era of the discoveries, the founding of the Estado da Índia, the expansion in Morocco and the great flowering of Renaissance culture in Portugal. This dynasty died out in 1580 and was succeeded by the Habsburg dynasty when Portugal was incorporated into the Spanish monarchy between 1580 and 1640. During this period the great expansion of settlement in Brazil began, but the Estado da Índia came under increasing pressure from resurgent Asian states and from attacks by the Dutch and English. With the king far away in Madrid, Portugal was reduced to being little more than a province of the Habsburg monarchy. The Braganzas were to inherit a monarchical culture that had taken root over three centuries and was firmly embedded in a range of institutions, ceremonies and practices. The revolution that brought the new dynasty to the throne did not intend to overthrow or even alter this monarchical tradition, but rather to take possession of it to strengthen the legitimacy of its rule.

During the long centuries of Roman and Visgothic rule the Iberian peninsula had been part of a single state that reflected a self-evident geographical logic. Moreover, the Arab conquests, which began in the early eighth century, also led to the installation of a single Caliphate, which included the lands that later became Portugal. This geographical logic, immediately apparent to anyone glancing at the map of Europe, was never entirely cancelled out by historical events and the idea of the natural unity of the Iberian peoples did not disappear, briefly becoming a reality between 1580 and 1640 and frequently recurring up to the present in the secret correspondence of statesmen and the dynastic ambitions of both Spanish and Portuguese royal houses. If France, Germany and Italy eventually experienced national unification and the benefits of a single central government, it seemed to some to be only logical that the Iberian peoples should follow in their footsteps.

In 1139 Afonso Henriques, a vassal of the king of León, declared himself king in Portugal and, after significant amounts of gold had changed hands, had his title recognized by the Pope in 1143. Although the Portuguese monarchy had its beginning in these events, it took a long time before anything like modern Portugal took shape. Lisbon and the south had to be conquered from the Moors, but even after this was achieved the kingdom remained closely connected to its immediate neighbour. For a long time episcopal jurisdictions spanned the new frontiers, as did the governance of the Military Orders. Moreover, the leading aristocratic families of Portugal held lands across the border and were also vassals of the Castilian kings. Their loyalties were divided.

In 1383, on the death of D. Fernando (r. 1367–83), the legitimate heir to the Portuguese throne was his daughter Beatriz, married to Juan, the king of Castile. Backed by the French king and by a large portion of the Portuguese nobility, Juan tried to enforce his claim, unsuccessfully laying siege to Lisbon in 1384, and in 1385 facing a force consisting of English mercenaries and local Portuguese levies at the battle of Aljubarrota. The destruction of the Franco-Castilian army in the battle enabled a new dynasty to take the Portuguese throne.

The Avis Dynasty

The new king, D. João I (r. 1385–1433), was the illegitimate son of D. Fernando's father, D. Pedro I (r. 1357–67). He was Master of the Military Order of Avis, from which the dynasty derived its name. Only a minority of the nobility supported him and he had to use every means available to him in order to secure the future of his dynasty. His marriage with Philippa of Lancaster, niece of Edward the Black Prince and daughter of John of Gaunt, secured the recognition and alliance of England but at the cost of dragging Portugal further into the diplomatic and military quagmire of the Hundred Years War. D. João employed the services of eminent legal minds who successfully legitimized his claims before the Cortes in 1385 and engaged the brilliant literary talents of Fernão Lopes, and later Gomes Enes de Azurara, as royal chroniclers to record his struggle for the Crown and the glorious achievements of his reign.

D. João's successful expedition to seize the Moroccan port of Ceuta in 1415 proved popular and reignited some of the fervour of the Reconquista, the earlier wars against the Muslims in the Iberian peninsula. It provided employment for the military class that might otherwise have been a disruptive influence, as well as looking after the interests of those whose living was derived from trade, piracy and commerce in northern Africa.

Perhaps D. João's greatest advantage came from the success of his marriage, which produced five princes and a princess. His sons – his heir D. Duarte, Pedro, Henrique, João and Fernando – were endowed with titles, crown lands and positions of authority within the Military Orders. They became a bulwark to the throne and the foundation of a new nobility. Meanwhile Isabel (1397–1471), his daughter, was married to Philip the Good, duke of Burgundy (r. 1419–67), a marriage that was the most obvious sign that the Avis dynasty had 'arrived' on the stage of European royalty. A further successful marriage confirmed the status of the dynasty when, in 1454, Leonor (1434–1467), the eldest daughter of D. João's successor D. Duarte (r. 1433–8), was married to the Holy Roman Emperor, Frederick III (r. 1440–93), a courtship and marriage portrayed by Pinturicchio in a series of paintings in the Piccolomini Library at Siena Cathedral, produced at the height of the Italian Renaissance. Leonor became the mother of the redoubtable Emperor Maximilian (r. 1486–1519). The dynasty that had begun with the apparently hopeless quest of the young bastard Master of Avis was now recognized among Europe's most distinguished royalty.

The kings reflected the growing prestige of the Portuguese crown by adopting ever more elaborate titles. Originally known as King of Portugal and the Algarve, D. Afonso V (r. 1438–80) changed Algarve to Algarves (to include Morocco) and added 'daquem e dalem-mar em África' ('on this side and beyond the sea in Africa'). To this was added 'Lord of Guinea', and after the establishment of the Estado da Índia in 1504 (in effect a new kingdom added to the Crown) the royal title became more elaborate still. To the traditional titles were now added 'lord of the conquest, navigation and commerce of Ethiopia, Arabia, Persia and India'. As these titles suggest, Portugal itself was expanding its power and influence to the far corners of the world.

The Avis dynasty presided over the astonishing expansion of Portugal's maritime activity around the world. The part played by the infantes Pedro and Henrique in sponsoring oceanic voyages and island settlements in the Atlantic, and the diplomatic activity that secured Papal Bulls, enshrining Portugal's exclusive rights to navigation and ecclesiastical patronage, are well known, as are the Moroccan conquests of D. Afonso v 'O Africano', D. João I's grandson, and the exploratory voyages sponsored by D. João II (r. 1480–95), which led in 1488 to the discovery of a sea route round the foot of Africa and in 1494 to the treaty with Castile, which partitioned the world between the two countries for purposes of discovery, proselytizing and exploitation. Equally well known are the remarkable expeditions and conquests of the reign of D. Manuel I (r. 1495–1521) – from the first return voyage from Europe to India (1497–9) and the discovery of Brazil in 1500 to the founding of the Estado da Índia with its capital in Goa and the circumnavigation of the globe by the fleet commanded by a Portuguese renegade in the service of Castile, Fernão de Magalhães, in 1519–21.

During the fifty years that followed the establishment of the Estado da Índia in 1504, the Portuguese established around fifty commercial settlements, most of them fortified, that stretched from the East African coast to China and Japan. Shiploads of spices were brought to Europe but the Portuguese also achieved a dominant position in certain branches of Asian commerce, establishing a monopoly over the import of horses into India and in the supply of Japanese silver to China. Meanwhile sugar plantations were being developed in the Atlantic Islands and Brazil, and the networks of Portuguese commerce extended literally around the world as large Portuguese commercial communities grew up in Seville and in the Spanish cities in the New World. The wealth that reached Lisbon soon made it one of Europe's most cosmopolitan cities, while the import of thousands of slaves made it also one of the most ethnically diverse.

Dazzling as these achievements were, and important as was the role of the royal dynasty in sponsoring them, confining the historian's attention to these epoch-making events obscures the real thrust of royal policy, which was less single-mindedly focused on this national narrative of overseas expansion. As the historian Mário Domingues wrote, 'the Portuguese monarchs thought more about the convenience of the family than the independence of the kingdom.'[1]

Having won the recognition of Portugal as an independent kingdom in the twelfth century, it might be thought that the Portuguese monarchs would stoutly defend this independence and become a focus for emerging national sentiment. However, while kings like D. Diniz (r. 1279–1325) and D. Manuel I did preside over a flowering of Portuguese national culture and periods of impressive economic prosperity based on the expansion of maritime trade, many of the Portuguese kings preferred to act according to their own dynastic logic. Time and again marriages were sought with the ruling dynasty of Castile, marriages that had the clear intention of bringing together Portugal and Castile under the rule of a single monarch. These dynastic ambitions of the kings of Portugal would have seemed quite normal to an observer in the fifteenth or sixteenth centuries but they should give someone in the twenty-first century pause before seeking to identify the Crown as the true symbol of national identity, let alone the defender of national independence.

The ambitions of the Avis dynasty were firmly fixed on a dynastic union with Castile. D. Afonso V's sister, Juana, was married to Enrique IV of Castile (r. 1454–74), and D. Afonso V himself married her daughter (his niece), known as Juana 'La Beltraneja', and fought a war between 1476 and 1479 to try to establish his wife's claim to the Castilian throne – an early example of the marriage of uncle to niece that was to become a recurring practice in the Portuguese royal family. Opposed to him was Isabella (the Catholic), Enrique IV's sister. Had D. Afonso V been successful, his marriage would have created a union of the Crowns of Portugal and Castile instead of the union of Castile and Aragon that resulted from Isabella's success in the war and her marriage to Ferdinand of Aragon. D. Afonso V was succeeded by his son, D. João II, who arranged a marriage between his infant son, another Afonso, and Isabella of Castile's daughter by which the two children would be brought up together at Moura on the Castilian border, a prospective marriage union that came to nothing when Afonso was killed in a riding accident in 1491.

D. João II was succeeded in 1495 by his cousin, D. Manuel I, who married the heiress of Isabella of Castile, resulting in the birth of a prince, Miguel, heir presumptive to both thrones. However, Miguel's death in 1500 frustrated this attempt to unite the crowns. D. Manuel's active pursuit of a Castilian bride led him to adopt the strong measures against Jews that was the price he had to pay for the hand of Isabella's daughter. D. Manuel, in fact, married two Castilian princesses in succession and his son, D. João III (r. 1521–53), married the sister of the

Spanish king, Carlos v, in a double marriage that saw Carlos marry D. João's sister Isabella.

These marriages did eventually lead to a union of the two crowns in 1580 and to Portugal's absorption into the Habsburg monarchy. The pursuit of a dynastic union with Castile had been almost obsessively pursued over four reigns. Each of the marriages could have led to the end of Portugal's independence and they were arranged with this possibility clearly in the minds of the Portuguese kings.

Meanwhile, the Avis kings had steadily strengthened the position of the monarchy by vesting the Masterships of the Military Orders of knights in members of the royal family, and ultimately in the Crown itself, with the effect that the towns and fortresses of the Orders became, in effect, part of the royal patrimony.

Second only to their dynastic ambitions, the priority of the Avis kings and princes was expansion in Morocco. This was clearly the main aim of D. João I's sons, the infante Henrique (Henry the Navigator) and his elder brother D. Duarte, who became king in 1433. Moroccan conquests were then actively pursued by D. Afonso v, who was called 'O Africano' in recognition of his Moroccan ambitions. Meanwhile, further exploration and 'voyages of discovery' were farmed out to private enterprise. D. João II also sponsored Moroccan expeditions and expansion in Morocco was, after the Castilian marriage, the priority for D. Manuel as well.

Under the spotlight provided by the royal chroniclers, the personalities of the Avis dynasty achieve a sort of three-dimensional image that is rare in the later Middle Ages: D. Duarte, educated and an intellectual, author of *O Leal Conselheiro* (The Loyal Councillor); Henrique, who did not marry (very rare for a great nobleman at that time), achieved a reputation for sanctity; Fernando, held as a hostage in Morocco for the return of Ceuta; Pedro, the traveller in Europe, who seems to have opposed the wasteful Moroccan expeditions and whose regency for the young D. Afonso v ended in his death at the battle of Alfarobbeira in 1449, in Portugal's miniature version of the Wars of the Roses. D. Afonso v, a weak man under the influence of his powerful uncles, Henrique and the duke of Braganza, was profligate with the Crown's resources and embarked on a hopeless attempt to win the Castilian Crown. Later he went on his own quixotic embassy to the court of Louis XI of France, tried to abdicate and go to the Holy Land and ended his life sharing his rule with his son, D. João II. D. João II was the strong man who asserted royal power against the nobles, murdering his principal opponent, the duke of Viseu, with a dagger thrust in open court but who, after the death of his son Afonso, left no legitimate offspring and failed in the end to legitimize his eldest bastard, Dom Jorge. There was also D. Manuel I, with his strange mystical obsessions and his equally strange personal appearance (pale skin, green eyes and long arms reaching almost to the ground), whose name was given to a uniquely Portuguese style of architecture as well as to a codification of Portuguese law. The vivid personalities of the kings and princes of the Avis dynasty are not only part of the fabric of Portuguese history but have become enshrined in Portugal's sense of its national identity. In this respect, they are comparable to the Tudor dynasty in England.

Portuguese kings, of course, had queens, two of whom stand out: Philippa of Lancaster, strong-minded mother of five princes, who imposed her values and discipline on the court of D. João I, and Leonor, wife of D. João II, who is remembered as the founder of the Santa Casa da Misericórdia, the charitable brotherhood that extended overseas and became the focus for Portuguese identity in distant settlements in Asia, Africa and the Americas.

The Culture of Monarchy in Portugal under the Avis Dynasty

It has often been said that Portugal was not a feudal kingdom like France but that there was a 'strong tradition of centralized power resulting above all from its situation in the zone of the Reconquista'.[2] The power of the Crown was nevertheless limited in practice by the Church and the Military Orders, both of which initially had jurisdictions that overlapped the borders of the Portuguese and Spanish kingdoms. It would be only in the fifteenth century that the Military Orders were brought effectively under royal control.

The relationship of the Church and the Crown, a fraught issue in many European kingdoms, had features that make Portugal unusual if not unique. By the fifteenth century the foreign jurisdiction of Castilian bishops over the Portuguese Church had been brought to an end and two Papal Bulls issued in the 1450s conferred on the Portuguese Crown exceptional privileges with regard to the churches established in Asia and Africa. These privileges became known as the *padroado real* and allowed the Portuguese Crown to make ecclesiastical appointments, collect church taxes and summon Church councils. It made the king of Portugal the effective head of the Catholic Church in half the world. However, shortly after the ecclesiastical authority of the Portuguese Crown in Asia had been symbolically sealed with the creation of the archdiocese of Goa in 1530, the Crown in Portugal established a branch of the Inquisition on terms that made this body semi-independent of royal authority. A powerful rival to the power of the Crown had been unwittingly created and was to prove a significant check on royal absolutism until the late eighteenth century.

The Portuguese kings were not crowned in a ceremony presided over by the Church, but were acclaimed by the nobility and the people at a public ceremony during which the nobility took an oath of loyalty.[3] Nor was the succession dependent exclusively on hereditary right as the heir had to be formally accepted as such by the Cortes of the kingdom, often before the death of his predecessor. As well as recognizing the heir to the throne, the Cortes had the power to approve taxation and present petitions. In 1478, when D. Afonso v announced that he would abdicate the throne, the Cortes installed his son as king by acclamation, and when Philip II of Spain became king of Portugal his accession to the throne was formally accepted by the Cortes at Tomar, where Philip made extensive promises about his future relationship with the Portuguese. In time this declaration of the heir became the most important, almost the only important, task of the Cortes and was still being invoked in the succession crisis of the 1820s.

The power of the kings, although in theory deriving from God, was dependent to an unusual degree on the 'sanction of the people'.[4] The kings of the Avis dynasty remained respectful of the public support that had brought them to power and tried to remain in touch with public sentiment. Like most kings in medieval Europe, they were itinerant, moving about their kingdom from one castle or royal residence to another. In this way they showed themselves to the people and became accessible to petitioners and to the population at large. In pursuit of a policy of centralizing royal power, D. Manuel I began the building of a new palace, situated on the Lisbon waterfront, which became known as the Paço da Ribeira (the Riverside Palace). Before it the Indiamen rode at anchor and in the great square that faced it, the Terreiro do Paço, popular ceremonies took place including the autos-da-fé of the Inquisition and the burning of their victims. This remained the principal royal palace in Portugal until it was destroyed in the earthquake of 1755.

The establishment of a royal palace in the urban setting of the capital was a trend seen in many European states and brought to an end the age when kings and their courts moved around the country. A permanent residence for the king brought closer together the court and the administrative bodies of the state and enabled the court to become a centre for artistic and cultural patronage. It also allowed the personnel of the court, the office holders and the households of important members of the royal family to expand in number and influence.[5]

Although D. Manuel tried to make Lisbon the centre of his government, summoning the Cortes to meet there and making it 'the seat of a more sedentary Court and the centre of the great financial interests of the King', it was a long time before the kings were able to settle permanently in the city and cease the itinerant habits of medieval monarchy. According to Ana Isabel Buescu, the court of D. João III, D. Manuel's successor, was

> constantly fleeing the plague which, since the beginning of the reign, was ravaging the country, not sparing the capital. The court maintained a quasi-forced itinerancy and . . . only returned to Lisbon at the beginning of 1527. Only then did D. Catarina, [the new] queen of Portugal, come to know the capital of the kingdom and empire . . . In April of the same year, hearing of a new outbreak of plague, the court abandoned Lisbon once again. After a stay in Évora . . . prevented from returning to the capital, they departed for their palace at Almeirim.[6]

Because of the persistence of plague during that reign, the Cortes met, not in the capital, but at Tomar, Torres Novas or Almeirim.

The wealth coming to the Crown from the gold trade at Elmina and from the spice fleets, coupled with the gradually tightening royal control over the Military Orders, gave the Crown great reserves of patronage that brought the needy members of the nobility and the class of knights, the *homens ricos*, *fidalgos* and *cavaleiros* to court in search of commanderies in the Orders, postings in the growing empire overseas or simply maintenance grants (*tenças*) for loyal service to the Crown. This dependence on royal patronage immensely increased the power of the Crown, attached all classes to the dynasty and helped to keep the king in touch with national sentiment and the opinions of the elites. Crown patronage was concentrated in the *casa real*, the royal household, which included the separate households of the queens and infantes, and which included nobles, courtiers and other servants of

Dirk Stoop, *Terreiro do Paço* (Palace Square, Lisbon), 1662, oil on canvas.

the Crown. It was a large and complex interlinking of personal and family interests.[7]

At the same time the supremacy of the Crown within the kingdom was firmly established with a ceremony of oath-taking. The French historian Jean-François Labourdette explains how D. João II, coming to the throne in 1480, sought in this way to rein in the independent power of the nobility:

> The meeting of the Cortes, which the king summoned to Evora, in November 1481, was preceded by an innovation that surprised and angered the nobles. Before the assembly was even opened, João II imposed on all *alcaides-mores* [commanders of fortresses] a new ceremony. They had to take an oath and do homage for the fortresses that they held from the hand of the king . . . The lords had to take their oath 'to be good, loyal and true vassals, subjects and servitors, using the formula 'that you will obey, serve and fulfil all your orders, loyally and truly like loyal and true vassals are obliged to do for their king and lord'. They had then to kiss his hands 'as a sign of obedience, subjection and vassalage which we owe directly and truly to the king our lord'.[8]

Oath-taking and the kissing of hands – known in Portugal as the *beija mão* – was confirmed at the core of the rituals of royalty.

In contrast, popular institutions flourished under the patronage of the kings and gave rise to what today would be called civil society. The kings led personally some of the major religious processions, notably those celebrating Corpus Christi. The founding of the Misericórdias by Queen Leonor and the granting of statutes that incorporated municipal government, the *Senados da Câmara*, first in Lisbon but then throughout the empire, laid the foundations for a kind of local democracy, or at least self-government. Although D. Manuel I was the first king to be referred to as Majesty, the letters written to him by his soldiers, captains and governors referred to him only as *Senhor* and adopted an informal, even intimate, language as though the king was part of a peer group along with his captains.

The national culture promoted by the Avis dynasty was nothing if not diverse and inclusive. In spite of the decision reached in 1495 at the behest of Castile to expel all Jews who would not convert, the Crown was prepared to tolerate the Jews who did convert (known in Portugal as New Christians), bestow patronage on them and even to appoint them to the royal council, while guaranteeing that there would be no inquiry into their religious beliefs for at least twenty years. In this Portugal followed a distinctly different path from nearby Castile, and one that made room for some element of diversity. The large influx of black slaves into Portugal added to that diversity.

The Avis dynasty had from the first been sensitive to the ways in which popular opinion could be cultivated. A succession of royal chroniclers were appointed, often linked to the maintenance of the royal archives in the Torre de Tombo. Fernão Lopes was succeeded by Azurara, and he in turn by Fernandes de Lucena, Rui de Pina and Duarte Galvão. The most famous of all the chroniclers and keepers of the Torre de Tombo was João de Barros, whose great chronicle, the *Décadas da Ásia* (published 1552–1613), is still one of the fundamental sources for the history of the discoveries. The work of these chroniclers not only established an official version of events that enhanced the power and authority of the Crown but founded a significant historical and literary tradition. The court also welcomed visiting humanists, scholars, poets and dramatists so that Portugal found a notable niche for itself as the culture of the Renaissance spread throughout Europe – not least through the display of exotic animals brought back from the East: elephants and, of course, the famous rhinoceros whose image was engraved by Albrecht Dürer. In this way the court became an effective centre for national life and a promoter of art, Manueline architecture, literature and the distinctive religious culture that grew up in Portugal.

The ruling dynasty was anxious to establish a reputation for sanctity and this was systematically cultivated over the generations. The two sons of D. João I, Henrique and Fernando, were, each in his own way, held up by the chroniclers as models of sanctity, Henrique through his celibacy and Fernando, held hostage till his death in Morocco, as a martyr. D. Afonso v's second child, Joana, eventually entered a nunnery and acquired a reputation for sanctity, becoming known as the Princess Saint of Portugal, although technically only beatified, not canonized. The idea that the kings of Portugal were especially chosen by God to fulfil His divine purposes became rooted not only in the narrative of the chroniclers but in the minds of the kings themselves. The vision of D. Manuel I, derived from the mystic Franciscan ideologies of Joachim de Fiore, led him to believe that he was destined to liberate Jerusalem, an objective only partly modified by the needs of realpolitik. D. João III's piety also led him to believe in the divine purpose of his rule, while the crusading fervour of his grandson, D. Sebastião, was to override all the dictates of common sense and good policy and led Portugal to catastrophe in Morocco at the battle of Alcacer el Kebir in 1578.

The Later Fortunes of the House of Avis

D. Manuel I was succeeded in 1521 by his son D. João III, a king who soon became overwhelmed by the magnitude of the problems facing the kingdom. Although Portugal remained in close alliance with Castile, an alliance sealed by a double royal marriage in 1525 that provided the emperor Charles v with a Portuguese bride and D. João with the emperor's sister, and with a new partition treaty signed at Saragossa in 1529, D. João III kept his country, as far as possible, out of European conflicts. Portugal did not become involved in the Italian Wars or the religious wars engulfing Germany, the Low Countries and even France, though its factory at Antwerp, important for the sale of Asian spices and the purchase of armaments and silver, became increasingly threatened by warfare in the Channel and was closed in 1545.

Meanwhile in Asia the Portuguese position had to be shored up against challenges from the Ottomans, while French interlopers threatened the settlements in Brazil. At the same time, the defence of the Moroccan fortress towns drained the kingdom's resources and D. João

III was forced to abandon the expansionist policies of his predecessors. The most significant aspect of this was the decision to withdraw Portuguese garrisons from all the Moroccan towns except for Ceuta, Tangier and Mazagan. This was to be the end, or almost the end, of Portugal's ambitions for a *reconquista* in North Africa, the central policy of the Avis dynasty since 1415.

As the problems of running a worldwide empire grew, D. João III, who as a young man had seemed to be a fitting heir to the glories of the Manueline renaissance, became increasingly morose, reclusive and focused on religious questions – a psychology not uncommon in Catholic Europe after the Reformation.

A monarchy can survive one weak and ineffective ruler and anticipate a recovery under his successor, but what was to drag the House of Avis, like the House of Tudor in England, inexorably towards extinction was the failure to produce any heir at all. In spite of the precautions taken to avoid plague-stricken Lisbon, D. João III's nine children all died young. One daughter, Maria Manuela, married to Filipe, Infante of Castile, lived long enough to produce a son, the ill-fated Don Carlos, and one son, João Manuel, struggled into his teens and was married to Joanna of Austria. Before he died of diabetes a year later, he left his wife pregnant with a son who was to be D. Sebastião.

D. Sebastião

D. Sebastião was abandoned by his mother soon after his birth. She returned to Castile, and the young prince was only three years old when his grandfather D. João III passed away. For twelve years Portugal was ruled by a regency. No civil war resulted as had happened during the minority of D. Afonso V, but while D. Sebastião's Castilian grandmother, Catarina, was regent (from 1557 to 1562), Portugal came close to being a satellite of Castile and a process of the Castilianization of the ruling classes intensified, in particular the adoption of the Castilian language – a dangerous development as the ordinary people of Portugal remained deeply hostile to Castile.

D. Sebastião came of age and assumed control of the government in 1568, at the age of fourteen. He never married and when he was killed in Morocco at the battle of Alcacer el Kebir in 1578 he left no heir.

D. Sebastião's dramatic and tragic life has made him the most controversial of all Portugal's kings. As his biographer António

D. Sebastião painted by
Cristóvão de Morais,
c. 1570, oil on canvas.

Baños-Garcia wrote,

> It is seldom that a life as short as that of king Dom Sebastião of
> Portugal gives rise to such great interest and controversy in the
> history of a country. He lived for only 24 years but the traces of his
> disastrous life remain in the collective memory of the Portuguese
> with all the characteristics of a real obsession.[9]

D. Sebastião's foolhardy expedition to Morocco led directly to Portugal
being taken over by Castile and to a new dynasty of kings. Disastrous
as D. Sebastião's rule had been, however, his death turned him into a
hero and his memory became the embodiment of an anti-Castilian
popular nationalism. This status as a national saviour went back even
to the circumstances of his birth, as Labourdette wrote:

> The 'desired one' [D. Sebastião], before he was even born, was the
> symbol of survival and the guarantee of the greatness and eternity of
> the nation. In the messianic and mystical depths of the Portuguese
> soul, his 'marvellous' birth, glowing with the halo of a miracle, gave
> rise to the myth of a Sebastian given by Providence.[10]

For some historians the D. Sebastião who led the Portuguese, only too willingly, along the path to national disaster was a youth deeply flawed, an orphan brought up under the influence of extreme religious ideas, a person strong-willed but with a kind of autism that made him unable to hear, let alone listen to, what others were telling him, a psychological misfit who suffered from some congenital illness and from psychosexual problems that made him shun women and all ideas of marriage. For others, like his recent biographer, he was a tragic romantic:

> His ascetic life was that of a monk knight belonging to a medieval epoch. He seemed to be bound, as was his grandfather Charles v, more to the rhythms of the past than the present . . . His indifference to the female sex was the result of this omnipresent spiritual world, an incarnation of the model of monastic chastity . . . His life is a mystery of light and dark with flashes of a bittersweet taste.[11]

On D. Sebastião's death in 1578, the only surviving legitimate male of the House of Avis was the aged Cardinal Henrique, the last surviving son of D. Manuel. He was 66 years old, infirm and celibate. Aware that at his death there would be a contested succession, which would further ruin a weakened and bankrupt country, Cardinal Henrique sought means to prepare the way for the succession of Philip of Spain.

The Habsburg Kings

In the nationalist historical tradition of Portugal, the change of dynasty in 1580 was a usurpation and the sixty years of Habsburg rule when, for the only time in its history, Portugal was united with the Spanish kingdoms, was described as a 'Babylonian captivity' and the source of all the disasters that overtook the great empire that had been built during the reign of D. Manuel I. More recent historians, as is their wont, have muddied such clear streams of interpretation.

No matter whether Philip II of Spain's accession to the Portuguese throne was or was not a 'usurpation', the events that immediately followed the death of Cardinal Henrique in 1580 had something of the character of a coup or possibly even a revolution. The great merit of hereditary monarchy is supposed to be that it leads to orderly succession and political stability – but this fails when the line of succession becomes hopelessly blurred. At the time of D. Henrique's death there were no direct male heirs. None of D. João III's children had survived and the succession had to be traced back to the children of D. Manuel, Cardinal Henrique's father. Here the problem began, for the royal progeny had spread their descendants throughout Europe.

D. Manuel's eldest daughter, Isabella, had married Emperor Charles V and was the mother of Philip II of Spain. D. Manuel's second child had been D. João III, whose line had ended with D. Sebastião. His third child, Beatriz, had married the duke of Savoy and was the mother of a line of male dukes.

His fourth child was Luís. He never married but had an illegitimate son, António, who held the title of Prior of Crato (head of the Hospitaller Order in Portugal). The fifth child was Cardinal Henrique. The sixth was another boy, Duarte, who had married the daughter of the duke of Braganza and had two daughters. The first, Maria, married Alessandro Farnese, duke of Parma, the Governor of the Spanish Netherlands and the most successful of Spain's generals. They had a son, Ranuccio. His second daughter, Catarina, had married her first cousin, João, the duke of Braganza, and was the mother of Teodósio, seventh duke of Braganza. The resulting complications provided constitutional lawyers with a bewildering series of options.

If priority was to be given to the senior male descending in the male line then there was only one candidate, Dom António, but he was illegitimate. Although he tried to prove that his father had legitimized him and/or that his father and mother had been secretly married, he had the disadvantage that he and Cardinal D. Henrique had fallen out and the cardinal was determined to block his claim. It was even alleged that his mother had been a New Christian. If this was the case António himself would be considered of New Christian descent, hardly endearing him to the cardinal, who was the Inquisitor General.

All the other candidates descended either from D. Manuel's daughters or granddaughters. Here a conflict of the rules became apparent. Philip of Spain was the child of D. Manuel's eldest daughter and had strengthened his claim by marrying a daughter of D. João III, thereby establishing a secondary claim through his wife. Next came the dukes of Savoy, descended from D. Manuel's second daughter, Beatriz, and finally the descendants of Duarte's two daughters, the Farnese dukes descended from Maria and the Braganza dukes from Catarina. In the eyes of some, these two lines had precedence because they descended from D. Manuel's son and not from a daughter. If this was accepted the legitimate heir was the nine-year-old Ranuccio Farnese, but, for the obvious reason that his father was the trusted general of Philip of Spain, his claims were never pressed. Second to Ranuccio was Teodósio, the heir to the duke of Braganza. Philip II came third and the claims of the duke of Savoy a poor fourth.

However, the complicated calculations of the genealogists and constitutional lawyers were rapidly overtaken by events and by the demands of realpolitik. D. Henrique had prepared the way for Philip II to take the Portuguese throne but on the cardinal's death the Prior of Crato, Dom António, had himself declared king in Lisbon and began to raise an army. Philip at once despatched his army and a fleet, defeated Dom António's levies and in December 1580 entered Lisbon to take his throne. Subsequently he was to declare that, as to the throne of Portugal, 'I inherited it, I bought it and I conquered it' – whether this saying was real or apocryphal, it remains the definitive statement of a right to succeed to any throne.

The succession crisis of 1580 has many features in common with the crisis of 1383–5, when the throne was contested between Juan of Castile and D. João, the Master of Avis. The outcome, however, was to be very different. In 1580, as in 1383, a Castilian king claimed the throne through his marriage to a Portuguese princess. He was supported by the majority of the Portuguese nobility but opposed by a 'popular' candidate who was an illegitimate son of a previous Portuguese king and head of one of the Military Orders. In both cases the 'popular' claimant appealed for an English alliance and for military assistance. However, although the pieces of the jigsaw seem the same, they did not fit to produce the same picture. In 1580 the Castilian army proved too strong. There was no battle of Aljubarrota. The English military intervention came too late and the 'popular' claimant was unable to find a backer of the calibre of Nun'Álvares Pereira, who had rallied support for D. João I among the military nobility.

The Portuguese throne was now to be occupied by three Habsburg kings of Spain: Philip I (Philip II of Spain) who ruled until 1598, Philip II (Philip III) who ruled 1598–1621 and Philip III (Philip IV) from 1621 to the revolt of 1640, which ended Habsburg rule.

The union of the Crowns had long been planned by both royal families and Philip's accession was the crowning moment for a dynastic policy that frequently ran counter to national sentiment. It was also the culmination of a gradual absorption of the Portuguese nobility and cultural elite into the wider world of Castile. Many of the noble families of Castile and Portugal had intermarried and the mercantile elites had woven networks of commercial interest that linked the maritime empires of both kingdoms. The intellectual elite of Portugal had also become increasingly Castilianized and used the Castilian language for much of their writing. During the regency of Catarina, the grandmother of D. Sebastião, Portugal had become in effect a satellite of Castile.

In 1580 Philip made sure that the Portuguese nobility would support his cause through a judicious policy of confirming Portugal's autonomy before the Cortes of Tomar in 1581 and providing financial assistance for noble families trying to ransom captives held hostage in Morocco. Until March 1583 Philip resided in Lisbon and there were rumours that he might make it the capital of his Atlantic empire in place of the inland isolation of Madrid and the Escorial. However, after the citizens of Lisbon had been given a taste of the Baroque splendour of Philip's royal style, the city had to reconcile itself to being simply the principal seaport and arsenal for Spain's Atlantic fleet from where the great Armada set sail in 1588. Only on one further occasion, in 1619, did the king, then Philip II (III of Spain), visit Portugal, and the occasion was to secure the recognition by the Cortes that his son was heir to the throne.

How did the idea, image and practice of monarchy change during the Habsburg sixty years? The most immediate impact was that the king became more remote and the lines of communication with the Portuguese people became attenuated. Whereas the presence of the king in the centre of Lisbon had provided nobles, petitioners and those enjoying or seeking royal patronage ready access to the court, now it became necessary to go to Spain or to be content with what patronage the viceroys were able to dispense. The role that the Manueline court had played in promoting the Portuguese renaissance ceased and the Habsburg years were relatively barren culturally.

The Cortes, which had lost much of its influence during the Avis dynasty, only met when the king was in Portugal – three times during the sixty years and then only to deal with questions related to the succession. However, even though the person of the king was absent, the authority of the Crown and its control over the government grew. A Spanish system of governing Councils was introduced, a revised code of laws was promulgated and the office of Inquisitor was combined with that of governor or viceroy for much of the sixty years, thereby providing a remedy for what had become a dangerous division of authority between Crown and Church.

Sebastianism and the Idea of the Saviour King

The remoteness of the Habsburg kings, the absentee nobility, the increasingly heavy taxation and the losses overseas to the Dutch and English all helped to stimulate a groundswell of anti-Castilian feeling. Until his death in 1596, António, Prior of Crato, maintained his claim to the throne but, although he was supported by the French and English for their own purposes, his cause flickered and died in Portugal itself. Instead a series of individuals, claiming to be the dead D. Sebastião, attracted some popular support as well as backing among Portuguese exiles abroad. At least four false Sebastians emerged and were dealt with by the authorities, but the Sebastianist cult soon began to morph from support for a pretender into a more generalized hope or expectation that some figure, the *encoberto*, 'hidden one', would emerge to provide redress for popular grievances and lead the Portuguese people to what was perceived to be their destiny. Sebastianism was, according to Labourdette, an expiation for the collective responsibility for the national disaster,[12] and provided a political philosophy for the dispossessed and powerless.

The aura of Sebastianism was never quite to leave the Portuguese monarchy. As Francisco Bethencourt has observed, Sebastianism was

> used from the very beginning both as a mythical anchor of collective identity and as a weapon of political action to challenge or erode royal legitimacy. The originality of Sebastianism lies ... in the diverse uses of its mythical configurations; and in the long period of its existence, during which it assumed functions ranging from political weapon to tool of passive resistance ... Longing for the disappeared and failed king would in time be linked to the feeling of *saudade*, the nostalgia for a past that never had been and a future that never would be.[13]

In the seventeenth century the prophetic element in Sebastianism was elaborated by the great Jesuit preacher António Vieira into a systematic ideology according to which Portugal would bring about the birth of the 'fifth empire', the Christian empire in succession to the Roman, Greek, Babylonian and Egyptian empires. Vieira tried to pin his dreams of a saviour king onto the figure of the duke of Braganza, hoping in this way to shape a mystical ideology to support the restoration of Portuguese independence.

Dramatis Personae: The Braganza Monarchs and their Spouses

D. João IV (r. 1640–56) (O Restaurador – the Restorer).
Married Luisa de Guzmán.

D. Afonso VI (r. 1656–68 (deposed), died 1683) (O Vitorioso – the Victorious).
Married Marie Françoise of Savoy; marriage annulled 1668.

D. Pedro II (Regent 1668–83, r. 1683–1706) (O Pacífico – the Peaceful).
Married first Marie Françoise of Savoy and second Maria Sofia of Neuburg.

D. João V (r. 1706–50) (O Magnânimo – the Magnanimous).
Married Maria Ana of Austria.

D. José (r. 1750–77) (O Reformador – the Reformer).
Married Mariana Vitória of Spain.

D. Maria I (r. 1777–1816) (A Piedosa – The Pious).
Married her uncle D. Pedro III (r. 1777–86); declared insane 1792.

D. João VI (Regent 1792–1816; r. 1816–26) (O Clemente – the Merciful).
Married Carlota Joaquina of Spain.

D. Pedro IV (r. 1826), abdicated in favour of his daughter D. Maria II.
As D. Pedro I, Emperor of Brazil (r. 1822–31), abdicated in
favour of his son Emperor Pedro II. (O Libertador – the Liberator).
Married first Leopoldina of Austria and second Amélia of Leuchtenberg.

D. Miguel (r. 1828–34) (O Rei Absoluto – the Absolute King).
Throne disputed with his niece D. Maria II. Married Adelaide of Löwenstein.

D. Maria II (r. 1826–53, effectively 1834–53) (A Educadora – the Educator).
Married first Augusto of Leuchtenberg and second Ferdinand of Saxe-Coburg.

D. Pedro V (r. 1853–61) (O Esperançoso – the Hopeful).
Married Stephanie of Hohenzollern-Sigmaringen.

D. Luís (r. 1861–89) (O Popular – the Popular).
Married Maria Pia of Savoy.

D. Carlos (r. 1889–1908) (O Diplomata – the Diplomat).
Married Amélie of Orléans.

D. Manuel II (r. 1908–10), deposed (O Patriota– the Patriot).
Married Augusta Victoria of Hohenzollern.

Emperor D. Pedro II of Brazil (r. 1831–89).
Married Teresa Cristina of Naples.

3

Overview of the Braganza Dynasty and the Culture of Royalty

A French ambassador said of Emperor D. Pedro II, one of the last of the Braganzas to occupy a throne, that when he disagreed with what was being said, 'at such moments he has an astonishing resemblance to Philip III as painted by Velazquez'. The Braganzas were, indeed, haunted by heredity, and these physical and cultural traits marked the history of the family and can be seen clearly recurring through ten generations. Successive members of the family were guided by a devotion to the traditions of the monarchy which sustained it from the *coup d'état* that brought it to the throne in 1640 to the monarchy's final demise in Brazil in 1889 and Portugal in 1910. It is the purpose of this chapter to look at these traits and to view the family's history over the *longue durée* before embarking on chapters devoted to each of the Braganza rulers.

A Reflection on Sources

Although monarchs are usually close to the centre where decisions are made, the Braganza monarchs, until the nineteenth century when they had a German makeover, are often figures that are curiously two-dimensional. The Portuguese historian Caetano Beirão commented on the absence of contemporary memoirs, diaries, even letters, written by members of the royal family or by Portuguese close to the court. Reflecting on the numerous sources available for the study of the French and English royal families, he pointed out that

> In Portugal these historical sources are completely lacking and . . .
> none are lacking so much as for the reign of D. Maria I . . . Almost

no texts contemporary with the sovereign are known that furnish information about her sentiments in regard to the persons or the events of her time, her habits, her conflicts, her opinions and even about the life of her family.[1]

It is striking that even modern historians like Joaquim Verissimo Serrão have to rely on the official *Gazetta de Lisboa* for much of what they have to say about the royal family before the nineteenth century.

The Braganza family were not great letter writers or memorialists, and contemporary foreign gossip had it that D. Pedro II (r. 1668–1706) and his grandson D. Pedro III (r. 1777–86) were virtually illiterate. To this, however, there are interesting exceptions, three of them women. Catarina of Braganza (1638–1706), who became the queen of England, wrote numerous letters (many to her brother D. Pedro II) that have survived and formed the basis for Lillias Campbell Davidson's groundbreaking biography. Queen Mariana Vitória (1718–1781), married to the infante (later King) José (r. 1750–77), wrote regularly to her mother, the queen of Spain, and her letters, written in highly idiosyncratic French, were published in 1936.[2] D. Maria I (r. 1777–1816) also wrote to her relatives at the Spanish court in her own stylized handwriting – her last apparently sane letters being written in 1792, the year she finally lost control of her mental faculties and was relieved of the responsibilities of government. The letters written to relatives at the Spanish court, and archived in Spain, seem to show that the Braganza queens wrote their own letters and did not have secretaries to handle their private correspondence.[3] Of the later Braganzas, it was D. Pedro V (r. 1853–61) who left the most considerable literary legacy in the form of memoranda, diaries and personal letters. The emperor D. Pedro II of Brazil was a great letter writer, especially to his lady friends throughout the world, and his letters to the countess of Barral are of particular interest. He also irregularly kept a diary, especially during his visits to Europe.

The relative absence of contemporary Portuguese writing has meant that historians have had to rely on the observations of foreigners, many of which appear to provide vivid and personal detail. However, herein lies a problem. Foreign writers have, of course, their own perspectives and write with their own cultural understanding. Most have had clear political or even personal agendas and the rivalries of France and Britain lurk near the surface of many of the accounts. Some of these descriptions of Portugal and the Portuguese court are extremely

colourful and interesting and, not surprisingly, historians have been
tempted to make use them, for example William Beckford's brilliantly
written and utterly charming account of his stay in Portugal in the 1780s.[4]
Many, perhaps most, of these accounts, however, were compiled long
after the events they describe. Beckford published his reminiscences of
his time in Portugal forty years after the event. Nathaniel Wraxall's
memoirs, which include a detailed account of the Portuguese court of
D. José, were published in 1815, forty years after the death of that king.[5]
The memoirs of the so-called duc de Châtelet (actually written by Pierre
Dezoteux de Cormatin), on whom historians have relied for some of
the best anecdotes of the eighteenth-century Portuguese court, were
published in 1798, twenty years after the most recent of the events
described.[6] Laure Junot, whose husband had been ambassador in Lisbon
and later commanded the French army of occupation, also published
her memoirs more than twenty years after her experiences in Portugal.[7]
The same is true of some Portuguese accounts. For example, the *Elogio*
of José Bonifácio, which purported to give a detailed account of the life
of the young princess Maria, later D. Maria I, and included many examples of her early piety and learning, was produced only after the queen's
death in 1816, seventy years after some of the events he described.[8]

There is a temptation for an English-speaking historian to rely on
the numerous accounts of British visitors to Portugal, and to be guided
by Rose Macaulay through the pageant of personalities who came and
went between England and Portugal,[9] but it was the French who
observed and wrote about Portugal and Portuguese affairs with most
insight. Indeed, after the strange fading away of Portugal's own tradition
of history writing, it was French historians of the seventeenth and eighteenth centuries who laid the foundations for a coherent history of
Portugal and its empire. Michel Blouin, Sieur des Piquetièrre's *Relation
des troubles arrivez dans la cour de Portugal en l'année 1667 et en l'année
1668* (1674) was a contemporary account of the dethroning of D. Afonso
VI,[10] while in 1728 the Abbé René-Aubert de Vertot published his *Histoire
des révolutions de Portugal*, a carefully researched account of the restoration of 1640, which went through many editions and in September
1836 was being read by Princess Victoria, soon to become queen of
Great Britain, to inform herself about Portuguese history.[11]

Charles Dellon's account of his experiences at the hands of the
Goa Inquisition was also translated into English and became a fundamental source for those writing on the subject.[12] An important French

account of the Portugal of D. João v is the *Description de la ville de Lisbonne,* whose author is unknown.[13] It is significant that when José Saramago came to write *Memorial do convento* (*Baltasar and Blimunda,* 1982), his novel about the reign of D. João v, much of his detailed knowledge about the king, the court and the Portugal of his time came from French sources. Meanwhile Joseph François Lafitau produced an account of Portuguese overseas expansion in two magnificent volumes and Nicolas de La Clède published a two-volume *Histoire genérale de Portugal* in 1735.[14] As important as the work of the English memorialists is the *Etat présent du Royaume de Portugal en l'année 1766* by the future revolutionary general Charles François Dumouriez[15] and the diaries of the French ambassador, the marquis de Bombelles.[16] The crowning French achievement was that great work of the Enlightenment, the *Histoire philosophique et politique des établis-semens et du commerce des Européens dans les deux Indes* by the Abbé Guillaume-Thomas Raynal, published in 1773–4.[17]

Foreign visitors to Portugal loved to describe the strange and the exotic: the elaborate religious processions, the bullfights, the autos-da-fé, the crowds of beggars, monks and 'negroes' that filled the streets and the hallways of the noble palaces. And they scarcely disguised their contempt for this backward, superstitious and ignorant country. Few were interested in the strides towards modernity and enlightenment that were being made. For them Pombal had been a monster, an autocrat who had left the country ruined and the prisons full. That he had vigorously, and not unsuccessfully, given Portugal a modern and progressive makeover was largely ignored. By the late 1770s, when so many of the foreigners were writing, a new generation of students were graduating from the reformed university of Coimbra and Portugal was producing its scientists and mathematicians. As Mário Domingues noted, although foreign observers mostly commented on the religious obsessions of D. Maria I and her husband, she was at the same time giving her backing to a variety of initiatives to train military and naval engineers, to modernize the navy and organize a national system of primary education. Meanwhile, alongside their participation in religious festivals, the Portuguese nobility were among the first in Europe to make experiments with flight, using hot-air balloons.[18]

If contemporary Portuguese memoirs and descriptions of the court are lacking, there is also a lack of contemporary images of the royal family. Generally speaking, monarchs have been extremely sensitive about their image, understanding that ultimately their authority stands or falls on the way their public personality is projected. The concern with the ruler's image, so clearly seen in the self-projections of rulers of antiquity like Alexander the Great and Augustus, became a preoccupation of the Habsburgs who had their portraits painted by leading artists of the day like Titian and Velázquez, while in England Queen Elizabeth used royal portraiture as powerful and effective propaganda for her rule. Louis XIV of France took self-aggrandizement, through a carefully managed portraiture and imagery, to an even higher level. In Portugal, for some reason, less attention was paid to the image of the monarch. Catarina, Queen of England, is an exception and her portrait was made many times, according to the traditions of the English court. D. João V was very conscious of the need for the visual projection of royal power, but this took the form of religious art and the embellishment of churches rather than portraiture. Caetano Beirão, commenting on the 25 oil paintings and ten prints of D. Maria I that have survived, many of them copied from one or two originals, says they were the most numerous portraits of any of the rulers to date.[19] Indeed, the best-known Portuguese portrait of the eighteenth century is not that of one of the Braganza family at all, but the posthumous portrait of the marquês de Pombal by Louis-Michel Van Loo.

The situation changed with D. João VI (r. 1816–26) and subsequent members of the Braganza dynasty. D. João VI was a modest man, with few outstanding personal characteristics, but his portrayal in paintings and prints far exceeded in number that of earlier monarchs. This has not helped his reputation, as he had a most unfortunate face with a bulging forehead, a slightly open mouth and staring eyes, which those who drew his likeness seldom attempted to disguise. These ungainly features have made him one of the most easily recognized of all the Portuguese monarchs.

The Idea of Monarchy in Portugal

According to fifteenth-century jurists, the king ruled with an authority that was both human and divine in origin and he had power of life and death over his subjects.[20] However, the path from this legal definition of kingship to a fully functioning absolute monarchy was not straightforward. The Braganza kings of Portugal were not anointed and there was no crowning ceremony. In 1646 D. João IV dedicated his kingdom to Nossa Senhora da Conceição (Our Lady of the Conception), and had her crowned as queen of Portugal. From this time, no Braganza wore a crown and in portraits the crown always rests near them on a table. The idea survived, and was reaffirmed at the start of each reign, that there was a contract between the king and the people. This took the form of an exchange of oaths at a public ceremony known as the 'acclamation'. The monarch took an oath to serve God and the country and the people, through their representatives, took an oath of loyalty to the ruler. According to the French historian Jean-François Labourdette, this ceremony demonstrated the 'contractual origin of his power'.[21] The ceremony of 'acclamation' accompanied the Braganza monarchs to the end: the last such ceremony was the 'acclamation' of D. Manuel II in 1908.

When D. Pedro (Pedro IV of Portugal and Pedro I of Brazil) established the empire in Brazil, he was acclaimed in the traditional Portuguese manner but he also introduced a crowning ceremony, said to have been inspired by Napoleon's coronation as emperor on 2 December 1804. D. Pedro's successor as emperor, D. Pedro II (r. 1831–89), was also crowned as well as being 'acclaimed'.

One of the most impressive 'acclamation' ceremonies was that held at the start of D. Maria I's reign in 1777, as described by Jenifer Roberts:

> First came the heralds and knights-at-arms, followed by the aristocrats, the religious establishment, and the secretaries of state . . . Maria's consort [D. Pedro III] wore a cloak of flame colour stripes, his robes studded with diamonds. Over a long bag wig, he wore a hat adorned with white feathers and he carried a sword of solid gold . . . After several declarations were read in ringing tones, Maria knelt

Panoramic painting of Lisbon in the 1690s.

on a crimson cushion and, in a quiet voice, promised to govern her country well, administer justice, and guard the customs, privileges and liberties of her people. Her husband and sons paid her homage, her courtiers swore allegiance, and the royal standard bearer acclaimed her as queen.[22]

The heir to the Portuguese throne had first to be recognized by the Cortes, which sometimes had to adjudicate on matters related to the succession and to decide who was the rightful heir. At four points in Portugal's history the Cortes had been summoned at a time when the succession had been disputed: in 1385, 1581, 1641 (when João, duke of Braganza, was confirmed as king) and 1828 (when D. Miguel was recognized as king). But the Cortes was also summoned to 1654 and in 1674 to confirm the line of succession and to discuss the issues raised by the prospect of a female heir.

The succession was regulated by the so-called Lei Fundamental of Lamego. This law, supposed to have been promulgated in 1143 by the Cortes of Lamego, had been 'discovered' in 1632. It purported to regulate the succession to the throne and to exclude non-Portuguese from becoming king. Importantly it also decreed that a woman could inherit, but only if she married a Portuguese. In the event of her marrying a non-Portuguese she would forfeit her title. The so-called 'laws of Lamego' were in reality part of the anti-Spanish propaganda that was spreading during the 1630s and were used to justify the accession of the Braganzas to the throne in 1640.[23]

The deaths of the monarchs were also occasions for great ceremonial. In addition to the funerals and the ceremonial interment in the crypt of the church of São Vicente da Fora in Lisbon, there was the ceremony of the breaking of the shields. These wooden shields, painted black, were carried by the judges and were formally splintered to mark the fact that royal justice had ceased on the death of the king. According to Diogo Ramada Curto, writing of the funeral of D. João v in 1750, 'the principal rite of the breaking of the shields took place in Lisbon and in all the cities and towns of Portugal and its empire'.[24] The last time this ceremony was performed was on the death of D. Luís in 1889.

In theory the Braganza kings were 'absolute' monarchs and, as late as 1827, the arrival of D. Miguel in Lisbon was greeted by crowds shouting vivas for the 'rei absoluto'. The realities of monarchical power, however, were always very different from the theory. There was no escaping the fact, whatever the theorists might argue, that João, duke of Braganza, owed his throne to a *coup d'état* carried out by a faction of the nobility. After his death, another noble faction intervened in 1668 to depose D. Afonso VI and to replace him with his brother Pedro, and Pedro was continually made aware that he owed his position to noble consent, which might at any time be withdrawn. So dominant were the noble factions that the government of Portugal during this period has often been called a 'monarchy of the nobles'.

The gold discoveries in Brazil at the very end of the seventeenth century put the king, almost overnight, in control of vast wealth that had the effect of making the monarchy increasingly independent of noble and even clerical support. The Cortes lost any claim to influence and was no longer assembled even to confirm the succession. The king's power, however, was still limited by the privileges enjoyed by the nobility and by the Church, especially the latter with its extensive land and property holdings and the jurisdiction wielded by the Inquisition. The state structure inherited from the Spanish kings and confirmed by D. João IV was conciliar in form, the councils dealing with war, justice and the Military Orders being dominated, as of right, by the small group of leading noble families. In the eighteenth century conciliar government was gradually replaced in Portugal, as in the rest of Europe, by ministerial government, where power was wielded by the secretaries of state, answerable directly to the Crown. In Portugal there were three of these secretaries, whose competence covered foreign affairs and war, the navy and colonies, and the domestic affairs of the kingdom. The increasing power of the secretaries of state led eventually to one of their number, Sebastião José de Carvalho e Melo, better known as the marquês de Pombal, becoming dominant during the reign of D. José (r. 1750–77). The eighteenth century saw a steady shift of real power away from the nobility and towards a professional bureaucracy, a trend that was apparent elsewhere in Europe where Cameralist ideas were in the ascendant. It was this professionalization of the government that was such a marked feature of Pombal's government.

In the nineteenth century, after three very disturbed decades, both Portugal and the now independent Brazil settled down under constitutions that replaced royal absolutism with a constitutional monarchy.

Fears for the Succession

The Braganza monarchy was, from the start, plagued by insecurity. For the first 28 years of its existence its legitimacy was not universally recognized in Europe. Portugal was excluded from the Westphalia peace negotiations in 1648 and it was not until 1668, when the first two Braganza kings had come and gone, that Spain and the papacy finally recognized the new dynasty and the attempts of Spain to reassert its sovereignty over Portugal ceased. The lack of recognition from Rome had meant that no new bishops had been instituted for a whole generation and the Portuguese Church had almost ceased to function. After 1668 the legitimacy of the dynasty was not challenged, except briefly when Napoleon declared in 1807 that the Braganza dynasty had ceased to reign.

However, in spite of the recognition accorded in the 1668 treaty with Spain, insecurity persisted because successive Braganza monarchs found difficulties in producing an heir. D. Afonso VI (r. 1656–68) had no children and may not have been capable of having any; D. Pedro II and his first wife, Marie Françoise of Savoy, had only a daughter, giving rise to critical debates about the future of the monarchy in the Cortes of 1674, while providing her with a husband became a highly sensitive political issue. D. Pedro's second marriage in 1687 was more successful and produced four male children, but three years after the marriage of his successor D. João V to Maria Ana of Austria in 1708 no child had been born. The vow to build the palace-convent of Mafra if a child should arrive was followed by a birth, but of a daughter. When a son eventually came, he lived only two years. Eventually two male children secured the survival of the dynasty.

Of D. José's eight children only four girls survived, threatening once again a succession crisis when the heiress, Infanta Maria, would have to choose a husband. The Braganzas resolved this dilemma by having recourse to incest (condoned by papal dispensation) and D. Maria was married to her uncle Pedro. Royal incest also seemed to resolve the problem of possible foreign interference or even the succession of a foreigner, which threatened to revive the spectre of the Habsburg takeover in 1580. As if to underline the precariousness of the succession, which had led to her incestuous marriage, one of the portraits of D. Maria showed her pointing unambiguously at the Actas do Cortes de Lamego, the medieval law that was supposed to have laid down rules

47

of succession that would prevent a princess who was heir to the throne from marrying a foreigner.[25] D. Maria I and D. Pedro III had seven children but four of these were either stillborn or died in early childhood. An incestuous marriage once again recommended itself as a way of keeping the succession in the Braganza family and the heir, the infante José, was duly married to his aunt, D. Maria's sister, who was fifteen years older than him. The infante José died childless in 1788 at the age of 27 and the Crown passed to his brother, later D. João VI, married to a Spanish princess, Carlota Joaquina, who was his cousin. At first there were doubts whether Carlota would produce children and fears for the succession led to the Spanish infante Pedro Carlos, the only child of D. Maria's daughter Maria Ana Vitória and the Spanish prince Gabriel, being brought from Spain to Portugal by way of insurance. In the end D. João and Carlota had nine children, including two boys who survived to manhood, Pedro and Miguel. Doubts over whether D. João was really the father of the boys were not allowed to disrupt the succession.

Incestuous marriages, accompanied by ecclesiastical dispensations, continued. Of D. João VI and Carlota's children, three of the daughters married Spanish uncles and D. Miguel, their youngest son, was also betrothed to his niece, D. Pedro's daughter Maria da Gloria. Maria da Gloria herself later married her step-uncle, the duke of Leuchtenberg, who died shortly after the wedding. The decision of D. Maria II to marry for a second time with Ferdinand of Saxe-Coburg was made not only for sound political reasons but because of the known prowess of the Saxe-Coburg princes in the marriage bed. D. Maria II had eleven pregnancies and seven of her children survived, including four sons. This, it might be assumed, would ensure the survival of the dynasty but three of the princes died of typhoid in 1861. The last king of Portugal, D. Manuel II, died childless in exile in 1932. This created a succession crisis in the exiled royal family and the succession to the title of 'king' *in absentia* had to pass to a descendant of D. Miguel, the king who had been deposed in 1834. Meanwhile the Brazilian branch of the family was also threatened with a succession crisis when both the sons of Emperor Pedro II died young and the succession devolved on Princess Isabel. The declaration of the Brazilian republic in 1889 resolved the issue.

Glancing sideways from the main line of succession, the Braganzas were not a prolific family. Catarina, daughter of D. João IV and wife of Charles II of England, had no children. Her brother D. Pedro II's daughter, Isabel Luisa, never married and had no children, and of his sons, Francisco, António and Manuel did not marry and had no legitimate offspring. D. João v's daughter Bárbara, who married the king of Spain, also had no children. D. João v had three illegitimate sons but none of these married or had offspring. Of D. José's daughters, Maria Doroteia never married and Maria Benedita, who married her nephew, the infante José, had no children. D. Pedro v died without any children and his brother Augusto never married. Although D. Luís had two sons, one of these, Afonso, only married late in life and had no children.

Many of the children who were conceived were either stillborn or died young. One after another, first-born sons died before they could succeed, with a regularity that came to resemble a family curse. D. João IV's first-born son, Teodósio, died in 1653; D. Pedro II's first son, João, Prince of Brazil, died less than a month old in 1688; D. João v's eldest son, Pedro, died at the age of two. D. José's sons were all stillborn and D. Maria's eldest son died of smallpox in 1788 at the age of 27. D. João VI's eldest son, António Pio, died aged only six years old, and D. Pedro IV's son, João Carlos, also died as an infant. The curse continued into the Brazilian branch, with both of Emperor Pedro II's sons dying in infancy, and pursued the Braganzas to the end, with D. Carlos's eldest son, Luís Filipe, being murdered beside his father in February 1908.

Most of the early Braganza kings had illegitimate children, even the solid and respectable D. João VI, but although some of these were recognized and legitimized (D. João v's three bastard princes, the so-called *meninos de Palhavã*, lived in semi-royal state), there was no place for their mothers at the royal court, no *maîtresse en titre* as was the case in France. Both D. Pedro IV and D. Miguel had illegitimate children; their sister Isabel Maria, who acted as regent between 1826 and 1828, never married and is also believed to have had illegitimate children.

The problems with the succession were not made easier by the strain of mental instability that ran in the family. D. Afonso VI was removed from the throne by a palace coup in 1667, largely because of his perceived mental instability, while D. Maria I, after years on the verge of mental breakdown, finally succumbed to madness in 1792. Her sister Doroteia suffered from the same symptoms, as well as anorexia, and died at the age of 31.[26] Marianna, another of her sisters, also became mentally ill. D. João VI at times suffered from depression and in 1805 his wife, Carlota, tried unsuccessfully to have him declared insane.

The Braganzas were not alone with their problems, which all European royal houses suffered to a greater or lesser extent. In England Queen Anne's children all predeceased her, leaving the country with a disputed succession that led to two civil wars, while George III became incurably insane and his son George IV had no male heir, his only daughter dying before him. Indeed, although George III had nine sons, legitimate male heirs were in short supply and in the end his throne passed in 1837 to an eighteen-year-old girl, the child of a very late legal marriage on the part of her father. The precarious Romanov dynasty was only rescued when the throne was seized by a German princess, while the Spanish Habsburgs and Bourbons also notoriously suffered from mental instability and impotence. The frequent marriages between the Spanish and Portuguese royalty did not improve the genetic viability of either family.

Although four of the early Braganza kings had relatively long reigns – D. Pedro II, as regent and king from 1668–1706, D. João V from 1706–50, D. José 1750–77 and D. João VI as regent and king 1792–1826, to which might be added the 58-year reign of D. Pedro II, the emperor of Brazil – the family were not especially long lived and most suffered from declining health and vigour long before their deaths. In the duc de Châtelet's *Travels* there is the comment that 'all the males of the house of Braganza have an hereditary disease, the principal symptom of which is swelled legs'.[27] Many of them, beginning with D. João IV, did indeed suffer from gout and leg ulcers. It is also clear that many of the family also suffered strokes: D. Pedro III suffered his first in 1777, the year of the accession of his wife and himself to the throne. D. João V and D. José also suffered strokes of varying severity. When afflicted with ill health, the monarchs followed the custom of the Portuguese upper classes and visited the thermal baths at Caldas da Rainha: on one occasion D. Maria I spent seven weeks at Caldas, taking baths daily. Epilepsy was another problem. To Marshal Beresford, who commanded the Portuguese army from 1809 to 1820, is attributed the cruel remark that 'all the daughters of the [Braganza] family had fits, though they did not seem to have any political views.'[28] Of D. João VI's children, three, including his heir D. Pedro, were epileptic, and D. Pedro's eldest son died after a prolonged epileptic fit. D. Pedro II, the emperor of Brazil, also suffered from epileptic episodes as a boy.[29]

Whatever the reason, few of the Braganzas lived to old age and among the monarchs of the dynasty only D. Maria I reached the age of 70: D. João IV had died aged 52, D. Pedro II at 58, D. João V was 60 when he died, D. José was 63, D. João VI was 58, while D. Pedro IV died aged only 36 and his daughter D. Maria II died at the age of 34 (after giving birth to eleven children). D. Pedro V died aged 24 and his brother Augusto aged 41. Emperor Pedro II, in spite of his long reign and venerable appearance, was only 65 when he died. The last king, D. Manuel, died in exile at the age of 41 and his successor, the pretender Duarte Nuno at 69. D. Maria I, the one exception, was aged 81 but for the last 24 years of her life she was insane. Among the few striking exceptions in the family were the formidable Teresa, daughter of D. João VI, who died aged 81, and the second duke of Lafões, whose father had been the illegitimate half-brother of D. João V. He lived to be 87, in 1788 marrying a young wife while well into his seventies.[30]

In Portugal royalty was often expected to assume responsibility at an early age and some of the Portuguese monarchs were very young when they were deemed to be of age. D. Sebastião, the penultimate king of the House of Avis, had begun his rule at the age of fourteen. D. Pedro II assumed the role as 'governor of the kingdom' at the age of nineteen. D. João V had become king at seventeen and D. Maria II was only fifteen when she became queen. D. Pedro, the second emperor of Brazil, was deemed to have reached his majority when he was fourteen and D. Manuel, the last king, succeeded to the throne at the age of eighteen after the murder of his father and elder brother.

Spanish Marriages

Although one theme in Portuguese history has been the determination to remain independent of Spain, this always ran counter to the dynastic ambitions of the ruling families and presented a profound disjunction between public policy and private dynastic interest. Repeated marriages between members of the royal families of Portugal and Spain had been a feature of the fifteenth and sixteenth centuries, one of them being a 'double marriage', when Emperor Charles V and D. João III each married the other's sister. These dynastic entanglements had led, inevitably one must conclude, to the union of the crowns in 1580 and the sixty years of Portuguese subjection to Spain. By the eighteenth century Spanish marriages had once again become popular with the Braganzas, and double marriages were arranged in 1729, between the heir D. José and Mariana Vitória and the Spanish prince Ferdinand and Maria

Bárbara. A second 'double marriage' was arranged in 1785 between the infante João and Carlota Joaquina, while Maria Ana Vitória of Portugal was married to the Spanish prince Gabriel. Further down the line, Emperor Pedro II, in Brazil, reverted to this family tradition by arranging marriages for his sisters at the same time as his own to Teresa Cristina of Naples. The benefits of these marriages may in the end have outweighed the problems caused by inbreeding, as contact between the two courts was, on occasion, able to prevent political conflicts getting out of hand. D. José's Spanish queen, Mariana Vitória, was able to use her close family connections with the Spanish royal family to help end the war of 1762 and to bring about the important rapprochement in South America that was incorporated into the Treaty of Madrid in 1777. The French ambassador, the marquis de Bombelles, commented in 1786 that the ambassadors of Spain had direct and easy access to Queen D. Maria I, as did the ambassadors of Sardinia and Naples, which were part of the Bourbon 'family' of states, while the other ambassadors were received only 'rarely and always on ceremonial occasions'.[31] However, marriage and political rapprochement did not always go hand in hand. When D. João VI arranged marriages for two of his daughters, Maria Isabel and Maria Francisca, with their Spanish uncles, Portuguese forces were occupying the Spanish colonial territory that later became Uruguay and Spanish armies were manoeuvring on the frontier of Portugal threatening retaliation. It was long experience that gave birth to the Portuguese proverb 'De Espanha, nem bom vento, nem bom casamento' (From Spain there is never a good wind or a good marriage).

It is often assumed that inbreeding must be a bad thing – but history seldom exactly obeys the rules of science. According to Roderick Barman, D. Pedro II, emperor of Brazil, was the child of generations of inbreeding. His mother, Leopoldina, 'had four great-grandparents in place of the usual eight'. His paternal grandparents were first cousins and his grandfather (D. João VI) was the child of an uncle/niece marriage. 'Counting back five generations, the young prince [Emperor D. Pedro II] possessed only fourteen in place of the usual thirty-two great-great-great-grandparents.' Yet this sad tale of inbreeding produced one of the ablest and most intelligent of all the Braganza monarchs.[32]

Queens and Infantas

The Braganza story is not just about men. Queens and princesses have always played an essential role in maintaining the reputation and viability of monarchical institutions and in establishing the cultural and moral values that the monarchy is supposed to represent. Women, whether the wives of the Braganza kings or their daughters, were always central to the dynasty's concerns. Female offspring, even when they were not heirs to the throne, were essential to dynastic politics. They could be strategically married to other European royalty and were considered to be 'diplomatic chess pieces', to use Ana Pereira's felicitous phrase.[33] Luisa de Guzmán, the Spanish wife of D. João IV, has been seen as the strong influence behind the king, persuading him to accept the Crown in 1640 and, after his death, assuming the regency for their son D. Afonso VI. She it was who organized the defence of the kingdom against the Spanish and arranged the marriage of her daughter, Catarina, to Charles II of England. Catarina, for her part, gradually established her influence at the English court and returned to Portugal in 1692 to act as regent whenever her brother, D. Pedro II, was absent from the capital or had to surrender the reins of government through ill health. D. Afonso VI's wife, Marie Françoise of Savoy, played a central role in the political crisis of 1667–8 and was largely instrumental in persuading D. Pedro to act as the figurehead for the coup that led to D. Afonso's removal from the throne. She and D. Pedro then married. D. Pedro's second wife, Maria Sofia of Neuburg, was successful in bearing seven children and averting a possible crisis for the dynasty, as eventually was D. João V's wife Maria Ana of Austria.

Maria Ana's influence was felt in the excessive devotion that marked the public ceremonial of the monarchy during D. João V's long reign. She was an Austrian princess and through her the links with Austria became important in Portugal's development. When, after 1742, D. João V became increasingly ill and incapable of governing, she assumed a central role in political affairs and it was her influence that led in 1750 to the appointment as a minister of Sebastião José de Carvalho e Melo (later marquês de Pombal), who had been ambassador in Vienna and had married an Austrian noblewoman.

D. José's Spanish wife, Mariana Vitória, was often described as uninterested in political affairs and as being a devotee of the hunting field. However, she was briefly made regent after the king was injured in an assassination attempt in September 1758. Observers of the Portuguese court during D. José's reign attribute to her a strong influence over her husband, an influence that was most clearly visible in the way in which women were kept away from the court and were not allowed to perform in the opera or even to be present in the audience – a cultural curiosity in a Europe used to the diversity and promiscuity that was a mark of court culture. She is said to have played an important part in the diplomatic relations between Portugal and Spain and towards the end of D. José's life she became regent again. After his death in 1777 she assumed an important role advising and supporting the new queen, her mentally fragile daughter D. Maria I. She may have been one of the important influences that helped to prevent the victims of Pombal taking revenge on the fallen minister after 1777.[34]

D. Maria I, whose personal rule lasted from 1777 to 1792, in spite of her fragile nervous and mental state, was not unimportant in maintaining social cohesion and stability in Portugal during the years following the death of her father and in the era of the American and French Revolutions, when revolts flickered in Brazil and Portuguese society, bitterly divided after the experience of Pombal's rule, and threatened to split into irreconcilable factions.

Of all the Braganza queens of Portugal, however, Carlota Joaquina proved to be one of the most politically significant. Although denounced by contemporaries, and gleefully also by historians, as small and ugly, with a vicious temper and promiscuous sexual behaviour, she tried to play a political role after Spain was invaded by Napoleon and her family lost its throne. She planned to set herself up in the South American colonies as regent for her imprisoned brother, although these pretensions were swamped by the rising tide of popular revolution and the opposition of both Britain and her husband. After the royal family returned to Portugal in 1821, she became the rallying point for conservative forces in Portugal and, through her youngest son, D. Miguel, sought to oppose the liberal and constitutional forces at work there. In 1828 she had the satisfaction of seeing D. Miguel acclaimed king in Portugal, and died in 1830 before he was overthrown by liberal armies in the civil war.

Leopoldina, the sister-in-law of Napoleon, was betrothed in 1817 to the infante Pedro and arrived in Rio in November of that year to massive and expensive celebrations. This marriage renewed the Habsburg connection that extended back to the marriage of Maria Ana of Austria to D. João V. Leopoldina, however, was rather different from the earlier Braganza queens. She was a serious and well-educated woman with a deep interest in natural history. She spent a lot of her time in study and in maintaining a menagerie of rare animals. During the short period of her marriage to D. Pedro IV she had a considerable influence not only on her headstrong husband but on establishing the dignity and stability of the Imperial throne. She died on 6 December 1826 after suffering a miscarriage at the age of 29.

D. Pedro IV had a daughter, Maria da Gloria, and his ultimately successful attempt to place her on the Portuguese throne was a central issue in the civil wars of the 1830s, while her marriage to a Coburg prince was finally to bring some stability to Portugal and to the dynasty itself.

Perhaps the most influential 'queen' in the Braganza story was Princess Isabel, the eldest daughter of the emperor of Brazil. Although never in fact queen or empress, she played a major role in Brazilian affairs and acted as regent for her father on three occasions when he travelled abroad. It was she who famously persuaded the country's politicians to abolish slavery and signed the decree leading to the freeing of slaves in May 1888.

Music, Horsemanship and Hunting

The early Braganza monarchs managed the business of ruling without showing any particular administrative talent or intellectual flare. Music, however, was another matter. Successive generations of the family demonstrated a pronounced interest in music and real ability as performers. Music had been central to the life at the ducal court at Vila Viçosa where a large music library had been collected by D. João IV, who was a composer and musical scholar of note. The infanta Bárbara, D. João V's daughter and later queen of Spain, was a highly accomplished player on the harpsichord for whom Domenico Scarlatti, her teacher, wrote many of his pieces. She took Scarlatti with her when she married the heir to the Spanish throne and her influence helped to develop opera at the Spanish court.[35] D. José played the violin and his queen and daughters sang and performed at private concerts, one of which was given for the British officers who had accompanied the army sent in 1762 to defend Portugal.[36] Both D. João V and D. José were devoted to Italian opera: D. João built a magnificent opera house in Lisbon that

Trophies of the hunt at Mafra.

was destroyed in the earthquake, while D. José not only built an opera house for performances at Belém but had an opera company that accompanied him when he went on tour. He also had a theatre for operatic performances built at the hunting lodge of Salvaterra dos Magos. D. João VI, once he arrived in Brazil, took over the *fazenda* of Santa Cruz, which had been a Jesuit property. He revived the music school where the Jesuits had taught their slaves to play and sing and soon had a widely acclaimed slave orchestra, which performed at public and private functions. D. Pedro IV was also a noted musician and composer, receiving instruction from Sigismund von Neukomm, who had worked with Haydn and Beethoven. As well as the flute and violin he learned to play the bassoon, trombone, harpsichord and guitar. He was said to have composed music that impressed none other than Rossini.[37] His compositions were played in the royal chapel and for long it was believed that he was responsible for the words and music of the new national anthem of independent Brazil. D. Luís was also a highly skilled performer on the cello.

Like much of European royalty, the Braganzas were keen to demonstrate their horsemanship and to amuse themselves with hunting. D. Pedro II was a renowned horseman, said to have been one of the best in the kingdom, and his daughter Isabel, compared by contemporaries with 'Diana the huntress', was renowned for firing at wild boar from the saddle.[38] Catarina of Braganza, Queen of England, had clearly inherited the Braganza pleasure in hunting. An account of the expenditure of her household in 1671 showed wages being paid to 'the master of Her Majesty's bows; a yeoman of Her Majesty's bows; a groom of Her Majesty's bows; master of Her Majesty's bucks; two yeomen of her harriers'.[39] D. José and his queen had a riding school at their palace at Belém and spent a large part of the year moving from one hunting lodge and game preserve to another; the queen, Mariana Vitória, was as keen a rider as the king and insisted on attending hunts to the last. In 1778, when unable to ride, she followed the hunt, armed with a gun, in a sedan chair from which she allegedly shot three stags and thirteen deer. When she was only eleven she had written every week to her mother in Spain recording the number of rabbits she had killed.[40] Mariana Vitória's daughter, D. Maria I, in spite of her nervous condition and mental fragility, was also keen on riding and hunting. When her sister Doroteia died in January 1771, there were eight days of mourning after which D. Maria set off for Salvaterra to hunt boar and deer.

Taking Decisions

During the seventeenth and eighteenth centuries observers commented on the lack of decisiveness of the Braganza monarchs so frequently that it seems to have been an inherited failing. D. João IV had been so reluctant to make any decision about accepting the Crown that the whole success of the restoration had been threatened. D. Pedro II was notoriously slow to make decisions and, although D. João V was decisive enough when it came to matters of cultural significance, D. José, his son, again showed a hesitancy that made possible the dominance of Pombal over the policy and direction of the government. Pombal had many failings but indecisiveness was not one of them. D. José remained torn between his trust in his minister and his doubts about some of the actions that the minister took. D. Maria I, again, was frequently unsettled by the need to make difficult decisions and was torn between policies that pulled her in different directions and conflicted with her conscience. This uncertainty and hesitation contributed in the end to her descent into madness. D. João VI was notorious for his hesitations and slowness in making decisions. His hesitancy in 1807 nearly resulted in the decision to leave for Brazil being made too late, while his vacillations over the return to Portugal after 1815 and his uncertain handling of the liberal movement in the 1820s often left a power vacuum at the centre of Portuguese affairs. However, observers grudgingly acknowledged that on occasions D. João's slowness in making decisions was shrewd and deliberate and was a way of maintaining some measure of control in an increasingly volatile situation.

With the arrival on the scene of D. João's two sons, Pedro and Miguel, the trait of indecisiveness in the Braganza character seemed to have run out. Both were impulsive and energetic and were not only willing and able to take decisions but frequently moved ahead of events and seemed to take no account of the consequences of their actions.

Royalty and Public Opinion

Ruling dynasties have usually been deeply concerned with how their subjects saw them. To be seen as the guardians of the public interest and the fount of justice was always an important supplement to the assertions of a divine right to rule. 'No one can be loved by whom he is not known' is a saying attributed to the chronicler Resende;[41] to maintain popular support it was necessary for the monarch to be seen to embody widely held national values. It did D. Pedro II and, a century and a half later, D. Miguel no harm to be seen among bullfighters and to perform themselves in the bullring. Even those rulers who did not fight bulls themselves appeared at bull festivals, which, until the earthquake of 1755, were often held in the square before the royal palace. Bullfights were often associated with celebrations of royal births, marriages and birthdays when, after elaborate processions, ceremonial Masses and fireworks, the royal family and the crowd came together to indulge in this bloody spectacle. One such festival during the reign of D. Maria I involved killing 24 bulls and the following day a further 26.

One of the prerogatives of an absolute monarch was to do justice and to grant pardons or the remission of sentences. According to Kirsten Schultz, 'in bestowing a pardon, or commuting a death sentence, the prince regent [later D. João VI] exercised the virtues of a Monarch . . . not only as Sovereign, but also as a Father of his Vassals'.[42] This exercise of mercy (called *graças*) was often associated with occasions when the exercise of royal authority was on display, as, for instance, when the birth of a prince or princess was being celebrated.[43]

Linked to the practice of *graças* were the public audiences when the monarchs allowed any of their subjects to approach them with a petition. The early Braganzas had set days of the week for public audiences (apparently D. Pedro II had prostitutes 'brought to his public audiences' so that he could inspect them), but D. João VI allowed anyone to approach him at any time, even when he was taking the air in his coach or on foot. All petitions or requests for assistance were then considered by D. João's staff, which included the chief of police, before a reply was given. This public accessibility of the king continued until the reign of D. Pedro V in the 1850s, when it was discontinued, being replaced by two boxes, known as the *caixas verdes* (green boxes), placed outside the Necessidades palace, one of which was for petitions and the other for requests for alms.

However, it was at religious festivals that the Braganza rulers most frequently showed themselves in public and through which they sought to uphold popular beliefs and values. Participation in religious festivals, in particular the Corpus Christi day processions, regular attendance at Mass, visits to shrines and convents and the endowment and construction of churches provided much of the story of the dynasty from the seventeenth century to the nineteenth. Being present at the autos-da-fé, organized by the Inquisition, also showed the royal family to be in tune with national beliefs and values. As Mário Domingues wrote: 'Since Maria I was so devout, it is no wonder that during her reign the common people (*povo*) found in the church the principal source of their entertainments.'[44] Caetano Beirão, in his biography of D. Maria I, describes how

> During the Easter celebrations, there was a procession every Friday. That on Good Friday involved half the city. Before going out the Royal Family went to the church of São Roque to kiss the feet of the celebrated image. But that of Corpus Christi exceeded all in splendour. It took six hours to pass, so great was the number of brotherhoods, corporations, ecclesiastical and civil authorities that took part. By tradition the king and the princes walked in the procession. D. Maria and the princesses occupied a tribunal built at the gates of the Cathedral. It was considered the most ostentatious procession in the whole Catholic world.[45]

The relationship between the Crown and the Inquisition was more problematic. Both D. João IV and D. Pedro II tried to pursue economic policies that were not favoured by the Inquisition and, in its opposition to these royal policies, it demonstrated the extent to which it had support from all sectors of the population. In contrast D. João v tried to work with the Inquisition rather than against it and during his reign he was able to exert increasing royal influence over that powerful institution. It was only during the reign of D. José that the powers of the Inquisition were drastically curtailed. D. José's powerful minister, Pombal, appointed his brother as Inquisitor General, removed the Inquisition's censorship powers and put an end to the autos-da-fé.

During the eighteenth century the absolute rule of the Braganza monarchs found expression, above all else, in architecture, religious art and ostentatious public displays of piety. So extreme were some of these displays that they became notorious in a Europe that was becoming increasingly secular and were commented on by visitors to Portugal, who found them both fascinating and faintly horrifying. The vast sums of money that D. João v spent on constructing the palace/convent of Mafra, establishing the Patriarchal church, building churches and altars and promoting Portugal's primacy among all the Catholic powers in Rome were justified as an elaborate exercise in propaganda that would underpin the Crown's claims to absolute power and would culminate in the Portuguese ruling dynasty being accorded the title of 'Fidelissima' (Most Faithful) by the Pope. During the reign of D. José there was a scarcely disguised reaction to D. João v's lavish expenditure on the Church, as Pombal pursued his vendetta against the Jesuits, against Papal power and against the independence of the Inquisition and the Church in general. D. Maria i and her husband, however, were deeply devout and during her reign religious observance once again became paramount in the public projection of royalty. The queen's construction of the Estrella basilica and convent in Lisbon was an echo of the vast Mafra project of her grandfather. However, it was her devout mentality, so anachronistic in the Europe of the French Revolution, that turned into an obsessive fear of hell and damnation and was largely responsible for bringing about her mental collapse.

A Court on the Move

In the fifteenth and sixteenth centuries the Portuguese monarchs habitually moved between a number of royal residences. This was common practice for rulers at the time who, like Queen Elizabeth in England, felt the need to maintain their authority through appearing in person in different parts of their kingdoms and spreading the cost of their courts around different local economies. In Portugal the kings often found it necessary to move out of Lisbon to avoid the plague, which was endemic in the city. When the duke of Braganza became king he brought as part of his 'endowment' the ducal family properties, notably the palace at Vila Viçosa. The royal palace, the *paço da ribeira*, was located in the heart of the capital, so the royal family often moved from Lisbon, especially during the summer months, to stay at Vila Viçosa where there was an extensive *tapada*, or game reserve. Only one monarch, D. Pedro II, never stayed in the ducal palace.

Gradually the royal family acquired or built other residences. D. João IV established the Casa do Infantado, an endowment for the younger branch of the royal family, and the *senhors* of the Casa built their own residences: Francisco, duke of Beja, built the Quinta Real at Caxias and D. Pedro III the palace at Queluz. Meanwhile the royal hunting reserve at Salvaterra dos Magos was also enlarged to house the whole court for months at a time, including the construction of an opera house. Mafra, the palace built by D. João V 30 kilometres from Lisbon also had a hunting reserve and the court sometimes removed to Alfeite, near Setúbal, where the Academia de Guardas-Marinhas (naval college) was established at the end of the century. There was also the old royal palace in Sintra, where the unfortunate D. Afonso VI had ended his days as a prisoner. A palace was also built at Vendas Novas to house the court when it transferred itself to the frontier to greet the arrival of the infante José's bride, Mariana Vitória, in 1729; after this one event, the palace was seldom used. Following the destruction of the *paço da ribeira* in the 1755 earthquake, the more modest Bemposta palace was used for official functions in the city while the royal family enlarged a residence at Belém with a wooden building, the so-called *barraca real* (royal shack), where, according to the marquis de Bombelles, there was a menagerie 'where very curious animals are kept'.[46] When fire destroyed the *barraca real* in 1794, a start was made on a new and very grand palace at Ajuda where a botanical garden was already in existence.

Throughout the seventeenth and eighteenth centuries the court regularly moved between these residences. As many contemporaries commented, these moves entailed the court taking with it the whole contents of the palace – furniture, soft furnishings, bedding and even kitchen equipment – as the provincial palaces and residences were not fully furnished. As members of the royal family had a passion for opera, theatres were built not only in Lisbon but at Belém, Queluz and Salvaterra and a whole opera company accompanied them on their travels. William Beckford commented on this in 1787:

> The Queen of Portugal's chapel is still the first in Europe, in point of vocal and instrumental excellence . . . Wherever her Majesty moves they follow; when she goes a hawking to Salvaterra, or a health-hunting to the baths of Caldas. Even in the midst of these wild rocks and mountains, she is surrounded by a bevy of delicate warblers, as plump as quails, and as gurgling and melodious as nightingales.[47]

A detailed and lively account of one royal progress is contained in a letter written by Philadelphia Stephens, the daughter of William Stephens, the owner of the Marinha Grande glass factory. In July 1788 D. Maria I and her sons visited Marinha Grande, bringing with them five beds and all the trappings:

> The Prince [of Brazil] and Princess's bed was very large and elegant. The stands were iron gilt, the boards painted white. Over them was a crimson buckram covering with crimson damask valance fastened to it. The headboard was covered with crimson damask, over which was a case of a most beautiful fine muslin worked with small spots of silver, the edges trimmed with an elegant blond lace plaited on pretty thick . . .

The queen's 'bedstead was the same as the princesses but smaller'.[48] Stephens purchased a hundred additional beds for members of the entourage. Knowing the tastes of the royal family, he had had a theatre constructed for the occasion where plays were performed by workers in the factory.

In the nineteenth century D. Maria II preferred to reside at Belém away from the radical turmoil of the city, where she could be protected, as she was on more than one occasion, by marines landed from British warships. Meanwhile, her husband Ferdinand took advantage of a lull in the political turmoil in the early 1840s to build a romantic castle, the Pena Palace, on a mountain top at Sintra. The death throes of the Braganza monarchy are closely associated with the royal palaces: D.

Carlos was staying at Vila Viçosa and left the ducal palace on 1 February 1908 to go to his death in the streets of Lisbon, while his son D. Manuel took refuge at Mafra when the republican coup erupted in Lisbon and from there went sadly into exile.

Court Etiquette and Customs

Elaborate court etiquette can appear to a twenty-first century observer to be among the more absurd aspects of royalty, but it could serve its purposes. The British diplomat Marcus Cheke, writing about the pre-revolutionary monarchy of Portugal, commented: '[Queen Carlota Joaquina] was, in fact, one of those royal beings of the eighteenth century whose passions and whose whims knew no bridle save the formal restraint imposed by the elaborate, minute etiquette of their courts.'[49]

Until the French Revolution sent the Portuguese court into exile in Brazil, the Braganza court was, by European standards, dull, formal and antiquated. Court life was dominated by frequent religious observance, as saints' days were solemnly observed and courtiers and the royal family took an active part in major public rituals like the Corpus Christi day processions. Royal birthdays were occasions for the ceremony of *beija mão,* when courtiers, diplomats and other dignitaries formally kissed hands with the members of the royal family. The marquis de Bombelles describes the *beija mão* that took place on D. Maria I's birthday, 17 December 1786, which he compares unfavourably with a similar ceremony at the Neapolitan court. Long files of people approached the throne, kissed the hand of the queen and of the princes and princesses of the royal family. They then retired through the same door through which others were trying to enter, with the result that the congested passage was 'choked, which considerably prolongs a ceremony that was already long and boring enough without this embarrassment'.[50] The next day the ambassadors all had to attend court again to celebrate the queen's Name Day, which they did with short flowery speeches that she received 'with infinite grace'. A *beija mão* held by D. João VI on his return from Brazil in 1821 is said to have lasted all day from eight in the morning.[51]

The *beija mão* was finally discontinued by D. Pedro V but it took a few more years before D. Maria II's widower, D. Fernando (Ferdinand of Saxe-Coburg), learnt the lesson that the days of hand kissing were over. After the fall of Napoleon III, the ambassador of the French Third

Republic was confronted by D. Fernando, who held out his hand to be kissed. The ambassador is alleged to have examined the hand and commented 'What a diamond! What a ruby! What an emerald! And what a privilege to be permitted to inspect such precious stones at such close quarters!'[52]

Mariana Vitória, writing to her mother, the queen of Spain, during the reign of D. João V, frequently remarks on the boredom of court life, enlivened for her only by visits to convents. She had to try to find her own amusement and in March 1745 she wrote:

> As I am very fond of riding I amuse myself with this and with singing when I return, or if I do not go out. For some months, I have had another amusement which is to go to play [at cards?] in the evening at the apartment of some *fidalgos* who are there and who belong to the household, because no other person enters unless he is an official. This is a very important thing for this country because I believe that the Queen [Maria Ana] never does this. Although, my Prince [José, her husband] is not as attached to these customs as they are, he does all he can to give me pleasure.[53]

Courtiers were not allowed to sit in the royal presence, a custom still being painfully and tiringly observed during the reign of D. Maria I.[54] The duc de Châtelet records:

> This court, during the reign of Joseph I [D. José], though ceremonious, was not so gloomy as at present: it was not an absolute stranger to diversions. Since the king's death, a wonderful alteration has taken place in this particular . . . The royal family never dine in public, and when you go to the palace, you cannot find so much as a seat. The secretary of state, and the ministers, are obliged to write upon their knees . . .[55]

Laure Junot recalls in her memoirs a visit to Queen Carlota Joaquina,

> When I entered the Princess of Brazil's drawing-room, all the *damas de honor* were seated – guess, reader, where? On the floor! Yes! On the floor! With their legs crossed under them, like tailors, or rather like the Arabs, who have bequeathed this among the many other customs they have left to the Peninsula.[56]

The bizarre world of eighteenth-century court life, and the strange and savage rituals that were sometimes inflicted on royalty, can be illustrated by a letter which the young Mariana Vitória, then aged 25, wrote to her mother in July 1743:

> So that you can see, my dear mother, the stupidities which are recounted here, I will recount this to you: my Prince [José] because of an injury to his hand which for a long time has caused him pain, was advised that a bull should be brought and that it should be killed and his hand should be placed inside it to strengthen it. At the same time, it was said that the bull that was brought was for the king to be placed inside and that the flesh should not be eaten because it remained enraged [poisoned?] from the bad humours that remained in it. See if there can be anything more mistaken. All the others [stupidities] are the same and I am told so many that it makes me angry when I am told of them.[57]

The marriages of the Braganzas were very public affairs. Betrothals and proxy marriages were accompanied by ostentatious ceremonial.[58] The celebration of marriages often took place when princes and princesses were only adolescents and the signs of consummation, successful or otherwise, were the subject of public discussion. The infante José (eldest son of D. Maria I) married his aunt at nineteen; D. João V was also nineteen when he married his sixteen-year-old bride; Mariana Vitória was only fourteen when her marriage to the future D. José was consummated and Carlota Joaquina was fifteen when the infante João (later D. João VI) decided she was old enough to consummate the marriage. D. Maria II married for the second time at the age of sixteen Ferdinand of Saxe-Coburg, who was only nineteen. As late as the 1860s, D. Luís, anxious to obtain an heir, married the fifteen-year-old Maria Pia and was rewarded with a son less than a year later.

The periods of young princesses were openly commented upon, even in diplomatic circles, and the brides were accompanied to bed by ladies-in-waiting and other members of the family. In his sermon given to celebrate the birth of Maria Bárbara in December 1711, the bishop of Angola compared princesses to the 'moon'. Just as the moon becomes full every month, so it was hoped she would give birth every year.[59] Giving birth was also a public affair with numerous councillors, clerics and family members present. The miseries of being a pregnant princess can scarcely be imagined, given the crude state of obstetrics at the time. Poor Maria Isabel, daughter of D. João VI and Carlota Joaquina, and married to Ferdinand VII of Spain, was in labour with a baby already dead. The doctors thought she herself had died and had begun to cut her open when the operation brought her back to consciousness. She died some hours later in great pain.

Death was a frequent visitor to the Braganza dynasty, taking away infant princes and princesses and cutting short the lives of many of those who managed to grow to adulthood. Funerals were among the great occasions when royalty displayed its authority to the people. Before the body was buried a *beija mão* of the deceased was held for all the great and good in the kingdom to pay their final respects. Burials were also public affairs marked by the pealing of bells, gunfire and the inevitable religious processions that accompanied the bodies of the dead to their final resting place. As a ducal family the Braganzas had been buried in the mausoleum at Vila Viçosa, but D. João IV began the practice of burial in the great church of São Vicente da Fora in Lisbon, making provision in his will for the bodies of his children who had predeceased him to be moved to the new royal mausoleum.

Of the royal funerals none was more bizarre than the two funerals of D. Maria I. Interred in Rio with full honours after her death in 1816, she was disinterred and carried to Lisbon in 1821 where the coffin was opened and the putrefying corpse was dressed in black clothes, while courtiers, nobles and important people of the city came once again to kiss the hand of the long-dead queen.[60] The whole scene must have recalled the legend of Inês de Castro's corpse being enthroned by D. Pedro I for the courtiers to pay their homage. D. Pedro IV, the first emperor of Brazil, was not far behind in tragic sentiment. When he heard that the illegitimate daughter he had sired with the French actress Naomi Thierry had died when only six months old, he had the baby corpse enclosed in a tiny coffin that he kept in his study until he left Brazil for Portugal ten years later.

The Braganzas were a strange and, in many ways, tragic family but this makes their story an apt reflection on the strange and, ultimately, tragic story of monarchy itself.

4

The Rise of the Braganza Ducal Family and the Reign of D. João IV

W hile the dramatic events of the 'long fifteenth century' from 1383 to 1521, which saw the rise of the Avis dynasty in Portugal, were unfolding, Portugal acquired a sort of parallel royal family. This family, often a shadowy influence in the background as major decisions were made at court, steadily grew in importance and occasionally commanded the national stage. D. João I's bastard son, Afonso, born in 1377 before D. João became king, had been made Count of Barcellos. He had married the only daughter of Nun'Álvares Pereira, the warrior nobleman, who had provided effective leadership during the war against Castile. Nun'Álvares, although himself illegitimate, became something of a national hero, his military exploits being gradually overtaken in the national imagination by his reputation for mysticism and sanctity, so that in 2009 he was canonized by Pope Benedict.

The House of Braganza

The count played a major role in the affairs of the kingdom after the death of D. Duarte in 1438. At first he supported the regency of the infante Dom Pedro, who rewarded him in 1442 with the title of duke of Braganza, his ducal seat and the centre of his power being in the northern city of Guimarães. The duke bore the royal arms of Portugal mounted on a cross. Endowed with extensive lands, he became the richest nobleman in the kingdom and his family the most important in Portugal after the royal family itself.

The newly created duke subsequently quarrelled with Dom Pedro and transferred his interest to the Queen Mother, playing a major role at the decisive battle of Alfarrobeira in 1449, fought between the factions supporting the Queen Mother and Dom Pedro, in which Pedro was defeated and killed. Until his death in 1461, aged 84, Duke Afonso remained dominant in the affairs of the kingdom alongside the infante Henrique (Henry the Navigator).

He was succeeded by his son Fernando, who acquired the title of count of Arraiolos (from his grandfather Nun'Álvares Pereira) and marquis of Vila Viçosa, extending the family's influence from the north to the central regions of Portugal. Fernando died in 1478 and was succeeded by his son, also called Fernando. Duke Fernando II was suspected, probably correctly, of intriguing with Castile, and his life came to an end in 1483 with public execution at Évora, in the heart of his ducal domain. The lands of the dukedom were confiscated and the family exiled. However, on the death of D. João II in 1495, his successor, D. Manuel I, restored the lands and the dukedom to Jaime, who became the fourth duke of Braganza.

In 1502 Jaime began the construction of a palace in the Manueline style outside the town walls of Vila Viçosa, but he is principally remembered in Portuguese history as an advocate of expansion in Morocco. In 1514 he commanded an army that won a major battle at Azamor in Morocco, which is the subject of a giant mural in the palace at Vila Viçosa. His first marriage ended in 1512 when he suspected his wife of adultery and had her killed. By his second marriage he had a son,

The ducal palace of Vila Viçosa.

Constantino, who became viceroy of India in 1558 and, among other measures, brought the Inquisition to Goa.

Duke Jaime was succeeded in 1532 by his son Teodósio, who became Constable of the kingdom. He proceeded to give a new layout to the square outside the palace and transformed the palace itself, giving it an elegant Mannerist facade and a *sala de música*. He brought the Braganzas once again close to the Crown by marrying his sister Isabel to Dom Duarte, the younger brother of the king, D. João III. Their daughter Catarina was married to Teodósio's son João, a marriage of first cousins that was to lead in time to the Braganza claim to the throne.

João became the sixth duke in 1563 and, when Cardinal D. Henrique died in 1580, he was considered to be one of the possible claimants for the throne through his wife and her mother. However, displaying a caution that was soon to become the hallmark of the family, the Braganzas did not press their claim, leaving the field clear for Philip II of Spain to contest the succession with António, the Prior of Crato. João's son, Teodósio II, at the age of ten, joined D. Sebastião's army that invaded Morocco and was taken prisoner at the battle of Alcacer el Kebir in 1578.

During the sixteenth century the dukes of Braganza turned the ducal palace at Vila Viçosa into a centre of culture and intellectual patronage. In particular they began to assemble the music library for which Vila Viçosa became famous. Teodósio II, the seventh duke, died in 1630 and was succeeded by his son, who was to become king of Portugal as D. João IV.

The Crisis of 1640

After 1580 Portugal was part of a dynastic Spanish state in which separate kingdoms and provinces, with their own laws, institutions and political identities, were united solely by having a common sovereign. It was tension arising between the different components of this segmentary monarchy, exacerbated by religious issues, that had caused the revolt of the Netherlands in 1568. Taxation in the kingdom of Castile had always been the 'Crown's traditional mainstay'[1] and had formed the largest part of the royal revenues. In Portugal, by contrast, taxation had been relatively light and the government had been more dependent on the profits derived from the royal trade monopolies. When war broke out in Europe in 1618, the financial strain caused Olivares,

Philip III's principal minister, to present plans for a national system of defence to which the Portuguese would have to contribute, a project known as the Union of Arms. In 1628, after failing to get local estates to consent to higher defence contributions, Olivares began to impose these directly in the different regions of the monarchy.[2] During the 1630s the strains of constant warfare began to take their toll. New taxes were imposed and others extended, notably taxes on salt. Higher taxes, coming on top of poor harvests, led to outbreaks of social revolt and it was not only the poor who rose in violent protest but the provincial elites who bitterly resented the encroachment of central government.

Growing social tensions could be felt in popular hostility towards the New Christians and in continuing manifestations of Sebastianism. Outbreaks of anti-Castilian feeling were also becoming more common. In 1611 a crowd had attacked the viceroy's palace in Lisbon, and when Philip III eventually visited Lisbon in 1619 in order to get the Portuguese Cortes to recognize his son as heir to the throne, he had to wait at Belém for the arrival of Spanish warships and an escort of soldiers before entering the city.

With Portugal increasingly required to raise money for its own defence and that of its empire, fresh taxes were directly imposed from Madrid to fund the general war effort and these led to further unrest. In 1637 rioting broke out in Évora against the collection of the new taxes. The Spanish believed that agents of Cardinal Richelieu were behind the disturbances and there is clear evidence that the cardinal, through Jean de Saint-Pé, his consul in Lisbon, was trying to make contact with groups in Portugal who were believed to be plotting a revolt against Spain. The outbreak in 1637, however, had all the characteristics of a spontaneous popular outburst, encouraged by officials of the town councils but motivated by belief in a moral economy that was being eroded by the necessities of war. The rioting spread throughout the south of Portugal and there were rumours of a mysterious young man, known as *manuelinho*, whose name appeared on some proclamations as though leader of the revolt. Hipólito Raposo, in his biography of D. Luisa de Guzmán, points out that *manuelinho* was the name by which an inoffensive madman was known locally and that 'behind this mask were the restless manoeuvrings of some of the regular clergy, principally the Jesuit fathers.'[3]

What began as opposition to further taxation soon threatened to become something much more serious and 'the popular movement, anti-fiscal in its origin, rapidly became nationalist and anti-Castilian.'[4] To Olivares's anger the Portuguese nobility appeared reluctant to take any action and Spanish troops were eventually sent to suppress the revolt. As António de Oliveira put it, 'the members of the "seigneurial class" (clergy and nobles) had a two-faced attitude towards the Crown: of support when it would benefit them; of opposition when their privileges were infringed by the Monarch.'[5] They now became concerned that, if the demands from Spain for money and men continued, there would be further outbreaks and disturbances that would have serious consequences for the whole social order in Portugal.

In 1639 Spain suffered a disastrous and debilitating defeat when its fleet was comprehensively defeated by the Dutch admirals de With and Tromp off the English coast with the loss of sixty ships. In the summer of 1640 revolt broke out in Catalonia. Initially, this was a popular rising against the billeting of the royal army in the provinces but it soon became a widespread rebellion against Castilian overrule and the burdens of the war. The murder of the viceroy Conde de Santa Coloma on 7 June made it clear to Olivares that he had a full-scale rebellion on his hands.

The Lisbon *Coup d'État*

By 1640 a significant section of the Portuguese church and nobility had become thoroughly alarmed at the deterioration of the fortunes of the monarchy. The war in Europe was going badly and there seemed to be no way of stemming the losses in Brazil and in the Estado da Índia. It was widely believed that the Spanish Crown was planning to undo the agreement that had sealed the Union of the Crowns at Tomar, and was plotting a *coup d'état* to establish the Union of Arms. This would mean nothing less than Castilian dominance in Portugal. After the revolt of 1637, Philip IV was rumoured to have told a delegation of Portuguese notables summoned to Madrid that he now considered the Tomar agreement at an end.

It is not clear when the idea of breaking away from Spain began to take shape in Portugal, but in the late 1630s it started to appear as an increasingly attractive option. Many of the elite believed that, if Portugal broke away from Spain, the attacks of the Dutch on Portuguese colonial possessions would cease, commerce with the Netherlands would be restored and Portugal would be free to conclude advantageous alliances with Spain's enemies. Meanwhile, the popular cult of Sebastianism remained focused on the return of the messianic figure of D. Sebastião, who would free Portugal from foreign bondage. In Sebastianism 'a nostalgia for a past golden age and the feeling of national humiliation felt by a people in the face of a foreign occupation' came together with 'the messianic aspirations of a community unable to decide its own destiny'.[6] At a more mundane level there were those who looked forward once again to having a king who would dispense patronage from a court in Lisbon. These discontents were secretly encouraged by Richelieu's agents, who promised money and support.

However, it was the revolt in Catalonia that concentrated minds both in Madrid and Lisbon and brought matters to a head, just as later, in 1820, it was a revolution in Spain that was to launch a corresponding movement in Portugal. When orders arrived from Madrid for the Portuguese nobility to join the army gathering against Catalonia, many were persuaded of the need for action. Rumour spread that 'this last summons for the nobility to attend the king, was only a specious pretence to force them out of their own country, lest their presence might prove an obstacle to some cruel design which was doubtless on foot'.[7]

Olivares had long doubted the loyalty of some of the Portuguese nobility and had tried to deal with the problem by placing his own men in charge of Portuguese affairs both in Lisbon and in the Council of Portugal. He had also planned to forestall the possibility of the duke of Braganza assuming the leadership of an anti-Castilian movement and in 1634 had sent a member of the royal family, Margaret of Savoy, a person who would outrank Braganza, to act as viceroy in Lisbon. He also tried to lure the duke away from Portugal by offering him the governorship of Milan, but the appointment had been refused. As soon as information about the Évora rising of 1637 had reached the rest of Europe speculation had been focused on the duke of Braganza and, in a letter written that year, the Dutch lawyer Hugo Grotius had observed that 'those who . . . wish to foment the beginnings of a revolt ought to give aid and support to the Duke of Braganza'.[8] In 1639, alarmed at this prospect, Olivares offered the duke the still more prestigious post of viceroy of Naples. Again he turned it down.

It was the duke of Braganza's ancestry (he was the great-grandson of D. Manuel) rather than his ambition that made him dangerous. 'His birth, his riches, his title to the Crown, were not criminal in themselves, but became so by the law of policy', as the Abbé Vertot put it in his famous *History of the Revolutions of Portugal*.[9] The duke's grandfather had declined to contest the throne with Philip II in 1580 and, although seditious rumours had surrounded his father Teodósio, João, who had succeeded to the dukedom in 1630, was not preparing to head any rebellion. He was a studious and cultured man, an accomplished composer and musician who liked a quiet life. He had never countenanced anti-Castilian plots, notably in 1637 when crowds urged him to lead a revolt against Spain.

Because the duke of Braganza showed so little indication of being prepared to lead a revolt, Richelieu appears to have toyed with the idea of supporting the candidature for the Portuguese throne of the grandson of Dom António, the Prior of Crato. The plotters for their part considered approaching other noblemen of royal descent or even declaring a republic. Allegedly the duke was asked whether, in that case, he would serve the republic or Spain – to which he replied that he had 'decided never to go against the common sentiment of the Kingdom'.[10] It may have been that, added to the urging of his wife Luisa de Guzmán (sister of the duke of Medina Sidonia and cousin of Olivares), which eventually persuaded the duke of Braganza to accept the Crown.[11]

Soon after the outbreak of the revolt in Catalonia, Olivares appointed the duke of Braganza to be Governador-Geral de las Armas (in effect commander of the royal forces in Portugal), ostensibly to organize the defences of Portugal against an attack by the French that was considered imminent.[12] The Abbé Vertot thought that Olivares planned to have the duke arrested when he left his ducal seat of Vila Viçosa to make a tour of the country's fortresses, but it is more likely that this appointment was a last-minute attempt to secure the duke's loyalty by giving him a high command. Either way it had the effect of giving Braganza a quasi-viceregal profile in the country as he toured Portugal dispensing largesse. According to Hipólito Raposo, 'his majestic appearance before the people made him appear as the charmed figure of a liberator. In short he was the incarnation of Hope.'[13]

The plot to overthrow Spanish rule was concocted by members of the minor nobility and it is not certain that the duke knew exactly what was being planned, though some of his followers certainly did and his business agent in Lisbon, João Pinto Ribeiro, was one of its leaders. One thinks of the situation in April 1974 when junior army officers plotted the *coup d'état* against the Caetano regime without General

A German print of 1641 shows the 1640 murder of Vasconcellos and the accession and coronation of D. João IV.

António de Spínola, the man who was to agree to become president of the new republic, having any direct part in it. The coup was originally planned for March 1641 but had to be brought forward as the duke had received a direct command from the king to present himself in Madrid. As Thomas Carte wrote in his *History of the Revolutions of Portugal*, the duke 'sent word to the conspirators of his being so pressed that he had no more pretexts for delay, and must either go to Madrid, or the enterprise be executed immediately'.[14]

While the revolt in Catalonia flared seemingly out of control, on 1 December 1640 a small group of armed men entered the viceregal palace in Lisbon and arrested Margaret of Savoy. There was no resistance but, unlike the coup in April 1974, there were a few casualties. Miguel de Vasconcellos, the unpopular secretary to the viceroy, and one of his assistants were murdered, but proposals to do away with the strongly Hispanophile archbishop of Braga were abandoned because of the outrage this would cause.[15] Margaret of Savoy was forced to sign orders to the Spanish garrisons to hand over their fortresses and then took refuge in a convent. Braganza himself hurried to Lisbon where he was declared king on 7 December and acclaimed as D. João IV at a ceremony at the Paço da Ribeira a week later. One by one the towns of Portugal accepted the new regime and the three Spanish galleons in the Tagus and all the fortress garrisons (except those at Angra in the Azores and Ceuta in North Africa) surrendered. As nearly as possible, it was a bloodless coup in which the Lisbon crowd had played little part beyond that of noisy but peaceful acquiescence and the lighting of bonfires in celebration. Portugal once again had its own *rei natural* – its native king.[16] One Spaniard is alleged to have summed up the coup, saying that 'John IV was very happy, since his kingdom cost him no more than a bonfire, and Philip IV much otherwise, who had been stripped of so sure a crown only by acclamations and illuminations.'[17]

There are interesting comparisons to be made with the earlier occasions in 1383–5 and 1578–80 when the independence of Portugal was at stake. On the previous occasions, most of the upper nobility and senior churchmen had been strongly pro-Castilian and rallied to the Castilian cause. This class had either gained or hoped to gain substantially from a union with Castile, already had family alliances with the Castilian nobility and were, in cultural terms, largely 'Castilianized'. In 1640 many of the principal nobles of Portugal, including Braganza's

Veloso Salgado, *Acclamation of D. João IV*, 1908, oil on canvas.

own brother, remained loyal to Spain. An example was Dom Francisco de Melo, who commanded the Spanish army of Flanders and, after the victory over the French at Honnecourt in 1642, was made a grandee of Spain. The higher clergy, led by the archbishop of Braga and the Inquisitor, Dom Francisco de Castro, also supported Philip, though here there was a notable exception as the archbishop of Lisbon strongly backed the revolt. There was some hesitation in the empire as well and it was not until later in the year that Salvador de Sá, governor of Rio, declared for the new king. The success of the coup that brought about the Restoration in 1640 was almost entirely due to the fact that Spain was totally preoccupied with the war in the Low Countries against France and with trying to suppress the revolt in Catalonia.

Braganza: A Tragedy

In 1775 a play about the Portuguese revolution of 1640, written in pseudo-Shakespearean blank verse by Robert Jephson, was performed in London. Now forgotten, this play shows the extent to which a particular version of the events surrounding the Restoration of 1640 had by then come to be accepted. The revolution is described in the Prologue as

> A nation struggling with tyrannic might;
> Oppression rushing on with giant strides;
> A deep conspiracy, which virtues guides;
> Heroes, for freedom who dare strike the blow,
> A tablature of honour, guilt and woe.

Braganza's early reluctance alarms the conspirators, one of whom, Almada, says:

> Urge how the Duke's affection to his country,
> His right unquestionable to her crown,
> First mark'd him for the victim of false Spain;
> That his commission as high admiral,
> His general's staff, and all the lofty pomp
> Of his high sounding titles, were but meant
> As gilded snares to invite him to his death.

Ribiro, Braganza's agent in Lisbon, later counters these doubts about the duke's resolve:

> . . . O you wrong him.
> I know his noble nature – Juan's heart
> Pants not with selfish fear – His wife, his friends,
> An infant family, a kingdom's fate,
> More than his own, besiege his struggling soul;
> He must be more than man, who will not hear
> Such powerful calls, and less, who can despise them.

In persuading the duke to act, the encouragement of 'the Dutchess' (Luisa de Guzmán) is all important:

> I have a woman's form, a woman's fears,
> I shrink from pain and start at dissolution.
> To shun them is great Nature's prime command;
> Yet summoned as we are, your honour pledg'd,
> Your own just rights engag'd, your country's fate,
> Let threat'ning death assume his direst form,
> Let dangers multiply, still would I on,
> Still urge, exhort, confirm thy constancy,
> And though we perish'd in the bold attempt,
> With my last breath I'd bless the glorious cause,
> And think it happiness to die so nobly.

To which the duke replies:

> O thou has roused me – From this hour I banish
> Each fond solicitude that hover'd round thee;
> Thy voice, – thy looks – thy soul are heaven's own fire.
> 'Twere impious but to doubt that pow'r ordain'd thee
> To guide me to this glorious enterprize.[18]

There was nothing theatre audiences liked more than to hear of Spanish oppression, which still raised shivers in the average Englishman as it had in the sixteenth century when Theodore de Bry was illustrating the horrors of the Spanish conquests in America and the Armada was collecting in the port of Lisbon waiting to sail for the conquest of England.

D. João IV

D. João, 8th duke of Braganza, had been born on 19 March 1604 and was a rather reluctant king. His natural disposition was to pursue his musical interests and to remain at Vila Viçosa where his father had assembled a music library. D. João was taught music by an English *mestre da capela* and was not only a performer but wrote about music (his *Defensa de la música moderna contra la errada opinion del obispo Cyrilo Franco* was published in 1649). He also composed music for the ducal chapel, some pieces of which are still performed today.

Although, as the new king, D. João brought a royal court to Lisbon, which once again became a focus for political activity and

D. João IV.

national culture, he remained a modest man who did not indulge in exaggerated ceremonial and elaborate displays of conspicuous consumption. He himself dressed mostly in black and had had to bring furniture and tapestries from his ducal palace at Vila Viçosa to give the Ribeira Palace in Lisbon some semblance of a royal residence.[19] Every Wednesday and Friday he gave public audiences and on Saturdays received *fidalgos*. On occasions, he sat in the *Relação* (the high court) and had a reputation for being a lover of justice.[20] A French agent left a description of him after he became king:

> He is of medium stature and of an extremely strong and robust constitution to which his previous way of life has greatly contributed. For when he was Duke of Braganza he spent the greater part of his time hunting, of which he was passionately fond. When he was at his palace of Vila Viçosa he diverted himself with music at which he is very skilled, and which is the sole pastime he pursues. He himself composes most of the pieces that are sung in the chapel where the services are performed with greater ceremony than anywhere else in Christendom.[21]

He had succeeded his father, Teodósio, as duke of Braganza in 1630 and three years later married Luisa de Guzmán, daughter of the Spanish duke of Medina Sidonia. She was to become, in many respects, the strong personality that guided the first twenty years of the Portuguese Restoration.

A portrait of the royal family was provided by the English priest and aspiring poet Richard Flecknoe, who was in Lisbon in 1648:

> The king is an honest plain man, changing nothing of the Duke of Braganza by being King of Portugal; faring as homely as any Farmer, and going as meanly clad as any Citizen . . . his ordinary Exercise is Hunting, and Musick . . . But for the Queen, she has more of the Majestick in her, and if she be not King, her ambition 'twas that made the King. She has a goodly presence, a stately gait, and uses the Trowel in painting . . . For Prince Theodosio her eldest son, he is a Prince of great expectation, learned, and of great wit and courage, of person tall and slender, about some 18 years of age.[22]

LOVISE DE GVSMANS, ROYNE DE PORTVGAL
ET DES ALGARBES. *etc.*

Montcornet ex

Luisa de Guzmán,
1640–60, engraving.

Print showing D. João IV
and Luisa de Guzmán
in front of a monastery.

Establishing the New Regime

The new king faced challenges of great complexity. Overthrowing a legitimate, acclaimed sovereign was deeply disturbing to the accepted ideas of the time. So D. João firmly based his claim on legitimate descent from D. Manuel, alleging that the Habsburgs had been usurpers and, for good measure, tyrants, as political theory recognized the right to dethrone a 'tyrant'. At home he faced the hostility of a large group of nobles and churchmen who continued to support the Habsburgs. In 1640 it had been the local town authorities, the minor nobility, the lower clergy and, most importantly, the Jesuits who had been the initial supporters of the Restoration. In October 1641 there was an attempted counter-coup, in which the archbishop of Braga, the Inquisitor and some leading nobles were involved. After this was defeated, the property of the nobles who had actively opposed the Restoration was sequestrated and used to establish the Casa do Infantado, the endowment set aside for the second son of the king. D. João was then able to win back most of the old noble families to support Portugal's independence. However, like his contemporary Charles I of England, who had tried to fend off the hostility of Parliament by sacrificing his chief minister, the Earl of Strafford, D. João was forced to give way to the demands of the Cortes that his principal adviser, the secretary Francisco de Lucena, be tried for treason and executed. More fortunate than Charles I, D. João's sacrifice of Lucena calmed the hostility of the Cortes and consolidated his rule.[23]

D. João's younger brother, Duarte, was serving with the Habsburg armies. He had refused to join the conspiracy against Spanish rule but he was imprisoned after the events of 1640 and held as a hostage, first in Austria and then in Spanish-ruled Milan. In spite of diplomatic efforts to obtain his release, he died, still a captive, on 3 September 1649.[24] Dying a prisoner in the hands of the enemy, it was perhaps inevitable that he should be treated in Portugal as a martyr and compared to the infante Santo, D. João I's son Fernando, who had died a captive in Morocco in 1443.[25]

Though D. João always made it clear that D. Sebastião was dead and the hopes of Sebastianists were futile, he benefited to some extent from the belief that the Restoration was, in some way, the fulfilment of the prophesies embedded in Sebastianism, that a 'hidden one' would come to establish the Fifth Monarchy that was Portugal's destiny. The main protagonist of these ideas was the Jesuit António Vieira, who became a favourite court preacher and who urged D. João to adopt an active and innovative policy towards Brazil. During his reign, measures were taken to defend the Brazilian Indians and to allow the Jesuits to extend their protection over them. Vieira also advocated the formation of a Brazil Company, on the model of the Dutch West India Company, to promote trade with Brazil and to counter the spread of Dutch influence.

To make this policy a success it would be necessary to attract investment from New Christian merchants. This aroused the opposition of the Inquisition, which had been hostile to the Restoration and had a deep-rooted suspicion of the Jesuits and their missionary activities in Asia and the Americas. The Inquisition now began a phase of active persecution of the New Christians in direct opposition to royal policy, with the result that the Brazil Company rapidly failed. To counter the influence of the Inquisition, when the Inquisitor General, Francisco de Castro, died in 1653 no new Inquisitor was appointed until 1671.

The greatest dangers for the newly independent Portugal, how-ever, lay in the international arena. Spain, of course, did not recognize Portugal's independence and sooner or later could be expected to try to reconquer the kingdom. And Spain had an ally in the papacy, which also refused to recognize D. João and applied sanctions against Portugal by refusing to institute new bishops to Portuguese sees. This quarrel was not one sided: the Pope did offer to institute bishops without any reference to the legitimate king of Portugal but D. João refused the compromise and continued to have the revenues of the vacant sees paid into the royal treasury.[26]

In Europe, the Portuguese revolt at first seemed to promise a new alignment of anti-Spanish forces. The Portuguese government believed that, with a desperate lack of military and financial resources, it would soon have to face a major military assault from Spain. One of D. João's first acts was to create a Council of War, but Portugal had no army to speak of, no frontier defences in good repair and a fleet that was badly weakened by the struggle with the Dutch. Foreign assistance seemed the only hope and the king immediately sought an alliance with the Dutch, who agreed to a truce in Europe and even sent some warships to protect Lisbon. However, no agreement was reached on a cessation of hostilities in Brazil, where the Portuguese refused to recognize the Dutch conquests. In the east it took some time before any truce was registered, and in the meantime, before any peace could be finalized, the Dutch commanders stepped up their attacks and in 1641 took Malacca, as well as Luanda and São Tomé in western Africa. Moreover, before commercial contacts could be normalized, the Dutch demanded extensive commercial concessions in Portugal, including freedom of worship and the exclusive right to lease ships to Portugal.

D. João also sought an alliance (a *liga formal*) with France, which had encouraged the revolt. The Portuguese proposal was for two marriages that would link the French and Portuguese royal families. The negotiations continued over a period of four years (1643–7) and, had they been successful, would have resulted in a marriage between the heir to the Portuguese throne, the infante Teodósio, and a niece of Louis XIV. So anxious was D. João to achieve the recognition and security that the French marriage would bring that he secretly made a suggestion that he would abdicate his throne in favour of Teodósio and would reserve for himself a dominion carved out from the Azores and northern Brazil. This suggestion, fantastic as it sounds, is a startling anticipation of events in the 1820s when D. Pedro IV first separated Brazil from Portugal as an independent country, declared himself emperor and then abdicated his Portuguese throne in favour of his young daughter. The other half of the matrimonial bargain would have seen the infanta Joanna married to Charles Manuel of Savoy. However, the French were to prove reluctant to make any formal commitments to the new regime and it soon became apparent that they considered Portuguese independence to be something over which bargains could be struck in any general European peace agreement. This became clear in 1648 when Portugal was excluded from the general negotiations for a European peace. As a result, it was not formally part of the settlement of Westphalia, which political scientists now consider to be the foundation of the modern state system in Europe. In the event, both Teodósio and Joanna died in 1653 while still teenagers.

In 1642 a treaty was signed with England allowing Portugal to recruit ships and men and granting the English the same privileges as the Dutch. However, 1642 saw the outbreak of the Civil War in England, which made the treaty of little practical value. This, however, did not prevent D. João from putting out feelers in 1644 for a marriage between the infanta Catarina and Charles, the Prince of Wales.[27] With the establishment of Cromwell's Protectorate there were renewed negotiations that culminated in a new treaty in 1654. This treaty, which was to govern Anglo-Portuguese relations until the nineteenth century, granted extensive privileges to the English merchant community. These included the right to establish 'factories' (corporate organizations to protect the interests of merchants), freedom of worship and immunity from interference by the Inquisition, and the right to appoint Judge Conservators to adjudicate disputes between the English community and the Portuguese. The terms of this treaty enabled the English to establish themselves as the dominant capitalist class in Portugal.

If D. João's diplomacy seemed to offer little immediate help to Portugal, his policy towards Brazil had notable success. In 1648 a revolt broke out against Dutch rule in the north. The revolt was supported by the southern captaincies and the governor of Rio, Salvador de Sá, organized an expedition that crossed the Atlantic and recaptured Luanda and São Tomé. In Brazil itself, the Dutch were gradually forced back to their fortified towns on the coast and in 1656 finally surrendered to the Portuguese. Portuguese rule in Brazil was never to be seriously challenged again until the independence movement of the 1820s. The king died in 1656, the same year that saw his policies achieve their greatest success.

D. João's Family

D. João and Luisa de Guzmán had seven children. Two of these, Ana and Manuel, died in infancy and the heir, Teodósio, in 1653 at the age of nineteen. This was a major disaster for the regime. The conde de Ericeira in his monumental history of the Restoration wrote of him:

> The inclinations of prince Teodósio were such as were necessary to make a perfect prince. As well as good judgement, he built his life on a secure base of the fear of God and during the eight years that I was continually with him, from [the ages of] seven to fifteen, I admired in him to the highest degree gifts of generous piety, sovereign modesty, admirable judgment and outstanding bravery.[28]

The infanta Joanna also died in 1653 at the age of eighteen. However, the royal couple were more fortunate than D. João's predecessor, D. João III, all of whose children predeceased him. Three of D. João's children survived: Catarina, born in 1638, Afonso born in 1643, who became heir to the throne on the death of Teodósio, and Pedro, the last child, born in 1648. In 1654 the title of Prince of Brazil was bestowed for the first time on Afonso.

D. João IV also had an illegitimate daughter, Maria, who was born in 1644. She played no part in the life of the court and her mother was of humble origins and was in no sense a *maîtresse en titre*.[29] D. João saw little of her during his lifetime but made extraordinary provision for her in his will, bestowing on her the *Comenda Maior* of the Order of Santiago, the revenues of four towns and, in addition, 50,000 *cruzados* to enable her to establish her own *casa* (household).[30]

D. João IV died on 6 November 1656, aged 52, leaving the queen, Luisa de Guzmán, to act as regent for his heir, D. Afonso VI, who was still a minor.

5

The Children of D. João IV

D João IV, reluctant monarch though he was, had steered Portugal through difficult times. By the end of his reign Portuguese society was much more united and the factions that had supported the Spanish connection had faded away. The country had fought off a Spanish attempt at reconquest and Brazil and Angola had been won back from the Dutch. Portugal's survival was far from guaranteed but it was less in doubt than it had been when the restoration coup was mounted in December 1640. On the other hand, Catalonia, which had also tried to break away from Spain in 1640, had been brought back under the control of Madrid.

Although D. João's heir, Teodósio, had died young, as had five of his other children, the king had three adult children still living at the time of his death, two of them sons. The succession was nevertheless a difficult moment for Portugal. The heir D. Afonso VI was a minor and the regency fell to his mother Luisa de Guzmán, who was Spanish. Portugal had been ruled by a Spanish queen mother during the minority of D. Sebastião in 1557 – history may not have been repeating itself but its patterns were recurring. Luisa was a strong and determined woman who had, from the very beginning, supported the Restoration and, in the eyes of many people, had been largely responsible for persuading her husband to accept the Crown. She had been a firm believer in the importance of the English alliance and her plan was to seal this with a royal marriage. In 1387 it had been an English princess coming to Portugal that had strengthened the new dynasty of Avis; now it was to be a Portuguese princess, Catarina, sent as a wife to the newly restored Charles II of England, that was to do the same for the new dynasty of the Braganzas.

Catarina of Braganza, Queen of England

Spain and France had made peace in 1659 and an alliance between Portugal and France seemed increasingly unlikely. The 1654 treaty with the Cromwellian regime had been signed between two countries fearful of Dutch maritime and commercial supremacy, but by 1656 the Dutch had been expelled from Brazil and Angola. The enemy now was Spain and Luisa knew that Portugal would have difficulty facing this threat alone.

Portuguese infantas, like their sisters in other countries, had usually been entered into the dynastic marriage market but few of these princesses were to leave their imprint on history compared with Catarina. She had been born in 1638 at Vila Viçosa and had received a sheltered and pious upbringing in a convent in Lisbon. After her father's death in 1656 she resided in the royal palace and, according to Thomas Maynard, the English Consul, 'hath hardly been ten times out of the palace in her life'.[1] At the age of eighteen her father left her an endowment to maintain a small court but she remained unmarried, possibly because her mother continued, even during the Cromwellian period, to hope for an English match. In 1662, already 24 years old and still unmarried, she was a valuable piece in the game of diplomatic chess.

The idea of a marriage alliance between England and Portugal went back at least as far as 1644 when D. João IV had approached Charles I with the idea of a betrothal between Prince Charles (later Charles II) and the six-year-old Catarina. With Charles II now restored to his throne, agents passed between the two courts, the Portuguese negotiator being Dom Francisco de Mello, Catarina's godfather. Although Spain tried hard to prevent the marriage, even going so far as to offer to provide some Protestant princess with a dowry if Charles would give up the Portuguese marriage, in June 1661 the deal was sealed. Catarina was to be married to Charles with an impressive dowry, which consisted of half a million pounds and the cession of Tangier and Bombay. Charles was receptive to the plan. He needed a bride and an heir to his throne. He was also extremely short of money and deep in debt. He is on record as having said, 'I hate Germans or princesses of cold countries', whom he described as 'dull and foggy'.[2]

The English marriage was the crowning achievement of Luisa's life. Offering a huge dowry was shrewd and rather unscrupulous as she knew that Portugal could not pay the full amount promised but that

Dirk Stoop, *Catherine of Braganza*, c. 1660, oil on canvas.

it was improbable that Charles would publicly reject his wife on this account. Her willingness to surrender Tangier, a North African posses-sion, and Bombay in western India to England was a continuation of a long trend in Portuguese overseas policy – to reduce profitless com-mitments in North Africa and to make Brazil rather than the Estado da Índia the priority for the kingdom's limited resources.

Catarina sailed for England at the end of April 1662, accompanied by her *Casa*, a household that numbered a hundred, including, besides her ladies-in-waiting, six chaplains, four bakers, a perfumer and a hairdresser.[3] She landed at Portsmouth on 14 May. John Evelyn visited Hampton Court soon after Catarina's arrival in London and on 30 May recorded in his diary:

The Queen arrived with a train of Portuguese ladies in their monstrous fartingales, or guard-infantes, their complexions olivader and sufficiently unagreeable. Her Majesty in the same habit, her fore-top long and turned aside very strangely. She was yet of the handsomest countenance of all the rest, and though low of stature, prettily shaped, languishing and excellent eyes, her teeth wronging her mouth by sticking a little too far out; the rest, lovely enough.[4]

A similar favourable opinion of Catarina made its way to the Verneys in rural Buckinghamshire. Sir John Leeke's daughter Dorothy, related to the Verneys by marriage, wrote in May 1662: 'My sister says the queen is very hansom, and I hear very stricte in hir carage, and all that is with hir modest and reserved. I hope it will work upon some of our wild ladys to make them more grave.'[5] A hope that was not to be realized.

Catarina was to make a considerable impact on English history but the start of her marriage was not auspicious. As Lord Clarendon, the Lord Chancellor and great historian of his own times, wrote:

The queen had beauty and wit enough to make herself very agreeable to [the king] . . . but the truth is, though she was of years enough to have had more experience of the world, and of as much wit as could be wished, and of a humour very agreeable at some seasons; yet she had been bred, according to the mode and discipline of her country, in a monastery, where she had only seen the women who attended her, and conversed with the religious who resided there, and without doubt in her inclinations was enough disposed to have been one of that number. And from this restraint she was called out to be a great queen . . .[6]

Moreover

there was a numerous family of men and women that were sent from Portugal, the most improper to promote that conformity in the queen that was necessary for her condition and future happiness, that could be chosen: the women for the most part old and ugly and proud, incapable of any conversation with persons of quality and a liberal education. And they had desired and indeed had conspired so far to possess the queen themselves, that she should neither learn the English language, nor use their habit, nor depart from the manners and fashions of her own country in any particulars.[7]

The unfortunate Catarina reacted hysterically to the presence of the king's mistress, Lady Castlemaine, and to the proposal that she be made a lady of the queen's bedchamber. The whole dispute alienated the king, isolated her in the court and for some time prevented her from playing any positive role as queen. Sadly for her, she also failed in what was the first duty of a queen and never succeeded in having a child. In 1666 there were rumours that she had miscarried but 'some of the women who had more credit with the king assured him, "that it was only a false conception, and that she had not been at all with child"'. Bishop Gilbert Burnet, who did not have a very high opinion of Catarina, was nevertheless certain that she had miscarried[8] and it seems that in all she may have suffered three or possibly four miscarriages.

Gradually Charles and his queen reached an understanding. Most of her Portuguese attendants returned (or were sent back) to Portugal and Catarina began to accompany the king as he made his progresses through the country or went to his retreat in the great park at Windsor. She adapted to the manners and dress of the English court and learned to dance. In 1670 she was sufficiently at home in England to take part in an adventure that acquired some notoriety. While the court was at Audley End, she and the duchesses of Richmond and Buckingham dressed as peasant women and went to a local fair. There they were recognized and had to escape from the crowd back to Audley End. Rumours of this and other escapades reached Sir Ralph Verney. In October 1670 he records that John Digby, son of Sir Kenelm Digby, had wagered £50 that he could walk five miles in an hour which he tried to do barefoot and naked but for a loincloth. Meanwhile 'the Queen, for a joke, in a disguise rid behind one to Newport (I thinke Faire) neare Audley Inne to buy a paire of stockins for her sweetheart [presumably Charles]; ye Dutchesse of Monmouth, Sr Barnard Gascoigne & others were her comrads.'[9]

Gilbert Burnet records that:

At this time [1668] the Court fell into much extravagance in masquerading, both King and Queen, and all the Court went about masked, and came into houses unknown, and danced there with a great deal of wild frolick. In all this, people were so disguised, that without being on the secret none could distinguish them.[10]

On one occasion the chairmen sent to carry the queen after a party failed to recognize her and left her in the street. All this was a far cry from the staid and prudish young woman who had arrived in England in 1662.

Although no great beauty, Catarina with her slightly protruding front teeth soon became a familiar sight as she accompanied her husband on his progresses or conferred her queenly patronage in different parts of the country. She appeared with Charles, portrayed in popular prints and on the earthenware plates and pots made in London and Bristol in imitation of Delft pottery. Her visit to Sandwich in 1672 was recorded in a series of paintings, and one regiment of the army, the Tangier Regiment, which later became the Queen Dowager's Regiment of Foot and finally the Queen's Royal West Surrey Regiment, adopted Catarina's badge of the Paschal Lamb. A fine portrait of Catarina remains in the officers' mess of what is now the Princess of Wales's Royal Regiment. Unlike most Elo of Charles's court, Catarina was simple in her tastes. In June 1664 Samuel Pepys was taken by James Pearse, Groom of the Privy Chamber of the Queen, to see Catarina's private apartments where 'she had nothing but some pretty pious pictures and books of devotion. And her holy water at her head as she sleeps, with a clock by her bedside wherein a lamp burns that tells her the time of the night at any time.'[11]

King Charles II and Catarina of Braganza, from William Salmon's *Polygrafice* (1685).

The queen in danger

As hostility towards Roman Catholicism rose in England, Catarina became an object of public suspicion and hostility. By the terms of her marriage contract, she maintained a private chapel, served by priests, that developed its own musical tradition. It was alleged that she was the centre of a group of influential Catholics who surrounded the king and were leading him to become a convert to Catholicism. Moreover, the fact that she had not given birth to an heir was also held against her, as it left the Catholic James, duke of York, as the heir to the throne. Pressure grew to have the marriage annulled, a story even being put about that there had been irregularities in the form of her marriage with Charles. According to Gilbert Burnet, a number of exceedingly bizarre suggestions were advanced for getting rid of Catarina. One of them, originating with the duke of Buckingham, involved having her kidnapped and sent to a distant colony, the marriage then being annulled on the grounds of desertion.[12]

More dangerous for Catarina were the allegations that she was the centre of a Catholic conspiracy to do away with the king. Such accusations, in the fevered atmosphere in England caused by the so-called 'Popish Plot', might well have led to the queen's trial and even execution – making way for Charles to marry a Protestant bride. Catarina, however, had never sought to play any part in politics and Charles was firm in her defence. 'The Queen is the subject now of great consultation, whether for Portugal, or a closer place, or the continued favour of him that fears no colours nor is sensible of any Danger; but the Qu. shows herself in the Park & is very merry', wrote John Stewkeley to his Verney in-laws in December 1679.[13]

Catarina was directly accused by Titus Oates himself, but the king came strongly to her defence. He is reported by Burnet to have said 'she was a weak woman, and had some disagreeable humours, but was not capable of a wicked thing: And, considering his faultiness towards her in other things, he thought it a horrid thing to abandon her.'[14]

Dryden wrote of this attempt to implicate the queen in his satire *Absalom and Achitophel*:

> No less than Wonders now they will impose
> And Projects void of Grace and Sense disclose.
> Such was the Charge on pious Michal [Catarina] brought,

Catherine of Braganza, painted by Peter Lely, second half of the 17th century, oil on canvas.

> Michal that ne'er was cruel e'en in thought,
> The best of Queens, and most obedient Wife,
> Impeach'd of curst Designs on David's [Charles] life!
> His Life, the Theam of her eternal pray'r,
> 'Tis scarce so much his Guardian Angels Care.[15]

Catarina was fortunate to survive these troubles because earlier in her life she had written letters that might have been used against her. According to Agnes Strickland, she had sent a letter to the Pope seeking his protection for Portugal, in which she had said 'that neither the desire of crowns or sceptres had induced her to become queen of England, but her wish of serving the Catholic religion'.[16]

Catarina's influence

In spite of failing to produce an heir, Catarina, it has been claimed, had a considerable influence on her adopted country. The American author Gertrude Thomas made sweeping and largely unsubstantiated claims about the way that influences from Portugal came to shape English taste. Catarina's dowry and

> the hundreds of Portuguese artisans that followed her to England brought to the beauty-starved English a fascinating amalgamation of designs, materials, and customs divergent in origin, yet oddly blended together through generations of use in Portugal. In England this foreign influence shaped the turn of a chair leg, popularized the use of woven cane, made fashionable a cup of tea, and further dramatically enriched English living in countless unexpected ways.[17]

Claims have even been made that Catarina introduced the English to marmalade – although Portuguese *marmelada* was, and is, made from quinces, not oranges.

It was through the presence of so many Portuguese in the English court that the Portuguese language first became widely known in England and two of Catarina's English entourage, John Steven and his brother Richard, translated the historical writings of Manuel de Faria y Sousa into English.[18]

Catarina had been granted a considerable annual income of £40,000 to which was added the dowry of Charles I's wife, Henrietta Maria, after she died in 1667. She used some of her wealth to become a significant patron of art and music. Although it took her some time to adjust to the life of the English court, she soon assumed a new and more regal image. There is a striking difference between the staid portrait of Catarina as a naive young girl, painted by Dirk Stoop at the time of her arrival on England, and the splendid regal portraits of her by Jacob Huysman painted two years later in 1664. In particular she patronized the painter Benedetto Gennari, who also enjoyed the patronage of Mary of Modena, the duke of York's Italian and Catholic second wife. Catarina also brought over Italian composers and musicians and through her patronage Italian music became popular and influential in England.[19]

After she moved to Somerset House in 1667 Catarina's court became a centre of cultural opposition to the dominant French influences that surrounded Charles and which came to him through his sister, the duchess of Orléans, and his French mistress, Louise de Kérouaille. Catarina's hostility to France and French influence was the nearest she came to taking a political stance and in this she was closer to popular sentiment in England than her husband.[20]

The dowager queen

After the death of Charles in 1685, the accession to the throne of the Catholic James II gave Catarina considerable security and she was one of those present at the birth of Mary of Modena's son, the future Old Pretender, in 1688. Moreover, she was astute enough to adapt to the changing circumstances when the revolution of 1688 brought William and Mary to the throne, her known hostility to France helping her to adjust to the new regime.

She had wanted to return to Portugal after her husband's death but there were problems in travelling caused by the European war and later the opposition of the exiled James II to the idea of her travelling through France. Meanwhile, it seems that she was not on good terms with Queen Mary and tried to move out of London to some country seat. Apparently, she contemplated acquiring either Chatsworth (in Derbyshire) or Knole (in Kent) as a residence, both at a considerable distance from the capital. Rumours once again circulated that she was involved in a Catholic conspiracy to poison Queen Mary and she reported this in a letter to her brother, D. Pedro II, in Portugal, adding, 'I lack him who defended me on a like occasion' – a reference to Charles's refusal to countenance any involvement of Catarina in the investigations into the Popish Plot.[21]

It was not until 1692 that all the diplomatic pieces were in place and she was able to make the journey back to Portugal, her leisurely procession through France taking six months. She arrived in Portugal with an English entourage just as, thirty years earlier, she had arrived in London with her Portuguese 'family'.

Catarina became an important figure in Portugal during the last ten years of her life, helping to turn her brother D. Pedro's policy in a more Anglophile direction, one result of which was that Portugal joined the Grand Alliance in 1703 and signed the famous Methuen Treaties, which were to tie Portugal closely to Britain both economically and politically for the next century. She had the palace at Bemposta built as her residence. She took over the reins of government in Lisbon as regent, first in 1701 and then in 1704 when D. Pedro accompanied his armies to the frontier, and finally, for nearly a year, in 1705 when D. Pedro was too ill to handle the affairs of the government.

Catarina died in December 1705, aged 67, and was initially buried in the Jeronimos monastery at Belém before being moved to São Vicente da Fora, the mausoleum of the royal family.

She remains perhaps the most loved and respected of all the members of the Braganza dynasty.

D. Afonso VI

Afonso had succeeded to the title of Prince of Brazil when his elder brother Teodósio died in 1653. At his father's death he was thirteen years old, a year short of the age when kings of Portugal were deemed to have reached their majority. From the start, it was widely held that he was not fit to be king and this judgement was repeated many times throughout the rest of the century, clearly, in part, as a justification for the coup that dethroned him in 1667.

The birth of a 'black legend'

Sir Robert Southwell, the English ambassador to Portugal, wrote a series of lengthy dispatches that, taken together, form one of the most detailed contemporary accounts of the events that led to the political crisis of 1667–8. In a dispatch written to Lord Arlington in November 1667, he sets out the problem posed by the personality of the king:

> The King . . . being in his childhood blasted on his right side, and the Doctors taking a destructive method to cure him by drawing out his blood, left not only that part of his body ever since in a paralytic estate, but his soul and understanding so eclipsed, and so broken, that as no education could ever have made him perfect, so the want of all, hath left him crude and miserable. However he hath some glances and short fits, wherein his discourse appears

not only very tolerable, but with sparks of good apprehension: Yet these fits soon vanish, and seldom return; nor is he sensible of the variation, but all seasons seem to him alike.[22]

This was a contemporary estimate. Six years later, when the idea of restoring D. Afonso to his throne was still a possibility, a detailed account of these events was published in French by Michel Blouin, Sieur des Piquetièrres, interpreter to the French ambassador in Madrid, entitled *Relation des troubles arrivez dans la cour de Portugal en l'année 1667 & en l'année 1668*. In 1677 an English translation appeared with the title *The Portugal History; or, A Relation of the Troubles that happened in the Court of Portugal in the years 1667 and 1668*.[23] In this near contemporary account, Blouin wrote:

Afonso VI, King of Portugal, c. 1719, painted by Domenico Dupra.

Afonso who had been taken at the age of three years with a malig-
nant fever, and with a palsie, which had caused a weakness on his
right side, inspite of all remedies, even that of the baths themselves,
having made use of them twice at Obidos, had hardly attained to
the age of seven years, but they perceived his malady had not only
taken away the vigour of his body, but also of his mind.[24]

However, when John Colbatch, the English chaplain in Lisbon, came
to repeat this story in a book published in 1700, he added that, although
'it is said, all his right side became withered, from head to foot, inso-
much that he remain'd lame ever after, on that side; but they that tell
this, accuse him likewise of delighting to ride the most fierce and
un-manageable horses and to encounter with wild bulls.'[25]

D. Afonso had almost certainly been the victim of meningitis,
or possibly some other infection, which damaged the left hemisphere
of the brain and affected his movement and speech. Its effects were
not always very apparent, however, especially when he was fully clothed.

As a teenager, he freed himself from the restrictions of the court
and the discipline that his various tutors tried to impose. In particular
he had favourites and friends who would

entice the king down into the stable yard of the palace, and there,
together with a lewd rabble of grooms, blacks, and moorish slaves,
entertain His Majesty with wrestling, boxing, throwing the bar,
darting knives, setting dogs to fight, the young king making one
amongst them, and what he learnt from the conversation of this
vile crew, he afterwards, on some occasions, put in practice . . .
they represent him also as guilty of many extravagancies on the
account of lewd women, as in truth, his vicious inclination to them
were apparently the cause of most of the disorders they lay to his
charge.[26]

Numerous stories were told of the street brawls in which the king
became involved. Rumours of this behaviour reached London and
Samuel Pepys heard from Captain Lambert of the *Norwich*, 'That
the King is a very rude and simple fellow; and for reviling of someone
a little time ago and calling of him cuckold, was run into the cods with
a sword and had been killed had he not told them that he was their
king'.[27]

A story typical of Afonso's behaviour is recorded in the account written by Michel Blouin. Although there was someone who slept in the corridor outside the king's room to keep a watch on him,

> he went out of his chamber with a ladder of ropes, followed by Antony, and John de Conti, and some other braves, all armed as well as he, who seemed to breathe nothing but blood, and slaughter . . . With these people he ran thorow the streets, and entered those scandalous places, where they did a thousand violences to women. There was never a night that they went out thus, but on the morning were recounted Tragick stories: In fine he was feared everywhere as a wild beast.[28]

In a memorandum to D. Afonso's mother, Queen Luisa de Guzmán, the king's tutor, the conde de Odemira, wrote 'it is difficult to remove him from the company and abominations of moors, and negroes, which are taken so badly by the nobility and the people'.[29] And the conde de Ericeira, in his history of the Restoration of 1640, which he continued to the end of D. Afonso's reign, wrote: 'he was a king weak in body and mind, destitute of virtues and blindly devoted to men who were insolent and villainous'.[30]

By the eighteenth century the accepted narrative that D. Afonso was physically, intellectually and psychologically unfit to rule was being challenged. Pedro Mariz, admittedly writing eighty years after the events of D. Afonso's reign, painted a rather different picture. 'The king D. Afonso had an excellent presence, blue eyes, perfect nose and hair long and fair . . . although of medium size he was very strong as a rider.'[31] This revisionist trend has continued and today historians tend to see the events that led to his deposition much more as a messy political *coup d'état*, the main objective of which was to get rid of D. Afonso's principal adviser, the conde de Castelo Melhor.

Nevertheless, on D. Afonso's accession it seemed as though Portugal was threatened with rule by a young, inexperienced and uncontrolled adolescent, a recurrence of the experience that it had undergone when the young D. Sebastião had attained his majority in 1568, though it seems that D. Afonso's behaviour was much more disruptive and irresponsible than D. Sebastião's had been.

Luisa de Guzmán remained as regent for some years after D. Afonso attained his majority and there was some suggestion that, in order to maintain her position, she made her son's scandalous behaviour as public and widely known as she could. Certainly she had a very low opinion of her son and in her will named his brother, Pedro, as the person to carry out her last wishes.[32]

In 1662, when D. Afonso was nineteen years old, a group of nobles decided to put an end to the bad influence of his friends, especially the Conti brothers who had been given apartments in the palace, and had five of them kidnapped and put on board a ship to Brazil. The king was outraged when he found out and this apparently persuaded him to assert himself against his mother and the dominant clique at court. In this he had the assistance of the conde de Castelo Melhor, who thought he could use D. Afonso to establish his own supremacy at court. In a struggle for power, the Queen Regent lost out and retired to a convent, leaving Castelo Melhor the dominant person in the kingdom. The events of June 1662 were undoubtedly a *coup d'état* of a kind and set a precedent for the coup that followed five years later. However, it should also be seen as a struggle between two ideas of monarchy, between the older idea that the king ruled through his Council, and with its consent, and the new concept of royal absolutism stemming above all from France, where the direction of affairs was invested in trusted ministers.

Luisa de Guzmán died in 1666, aged only 52. Lady Fanshawe, the wife of the English ambassador, met the queen many times during her stay in Lisbon and in her memoirs spoke warmly of her: 'Truly she was a very honourable, wise woman, and I believe had been very handsome. She was magnificent in her discourse and nature, but in the prudentest manner; she was ambitious, but not vain; she loved government, and I believe the quitting of it did shorten her life.'[33]

Lady Fanshawe records that in February 1663, 'the King intended to go into the field and lead his army himself . . . but the Council would not suffer him to go, and so that ended'.[34] She says little more about D. Afonso except that he was very fond of hunting.

Castelo Melhor continued Luisa de Guzmán's policy of maintaining a close alliance with England and, with the help of English soldiers sent to Portugal, significant victories were won against the Spanish, which earned D. Afonso the sobriquet of 'The Victorious'. However, he also sought, once again, to form an alliance with France and this was to lead indirectly to his downfall. At the time, peace with Spain had not yet been made and an alliance with Louis XIV was seen as the best guarantee for Portugal's continued independence. The

Marie Françoise of Savoy, from Nicolas de Larmessin's *Les Augustes représentations de tous les rois de France* (1690).

alliance was to be sealed with a marriage to a cousin of Louis XIV. In 1666, when D. Afonso was 23 years old, the young king was betrothed to Marie Françoise (known in Portugal as Maria Francisca) of Savoy.

The new queen arrived in Lisbon on 2 August 1666. She was greeted with great ceremonial including a barge laden with flowers, apparently to disguise the foul smell given off by a city without proper drains.[35] Soon after the marriage, to use John Colbatch's words, 'Afonso began to express an extraordinary coldness towards her, and in a short time he estranged himself very much from her company'.[36] Later this came to be attributed to the fact that the marriage was never consummated. However, in letters written soon after her marriage, Marie Françoise appeared happy enough with her marriage, describing D. Afonso as 'the most honest man in the world' and hoping soon to have a child.[37]

D. Afonso loses his throne

France had made peace with Spain in 1659 and active support from that quarter for Portugal was never likely to be forthcoming. However, the arrival of another strong-minded queen was to influence Portugal's destiny in almost as profound a way as had the arrival of Luisa de Guzmán.

For whatever reason, the marriage between D. Afonso and Marie Françoise was a disaster and precipitated a crisis for the monarchy. This might well have proved fatal had the military reforms carried out under the direction of Luisa and the active assistance of England not fended off the Spanish victory that would have meant the end of Portugal's independence.

The events of 1667–8, which were to lead to D. Afonso losing his throne, can be briefly stated. Marie Françoise, discovering the drawbacks of being married to a mentally unstable husband, not the least of which was that he appeared to be unwilling or unable to consummate the marriage, soon struck up a liaison with his younger brother Pedro, and together they forced Castelo Melhor into exile and then persuaded the king to abdicate – a situation officially recognized by the Cortes in January 1668. D. Pedro did not assume the crown but became regent (Governor of the Kingdom was the official title), while D. Afonso was sent to protective custody in the Azores. A formal inquiry into the king's impotence resulted in the royal marriage being annulled and shortly afterwards Marie Françoise and D. Pedro were married and obtained a papal dispensation. Nine months later Marie Françoise gave birth to a daughter, Isabel, providing a frail line of continuity for the Braganza dynasty.

This outline of the story does not do justice to the controversy that has surrounded these events. It was clear at the time, and has become still clearer since, that what happened in 1667–8 was a *coup d'état* carried out by a faction of the nobility headed by the duke of Cadaval with backing from France and, at the very least, the connivance of the infante Pedro.[38] The real objective was to oust Castelo Melhor from power and to restore a more traditional order to Portuguese politics. D. Afonso had to be sacrificed to achieve this objective. The conde de Ericeira in his monumental work *História de Portugal restaurado*, the first part of which was published in 1678 and which became the narrative on which most subsequent histories were based, wrote of a court 'in a state of confusion and disorder where passions so diverse were indulged that there were more deaths that were violent and unworthy than in a glorious declared war'.[39] Castelo Melhor was banished from the kingdom in September 1667 and immediately afterwards Marie Françoise fled to a convent from which the king made an unsuccessful attempt to remove her by force. The queen thus played a key role in the crisis, deserting her husband and threatening to demand the repayment of her dowry. Meanwhile the king's servants were dismissed from the palace and he himself was placed under what was effectively house arrest.

Rumours of the king's impotence were already current. Sir Robert Southwell reported to London: 'For women he had a kind of seraglio, doting on them (as they themselves affirm) without any effect'. He claimed that Castelo Melhor tried to hide D. Afonso's sexual malfunction by having in his house a child whom he alleged was D. Afonso's bastard: 'to silence the imputation of insufficiency, [Castelo Melhor] kept in his house a child (of four years old) under the name of his daughter, which is now called a cheat, and made a theme of derision'. He was also clear that Marie Françoise had known exactly what the situation was before she left France:

> It is manifest, that the Queen was not herein ignorant in any tittle, before she left France, or was engaged in marriage; but being a Lady of boundless ambition, and her desires to govern prevailing over all other passions, the defects of this Prince, and the dissuasions she received against him, were but as so many incentives to warm her in her undertaking.[40]

In December 1667 an ecclesiastical court in Lisbon considered the case for annulling the marriage. It heard evidence of the most intimate kind, not only from the queen but from a number of women with whom, it was alleged, D. Afonso had unsuccessfully attempted to have sexual intercourse. The sexual lives of royalty had always been a public matter but seldom were the details of the bedroom brought out into the open in such a humiliating way.[41] At the end of March 1668 the marriage was annulled and shortly afterwards Marie Françoise and the infante Pedro were married. She was already in the early stages of pregnancy.

The queen's remarriage to her brother-in-law, scandalous at the time, nevertheless 'resolved various pressing questions', as the *Nova*

História de Portugal puts it.[42] Joaquim Verissimo Serrão, though more sympathetic to D. Afonso than many historians and doubtful of the allegations of impotence, agreed that it was 'a solution to a crisis which, in the European context, had threatened to compromise the Restoration'.[43] Maria Paula Marçal Lourenço, in her chapter in *História dos Reis de Portugal,* comments on how ironic it was that the king, who received the sobriquet of 'The Victorious' and who had presided over the rout of the Spanish armies, should have suffered defeat both in his personal life and as a king, and that this defeat should have been inflicted by his brother, who was known as 'The Peaceful'.[44]

Poor D. Afonso was sent as a prisoner to the Azores in 1669, after plots to free him had been discovered. Isolated and virtually confined to his apartments, he became increasingly unstable. In 1673 a conspiracy to restore him to the throne was uncovered and in 1675 he was brought back to Portugal and imprisoned in the old palace at Sintra where, it is alleged, his endless pacing of his room wore away the tiles in the floor. He died there in 1683 aged 40.

This contest between two brothers, who came to represent two opposed visions of the constitutional order of the kingdom, was to be repeated in the early nineteenth century in the struggle between D. Pedro and D. Miguel for the true inheritance of the Braganza dynasty and for the future of Portugal.

D. Pedro II

D. Pedro, the third of D. João IV's sons, was born in 1648. He had little immediate prospect of succeeding to the throne and as a youth lived the same kind of rowdy and disordered life as his brother D. Afonso. He was exceptionally strong and an excellent horseman. He also entered the bullring himself to fight the bulls. He did not receive the education a future king might have expected and it was alleged that he was only semi-literate. When the heir to the throne, his brother Teodósio, died in 1653, he moved up in the order of succession and was endowed with the Casa do Infantado, which D. João IV had created from the confiscated estates of supporters of the Spanish kings, to provide for the second son of the dynasty. In 1662, having reached his majority at the age of fourteen, he moved out of the royal palace into the Castelo Rodrigo, a magnificent residence that had been confiscated from the Corte Real family after the failed coup of 1641. From this

D. Pedro II, engraved
portrait by Gerard
Edelink.

Pierre II, Roy de Portugal

time, a number of nobles formed his entourage and constituted a rival court to that presided over by his brother D. Afonso.[45] As D. Afonso's behaviour created more and more problems, it seems that D. Pedro became increasingly his mother's favourite and, when she died, he was entrusted with administering her will.

The problem of the succession

In the early period of Castelo Melhor's ascendancy there is evidence that D. Pedro and his brother were quite close and would attend functions together but, as opposition to the rule of Castelo Melhor grew among the inner circle of nobles, D. Pedro became the focus of the opposition. He appears to have become the confidante of the queen Marie Françoise and it is likely that they became lovers before the palace coup, in which the queen was a central figure, led to the removal of D. Afonso from the throne.

Although the coup was successful, D. Pedro was only nineteen and made clear his unwillingness to become king while his brother was still alive. His position as effective ruler was regularized to some extent by the Cortes that met in January 1668, where it was decided that D. Afonso was still king but that Pedro would assume the government as *curador e governador do reino*.[46] D. Afonso's marriage to Marie Françoise was annulled and in April 1668 she and Pedro formalized their relationship. She was already pregnant with the daughter who was to be her only child. However, this marriage and the birth of a child did not bring about the expected stability and soon the question of the succession once again came to dominate politics. Although Marie Françoise had been a central figure in the reconfiguration of the monarchy, she failed to produce a male heir and her one child, Isabel Luisa, was for a long time the sole frail hope of the Braganza dynasty. It was not clear what constitutional law applied and, after a conspiracy to restore D. Afonso to the throne was uncovered in 1673, it became urgent to settle the question of the succession. The following year the Cortes was summoned to resolve the issue and declared Isabel to be the heir to the throne when D. Afonso and D. Pedro should both die. But the question of who would come after her remained unresolved. The Cortes, summoned in 1679 when a marriage was proposed between the infanta and a foreign prince, tried to invoke the so-called Laws of Lamego to prevent this marriage taking place. In the end, after fifteen possible marriage partners had been discussed, Isabel Luisa died unmarried, only 21 years old. Appropriately she was known as the *sempre noiva* – the 'always engaged', but never married.

D. Afonso meanwhile lived on and in 1675 was brought back to Portugal and lodged, a prisoner, in the old palace in Sintra. Although incapable, his very existence was a cause of some instability and he remained a focus for factions opposed to D. Pedro's government – his return in 1675 had been the occasion for popular demonstrations – and there was always the fear that a faction of the nobility might try to reinstate D. Afonso and oust D. Pedro from his regency. This perforce made D. Pedro excessively cautious and conciliatory in making decisions.

In 1683 D. Afonso died aged only forty and D. Pedro became king in his own right, with Marie Françoise now queen of Portugal for the second time. Her second reign is remembered for her patronage of Josefa of Óbidos, a female painter who became the best-known Portuguese artist of the century. However, her reign did not last long, for she died the same year, leaving D. Pedro free to marry again. The choice of a bride presented the king with a difficult decision as it would commit Portugal either to the French or the Habsburg side in the increasingly polarized affairs of Europe. In the end, in 1687, the choice fell upon Maria Sofia of Neuburg, a daughter of the Elector Palatine whose sisters were already married to the king of Spain and the emperor. Although this marriage aligned Portugal with Habsburg interests, there was another consideration almost as important. The choice of Maria Sofia had been in part determined by the known fertility of the family from which she came: her parents had had 23 children, seventeen of whom had lived.

D. Pedro's new bride soon performed her pre-eminent wifely duty. Her first child, a son christened João, died, but on 22 October 1689 she gave birth to another boy, a new prince of Brazil, also christened João, the much-needed heir to the throne and all the Braganza titles. Maria Sofia was to have five more children, three of them boys. In 1697 another Cortes settled the succession on the infante João. For the first time since the death of D. Manuel I in 1521 Portugal had an assured succession.

D. Pedro also had illegitimate children. Luísa was born in 1679 to a palace servant and was legitimized after the death of Marie Françoise. Her family were of humble origin but her brothers were familiars of the Inquisition and her *limpeza de sangue* (purity of blood) was officially recorded.[47] Perhaps the most important of the illegitimate children was Miguel de Braganza, whose descendants were the dukes of Lafões.

Foreign observers give their opinion of the king

Portugal had reason to be grateful for the long and relatively stable rule of the regent/king D. Pedro, but he was a very different man from his father. D. João IV had been an educated and cultured man, D. Pedro, on the other hand, according to the English chaplain John Colbatch, 'hath not been brought up to letters; some say, we may use the term in the strictest sense: But 'tis certain, the Publick dispatches are neatly signed with his own hand. However, considering the manner of his education he can have but little of what we generally call learning.'[48] This was Colbatch's delicate suggestion that the king was rumoured to be illiterate, though able to sign his name.

Colbatch described the king in a book that was published in 1700 towards the end of D. Pedro's life. It is a not unattractive portrait:

D. Maria Sofia of Neuburg, 1690s, oil by António de Oliveira de Louredo.

D. Pedro II, King of Portugal, oil on canvas.

He is of a robust and vigorous constitution, tall of person, somewhat above the ordinary size, and proportionately big; of wonderful
strength, and great activity of body, as appears still be the proof he
makes of both, at his ordinary exercises and diversions. He is of a
grave and comely aspect, hath nothing of haughtiness in his looks;
but on the contrary, such an air of modesty, as may be thought unusual in persons of his rank: He appears somewhat uneasie, when
gazed upon by a multitude; and one may discern a little disorder
in his countenance, when he is speaking in publick, to such as he
is not used to. He wears a long black perruque; and when he appears
in publick, is always habited in black, with a cloak, and long lace-
band, which is the common wear, among people of any fashion,
about the town . . . This prince is of quick apprehension, and a
piercing judgment, sensible, thoughtful, and inclinable to melan-
choly, which of late years has grown much upon him.[49]

This description is largely borne out in another contemporary
account of the king that is less guarded in its language. According to
A. D. Francis, who published the translation, the anonymous *Mémoire
touchant le Portugal* was apparently prepared for the use of a 'great lady
and also the newly appointed nuncio': 'King Pedro is very tall and has
a very dark complexion but is good looking. He is an excellent horseman; nobody is as strong as he is; he has broken with his two hands a
horseshoe and stopped a bull, holding it by its horns.'[50] A later account
alleged that the king's habit of going into the arena to fight the bulls
so terrified the queen that bullfights were banned except on special
occasions.[51]

In his tastes D. Pedro was like his brother:

The King does not like persons of quality, and does not hide his
pleasure when he has got rid of them . . . He passes his time with
junior officers of his household, who bring him all the gossip . . .
He likes to have a few mulattoes about him, as they have more
spirit than the Portuguese; he has several, who act incognito for
him in the town. He likes to make them fight and often takes part
himself.

This sounds very like the type of behaviour that was deemed to have
made his brother, D. Afonso, unfit to rule.

He is very fond of women and he is not particular; he has never been attached to any woman of standing but very few in the service of the palace, even the lowest, escape his attentions. He likes to hear of all the gay girls in the town and to have a look at them; he has them brought to his public audiences; he goes to them at night escorted by a single mulatto, visiting two or three houses in a night. As this sort of adventure is common in Lisbon, he has several times been attacked and even robbed . . . he likes black girls and has had several black babies, whom he sends off to the Indies.

Whatever may have been the case with D. Afonso, impotence was never D. Pedro's problem and he acquired during his lifetime a considerable reputation for his amorous escapades, as John Colbatch wrote.

I never heard that he had any favourite of the sex, unless it were one French woman . . . Those he has had his commerce with are said to be of the lowest rank, and very many, and not all of the same colour. He has not as yet acknowledged an unlawful issue, save one daughter, whose mother was a mean person.

The anonymous author of the *Mémoire touchant le Portugal* also asserts that the king once stabbed to death a nobleman whom he found in the room of a 'maid of the infanta' with whom the king was in love. 'Naturally the king caught the sickness [venereal disease], but he has never done anything to cure it, and owing to his strength has suffered less from it than most.'[52]

D. Pedro never drank alcohol and imposed this abstinence on the court and, rather strangely, according to Colbatch, 'eats commonly alone, and sometimes (as they say) sitting on the floor, according to the ancient custom of the country . . . with a flat piece of cork under him, seldom more than one attendant waiting on him while he eats.'[53] Apparently he regularly fasted once a week. This vision of Portuguese royalty contrasts rather starkly with the behaviour of the Sun King, Louis XIV, and his court of Versailles.

However, those who frankly commented on D. Pedro's sexual escapades all agreed that he was pious and charitable and took his kingly duties seriously, holding audiences twice a week, occasions when ordinary citizens could present petitions. The portrayal of D. Pedro by

Carlo Fontana, *King Pedro Asleep on a Wooden Board*, 1707, print (decoration for the memorial service to King Pedro II of Portugal, Rome, S. Antonio de' Portoghesi).

these two foreign writers is largely borne out by the near-contemporary description of him given in the *História Genealógica da Casa Real Portuguesa*.[54]

Serrão suggests that D. Pedro had a heavy conscience over the way he had treated his brother D. Afonso, which explains his scruples about accepting the Crown while his brother was still alive and that he always 'did everything to gain the approval for what he did from his sister Catarina, Queen of England'.[55] D. Pedro was not a man to make rapid decisions, and important matters were referred to the Council of State, a slow and cumbersome decision-making process that observers also attributed to D. Pedro's uncertainty about his position as head of the government, subject very much to the influence of the major noble families who had placed him in power.

A peaceful reign

D. Pedro was able to conclude peace with Spain and the papacy in 1668, which enabled Portugal to resume its place in the community of European states. Until coerced into joining the Grand Alliance in the last years of his reign, D. Pedro firmly maintained Portugal's neutrality, as Europe became embroiled in Louis XIV's wars of expansion. In this

Harquebusier's armour
of Pedro II, *c.* 1680s.

he was to establish a pattern that can be traced in Portuguese policy
for the next 150 years. He was also, by inclination, a reformer and
tried in many ways, as his father had done before him, to modernize
Portugal's economy and place the empire on a sounder administrative
and economic footing. In particular, he is remembered for the support
he gave to the Conde de Ericeira in his attempt to establish new indus-
tries in Portugal and to form commercial companies to operate the
colonial economies in place of the antiquated system of captaincies
and monopolies. In these endeavours he was supported, as his father
had been, by the Jesuits and their leading protagonist, António Vieira,

but was opposed by a formidable combination of the privileged noble families and the Inquisition. In his long struggle with the Inquisition Pedro tried to enlist the support of the papacy, but in the end was unable to prevent either the persecution of New Christians associated with this new economic order or even the attempt of the Inquisition to prosecute Vieira himself.

D. Pedro's policy of neutrality faced its ultimate challenge when the Grand Alliance of England, the United Provinces and the Habsburgs was formed to confront Louis XIV and the prospect of a Bourbon inheriting the Spanish throne. The archduke Charles, the Habsburg claimant to the throne of Spain, was determined to press his claims with an invasion of Spain, and Portugal had to choose between the protection that would be provided by the sea power of the Dutch and English if it joined the Grand Alliance and the risk of attacks on its maritime empire if it sided with the French.

After lengthy negotiations and much hesitation Portugal joined the Grand Alliance and a commercial treaty, always known as the Methuen Treaty, was signed with England, whereby Portuguese wines would have a tariff preference in the English market and English woollens would have free entry into Portugal. Portugal gained little from participating in the war and for the next century remained economically and politically dependent on Britain.

D. Pedro, however, did not live to see the end of the war, dying on 9 December 1706, aged 58.

Dramatis Personae

D. João v (born 1689, r. 1706–50), married in 1708 to Maria Ana (1683–1754), daughter of Emperor Leopold

D. João v's brothers

Francisco, duke of Beja (1691–1742)

(João de Bemposta, illegitimate son of Francisco)

António (1695–1757)

Manuel, count of Ourem (1697–1766)

D. João v's illegitimate siblings

Luísa, married the duke of Cadaval

José, archbishop of Braga

Miguel, married daughter of the Prince de Ligne, father of Pedro-Henrique, duke of Lafões

Children of D. João v and Maria Ana

Bárbara (1711–1758), married Ferdinand vi of Spain

José, later D. José (r. 1750–77), married Mariana Vitória

Pedro, later D. Pedro iii (r. 1777–86), married his niece D. Maria i

Illegitimate children of D. João v, known as the meninos de Palhavã

António de Braganza, son of Luísa Inês Antónia Machado Monteiro

Gaspar de Braganza, son of Madalena Máxima de Miranda; became archbishop of Braga

José de Braganza, son of Mother Paula da Silva; became Inquisitor General

Another acknowledged illegitimate child

Maria Rita de Portugal, daughter of Luísa Clara de Portugal

Ministers

Diogo de Mendonça Corte-Real

Cardinal da Mota

Alexandre de Gusmão

6

D. João V: The Golden Age

The table of dramatis personae set out opposite shows the complex family relationships, both legitimate and illegitimate, of the Braganzas during the reign of D. João V and is needed to make sense of the history of this period.

Baltasar and Blimunda

It is now difficult to see the reign of D. João V except through the baroque imagination of the Nobel Laureate José Saramago, who gave the king and his great building project at Mafra star billing in *Baltasar and Blimunda* (*Memorial do Convento*, 1982), which is perhaps his best-known novel.

D. João, constrained by the demands of kingship and the strait-jacket of royal etiquette, struggles, without much joy, to make his wife pregnant and to fulfil his vow to build a convent for the Franciscans if his efforts prove successful. The project grows to dominate the lives both of the king and the tens of thousands of ordinary workmen who are conscripted to build it. 'All is vanity, to desire is vanity, to possess is vanity',[1] comments the author.

In the ironic and detached gaze of the narrator in the text, all is not as it seems in the baroque world inhabited by D. João. The daily life of the king is filled with elaborate religious theatricality: 'Praise be to God who has to endure such ceremonies.'[2] The great statues of saints that are to adorn the basilica arrive from Italy and stand together in the moonlight 'like pillars of salt' – 'if this is sanctity what must damnation be like?'[3] 'Some mistake the olive branch for a gesture of peace when it is all too clear that it is kindling wood for the funeral pyre' and justice means 'a thousand cruzados to put on the scales, which is why Justice holds it in her hands'.[4] The infanta Bárbara on the way to meet her husband sees what appear to be prisoners in chains on the way to prison, but they are in fact skilled workers being taken to the building work at Mafra.[5]

How is Mafra to be afforded? The treasurer tells the king, 'If Your Majesty will permit me to speak frankly, I am of the opinion that we are facing bankruptcy. . .' 'Thanks be to God, [says the king] there has never been any lack of money.' 'That is true [says the treasurer] but my experience as treasurer has taught me that the most persistent beggar is the one who has money to squander, just like Portugal.' So 'a royal courier was despatched in haste to Mafra with strict orders from His Royal Majesty that the mountain be razed without delay.'[6]

Against the backdrop of the construction work on the vast palace/ convent, the central narratives of the novel concern the love of a soldier called Baltasar, who has lost his hand in the wars, and a woman with powers to see past the material here and now. They participate in the successful building of a flying machine, kept aloft by human will. The secondary narrative is equally symbolic as teams of oxen and hundreds of men struggle to bring a single huge block of stone to Mafra, also a triumph of the human will. When it arrives 'everyone was astounded at the dimensions of the stone. It's so huge. But looking up at the basilica, Baltasar murmured, "It's so small".'[7]

Meanwhile, the hollow pomp of royalty is everywhere subverted. A night-time story is told of the Queen and the Hermit. After they had disappeared together and the king had failed to find them, 'the Hermit ceased to be a Hermit and the Queen stopped being a Queen, but it was never discovered whether the Hermit succeeded in becoming a man or the Queen succeeded in becoming a woman.'[8] As for the realities of religion and daily life, 'Lisbon stinks, but the incense bestows meaning on this putrid stench of decay, a stench that comes from the wickedness of the flesh' and 'we shall never know what the inhabitants of Lisbon enjoyed more, autos-da-fé or bullfights'.[9]

D. João V and Absolute Monarchy

D. João v became king at the age of seventeen and was to preside over Portugal's golden age. Gold had been discovered in Brazil in 1697 and by the time of his accession in 1706 bullion was flowing into Portugal and into the royal coffers in substantial quantities. The riches of Brazil were, in a very short time, to transform Portugal and its monarchy.

Absolute monarchy and divine right has always been just an ideal: the realities of power are that kings have to operate in alliance with influential groups in society who look to the king to support their sectional or class interests. The art of being an absolute monarch was not to become dependent on any one powerful group in society but to achieve a balance or, more often, to be successful in playing one group off against another. Half-hidden in the shadows behind the public ceremonies that glorified the absolute monarch was the idea that the king was chosen by the people and that his power derived from a contract made with his subjects. As Bishop José de Mascarenhas stated in a memorandum sent to the Cortes in 1674, when the public good demanded it, 'the people, legitimately assembled, could depose [the king] and deprive him of the royal dignity'.[10]

D. João V by Nicolau Nasoni (1691–1773).

During the regency and reign of D. Pedro II, the Crown had been relatively weak. The king had neither the resources nor the capacity to transform his regime into the kind of absolute monarchy that was emerging elsewhere on the continent. Although the influence of the Cortes was largely limited to dealing with questions related to the succession, D. Pedro II himself never broke free from the influence of the noble factions that had brought him to power in 1668 and which, in alliance with the Inquisition, frustrated at every turn his attempts at economic reform and modernization.

D. João V was, from the outset, in a wholly different position and was able to assert his pretensions to absolute monarchy beyond anything his father or grandfather had been able to imagine, and the source of this new authority was the vastly expanded revenues he enjoyed. Between 1726 and 1731 annual imports of gold varied between six and eight tons and this quantity rose between 1740 and 1755 to between fourteen and sixteen tons.[11] From this the king was able to levy the traditional royal fifth, or 20 per cent tax. The Crown also benefited from the vastly increased customs revenue as Portugal enjoyed a consumer boom that sucked in imports from abroad. By the 1730s, diamonds were also being mined in Brazil. D. João now had the riches to realize his vision of a new age of Portuguese greatness over which he would preside. From being one of the poorest monarchies in Europe, Portugal and the Portuguese king became bywords for wealth and lavish expenditure.

A Complicated Family Life

D. João V's uncle, D. Afonso VI, may have suffered from sexual malfunction but his father, D. Pedro, had no such problem and left many children, legitimate and illegitimate. D. João had three brothers whose existence seemed to guarantee the survival of the dynasty. All three, however, were to die unmarried and without legitimate descendants. The eldest, Francisco, duke of Beja, commanded the Portuguese naval contingent against the Turks in 1717. According to the *Description de la ville de Lisbonne*, an account of Portugal published in Paris in 1730 by an unknown author,[12] he was 'a fine man who in spite of his obesity was very lively . . . and devoted most of his time to hunting'. The *Nova História de Portugal* suggests that he tried to woo his brother D. João's queen in an apparent attempt to steal the crown, in a repeat of the events of 1667–8, which had seen D. Pedro II steal the throne from his brother D. Afonso VI.[13] And the Portuguese historian Joaquim Verissimo Serrão agrees that Francisco wanted to replace his brother on the throne and that he intended to use D. João's absence, should he set out on the grand European tour that he planned, to 'gain the good favour of the queen' (*ganhar as boas graças da rainha*).[14] Francisco built the Quinta Real at Caxias as his residence. The bizarre behaviour of princes is often unlocked from their psyche when they feel themselves to be immune from the processes of the law and Francisco is reported to have enjoyed sitting in his river palace firing pot-shots at sailors on the shipping in the Tagus. He died in 1742, aged 51.

Francisco had two illegitimate sons by a nun, Marianna de Sousa. The younger son, known as João de Bemposta, was later legitimized and became commander of the navy. He was a close friend of the English naval captain Augustus Hervey and features in the latter's journals. In 1748 Hervey recorded, 'he made his palace as my own. I used to dine there, lay there, and used his equipages just as I pleased.'[15] Four years later, on returning to Lisbon, Hervey 'went in one of Don João's barges nine leagues up the river to St Mora, a palace of his. He received me with near twenty horsemen at the water-side and carried me a boar-hunting.'[16]

The second of D. João V's brothers was António, who lived a very retired life and died in 1757. He never married but had one illegitimate son. The third brother, Manuel, Count of Ourem, left Portugal without the king's authorization at the age of eighteen and took service in the Austrian army commanded by Prince Eugene of Savoy, which was fighting the Turks. He fought in the campaigns of 1716–18, rising to the rank of Maréchal de Camp when he was aged just twenty-one. For the next fifteen years he lived at the Austrian and Russian courts. He was one of a group of Portuguese, the best-known being Manuel Teles da Silva, Duke Silva-Tarouca, who became influential at the Austrian court and helped to build the close ties that linked the Braganzas with the Austrian Habsburgs, ties which lasted into the nineteenth century. He was in Russia in 1730 when it was rumoured that he was a suitor for the hand of the Tsarina Anna,[17] and in 1733 his name was even put forward as a possible candidate for the throne of Poland.

D. João V also had three 'natural' siblings. Luísa married the second duke of Cadaval and, after his death, his brother Jaime, the third duke; she died in 1732. José became archbishop of Braga. Miguel, who was born in 1699, drowned in the Tagus while returning from hunting at the age of just 25. In 1715 Miguel, then aged sixteen, had married the daughter of the Prince de Ligne, by whom he had two sons. The elder, Pedro-Henrique, born in 1718, was made duke of Lafões by D. João v. His younger brother, João-Carlos, born in 1719, inherited the title and survived the century, dying in 1806; he was the founder of the Real Academia de Ciências. The Ducal House of Lafões became one of the premier noble families of Portugal, following a pattern familiar in the life of Charles II of England, who had also created a new nobility by granting titles to his mistresses and their children.

The Austrian connection had been established by D. Pedro II when he married Maria Sofia of Neuburg, whose sister was the third wife of the Habsburg emperor Leopold I, and had been confirmed when Portugal joined the Grand Alliance against Louis XIV. The links with Vienna were strengthened by the young D. João V in 1708, two years after coming to the throne, when he married Leopold's daughter Maria Ana, who was his first cousin (their respective mothers being sisters). This marriage confirmed Portuguese commitment to the Grand Alliance and to the cause of the archduke Charles in his quest for the Spanish throne. Maria Ana was escorted through the Channel to Portugal by a fleet of eighteen English warships led by the hundred-gun *Royal Anne*.[18]

It was three years before Maria Ana became pregnant, in spite of the earnest efforts of the king, described in the early pages of *Baltasar and Blimunda*. Her first child was a girl, Maria Bárbara, who eventually married Ferdinand VI of Spain. A son, Pedro, followed but he died in infancy at the age of two, and it was not until June 1714 that Maria Ana gave birth to the infante José, an event greeted, unsurprisingly, with relief as it seemed to promise the survival of the dynasty, which had once again seemed in doubt. Maria Ana gave birth in all to five male children between 1712 and 1723: Pedro, Carlos who died aged nineteen in 1736 and Alexandre who died at four years old from small-pox. José (born 1714) became king in 1750, and Pedro (born 1717) succeeded him as King D. Pedro III in 1777. The queen was, from the early days of her marriage, made aware of D. João's sexual prom-iscuity and made sure that the women with whom he was indulging himself were kept away from the court. Apart from D. João's regular conjugal visits, she led an isolated life. According to José da Cunha Brochado, 'this princess lived in her apartments conversing with her

German ladies and playing with her dogs. She made visits to the king her husband and then returned to Germany, which is to say to her apartments.'[19]

D. João's Daughter Maria Bárbara

The royal couple's eldest child was Maria Bárbara, who was born in 1711. In various ways she left her imprint on history. Her birth, as has been shown above, followed the vow that D. João made to build a convent at Mafra if his wife conceived. Although she was not the hoped-for male heir, the king, in fulfilment of his vow, went ahead with his vast and ambitious plans for Mafra.

Maria Bárbara survived smallpox early in life and in spite of the scars left by the disease was considered attractive, being described by the French ambassador at the time of her marriage as a princess 'of the best character and disposition, extremely gentle, polite, attentive and obliging'.[20] The famous Italian composer Domenico Scarlatti was persuaded to come to Portugal to be her music teacher and he later followed her to Spain, where he and his pupil had a considerable impact on the musical culture of the Spanish Court. Maria Bárbara became an accomplished player on the harpsichord, though it has been suggested that some of Scarlatti's later works, which were composed for her, were made somewhat less difficult to play as they were written with the limitations of her skills in mind. Maria Bárbara was also an unusually well-educated woman, as can be seen from the details of her personal library, which have survived. This included a variety of works in Italian, French and German as well as Portuguese and Spanish.[21]

In 1729 Maria Barbára was married to Ferdinand, the heir to the throne of Spain, in a double marriage that saw the Spanish princess Mariana Vitória arrive in Portugal to marry the infante José, a repetition of the famous 'double marriage' of 1525. Sadly, Maria Bárbara and Ferdinand did not have any children.

D. João's Mistresses and the Nuns of Odivelas

As well as the six legitimate children that he had with his queen, Maria Ana, D. João had numerous illegitimate children, at least four of whom he formally recognized. Throughout his reign he was tireless in his pursuit of women though, unlike Charles II of England and Louis XIV of France, they were never allowed to establish themselves at court. Although these affairs naturally caused distress to his pious queen, there is little sign that contemporaries seriously disapproved. D. João was, after all, the contemporary of Augustus the Strong of Saxony, who was believed to have had more than 360 illegitimate children. In some ways, the proven virility of the king enhanced his power and authority, drawing on ancient and scarcely acknowledged beliefs about the nature of divine kingship.

His first affair, which began in 1704 when he was fifteen, was with one of the queen's ladies-in-waiting, Filipa de Noronha, who was seven years his senior. The affair continued after his marriage to Maria Ana in 1708 and lasted until 1710. Filipa had one child by the king.[22] Towards the end of his liaison with Filipa, D. João became a regular visitor at the convent of Odivelas, already much frequented by the Portuguese elite in search of sexual adventures.

Like Louis XIV of France, D. João's private life was the subject of much contemporary gossip and subsequently of fascinated comment by historians. According to Charles Frédéric de Merveilleux, a Swiss doctor and naturalist, 'the king was accustomed to go every afternoon to [the convent at] Odivelas accompanied by his confessor, a doctor, a major-domo and one other servant as well as his coachman'.[23] Over the years he appears to have had affairs with at least three of the nuns including the Reverend Mother, Paula da Silva. In 1714 António de Braganza was born, son of the French nun Luísa Inês Antónia Machado Monteiro, and in 1716 Gaspar de Braganza, the child of the nun Madalena Máxima de Miranda. She was visited a number of times by Augustus Hervey and became 'a great friend of mine afterwards'.[24] Gaspar later became archbishop of Braga. José de Braganza, who became Inquisitor General, was born in 1720, the son of Mother Paula da Silva, who had already had a number of lovers before D. João. D. João's liaison with Mother Paula lasted for some years and the king had a luxurious house built near the convent where he entertained his lover. These three male children were all officially recognized as D. João's sons and were collectively known as the Children of Palhavã (os meninos de Palhavã) after the Palace of Palhavã where they lived at the king's expense. All three entered the Church in one capacity or another and remained celibate.

In a striking instance of 'don't do what I do, do what I say' the king is reported to have tightened up the regulations covering visits by laypeople to convents to the extent that 'even the nuns complained of the rigour of the royal orders which reduced them to a seclusion little suited to their inclinations'.[25] While still visiting Mother Paula, the king apparently became enamoured of a gypsy known as Margarida do Monte. When she refused to give up her liberty, the king had her incarcerated in a convent where she was forced to wear a nun's habit. When he found out that she was being visited by former lovers, he is alleged to have had them killed.[26]

The notoriety of the convent at Odivelas became legendary and was soon the stock-in-trade of foreigners writing about their travels in Portugal. In 1772 Richard Twiss, travelling through Portugal, visited

> the convent of Odivelas, where it is said that three hundred beautiful nuns formed a seraglio for the late king; had each one or more lovers, and were the most attracting mistresses of the Portuguese nobility. At present but a very few of these nuns are living, and they are become old and ugly; so that this convent is no longer a scene of debauchery. A French author speaking of it, says 'I was assured that the famous *Portuguese Letters*, of which we have a French translation, came out of this tender, gallant, and voluptuous monastery'.[27]

It is of interest that Richard Twiss should have associated Odivelas with the famous *Lettres portugaises* (Letters of a Portuguese Nun), which had originally been published in 1669 and which is now thought to have been a work of fiction by the Comte de Guilleragues, Louis xiv's ambassador to the Ottoman court. The Odivelas convent and its inmates had certainly been a place for the nobility to seek recreation as early as the reign of D. Pedro, when the *Lettres portugaises* were written.[28]

D. João's love life was characterized by such unrestrained excess that his health was ruined and it became necessary for him to rely on chemical stimulants. However, it was also marked by a certain amount of good taste. In 1729 he began an affair with Luísa Clara de Portugal, a lady of the queen's household, whose surviving portrait has a beauty and charm that can still be captivating. She was already married with three children when she met the king and soon became pregnant again. Her daughter was known as Maria Rita de Portugal. At the same time the king also had sexual relations with one of Luísa's servants. Luísa

Thomas Rowlandson's 1811 print *Pastime in Portugal, or A Visit to the Nunnerys.*

herself apparently had an affair with D. João's nephew, the duke of Lafões, which so infuriated the king that he planned to have his nephew castrated.[29]

It is no wonder that the infante José's wife, Mariana Vitória, once she became queen, would only allow old and ugly women among her ladies-in-waiting.

D. João's Style of Kingship

D. João is described in the *Description de la ville de Lisbonne* as a conscientious ruler who took his duties seriously. He had received a classical education from Jesuit tutors and had a good knowledge of French and Spanish. He was of stature above the average, with a good presence and an agreeable face with a dark complexion. He dressed in the French manner and all his clothes came from Paris.[30] D. João was clear from the outset that he was king by the grace of God, not by the will of the people – and he had the wealth to impose this understanding of what a ruler should be. However, like all supposedly absolute monarchs, he was very dependent on his closest advisers as well as the tacit support of the privileged classes – and, as it proved, of the English. The kingdom was administered by long-serving ministers, Diogo de Mendonça Corte-Real, who was the principal secretary of state from

1707 until his death in 1736, and Cardinal da Mota, who died in 1747. In addition, the king had a private secretary, Alexandre de Gusmão, a man of Brazilian origin, who served D. João from 1728 until the king's death in 1750 and who was a great advocate of the modern ideas of the Enlightenment. Among D. João's closest advisers should also be numbered Nuno da Cunha, the Inquisitor General, who held his post throughout the reign from 1707 to 1750 and who was a close friend of both Gusmão and the king. Abroad D. João was served by Luís da Cunha, who held diplomatic posts in London, Madrid, Paris and Brussels and represented Portugal at the negotiations leading to the Treaty of Utrecht in 1713.

These men provided a virtually unbroken stability to the administration and from early in his reign D. João left the daily running of the government to these trusted servants. In 1713, when he was aged 24, the French minister in Lisbon reported that 'there are complaints of the little attention he pays to his affairs and of the time he spends on matters of small importance regarding the ornaments to his chapel', and two years later that 'the king only listens superficially to the foreign ambassadors. They have to ask for an audience for a long time before getting it and the matters which they raise with him are always sent forward to his ministers.'[31]

The ministers and leading nobles, especially early in the reign, were able to impose some restraint on the young king and prevented him following his inclination to travel abroad to visit England and Rome.[32] However, as he grew more confident in his role, he was prepared to deal strictly with members of the nobility who caused him trouble, sending them into exile in the provinces. Merveilleux reported that on one occasion he exiled 35 of the leading court nobles and that 'the court appeared deserted'. He also recorded that D. João, addressing one of the courtiers, had said of the nobility: 'King D. João iv loved them, D. Pedro feared them but I, who am your master by law and inheritance, do not fear you and will only love you when your behaviour is worthy of that reward.'[33]

The king demanded obedience and respect, but this had to be earned. In 1723, when there was a serious epidemic in Lisbon, he not only remained in the capital but continued to hold his weekly audiences for the general public.[34] These audiences were taken very seriously by D. João, as they had been by his father. According to Merveilleux,

The audience begins with the men and ends with the women. They speak on their knees to the king who is seated on a throne, beneath a canopy and behind a table on which is placed a basket full of small packets of gold coins which His Majesty distributes charitably to those of his subjects who seem most in need, especially artisans and women.[35]

In contrast to his love of religious pageantry and his indulgence in sexual adventures with nuns, D. João lived a rather private and simple life, eating on his own and seldom going to the royal country retreat at Salvaterra to hunt, like other members of his family. His court, if his daughter-in-law Mariana Vitória is to be believed, was dull in the extreme.

D. João V and the Enlightenment

Frederick the Great of Prussia, who came to the throne of Prussia in 1740, towards the end of D. João's reign, famously described the Portuguese king:

> Dom João was known only for his strange passion for Church ceremonies. He obtained a papal brief giving him the right to a patriarch; and by another brief he was allowed to perform mass except for the consecration. His pleasures were priestly functions and his buildings convents; his armies were monks and his mistresses, nuns.[36]

The formal and theatrical aspects of religion did indeed dominate D. João's vision of himself as absolute monarch. He wanted to make Portugal once again recognized as a great European state but, unlike his contemporaries in Prussia and Russia, he did not seek to do this through military might. Instead he sought to establish Lisbon as the second Rome, the seat of a Patriarch with a patriarchal church to rival St Peter's. D. João's agents abroad were instructed to observe and report on the ceremonies conducted in other European courts,[37] and in Portugal it was theatrical religious observance that dominated court ritual and huge sums of money were lavished on churches and their decoration. As Angela Delaforce put it, 'The king intended to create an official state art that would reflect a new image of the kingdom and that would celebrate the prestige and glory of the absolutist monarchy he had created.'[38]

As this is so foreign to modern ideas of how a wise ruler should manage his country's affairs, it is easy to dismiss D. João V's reign as one in which opportunities for Portugal to modernize and to play a part in the development of European civilization were missed. The massive expenditure on churches, church ceremonies and ecclesiastical magnificence seem to fit uneasily into the Europe of the Enlightenment.

D. João V, however, would not have considered that his conspicuous expenditure on religious art and ceremony were at all incompatible with the ideals of the Enlightenment. He saw himself not only as a devout Catholic but as a great patron of enlightened thought.[39] Through his lavish expenditure he aimed to put Portugal in the forefront of architectural and artistic achievement. Although much of the artistic work commissioned to adorn his churches was carried out by foreign artists, principally Italians, he also encouraged Portuguese artists with the result that, by the end of his reign, Portugal had begun to produce artists and craftsmen of note. A purely Portuguese tradition in church ornamentation was encouraged, and the churches built in this period were decorated with *talha dourada* (gilded wooden carving) and scenes depicted in blue-and-white tiles (*azulejos*), which adorned not only the insides of churches but public buildings and even the formal gardens of aristocratic palaces.

The artistic style favoured by D. João was the baroque of Rome and, as he was unable to visit Rome to see its great buildings for himself, he ordered scale models to be made, including one of St Peter's, which were assembled in his palace in Lisbon. In collecting these models of famous buildings, the king was following in the footsteps of his Avis predecessor D. João III, who had ordered a model of the Colosseum to be made.[40]

D. João thought of himself as a patron of learning. In order to place Portugal on a footing to rival the other courts of Europe he founded in 1720 the Real Academia de História to be a focus for the collection and preservation of archives and the publication of works on Portuguese history. He also issued decrees to prevent the 'destruction of the artistic and cultural patrimony of the kingdom' and for the preservation of antiquities and ancient monuments.[41] The emphasis on Portugal's history was part of the plan to enhance the standing and reputation of the kingdom in the rest of Europe. The king also founded and lavishly

Pompeo Batoni, *D. João v of Portugal, c.* 1707, oil.

endowed the Academia di Belli Arti Portoghese in Rome. However, the intense religious atmosphere of Portugal during this period, the continued activity of the Inquisition and the dominance of ecclesiastics in Portuguese affairs meant that access to the scientific and rationalist writings of the age was not readily available, and many Portuguese intellectuals found it necessary to go abroad to study and pursue their scientific interests.

D. João also spent lavishly on building the royal library and on the collection of works of art. His ambassadors were given the task of purchasing private collections of books, manuscripts, scientific instruments and artworks when these came on the market and he would probably be better remembered as the builder of one of the great libraries and art collections of the age if most of his acquisitions had not perished in the earthquake of 1755.

As well as art and architecture, D. João was a great patron of music. In this he was following in the tradition of the Braganzas, his grandfather having been a noted musician and patron of church music. Again, it was Italian music that was favoured and Domenico Scarlatti was brought from Rome with a company of singers to serve as Maestro di Cappella for the new Patriarchal church and to teach music to the infanta Maria Bárbara. In 1719 the king ordered the construction of a magnificent new opera house in Lisbon. This building was designed to stage Italian operas in a suitably magnificent setting. The opera house was completed in 1737 but was another of the casualties of the earthquake in 1755.

The king is also remembered for encouraging the Lisbon municipality to build the great aqueduct known as the Aguas Livres, which was completed in 1738 to provide a water supply for the city, and for establishing the Royal Silk Factory at Rato, which became the centre for industrial entrepreneurship in the capital.

John Clark's 1809 depiction of the aqueduct of Alcântara.

Of D. João's religious enterprises, the three of which he was undoubtedly most proud, and which he saw as fitting monuments to his reign, were the building of the palace/convent at Mafra, the establishment of the Patriarchate and the granting by the Pope of the title of Fidelissimo (Most Faithful), which henceforward was to be one of the titles borne by the Braganza monarchs. The Patriarchate was established with privileges and ceremonial to match that of the Pope. The Patriarch even had a college of canons who wore scarlet robes like the Roman cardinals. The title of Fidelissimo was granted late in D. João's life and was in many ways the crowning achievement of his policy to use religion to establish his credentials as an absolute monarch, though today it is the building of Mafra that is the most visible of these accomplishments.

Mafra

By 1711 D. João and Maria Ana had been married three years and had not been able to conceive a child. D. João had made a vow to build a convent for the Franciscans at Mafra if his queen should become pregnant and in December that year the infanta Maria Bárbara was born. D. João now proceeded to fulfil his vow and the idea of the convent at Mafra took hold. With the signing of the Treaty of Utrecht in 1713, Portugal was at peace and gold was flowing into the country from Brazil. What had originally been conceived as a small house for thirteen friars grew in the royal imagination into something to rival the famous Escorial palace-convent complex built by Philip II of Spain, and perhaps even Versailles itself. The foundation stone of Mafra was laid in November 1717. The same year the papacy agreed to the establishment of the Patriarchate in Lisbon. Portugal, D. João hoped, was on its way to becoming the leader of the Roman Catholic world.

To construct the palace-convent in the comparatively remote location of Mafra, 30 kilometres from Lisbon, roads and harbour works had to be built and quarries opened. There were strikes by unpaid workmen and a growing chorus of complaint at the taxation levied to pay for this costly white elephant. Joaquim Verissimo Serrão wrote that 'the construction of Mafra has, then, in its final monumental state, to be seen in terms of artistic patrimony and not in terms of profitability, which it could never justify in material terms'.[42] However, he also pointed out that the wages of the workforce and the sums spent on materials for the building all boosted the circulation of money and aided the national economy.

The king took a great personal interest in the building and was reported to spend time 'living informally among his craftsmen'.[43] The same had been true of the building of the Patriarchal church. When in 1719 the Italian architect Filippo Juvarra arrived in Lisbon, it was said that he 'always travelled with the king in his carriage as they conferred over the planning of the new building'.[44]

Mafra stands with the Bourbon palace of Caserta in southern Italy as one of the great follies of the baroque age. It was a vast monument to the idea of Catholic absolute monarchy, wholly inappropriate and out of scale for a small and relatively backward country. The designs, which were modelled on the baroque architecture of Rome, were the work of the principal architect and supervisor of the work, a German called Johann Friedrich Ludwig (known in Portugal as João Frederico Ludovice), who had trained as a goldsmith in Ulm and Augsburg before travelling to Rome. Like his near-contemporary Christopher Wren, he was not a professional architect and came late in life to the design of buildings. As well as Ludwig, many other architects worked on the details of the design, which were finalized in Rome. In 1728 the original design was enlarged to make provision for three hundred friars and, as the king decided that the basilica was to be consecrated on his birthday on 22 October 1730, vast numbers of workmen, perhaps as many as 52,000, were drafted in to complete that part of the work.

As well as a basilica and convent, the buildings included a royal palace, a massive library and accommodation for the Patriarch. When completed in 1750, the year of D. João's death, this immense complex consisted of 880 rooms, had 4,500 doors and 154 staircases. Its principal facade was 232 metres in length, longer than that of the Escorial, which is only 207 metres. Versailles, with its wings, had a total facade of 402 metres and covered 6.7 hectares, while Mafra covered only 4 hectares – but Versailles had only 700 rooms and 67 staircases.

This vast structure was seldom used by the royal family and was too distant from Lisbon to be the principal royal residence. After the destruction of the Ribeira palace in the earthquake of 1755, the royal family preferred comparatively modest residences at Belém or Queluz on the outskirts of Lisbon. William Dalrymple, who visited Mafra in 1774, reflected: 'Here centers pride and poverty, folly and arrogance; a stately palace with bare walls, a sumptuous convent for supercilious

The palace/convent of Mafra.

priests.'[45] William Beckford, who first saw it in July 1787, thought 'The distant convent of Mafra looked like the palace of a giant, and the whole country round it as if the monster had eat it desolate.'[46] When Beckford visited Mafra itself in the following month, he was followed wherever he went 'by a strange medley of inquisitive monks, sacristans, lay-brothers, *corregedors*, village-curates, and country beaux with long rapiers and pigtails'. He fled into the palace gardens planted with 'wild thicket of pines and bay-trees, several orchards of lemon and orange, and two or three parterres more filled with weeds than flowers. I was much disgusted at finding this beautiful enclosure so wretchedly neglected, and its luxuriant plants withering away for want of being properly watered.'[47]

Nevertheless, Mafra was, in its own way, an architectural masterpiece and was magnificently embellished with statuary, marble and artworks, mostly by Italian artists. After D. João's death it was to become a centre for training Portuguese sculptors. Like the Escorial it boasted a magnificent library, which, unlike the royal library in Lisbon, survived the earthquake of 1755 and can be visited today in all its gloomy magnificence, its thousands of volumes dusty and unread, a veritable graveyard of forgotten books.

Considering the vast and costly nature of Mafra, one wonders if D. João ever considered how inappropriate it was that his convent should be a house for Franciscan friars, supposedly the followers of St Francis, whose life had been marked by a devotion to holy poverty. However, as the narrator in *Baltasar and Blimunda* says, 'St Francis of Assisi was content with a wilderness, [but] he was a saint and is now dead.'[48]

D. João and the Inquisition

In 1742 the French ambassador Théodore Chevignard de Chavigny wrote that among the king's favourite distractions was being present at autos-da-fé, which he described as 'a miserable ceremony but too disgusting for more to be said'.[49] D. João did indeed make a point of being present at the Lisbon ceremonies, the proceedings of which took place in the Terreiro do Paço below while he watched from a balcony of the royal palace. During his reign the Inquisition showed a marked revival in activity, but the king's relationship with the Holy Office was far different from that of his father. During D. Pedro's reign the Inquisition, which had been hostile to the Restoration and accession to the throne of the Braganzas, was engaged in a long drawn-out struggle with the Jesuits, who backed the king's economic reforms and more lenient approach to New Christians. In contrast to his father, D. João V was determined to work with the Inquisition rather than against it, and in so doing he was able to exert a strong influence over the way it conducted its affairs. He was aided in this by the appointment of Nuno da Cunha as Inquisitor General in 1707. Nuno was a man of European-wide experience and had been a member of the party that had escorted Queen Catarina from England back to Portugal in 1692. He had been profoundly influenced by the thought of the Enlightenment and he and the young king shared a desire to see Portugal more fully in tune with the European culture of the age, a trend which was widely welcomed by Portuguese who had gone abroad to study or find opportunities for a career, and by a growing class of educated professionals in Portugal itself.

During D. João's reign many of the familiars of the Inquisition were educated medical men whose influence was seen in the new direction taken by Inquisition activities. With the connivance and probably active encouragement of the king, the Inquisition increasingly turned its attention from those accused of being crypto-Jews to those

Auto-da-fé in the Terreira do Paço.

practising magic, or the occult arts, most of whom were probably simply practitioners of folk medicine. This was a kind of 'witch hunt' that grew in intensity in Portugal just at a time when witch hunting and witch trials were dying out elsewhere in Europe. It may seem anomalous that witch hunting should increase in Portugal at a time when the king was trying to portray Portugal as being in the forefront of modern European culture, but to D. João and Nuno da Cunha the war on magic and folk medicine was part of an attempt to eradicate superstitious practices and to bring Portugal into line with the rational thought and practice of the age.[50]

D. João on the European Stage

Throughout his reign D. João was determined that Portugal should rank alongside the major European powers but he wisely limited this competition to the magnificence of his court, his palaces, his patronage of the arts and his ecclesiastical and secular ceremonies. Portugal's participation in the Grand Alliance against Louis XIV had brought no gains and had exposed its colonial possessions to French assaults, the French occupation and plunder of Rio de Janeiro in 1710 being the most memorable. Thereafter, D. João and his ministers were determined to remain neutral in European conflicts. The one exception was the decision to despatch warships to join the combined fleet sent against the Turks in 1716. The main purpose of this departure from neutrality, however, was to assist the diplomacy of the marquês de Fontes in Rome, which resulted in the archbishopric of Lisbon being raised to the rank of a Patriarchate.

After the end of the War of the Spanish Succession, D. João and his ministers successfully maintained Portugal's neutrality in European affairs. By neutrality the king was understood to mean the non-participation in wars, not the avoidance of alliances. In 1729 a double marriage was arranged with the Spanish royal family. This marriage brought the Bourbon Mariana Vitória to Lisbon to marry the infante José, and at last brought to an end nearly a century of confrontation and warfare between Portugal and its powerful neighbour.

According to Joaquim Verissimo Serrão, 'João V many times assumed the role of arbiter among the nations of Europe and demanded the marks of deference which were the privilege of the major states and that [his] ambassadors should always behave as representatives of a great monarch.'[51] However, Portugal's neutrality and security, in the last resort, rested not with the Spanish marriage but with the English alliance and D. João's reign saw English influence in Portugal at its most dominant.

The Last Ten Years

In 1740 the king suffered the first of a series of strokes and ceased to be as active as before. Life at court during the last ten years of his reign is described in Mariana Vitória's letters to her mother in Madrid. It is a story of a dull court, often in mourning for the death of some dynastic relative, relieved only by visits to churches and convents and with little to entertain a young princess. In March 1745, in mourning for the death of her grandmother, she wrote, 'the King thinks of nothing but the Patriarchate and the Queen does nothing; we live the most contemptible life in the world. If I did not have the liberty to go out sometimes, I do not know how I would be able to live.'[52]

The queen, Maria Ana, her childbearing days over, now increasingly assumed a major role in the nation's affairs and the Austrian Habsburg influence grew. It was she who, famously, had the Portuguese ambassador in Vienna, Sebastião José de Carvalho e Melo (the future marquês de Pombal), who had married an Austrian princess, recalled in 1749 to take up the post of Minister of Foreign Affairs, an appointment with momentous consequences for the future.

During the final months of D. João's life, the important Treaty of Madrid was signed with Spain. This recognized that the frontiers of Brazil had expanded far beyond the notional boundary agreed in the Tordesillas Treaty of 1494 and transferred to Portuguese jurisdiction the Jesuit missions in what is now Paraguay. The year 1750 also saw the completion of Mafra, which more than anything else had come to symbolize D. João's ambitions and his achievements. The king died on 31 July 1750, aged only sixty.

7

D. José: The Reformer

A fine equestrian statue of D. José today occupies the centre of what was once the Terreiro do Paço and is now the Praça do Comercio, but he remains an indistinct figure, lurking in the deep shadow cast by his great minister the marquês de Pombal, who presided over the affairs of Portugal for the whole of his reign. Although royal absolutism reached its peak during D. José's reign, it was very much absolutism in spite of the king. In his portraits, notably the frequently reproduced family portrait attributed to Joana do Salitre, D. José, dressed in all the paraphernalia of royal power, nevertheless seems lost and somehow out of his depth, as though he was a household servant dressed up to play the part of the monarch.

Was D. José really the nonentity, dominated by the powerful personality of his minister, that writers have often claimed him to be? Or was he a real influence behind the policies carried out in his name? One thing is certain, Pombal, for all his political skill and forceful personality, could not have survived without the unquestioning trust placed in him by the king. This was brutally revealed when D. José died and Pombal's power and influence expired with him. The French historian Jean-François Labourdette summed up the relationship when he wrote, 'Pombal, like Richelieu, became all powerful because . . . Joseph I considered him the only person able to bring about the reforms that were called for in reaction to the previous regime.'

After the 44 years of the reign of D. João V, dominated as they had been by the king's passion, possibly even obsession, for ecclesiastical grandeur, there was bound to be a reaction, but in one important respect D. José's reign should be seen as a continuation of that of his father. D. João V had sought to make royal power supreme and he had

Attributed to Joana do Salitre, *Allegory of the Acclamation of King José I, c.* 1750.

done this through his lavish expenditure, his attempt to establish Lisbon as the Second Rome and his new title of Most Faithful, while working with the Inquisition rather than forcing confrontations with that formidable body. D. José was no less an absolute monarch but he sought other means to make this power effective. With his aspirations brought into sharp focus by his minister, he was to strike at the influence of the leading noble families and the Church. Although these vigorous and often violent policies were seen by contemporaries to be the work of Pombal, they were, for the most part, measures that the king himself wanted to see implemented.

D. José, the Man and the King

D. José was aged 36 when he came to the throne. He was no teenage king like D. Afonso or even like his father D. João v. Yet he had been kept from having any say in the nation's affairs, first by his father, who, it is said, had always favoured his brother Pedro, and then by his mother as she increasingly took over the reins of power.

When he became king, D. José had to don the mantle of Braganza royalty, and family tradition somehow made it inevitable that the twin passions he would indulge were music and hunting. In this he was encouraged by his wife, Mariana Vitória, who shared his tastes. Nathaniel Wraxall, who saw the royal family during a visit in 1773, left a detailed and not unsympathetic description of the king, then in his 57th year:

> He was of a good stature, but inclined to corpulency: his features regular, his eye quick and lively, if a habit of holding his mouth somewhat open, had not diminished the expression of intelligence, which his countenance would otherwise have conveyed. In his cheeks he had a high scorbutic humour . . . Never had any Lusitanian Peasant coarser or darker Hands. One could not look at him, without recollecting how near are the Shores, and how similar are the Climates, of Portugal, and of Africa.
>
> Two passions or pursuits, Hunting and Music, principally occupied his time, absorbed his thoughts, and divided his affections: nor was it easy to decide which of them possessed the strongest ascendant over him. In the former diversion he passed the far greater part of the day: to the latter amusement his evenings were

Portrait of the marquês de Pombal by Louis-Michel van Loo, 1766, oil on canvas.

principally or wholly dedicated, either in public, when at the Opera; or in private, with his family. No royal House in Europe was then so musical as that of Portugal. Joseph himself performed with considerable execution, on the Violin; and the three Princesses, his Daughters, all were proficients in a greater, or in a less degree, on different instruments. If he was prevented by the weather from going out to the Chace, the king had recourse for occupation, to his Manege [riding school]. On Sundays, he seldom or never missed attending the Italian Opera in Lisbon; but he likewise maintained another Opera at Belem, his residence near the Capital.[2]

Augustus Hervey had attended the opera in 1752, shortly after D. José had come to the throne:

It was built at an immense expense in his own palace, and was the finest theatre of its size in Europe, supported by marble pillars which had conveyances about each for water in case of fire. The king's box took up all the front and was most magnificently ornamented, as was the whole, for everything was the king's expense. The ladies were all in boxes and boxes for the foreign Ministers; the nobility were in the pit but there were only men (as at Rome) that sung and danced there . . . The tickets were difficult to get as the King had it purely for his own amusement, but there was a disagreeable ceremony for the men, for as you came in under the King's box, before you sat down you were to turn about and make a low bow to the Royal Family and another to the ladies, and this every time that you had occasion to go out or come in.[3]

The hunting excursions of the king and queen took the royal family to Mafra, Vila Viçosa and Salvaterra and were a misery for the courtiers who were forced to rise early to accompany the monarchs in the worst of weather, riding in draughty coaches that did not keep the rain out. The Spanish ambassador, the marques de Almodovar, spoke for many when he gave the king the nickname of His Pleurisy Majesty. The mere threat of a hunting expedition gave the countess de Tarouca a nervous seizure, while the conde de Val de Reis took to his bed and had a doctor come to bleed him.[4] The royal family hunted deer and wild boar but on occasion would set out by boat from Salvaterra to hunt the whales that sometimes swam up the river.[5]

JOSEPHUS PRIMUS XVII

D. José I, 1773.

When the court and the hunt adjourned to Mafra, where the palace buildings were empty and unfinished, a huge encampment was set up in the park.[6] This movement of the court and its personnel to the various hunting lodges has been compared to the movement of a nomadic tribe and was vastly expensive. It was D. José's version of the conspicuous expenditure that his father had lavished on churches and church ceremonial. However, this had all to be paid for from a treasury that was no longer receiving gold from Brazil in the quantities that D. João had enjoyed. Where D. João had relished display and luxury, seeing it as the essential prop of his absolute rule, his son went to the other extreme and was careless of the exterior trappings of royalty. According to Wraxall, he travelled in old and shabby coaches and, although he spent lavishly on maintaining an opera company, the 'attendants of the Court, having been unpaid for several years, were in the lowest stage of distress'.[7]

Salvaterra dos Magos

No discussion of the king's twin passions for hunting and opera would be complete without considering the royal retreat at Salvaterra. Salvaterra dos Magos is today a small town on the main road from Santarém to Lisbon. Away from the through traffic it has a few streets of old houses and a riverside resort, called Escaroupim, which can be reached by a narrow causeway across the flat, and sometimes flooded, fields that line the Tagus. The river at this point is half a mile wide and flows sluggishly on its way to the sea. It was here, a day's journey by river from Lisbon, that since the sixteenth century the kings of Portugal had their principal hunting lodge. The Braganza kings visited Salvaterra on a regular basis, usually during the three winter months after Christmas. However, it was D. José who gave Salvaterra a special significance. After the devastation caused by the Lisbon earthquake in 1755, the king was reluctant to reside in Lisbon. Instead he and the royal family inhabited a warren of wooden buildings at Belém. He also began to extend the palace and opera house at Salvaterra.

The royal family travelled to Salvaterra in a grand royal barge and a canal, which still exists, was dug to link the town and the palace complex to the river. At the landing point on the edge of the town the royal family visited the local church to give thanks for a safe journey before continuing to the palace.

According to the French general Charles François Dumouriez, the king, once installed at Salvaterra, 'is the most magnificent sovereign in Europe; there he entertains at his expense every foreigner who comes and who is known as an honest person; there he maintains a good opera, gaming tables and horses for hunting available for everyone'.[8]

A huge encampment grew up at Salvaterra for the court personnel, nobles, servants, grooms, horses and all the vast paraphernalia of the royal hunt. In addition, there were musicians, dancers and the singers who were the stars of the opera and who accompanied him everywhere as he progressed from one hunting lodge to the next. The king's constant attendance at the opera was such that his minister, Pombal, often had to come to him after midnight to get him to sign papers.

The palace itself dated from 1548 and had been enlarged during the reign of D. João v. However, it was during D. José's reign that considerable rebuilding took place under the supervision of José Joaquim Ludovice, son of the architect of Mafra, and Carlos Mardel, the engineer who was largely responsible for the rebuilding of Lisbon. The construction of the new palace, the theatre and the famous falconry (*falcoaria*), which along with the royal chapel is all that survives of the palace today, took place between 1756 and 1759. The design of the theatre was the work of Giovanni Carlo Sicinio Galli Bibiena, an Italian architect from Bologna, whose family included several of the most renowned theatrical designers in Europe. It was of considerable size with three tiers of boxes and total accommodation for five hundred persons.

The productions were on a lavish scale. According to a French guest at Salvaterra in 1766, the opera company had eighty personnel including dancers, singers and musicians. The orchestra consisted of thirty instruments and the whole was ranked 'one of the best operas there is in Europe'. A production of *Demetrio* by the favourite court composer, David Perez, was alleged to have cost 200,000 *cruzados* and had elaborate scenery and costumes embroidered in Milan in gold and silver thread.

The opera, which apparently lasted four hours, was the main attraction of any stay at Salvaterra. After it was over guests were invited to view the bodies of the game that had been killed during the previous day's hunt. The next day they were invited to the falconry. The king was attended there by guards, musicians and the *fauconniers* in scarlet uniforms fringed with gold. The queen attended 'dressed like an amazon

Royal chapel at Salvaterra dos Magos.

in scarlet trimmed with gold, with trailing skirt and a man's feathered hat and long hair, riding a magnificent Spanish horse'. However, apart from the opera and the flying of the falcons, Dumouriez commented, 'one gets bored very easily at Salvaterra'. After a day of wind and rain, he welcomed the offer of returning to Lisbon in the marquis of Marialva's barge.[9]

Salvaterra remained a favourite resort of the royal family until it was burned down in 1824.

Queen Mariana Vitória and her Daughters

D. José had married the Spanish infanta Mariana Vitória in 1729 when she was only ten years old. This marriage was one half of a marriage compact with Spain, his elder sister, Maria Bárbara, being married at the same time to the future king of Spain. Mariana Vitória had originally been intended as a bride for Louis XV of France and she had even resided for some time at the French court, but the negotiations fell through and, according to Dumouriez, 'the queen of Portugal retains a prodigious aversion towards the court of France.'[10] While still a girl at the Portuguese court, she wrote regularly to her mother in Spain describing the activities of the royal family, the hunts when she was able to kill rabbits, the visits to convents and the lessons she took in Latin and grammar.[11]

The marriage was consummated in 1732 when she was fourteen years old, and two years later a child, the future D. Maria I, was born. Between 1734 and 1746 D. José and his Spanish wife had a total of eight children, but four of them, including the only male child, were stillborn. The four surviving daughters once again raised the spectre of an uncertain succession that had been a recurring problem for the Braganza dynasty ever since it was first installed on the Portuguese throne. All four daughters were christened Maria Francisca and had to be distinguished by their third baptismal name. The eldest, Maria Francisca Isabel, was born 17 December 1734 and eventually succeeded as D. Maria I, but the other three had sad histories, common enough for princesses of the period. Maria Ana Francisca and Maria Francisca Doroteia died unmarried after unsuccessful attempts to find them husbands. Maria Ana was described as 'a beautiful person, well brought up and full of talent'.[12] An attempt was made to arrange a marriage with the future Emperor Joseph II, but this never materialized. The fourth daughter, Maria Francisca Benedita, married her nephew, D. Maria's son and heir to the throne, the infante José, but had no children.

Mariana Vitória was very devout in her own way and this had a considerable influence on the way her children were brought up. The Italian Joseph Baretti recorded that it was 'her custom to kiss the names of God, our blessed Lady and all the saints and angels in any book that she opens'.[13] After her last child was born in 1746, the queen devoted herself to hunting and outdoor pursuits – unusual for queens at that time. Nathaniel Wraxall painted a highly coloured portrait of the queen as he had known her towards the end of the reign. Jealousy, he maintained, was her guiding passion – mindful no doubt of the amorous adventures of D. José's father:

> The Queen of Portugal, though at this time she was considerably advanced towards her sixtieth year, yet watched every motion of her husband, with all the vigilant anxiety of a young woman. And in order the better to secure his personal fidelity, she wisely took care to remove from before his eyes, as much as possible, every temptation to inconstancy. The ladies in waiting, and Maids of Honour, who attended Their Majesties in public, must certainly have been selected for their want of all attractions; and they were besides, too far advanced in years, to be longer capable of inspiring any sentiment except respect. The Portugueze females who accompanied Catherine of Braganza in 1662, when she came over to England, in order to espouse Charles the Second, whose total deficiency in personal charms is so eloquently described in the 'Memoires de Grammont', could not possibly exceed in that particular, the Attendants on Marianna Victoria, wife of Joseph the First.[14]

Women were not allowed to perform in the theatre or opera, a ban that was attributed to the queen's jealousy but which was still in force after her death, when William Beckford commented in his inimitable manner on the men who acted female parts and

> the pleasing effect this metamorphosis must produce, especially in the dancers, where one sees a stout shepherdess in virgin white, with a soft blue beard, and a prominent collar-bone, clenching a nosegay in a fist that would almost have knocked down Goliath, and a train of milk-maids attending her enormous foot-steps, tossing their petticoats over their heads at every step.[15]

Poor D. José had to pursue his love affairs secretly and this secrecy was the indirect cause of some of the most dramatic events of his reign. Nathaniel Wraxall has more on this subject:

> Nor was her vigilance by any means confined to the opera. She displayed the same apprehensions, and took similar precautions,

Mariana Vitória by Alexis Simon Belle, *c.* 1725–6, oil on canvas.

against any rival or intruder in the King's affections, whenever he went to the Chace. Whether the diversion was hunting, or shooting, or falconing, she was constantly at his side. No woman in Europe indeed rode bolder, or with more skill. Her figure almost defied the powers of description, on these occasions. She sat astride, as was the universal custom in Portugal, and wore English leather Breeches; frequently black; over which she threw a petticoat which did not always conceal her legs. A jacket of cloth, or of stuff, and a cocked hat, sometimes laced, at other times without ornament, compleated the masculine singularity of her appearance. When, after having let loose the falcon, she followed him with her eye in his flight, she always threw the reins on her horse's neck; allowing him to carry her wherever he pleased, fearless of accidents. She was admitted to be an excellent shot, seldom missing the bird at which she fired, even when flying: but this diversion had nearly produced a most tragical result; as, a few years before I visited Portugal, she very narrowly missed killing the King with a ball, which actually grazed his temple. Few princes in modern Times, have had more hair-breadth escapes from danger or assassination, than Joseph I experienced.[16]

Suzanne Chantal wondered whether this was really an accident: 'It seems doubtful that a marksman as good as Marianna Victoria could have committed such a mistake.'[17]

Although the queen hated Pombal, she was not able to influence the king against him and had little impact on public affairs in Portugal while her husband was alive. She did, however, maintain close links with the court of Spain and, according to Dumouriez, 'by her negotiations averted the danger from the Spanish armies in 1762', when Spain and Portugal were briefly at war.[18] When her daughter, D. Maria I, succeeded to the throne in 1777 she became the principal adviser and support for the new monarch and undoubtedly had great influence in the early part of that reign.

D. José as Ruler

For the first few months of his reign D. José took an active interest in the affairs of state and began to impose his own personality on events. The British minister Abraham Castres reported in 1751:

> as to the king of Portugal's character, he bears an excellent one and is universally acknowledged to have shown more instances of justice and humanity than his late father had done through his whole reign. As he is extremely diffident himself and conscious his education has been greatly neglected, he showed at the beginning of his reign a greater suspicion of, than confidence in, his ministers, which occasioned at first great delays in the despatch of his affairs, but his ministers, particularly Carvalho [Pombal], when once he

began to obtain a competent knowledge of his affairs, began to establish their credit with him, and since then matters have been carried on with uncommon expedition, HM [D. José] having in some remarkable instances shown a docility and patience in despatching what was laid before him much greater than could be expected from a prince so little used to business.[19]

Although D. José had played little part in public affairs while his father was alive, he had resented the excessive expenditure on the Patriarchate. According to Marcus Cheke, 'the Patriarchal Church supported three hundred and forty prelates, canons, acolytes, chaplains, sacrists, choristers, and confessors. In addition, there were fifty-three minor officials, including organists, bell-ringers and a hair dresser.'[20] Reducing the power and influence of the Patriarch and the dominance that the priests had over the court was an urgent priority. So on his accession D. José was already predisposed to cut back on the expenditure on the Church and to limit its influence in public affairs.

However, the king, who lacked confidence and was socially awkward, soon took the line of least resistance and left the day-to-day running of affairs to Pombal. After the earthquake, he largely relinquished control of the government. Chantal, in her book *La Vie quotidienne au Portugal après le tremblement de terre de Lisbonne de 1755,* for which she was awarded a prize by the Académie Française, described the king living after the earthquake in a single-storey wooden house on the Ajuda hill:

> The king had nothing to do in the city where he went only to attend some religious ceremony. God would be praised, all the rest would be cared for by his minister. D. José had always had little inclination, and still less curiosity, [to concern himself] with the affairs of government and in the course of his reign he only summoned the Cortes once.[21]

Although, after the earthquake, Pombal seemed to be all powerful, D. José was nevertheless very present in the background and it was clear that the minister always had to gain the king's assent to whatever he wanted to do, and that this assent was not automatically forthcoming. Moreover, D. José would sometimes take decisions to which Pombal was strongly opposed. One such case was the king's appointment of Martinho de Melo e Castro to succeed Pombal's brother as Minister

Joseph Emanuel, King of Portugal by Miguel António do Amaral, *c.* 1773, oil on canvas.

of Navy and Colonies, an appointment that Pombal did not approve. Another was the decision in 1760 to arrange the marriage of the infanta Maria, the king's eldest daughter and heir to his throne, to his brother Pedro.[22]

When in September 1757 the king was injured by bullets fired at his coach, it appears that he not only agreed to the savage sentences passed on the conspirators alleged to have been involved in the incident but may even have been largely responsible for them. D. José also welcomed the subsequent purge that removed powerful and hostile nobles from the court. Moreover, as Pombal pursued his vendetta against the Jesuits and all priests who opposed him, he clearly had the backing of the king, who is alleged to have told the British envoy Lord William Lyttleton in 1768 that 'during the eighteen years he had reigned, nine had been disturbed by the machinations of ecclesiastics, and therefore he required him [Pombal] to take such measures as might effectually silence those turbulent spirits'.[23] Even so, Pombal had had to use great skill to manoeuvre the king into accepting the expulsion of all Jesuits from the Portuguese dominions and had to give way on the crucial matter of putting them on trial. It appears that it was the king who refused to allow the Jesuits, detained after the expulsion of the Order, to be tried or executed.

The king was more engaged with the affairs of the kingdom than is sometimes suggested. He supported the appointment of Count Lippe to command the Portuguese army in 1762 and took an active interest in his reforms. It is even reported that he 'went into camp to attend the annual manoeuvres'.[24] It is also recorded that when the Commercial College was established both Pombal and the king used, on occasion, to attend the oral examinations. D. José also took an interest in the navy and, according to Augustus Hervey, would sometimes accompany the Brazil fleet out over the Tagus bar.[25] These anecdotes suggest a king who was not exactly 'hands on' but who was well informed about important developments and, from a position in the background, was giving tacit approval to what his minister was doing.

There was certainly both give and take in the relationship between D. José and Pombal. According to Marcus Cheke,

> there is a story that on one occasion King Joseph was toying with the idea that all Jews in his realms should be stigmatised by being compelled to wear a white cap, and he confided this idea to his minister. When next admitted to the throne room Pombal was carrying two white caps, and on the King inquiring what they were for, he replied that one cap was for him and one for himself. For it is true that Jewish blood has been mixed, since remote times, in the veins of many of the noblest Portuguese families.[26]

Although D. José seems to have been complacent about Pombal's vendetta against the major noble families, according to Beckford, he was prepared to draw lines that Pombal dared not cross: "'Act as you judge wisest with the rest of my nobility", used to say the King Dom Joseph to this redoubted minister; "but beware how you interfere with the Marquis of Marialva".'[27] On the other hand, D. José allowed Pombal to get his way over the exile of the king's two half-brothers, the *meninos de Palhavã*, though he refused to allow a similar decree of exile to be imposed on his brother Pedro.[28]

The Exile of the *meninos de Palhavã*

In spite of being D. José's half-brothers, both António and José – but not Gaspar, archbishop of Braga – were exiled in 1760 to Buçaco, 250 kilometres north of Lisbon, after having come into conflict with Pombal. Various reasons have been put forward for this rather drastic measure against two close relatives of the king. An early version of these events appeared in the *Memoirs of the Marquis of Pombal*, compiled in 1843 by John Smith Athelstane, the private secretary of Pombal's grandson, the duke of Saldanha. According to this version,

> various persons were banished from Court at this period [July 1760] for intriguing with the Nuncio, or holding secret correspondence with the Jesuits . . . Dom António and Dom José, were, by the King's order, removed from their house at Palhavão under a strong guard and conducted to a convent beyond Coimbra where they were to remain.[29]

D. José was the Inquisitor General and he had refused to give his imprimatur to the *Dedução cronólogica e analítica*, the definitive defence of royal absolutism, which Pombal had had published. However, it was rumoured that there were other issues. In spite of their clerical vows, both brothers were thought to be intriguing to marry D. José's daughter Maria and so inherit the throne. At a more frivolous level, stories circulated that the princes had had a row with Pombal during which one of them had snatched off the minister's wig and struck him in the face with it.[30]

It was clear that Pombal was eager to take any opportunity to clip the wings of the Inquisition, that once powerful organization, and it was a clear indication of how the balance of power in Portugal had changed when the Inquisitor General could be exiled for seventeen years to the provinces.

The exiled princes were allowed to return to the Court only after the king's death in 1777. In May 1787 William Beckford was persuaded to visit Palhavã while the princes were away and he recorded his impressions in his diary:

Not an insect stirred, not a whisper was audible in the principal apartments which consist in a suite of lofty covered saloons, nobly proportioned, and uniformly hung with damask of the deepest crimson . . . No glasses, no pictures, no gilding, no decoration but heavy drapery . . . Stuck fast to the wall, between two of the . . . tables, are two fauteuils for their Highnesses; and opposite, a rank of chairs for those reverend fathers in God who from time to time are honoured with admittance.

Beckford was inspired by this visit to contemplate the futile lives of minor royalty, sentiments that he later repeated in his account of his travels written when the romantic critique of royalty was more the fashion:

What pains what application it must require on the part of nurses, equerries and chamberlains to stifle every lively and generous sensation in the princelings they educate, to break a human being into the habits of impotent royalty! Dignity without power is the heaviest of burdens . . . princes like those of Palhavã, without credit or influence who have nothing to feed on but imaginary greatness, must yawn their souls out and become in process of time as formal and inanimate as the evergreen pyramids of stunted myrtle in their gardens. Happier were those babes King John did not think proper to recognise.[31]

D. José and the Earthquake

D. José and the royal family were in Belém when, on 1 November 1755, an earthquake struck Lisbon with devastating force. Eighty per cent of the buildings in the city were badly damaged, and damage was turned into devastation when a tsunami flooded the lower parts of the city and fires raged for days throughout the ruins. Between 10,000 and 15,000 people lost their lives.

The king, it was reported, was thrown into confusion by the catastrophe. Confusion turned into long-term depression and he remained deeply affected by the trauma for the rest of his life. According to Nathaniel Wraxall:

Previous to the memorable earthquake of 1755, [the king] was considered as temperate, drinking usually water at his meals: but,

João Glama's painting of the Terramoto, 1756–92.

such was the effect produced on his mind, and so severe the
dejection of spirits, which he experienced . . . that it was appre-
hended, his health would be seriously affected by it. His physicians
prescribed the use of wine, as necessary to restore his Constitution.[32]

It was rumoured that the king was so overwhelmed that at one point
he stated his intention to abdicate. According to the Italian adventurer
Giuseppe Gorani, who was in Lisbon in 1765, Pombal found the king
'on his knees at the feet of his brother, the Infante Dom Pedro, asking
him to accept the Crown whose weight was too great for him, to which
the Infante prostrating at the feet of the Monarch replied to him,
begging him to continue wearing the Crown'. It was at this point, when
the princes felt 'abandoned by all the courtiers, that Carvalho [Pombal]
appeared to them like a guardian angel . . . consoling him and persuading him that the disaster was not as great as His Most Faithful Majesty
believed'.[33]

The king gave plenary powers to Pombal and other competent
nobles to deal with the chaotic situation caused by the earthquake and
this presented Pombal with the opportunity to redesign the city and in
the process to carry forward the far-reaching plans for economic and
social reform that he had in mind. Standing in the way of significant
change in Portugal was the power of the narrow group of noble families

who held so many of the positions of influence in the state, and the Church with its powerful institutions, the Society of Jesus, the Inquisition and the newly created Patriarchate. These powerful interest groups had thwarted change in D. Pedro II's reign, and D. João V had been only partly successful in co-opting them for his project to re-establish Portugal's position among the nations of Europe. Now the earthquake dealt a severe blow to the opponents of royal absolutism – the Inquisition, the Jesuit College, the Patriarchate and many of the noble palaces were destroyed. The royal palace located on the waterfront in the heart of the city was also destroyed. It was impossible to escape the message conveyed by the destruction of these hallowed buildings. The prestige of the Church and the nobility was fatally weakened and the new city that Pombal planned, and which slowly arose on the ashes of the old, was to be a city that was bourgeois and commercial in character, not clerical and aristocratic.

Most strikingly, the royal palace by the river was not rebuilt, and here D. José's dislike of Lisbon was instrumental. While his brother, Pedro, resided at Queluz, some miles from the city's perimeter, D. José himself continued to live among his horses and menagerie out at Belém, using the buildings of the convent of Necessidades, a beautiful building with gardens and a library, for formal functions in Lisbon. At Belém a complex of wooden buildings grew up to house the court. Where D. João V had built a palace to rival Versailles and the Escorial, his son and his son's family

> inhabited a long wooden range of apartments at Belem . . . The terrors and recollection of the Earthquake of 1755 were so deeply impressed in their minds that they preferred residing in a wooden building, however mean in its fabrication, or inconvenient, rather than encounter the perils annexed to a stone edifice.[34]

Beckford commented in November 1787, 'Nothing can be well shabbier. The audience chamber is a vile low barn, not above fourteen feet high, spread with greasy Persian carpets and hung with the coarsest hobgoblin tapestry.'[35] This wooden palace complex, known as the *barraca real*, the royal shack, was inhabited by D. José for the rest of his life, and after him by his family, until it burned down in 1794, after which a new palace was planned for the site at Ajuda.[36]

The Attempt to Assassinate the King

Late at night on 3 September 1758 a party of gunmen waylaid the coach in which the king was travelling after a clandestine visit to his mistress, the marquesa de Tavora. Only a week earlier D. José's sister, Maria Bárbara, the queen of Spain, had died and the court was supposed to be in full mourning. Two of the shots that were fired hit and injured the king. It took D. José nearly three months fully to recover and during that time Queen Mariana Vitória acted as regent. The plot behind the assassination was eventually uncovered and a number of the most senior aristocratic figures in the country were implicated. In January 1759 sixteen people were executed in a public spectacle that horrified those who witnessed it. Although there is no doubt that the king was injured in the incident, doubts have since been raised as to whether the assassins were really attempting to kill the king and whether some of those who were executed were involved at all.[37] The target of the assassins, it has been claimed, may have been the royal coachman, Pedro Teixeira. However, the aristocrats who were involved, the duke of Aveiro and the marquis of Tavora and his sons, had many grievances against the king. The marquis had served in Goa as viceroy between 1750 and 1754. He returned to find that his daughter-in-law, Theresa, had been for some time the king's mistress and that Pombal had replaced the leading court nobles and was installed as first minister. The young Theresa had been left alone in Lisbon when her husband had accompanied his father to Goa, and the philandering Augustus Hervey recorded in his journal in 1753 that he saw that the marquesa was 'very well with the King' and again in 1755 that, at the opera, 'I perceived the marquesa de Tavora was very well with the king; they did nothing but eye each other as much as they dared in the Queen's presence.' He also recorded another occasion when, at the theatre, he met the marquesa 'with whom I flirted, tho' I was on my guard, knowing I should ill pay my court by any assiduity there'.[38] The queen, well aware of her husband's infidelity, is alleged to have said to the former viceroy, after he had complimented the king on his horsemanship, 'and he rides still better when he is with your daughter'.[39]

The marquis of Tavora was one of a group of nobles who found themselves marginalized by Pombal. He had not been made a duke after his tenure as viceroy, as he had hoped, and it seems likely that he and his relative, Duke Aveiro, increasingly attributed what they saw as their humiliation to Pombal and the unquestioning support he received from the king. In this they were encouraged by Jesuits who had already been stripped of property, influence and power by the minister. If this analysis is correct, the conspirators believed that only by getting rid of D. José could Pombal be removed from power, although it is still not entirely clear why an attempt was not made to assassinate the minister rather than the king.

Whatever may have been the realities that led to shots being fired at the king's coach that night, the severest penalties were prescribed. It seems that Pombal and the king were determined to intimidate the noble families and make clear the consequences of any further conspiracies. It may have been the king rather than the minister who insisted on the severity of the sentences and D. José made sure he was present to witness the executions. It was only the intervention of the queen and the infanta Maria that prevented the execution of still more members of the two families. Infanta Maria, for her part, was profoundly affected by these events, which filled her with a deep sense of guilt that in the end contributed to her losing her reason.

D. José apparently led a charmed life. He had escaped death during the earthquake and now at the hands of assassins. Later he was to be grazed by a bullet fired by his wife in the hunting field and was

The attempted assassination of D. José I in 1758 in a sanguine drawing by Vieira Lusitano.

attacked at Vila Viçosa by a peasant infuriated at having had his cattle seized by the king's servants.

In fact, this attempted assassination was not the first attempt on a Braganza king's life. In December 1786 the marquis de Bombelles recorded the following story in his diary:

> In the time of Jean v, who the Portuguese call João Quinto, there was a courtesan who was very pretty but of a rather low class. The king, who was both devout and a libertine, wanted to know her. An ensign who was both amorous and jealous, unaware that his rival was his master, one day fired a shot that wounded his majesty. It was proved that the ensign was not guilty of regicide; he was sent to India where he served with distinction and earned promotion. His mistress also contributed to the leniency of his punishment. The king had found this pretty girl: she said that she would kill herself [s'étranglerait] if her lover was punished too severely.[40]

D. José's Final Years

During his final years D. José did not cut a very regal figure. Living in his sprawling wooden palace at Belém, he seldom appeared in public and the affairs of the kingdom were conducted by Pombal. In 1774 he had a stroke and during the last years of his life he was practically an invalid. One of his last acts, in February 1777, was to secure the marriage of his grandson, José, then fifteen, to his aunt Maria Benedita. Maria Benedita was a strong supporter of Pombal and it is probable that this marriage was a final effort by the marquês to save his position in the new regime that seemed imminent.[41]

The reality of an aged and increasingly decrepit monarch contrasted cruelly with the magnificent bronze statue of the king that was cast to form the centrepiece of the Praça do Comercio, and with some of the propaganda that Pombal organized to underpin the royal absolutism that he had worked so hard to establish. In 1775, two years before D. José's death, appeared a pamphlet entitled *Parallelo de Augusto Cesar e de Dom José o Magnanimo Rey do Portugal* (A Parallel between Augustus Caesar and Dom José the Magnanimous King of Portugal). The pamphlet contained what was probably the most inappropriate epitaph of a king ever written:

Statue of D. José I by Machado de Castro, 1775, in the Praça do Comercio, Lisbon.

To Augustus, Rome attributed all its splendour, so Portugal will be the eternal debtor to the king to whom will be attributed greatness and good fortune . . . Who cannot see in the beautiful representation of the happiness of the Romans in the time of Augustus a living image of what today Portugal experiences under the government of Dom José?[42]

D. José died on 24 February 1777, aged just 62 years. All Portuguese kings received a sobriquet. He was always known as *O Reformador* (the Reformer), a description that might more justly be applied to his great minister than to himself.

D. Maria I, Queen of Portugal by Giuseppe Troni, 1783, oil on canvas.

8

D. Maria I and D. Pedro III

Τ he story of Maria Francisca Isabel, D. Maria I, is one of the saddest in the narrative of the Braganza family. A devout and conscientious queen, she was overcome by the demands and stresses of her position and became mentally ill for the last 24 years of her life.

She was born on 17 December 1734, the eldest of D. José and Mariana Vitória's daughters. At the time of her birth her Spanish mother was sixteen years old and her father was twenty. She was an intelligent girl who impressed people with her memory, her diligence and her piety. After her death in 1816, exaggerated stories of her early precocity were circulated, forming a panegyric to the memory of someone who most people remembered only as a sad and mad old woman. According to these accounts, when she was just two years old she was already attending the royal ceremony of the washing of the feet of the poor and from an early age developed a special devotion to St Francis Xavier. It was alleged that, when still a girl, she gave away to the poor money that had been given to her to buy toys.[1] Her most recent Portuguese biographer wrote, 'her devotions came before everything else and dominated the spirit of D. Maria, constituting one of the fundamental traits of her personality'.[2] Nevertheless, in spite of her piety and devotion, she seems to have been better educated and perhaps more intelligent than most of her family.

D. Maria had received a careful education. She was brought up to speak Castilian with her mother and Portuguese with her father and had a good knowledge of French. Interestingly she was also taught an elaborate calligraphy, which she used all her life in her personal correspondence. Her letters 'were more drawn than written', wrote her biographer Caetano Beirão, and demonstrated that 'she had a mind that was scrupulous and ordered'.[3] A modern writer might add that, in the light of her later mental breakdown, this perhaps showed a form of obsessive compulsive disorder.

As she grew up, D. Maria's piety took possession of her and had a paralysing effect on her ability to make decisions and to deal with the realities of power and politics. Arthur William Costigan, in one of his letters to his brother Charles, tells a story, current at the time, that seemed to him to illustrate her religious obsession:

> Some thieves having lately broken into a country Church about four leagues from this, and rummaging about in the dark for plate and other plunder among the Altars, they happened to overturn or break open a Pix, which contained several consecrated wafers, which were found next morning strewed about on the ground near the Altar, and some of them were missing, which was reckoned still a greater misfortune. When these circumstances were reported to the Queen, they threw her into the deepest affliction: she shut herself up and was invisible for three days, after which, she said that all the misfortunes of her late father's reign and the judgments with which God had visited him, such as earthquakes, the expulsion of the Jesuits, and the war which followed, were altogether nothing, when compared to the grievous insult which had been offered to the body of our blessed Saviour himself, and which it became her duty to apologize for, after the most signal manner possible; and, after holding a consultation with the gravest and most orthodox divines, the whole Court were ordered into deep mourning for nine days, at the end of which there was a general procession from one great Church to another in the city at a considerable distance, in which the Queen herself and the Court walked in ceremony, and which they called the procession of the Disaggravation, and by performing of which they seriously think they have appeased the justly provoked wrath of the Deity.[4]

The duc de Châtelet, recording all the best court gossip during his stay in Lisbon in 1777, also had a story about D. Maria's piety: 'While I was at Lisbon, this princess [D. Maria] having granted a favour, which was disapproved by her confessor, was sentenced to fast eight days, and to tell her beads eight times.' Whether this story is true or not is less important than the fact that it was circulating, and was believed to be true.[5] The French ambassador, the marquis de Bombelles, recorded, somewhat wickedly, in his diary on 19 February 1787 that during the chaos and misrule that accompanied Carnival in Lisbon, 'the court and above all the queen were at prayer lest the madness of her people should displease God.'[6] Implicit in these stories was the idea that D. Maria's religion not only dominated her life but was impairing her judgement as ruler.

D. Maria believed that divine intervention had saved her life on more than one occasion. In 1753, shortly after her father's accession, when she was only nineteen, she became seriously ill with smallpox and her life was despaired of. However, she survived and attributed her recovery to the powers of a miraculous statue brought to her sickroom from the Graça convent.[7] Two years later she survived the earthquake, as she was with the royal family at Belém when the disaster occurred. With her family, she escaped into the palace gardens in her nightclothes and thereafter for a long time lived in a tent in the grounds. In November 1787 William Beckford gained clandestine admittance to the queen's bedroom in the barraca real, which, he said, 'is strewed over with books of devotion and saintly dolls of all sorts and sizes'.[8]

When it became clear that D. José and Mariana Vitória would not have a male heir, attention became focused instead on D. Maria and her marriage. As had happened in the 1680s, when it appeared that the heir to the throne would be the princess Isabel, the daughter of D. Pedro II and Marie Françoise, there was extreme reluctance to allow D. Maria to marry someone who was not Portuguese. In D. Maria's case attention became focused on close relatives within the royal family to provide a husband. Pombal appears to have thought that D. Maria's half-uncles, the meninos de Palhavã, illegitimate sons of D. João V, aspired to her hand and had them sent into exile to a convent in Buçaco. In 1760 it was eventually agreed that D. Maria should marry her full uncle, D. Pedro. This marriage had been suggested as early as 1749 by D. João V himself, when D. Maria was fifteen years old, but D. José had not liked the idea of his brother being raised to the position of co-heir and Pombal feared that D. Pedro might become a focus for opposition to the crown. It took some time for the minister's opposition to be overcome and, in the end, when a formal request for D. Maria's hand was received from the Spanish court, the marriage was brought forward to provide a diplomatic way of refusing Spain's proposal.[9]

D. Maria's marriage to her uncle Pedro took place on 6 June 1760 and proved to be a happy and fruitful one. When she eventually became queen at the age of 43, she had already given birth to seven children, though only three of these had survived beyond infancy: the infante José, the prince of Brazil, the infante João, who eventually succeeded her as D. João VI, and Maria Ana Vitória (named after her grandmother), who was later married to the Spanish infante Gabriel.

D. Maria's personal hostility to Pombal went back to the minister's suppression of the Jesuits and to his attempts to prevent her marriage with her uncle. In 1757 Pombal had persuaded D. José to remove all Jesuits from the court and to order them no longer to hear confessions. One of the casualties was D. Maria's own confessor, Timoteio de Oliveira. D. Maria was also aware that Pombal had tried to prevent her accession. As the young prince José, her son, grew up Pombal became convinced that he was more in tune with his own ideas and had made little secret of the fact that he thought the succession should pass to him, bypassing D. Maria and her uncle.[10] When Maria heard of this plan she protested to her father and told him she would never sign any document relinquishing her right to the throne. Pombal was forced to abandon the idea.

Pombal was not alone in his doubts about D. Maria's suitability to become queen. In 1777, the year of her accession, the duc de Châtelet wrote,

> She is a woman truly worthy of esteem and respect; but she does not have the qualities to make a great queen. No one is more humane, more charitable or more sensitive than her; but these qualities are spoilt by a devotion which is excessive and poorly understood. Her confessor who has an unlimited ascendancy over her employs her in acts of devotion and penitence, time which could more usefully be employed for the happiness of her people without harming the safety of her soul.[11]

William Beckford was also critical of the queen's judgement where her charitable duties were concerned. On 25 November 1787, he was down in the Praça do Comercio where there were

> vast crowds of people moving about, of all degrees, colours and nations, old and young, active and crippled, monks and officers.

D. Maria I and D. Pedro III by Miguel Antonio do Amaral, *c.* 1777, oil on canvas.

Shoals of beggars kept pouring in from all quarters to take their stands at the gates of the Palace and watch the Queen's going out; for Her Majesty is a most indulgent mother to these sturdy sons of idleness, and hardly ever steps into her carriage without distributing considerable sums amongst them. By this misplaced charity, hundreds of stout fellows are taught the management of the crutch instead of a musket, and the art of manufacturing sores, ulcers and scabby pates in most loathsome perfection.[12]

Ten years earlier Costigan had commented in much the same way:

Immediately on the Queen's accession to the Crown, a number of starving and unprincipled Foreigners, among whom I am sorry to include some of our own country of both sexes, availed themselves of her weakness and known disposition towards Catholicism, and pretending to become converts to the religion of the country, they took her for godmother at the time of their being baptized into the true church, by which means they insured to themselves her protection, and often also a trifling pension to live on.[13]

Apart from her devotions, which played a central role in her life, D. Maria inherited her parents' pleasure in hunting and, even when she began to show signs of mental instability, would often go to one of the royal hunting reserves. Like other members of her family she also took pleasure in music and would sing, sometimes with her sisters, before selected guests.[14]

In some respects she took more after her grandfather than her father. Like D. João V, D. Maria promised to build a convent, dedicated to the Heart of Jesus, if she gave birth to a son. Her first son was born in August 1761, named José after his grandfather, but it was only after she came to the throne that, as queen, she was able to fulfil her vow and plans were laid for the building of the Basilica of the Estrela. The religious complex of the Estrela cost five million *cruzados* (some estimates put it at nine million) at a time when the government was having to retrench to cover its debts. Mário Domingues wrote that 'it seemed as though she was the reincarnation of the spendthrift spirit of her grandfather.'[15] The convent attached to the Basilica was finished in 1781. Its inauguration was attended by the queen, who served a meal for the nuns with her own hands.[16] The church itself was eventually completed in 1790, when the son, whose birth it had been built to celebrate, was already dead.

Opinions on D. Maria's Reign

Mário Domingues took a decidedly positive view of D. Maria's reign:

The work of D. Maria I's government was truly notable in respect of education and the sciences and arts, with ministers of recognized clarity of intellect and competence willing and happy to give concrete form to the proposals of a lady who was intelligent and good, and who was inspired with an unmistakeable intent to contribute to the common good, while fulfilling conscientiously her duties as a Sovereign.[17]

Domingues points out that her reign saw the founding of the Royal Academy of Science (Real Academia das Ciências), the Schools of Art and Design and the Schools of Artillery and Fortification. The Casa Pia for the protection of orphans was also founded in her reign and plans were drawn up for a national system of primary education. The Teatro de São Carlos was built to replace D. João V's great opera house destroyed in the earthquake and was inaugurated in 1793 to celebrate the birth of the infante João and Carlota Joaquina's first child.

Mário Domingues went on to write: 'Since the remote times of Dom Manuel, *O Venturoso*, there have been few periods in the national history in which the administration revealed itself so focused on the resolution of the most serious problems facing the nation as in the reign of Maria I.'[18]

The marquis de Bombelles, the French ambassador, remarked after a meeting with the queen in February 1787,

> If this princess had moved in other circles and had had another husband, her reign, which was too mild and during which nothing had been done either for good or ill, would certainly have been distinguished by the use she would have made of the justice of her ideas and her principles.[19]

William Beckford, who loved to comment affectionately and without malice on the follies and eccentricities of the Portuguese upper class, had nothing but praise for the queen. Although he had not been officially presented, he was smuggled by the young Marialva into a side room where he could observe the court:

> Her manner struck me as being peculiarly dignified and conciliating. She looks born to command; but at the same time to make that high authority as much believed as respected. Justice and clemency, the motto so glaringly misapplied on the banner of the abhorred Inquisition, might be transferred with the strictest truth to this good princess . . . Nothing could exceed the profound respect, the courtly decorum her presence appeared to inspire.[20]

Another very positive picture of the queen comes from the description of her official visit to the glassworks founded by William Stephens at Marinha Grande. Stephens had been a protégé of Pombal and had benefited from the mercantilist policies of the minister, but he retained the favour of D. Maria.[21] This interlude in the queen's life is charmingly described by Jenifer Roberts in her biography *The Madness of Queen Maria* and is based on a lengthy letter written by Stephens's sister, Philadelphia, which is located in the West Sussex Record Office. D. Maria had visited the Stephens glassworks for the first time in 1786, shortly after the death of her husband, but she returned for a longer stay of three days in 1788.

The queen arrived with her whole family and was housed in Stephens's residence. She was accompanied by a retinue of guards, servants, attendant ladies and noblemen of the court. Philadelphia comments, 'You may guess a little more or less of the number of people belonging to Her Majesty's suite when I tell you that we had stables provided with straw and barley for six hundred beasts exclusive of the troops.' On arrival, D. Maria went first to inspect the accommodation provided for her ladies-in-waiting before visiting the glass factory where

> after satisfying her curiosity of seeing the people at work and applauding them all very much, came upstairs [to the packing room] and examined everything very attentively. After spending a little time here, they took a view of the other departments belonging to the Fabrick. In the cutting and flowering room, they sat some time admiring the work, the Queen and Princess both asking me a number of questions about our craftsmen.

The royal party were entertained by music, a theatrical production put on by members of the workforce and fireworks. The following day they made a formal visit to nearby Leiria, where 'the houses were all white-washed, the streets covered with sand, and the windows hung with curtains the same as on grand procession days'. On the final day the queen left Marinha Grande for a visit to Nazaré, where she watched fish being landed, even though there was an outbreak of smallpox in the town.[22]

This account of a royal visit, reminiscent of such visits made by monarchs in more recent times, provides a highly detailed account of D. Maria, her family and entourage, of the royal ceremonial, and of the practical details of the Portuguese court on the move. It is in many ways an attractive and sympathetic account, which contrasts with the often cynical and contemptuous comments published by other foreign visitors to Portugal.

The Queen Takes Charge

D. Maria i's accession to the throne in 1777 was greeted with eager anticipation throughout Portugal and there were, as her most recent biographer expresses it,

> hopes for the new regime, that is for better and more prosperous days, for actions in respect of justice and the eradication of despotism, which were all made clear in the sumptuous and enthusiastic act of *levantamento* (acclamation) and oath-taking perhaps more glossy and well attended than any previous one.[23]

The duc de Châtelet described the beginnings of D. Maria's reign:

> The coronation of the queen took place with great magnificence, amid the discharge of artillery and acclamations of an immense concourse of people assembled, from all quarters, to witness the ceremony. The queen alone seemed to take no share in the general joy. She was painfully affected. The principal nobles of the court had resolved to instigate the people to demand of her the head of the Marquis de Pombal. The queen was informed of their intention; she was apprehensive of danger from refusal; but though she disliked the statesman, she respected the friend of her father.[24]

Soldiers were called upon to control the crowd:

> A great number of spectators had forced their way through the guards into the gallery; the queen ordered them not be disturbed. As it was impossible for carriages to approach, she was herself obliged to go through the crowd to reach hers. This was the most delightful moment of her life. Some threw themselves at her feet, others kissed the skirts of her robe, and she was affected even to tears. The illuminations were brilliant; the ceremony was performed with equal tranquillity and pomp. At night the English nation gave a

magnificent ball to the principal inhabitants of this city, no doubt, in testimony of its gratitude; for it was that nation, the real sovereign of Portugal, which had been crowned in the person of the queen. Next day the people resumed the mourning which they had thrown off on the preceding day. Amidst the general joy occasioned by the fall of Pombal, an air of sadness universally prevailed, and the company, on quitting the ball hastened to the churches.[25]

It was hoped that the new reign would bring to an end the rule of Pombal, but Costigan reported that many feared that somehow the old minister would hang on to power, and that the nobles who attended the court following the death of the king came 'provided with their *facas de ponta*, stabbing knives, in order to have immediately despatched the old man, in case he made any such attempt'.[26]

At the very beginning of her reign D. Maria had to face the contentious legacy of the previous reign. At first she relied heavily on the advice of her mother and continued to do so until her death in January 1781. Already before her father had died, she had begun to arrange, with her mother's assistance, the release of some of those imprisoned by Pombal and, immediately following her accession, some eight hundred prisoners were released. Many had grown old in prison and the Spanish ambassador described this as like the 'resurrection of the dead'.

D. Maria also consulted her mother about the future of Pombal himself. Aware that many people wished him to be punished for his actions, she took a surprisingly lenient and humane decision to exile him to his estates, eventually agreeing to establish a tribunal to investigate his actions. Kenneth Maxwell explains that, before any verdict could be delivered, 'D. Maria cut the process short in 1781 by issuing an edict declaring Pombal deserving of "exemplary punishment" but instituting no proceedings against his person because of "his age and feeble condition".'[27] Pombal claimed in his defence that he had never acted except with the consent of the king, D. José, and this appealed to the queen's filial piety and persuaded her, in effect, to pardon him. In taking this course D. Maria may well have been influenced by her mother, but it nevertheless indicates someone who was able and willing to make her own statesmanlike decisions.

The Church, which had been greatly reduced in influence during Pombal's ascendancy, found a much more favourable environment under D. Maria. One of her first acts was to dispense with the presence at court of the cardinal da Cunha, who had been prominent during D. José's reign and had been one of the instruments the minister had used in the destruction of the Jesuits.[28] She also allowed the restoration of the court of the Papal Nuncio and granted pensions to the Jesuits freed from prison. D. Maria's confessor, Inácio de São Caetano, now became a prominent figure at court. He had originally been placed in this influential position by Pombal and had remained a close ecclesiastical collaborator of the minister. On Pombal's fall from power he retained his position and, more importantly, the confidence of the queen. He became possibly the most influential person at court until his death in 1787. In that year he had been made Inquisitor General, once again confirming how that once powerful and independent institution had come under royal control. Mário Domingues wrote of him: 'Without being a minister he exercised over the spirit of D. Maria an influence that was deeper and more decisive than all of the other ministers or secretaries of state who officially served her.'[29]

D. Pedro, who ruled alongside his wife as D. Pedro III, gave the impression to foreign observers that he was unused to dealing with the

D. Pedro III, 1745, oil on canvas.

affairs of the government. He was described by Dumouriez as 'un Prince dévote, sobre & silencieux',[30] but rumour had it that, like his namesake D. Pedro II, he was nearly illiterate. He spent much of the day attending religious ceremonies and took little part in political affairs. Châtelet described him as 'fanatically devout, reserved, gloomy, constantly engaged in prayers and processions; he never interferes in the least, with the government, and is, in every respect, the mere shadow of a sovereign.'[31] However, he clearly provided the queen with a great deal of emotional support, which enabled her to manage the stresses that came with being a monarch who both reigned and ruled.

The Double Marriage

In 1785 another double marriage was arranged between members of the Portuguese and Spanish royal families. The infante João was to marry the Spanish princess Carlota Joaquina, while at the same time Maria Ana Vitória was married to the Spanish infante Gabriel.[32] This double marriage, which echoed the double marriage of 1729, was seen by D. Maria as a diplomatic triumph. Spain and Portugal had had a tense relationship during the Seven Years War (1756–63), and the Spanish invasion of Portugal in 1762 was still a vivid memory. There had also been a series of conflicts in South America over the Jesuit missions, the Portuguese settlement at Colónia do Sacramento and the status of the lands on the Banda Oriental (the future Uruguay). It was hoped that the dual marriage would bring the two countries closer together and establish firmer and more peaceful relations. However, on the Spanish side the marriages appear to have reawakened the possibilities of once again assimilating Portugal through dynastic inheritance. In 1787 the Spanish minister the count of Floridablanca had referred to the marriages as uniting the two countries by ties of family and friendship 'while Portugal is not yet incorporated into the Spanish dominions through the right of succession'.[33] Closer relations between Spain and Portugal, however, were seen by the French as an obstacle in the way of France's plans to become the dominant influence at the Portuguese court.

D. Maria's Mental Breakdown

D. Maria's famed piety did little to disguise the fact that she was highly strung and found the pressures of her position very stressful. She suffered her first psychological breakdown in 1780, apparently brought on by having to sign the act retrospectively pardoning the nobles who had been executed following the attempt on her father's life. The queen was apparently torn between her desire to do justice to the condemned and her respect for the memory of her father who had signed their death warrants.

In 1781 the Queen Mother, Mariana Vitória, died and D. Maria's husband, D. Pedro III, died in May 1786. D. Maria had enjoyed a happy marriage with the man she always referred to as 'my uncle of my heart' or 'my beloved uncle and husband'.[34] She had been supported by her mother and her husband in the difficult decisions she had had to make and their loss left her isolated and alone. In February 1787 Bombelles reported court gossip to the effect that the queen had been overheard saying she wanted to enter a convent.[35] Beckford heard a similar story: in October 1787 the marquis of Marialva 'told me in the strictest confidence that the queen had thoughts of retiring from government, that she was worn out with the intrigues of the Court and sick of her existence'.[36] Beckford was not entirely sympathetic: 'I cannot but reserve a larger portion of pity for the miseries of two millions of human beings who in affairs of the most serious moment are equally the victims of her timidity and irresolution.'[37]

D. Maria's complete mental breakdown was precipitated by the death of her son, the infante José, in September 1788, followed in the next three months by the deaths of her daughter and son-in-law in Spain and by the death of her confessor, Inácio de São Caetano. These repeated blows fed D. Maria's fears for her father's salvation and her own guilt in relation to the events of his reign. In 1789 the outbreak of the French Revolution caused her acute anxiety. She had always been a depressive – contemporaries described it as melancholia – and it seems that this condition was made worse by acute anxieties caused by the religious conversations with her new confessor and the abbess of the Estrela convent. By mid-January 1792 her last letter to her Spanish cousin, King Carlos IV, had been written,[38] and her advisers recognized that she had become incapable of governing, her symptoms increasingly those of a severe bipolar disorder. Dr Francis Willis, who had apparently been successful in treating the madness of King George III, was summoned from England at great expense and subjected the queen to a brutal regime that included enemas, forced feeding and the strait-jacket. Her condition grew steadily worse and she was moved to Queluz to be away from the court and the bustle of Lisbon. Dr Willis finally tendered his resignation but his departure seemed to make D. Maria's condition worse still. After a fire destroyed the *barraca real* at Belém in 1794, D. Maria was housed permanently in an annexe at Queluz, where visitors reported hearing her constantly crying aloud. Meanwhile, her two unmarried sisters, Maria Ana Francisca and Maria Francisca Dorothea, also began to suffer mental breakdowns, suggesting a strong inherited tendency afflicting the royal family.

For the next ten years D. Maria lived the life of the insane, cared for but with a mind darkened and out of her control. She was seldom seen by anyone outside the palace circles but Laure Junot, the wife of the French ambassador General Jean-Andoche Junot, describes meeting her by accident in 1805 while out in the country:

> One day when I was strolling in a little solitary valley, in the neigh-bourhood of Cintra, where I used to go and botanize, I met three ladies, one of whom attracted my notice on account of her strange appearance and wild stare. It was a windy day, and her hair, which was as white as silver, was blown over her face and shoulders. As this appeared to annoy her, one of the females who accompanied her endeavoured to shade the hair from her face; but for this kind office she received a box on the ear, which I heard, though I was a hundred paces off . . . I think her attendants must have told her who I was; for as I withdrew I perceived that she was men-acing me with clenched fists, and darting at me looks which were absolutely demoniac.[39]

When the royal family finally decided to leave for Brazil in November 1807, D. Maria was taken aboard the ship of the line *Príncipe Real* and housed with her family in the state cabin for the two-month voyage. Apparently, from her confused conversation, she had no idea where she was going or why, but as she was being brought in a coach to the quay she is reported to have told the coachman, 'Not so fast! They are going to think we are fleeing' (*Não tão depressa! Vão pensar que estamos a fugir*). It is ironic that this exclamation, probably the most memorable single remark made by any member of the Braganza family, should have been made by the one who was completely insane.

Once in Rio, the queen was housed in the Carmelite convent in what became known as the Largo do Paço. She continued to be honoured as queen and her family visited her to kiss hands on ceremonial occasions, according to ancient Portuguese custom. When she was taken out for drives into the country 'people had to dismount from their horses, alight from their carriages, and kneel on the ground with bowed heads as the royal chaise passed by.'[40]

D. Maria eventually died on 20 March 1816 at the age of 81, by far the longest lived of the Braganza monarchs. Her body was prepared for burial with her right hand exposed for the family and courtiers to kiss one final time. When the new king, D. João VI, eventually decided to return to Portugal, D. Maria's coffin was brought back to Portugal and the queen was buried a second time, with full honours, in the Estrela basilica in March 1822.

The Infante José: The King Who Never Was

D. Maria's eldest son and heir, José, prince of Brazil, was born in 1762. Pombal had a say in the appointment of his tutors and as he grew he apparently adopted the secular and 'enlightened' views of the Pombaline era. In 1774 Pombal proposed that José should succeed to the throne on the death of his grandfather instead of D. Maria. This proposal was dropped and in February 1777 José was married to his aunt, Maria Benedita. This was the second incestuous marriage in the ruling family, which, according to religious ideas of the time, made him the brother of his own mother. Maria Benedita was eleven years older than the nineteen-year-old boy and the marriage produced no children.[41]

The marquis de Bombelles mentioned in his diary on 27 February 1787 that the prince, then 25 years old, was 'angry at being nothing in a country of which he would one day be the master'.[42] Later in the year he was, as he hoped, appointed as a member of the royal council. This was rather exceptional in the story of the Braganzas, as it had been far more usual for the heir to the throne to be excluded from access to affairs of state, as his grandfather D. José had been. The young prince had little opportunity to influence the affairs of the kingdom because in September 1788 he contracted smallpox and died. Apparently D. Maria had refused to allow him to be vaccinated.

When William Beckford eventually published the account of his stay in Portugal in 1787, he reported in detail a long conversation that he had had with José during a chance encounter near Sintra. According to him, José was particularly concerned with England's influence, which he saw as very detrimental to Portugal. However, there is doubt whether this meeting ever took place as there is no mention of it in Beckford's diaries for that year.[43] On other occasions when Beckford saw the prince, he was not impressed and recorded in his diary how, 'the Prince of Brazil [José] and João stalked about with their hands in their pockets, their mouths in a perpetual yawn, and their eyes wandering from object to object with a stare of royal vacancy'.[44]

José's death threatened the succession once again as his brother, the infante João, who was now heir to the throne, was betrothed to Carlota Joaquina but she was only thirteen and the marriage had not been consummated. Moreover, it was rumoured that the princess, who was abnormally small, would not be able to have children.

In Spain José's sister, Maria Ana Vitória, and her husband, the Spanish infante Gabriel, also died of smallpox in 1788, leaving a son, Pedro Carlos, who was brought to Portugal as a possible heir to the throne should the infante João and Carlota Joaquina not produce children. Pedro Carlos eventually married João's daughter (his first cousin) Maria Teresa and the couple had a son, the infante Sebastião, before Pedro Carlos himself died in 1812 at the age of 26. As for Maria Teresa, she outlived Pedro Carlos by fifty years. She led an extremely active and influential life and was perhaps the main inspiration behind the Carlist movement in Spain.

The Palace of Queluz

If the palace/convent of Mafra was the consummation of the grand aspirations that D. João v had for Portugal, the palace at Queluz stands above all as a memorial to D. Maria and her husband D. Pedro.

In 1654 D. João iv had created an endowment for the second sons of the royal family, known as the Casa do Infantado. The endowment was made up of properties confiscated from supporters of the Spanish Habsburgs and the Quinta of Queluz was one of these, formerly the property of Manuel de Moura, son of Philip's secretary Cristovão de Moura. The infante Pedro, later to be King D. Pedro iii, inherited the position of Senhor da Casa do Infantado in 1742 on the death of his

The Queluz Palace.

uncle, Francisco, duke of Beja, and in 1747 began the construction of the palace. From the start this was a private residence rather than a centre of national political life and D. Pedro lived there when his palace in Lisbon was destroyed in a fire in July 1751.[45] With Pedro's marriage to the infanta Maria in 1760 Queluz became one of the principal royal residences.

There was continuity between the two great palaces built by the Braganzas in the eighteenth century. Mateus Vicente de Oliveira, who was the architect principally responsible for the building of Queluz, had worked under Johann Friedrich Ludwig on the building of Mafra. If Mafra had been built in the heavy style of Roman baroque, Queluz reflected the aesthetic of French rococo with its lightness of decoration and its use of mirrors. The gardens however were very Portuguese with their clipped evergreen hedges and borders and the *azulejos* that decorated the ornamental canal.

In the 1780s apartments were added to the palace for the heir, Infante José, and then for the infante João and his Spanish bride Carlota Joaquina. When Queen Maria lost her reason she was housed in what was known as the Pavilion in Queluz while the main palace became the residence of D. João, who in 1799 formally assumed the regency. Carlota Joaquina continued to reside there after she separated from her husband and it became her favourite residence when she was not in retirement at Ramalhão. Her son, D. Pedro IV, was born at Queluz and eventually died there in 1834.

D. João VI in 1821 by Jean Philippe Goulu, tempera on ivory.

9

D. João VI: The Merciful

The infante João was a second son and only became heir to the
Braganza throne when his brother, José, died of smallpox on 11
September 1788. Until his death in 1826 at the age of 59, D. João's life
was plagued on the one hand by a mentally unstable and eventually mad
mother and on the other by a wife who despised him, whose reckless
behaviour threatened to bring the royal family into contempt and who
constantly interfered in politics in opposition to her husband. In spite
of these trials, and his clumsy and not very regal appearance, D. João
became one of the best-loved of the Braganza monarchs.

The Heir to the Throne

D. João was born on 13 May 1767 and at the age of fifteen had himself
survived a bout of smallpox. In 1785 he had been married by proxy
to the Spanish infanta, Carlota Joaquina, who was only ten years old,
as one-half of the double marriage celebrated between the Spanish
and Portuguese courts. 'We sent them a fish and they sent us a sar-
dine', was the popular comment when the insignificant and undersized
Carlota appeared in Portugal.[1] At thirteen Carlota was small, with
frizzy hair and a face that became ugly as she grew older. Her behaviour
was adolescent in the extreme, unruly and unpredictable, and she
acquired a reputation for ill-treating servants at the court. When the
infante José died, she rose, at the age of fourteen, to high precedence
in the kingdom as the betrothed of the new prince of Brazil. The
Braganza dynasty once again had very precarious prospects for survival
– and for retaining the respect of the Portuguese people. In February
1787 the marquis de Bombelles heard that the marquis de Louriçal,

the ambassador in Madrid who had negotiated the double marriage, was near to death. In a particularly malicious entry in his diary he reflected that the Portuguese people would never forgive him for having arranged a marriage

> which has given to D. Jean de Bragance a wife from whom it seems impossible he can have issue; it is said in jest on this subject that it is necessary to have faith, hope and charity for this ridiculous marriage to be consummated: faith to believe the Infanta is a woman, hope to believe she can have children and Christian charity for him to resolve to have them.[2]

In 1790, however, Carlota, then aged fifteen, was deemed ready, and she and D. João consummated their marriage.

D. João struck observers as being a heavy and dull young man with a head too large for his shoulders and a mouth that was open in what seemed to be a perpetual yawn, an appearance unsympathetically caught in a number of the portraits made at the time. Bombelles describes how, at the queen's name day reception, D. João 'stammered sulkily the words to which his blank countenance gave an added degree of insignificance'.[3] He suffered from poor health, being afflicted with haemorrhoids, ulcers, skin problems and sores on his legs. He was not a well-educated or cultured man, though, like most of his family, he took great pleasure in church music and in hunting. Indeed, when settled in Brazil after 1808, he presided over a kind of cultural renaissance in his new capital in which the royal theatre and chapel played a major part.

D. João's reign was a turbulent period for Portugal and its empire during which the very survival of the Braganza dynasty seemed in danger. The king was slow to make decisions and constantly appeared unable to make up his mind between different courses of action. In the end this very indecisiveness and lack of energetic engagement matured into a certain political shrewdness and were to earn him a grudging respect from his contemporaries. According to Marcus Cheke, during the ascendancy of the Constitutional Cortes in 1822, the king was on record as saying, 'it is my considered opinion that the best thing to do is to do nothing.'[4] The nineteenth-century historian Alexandre Herculano referred to D. João as having the 'proverbial craftiness of the peasant',[5] while A. H. de Oliveira Marques wrote that 'all witnesses agree in describing him as indolent, timorous and indecisive although many of the examples of "indecision" could rather be seen as consideration and prudence."[6]

In February 1792 D. João was suddenly thrust into the forefront of affairs when his mother finally succumbed to her mental illness and was considered incapable of ruling. At first he refused to assume the title of Regent, out of respect for his mother, and for several months no one presided over the affairs of the kingdom. When, towards the end of 1792, D. João was persuaded to assume the role of head of the government, he still refused the title of Regent, a refusal he maintained until 1799.

D. João and Carlota Joaquina

Although any affection that might once have existed between the prince and his eccentric wife soon evaporated, the two continued for a time to perform their conjugal duty and children came at regular intervals. In all Carlota defied the early predictions and had nine children. However, by 1801 the prince regent and his wife were living apart and it is doubtful whether Carlota's last three children, including the infante Miguel, were fathered by D. João.

The *barraca real* had burnt down in 1794 and plans were drawn up for a new royal palace at Ajuda, where work began in 1799. As the couple had now separated, Carlota continued to occupy the palace at Queluz or her *quinta* of Ramalhão, which had once been rented by William Beckford, and which she had bought in 1794. D. João increasingly took lonely refuge at Mafra. Effectively separated from his wife, he had a brief affair with Eugenia de Menezes, by whom he had a child.[7] In 1805 D. João became ill and Carlota and some of her cronies plotted to have him declared insane like his mother, so that Carlota could assume the regency. D. João eventually discovered what had been planned, which served to deepen the hostility between himself and his wife.

D. João and the French Revolution

D. João's reign was to be one long struggle to adjust to the changing world brought about by the French Revolution. Throughout the eighteenth century Portugal had depended on the close alliance with Britain for the protection of itself and its empire. The Royal Navy had, in effect, used Lisbon as a base and British forces had come to Portugal's defence when, during the Seven Years War, the Bourbon family compact between France and Spain had led to a Spanish invasion of Portugal. However, by the end of the century it was by no means clear that Portugal could rely on Britain as it had in the past. Britain's commercial dominance in Portugal was in decline and there were years when the balance of trade was in Portugal's favour. D. Maria's government was assiduous in trying to develop other trading partners and in 1788 a commercial treaty was signed with Russia. Far more important than the shifting balance of trade in weakening the ties with Britain was the rapid growth in France's military power. The conquests of the French Revolutionary armies in Italy, Switzerland, the Low Countries and Germany represented an unprecedented military threat, overturning a political balance that had, on the whole, been maintained for a century. Britain could not match the expansion of French military power, its army being undermanned and scattered throughout its empire, and instead concentrated on maintaining its sea power. Portugal's empire could be protected by the British navy but Portugal itself could not. A succession of British military missions reported on the poor state of Portugal's defences and the weakness of its armed forces, and concluded that Britain could not provide any guarantee of the security of mainland Portugal.

In 1793 Portugal had joined the First Coalition against France, along with Spain, incurring the hostility and suspicion of the French. With the collapse of the First Coalition and the French invasions of Italy, Spain changed sides and sought its own security through an alliance with France. Portugal was now exposed and in the short War of the Oranges in 1801 experienced another Spanish invasion and the loss of the frontier town of Olivença. Britain did not come to Portugal's defence but instead occupied the island of Madeira to prevent a French pre-emptive strike at the all-important shipping lanes of the Atlantic. The war proved what the British military missions had already concluded, that Portuguese armed forces were unable to defend the country against Spain, let alone against France. Portugal was forced to sign a humiliating treaty and to pay a large indemnity, but a final break with Britain was avoided when the general Peace of Amiens was signed in 1802.

The war began again in 1803 and soon moved close to mainland Portugal. Spanish treasure ships were seized by the British navy and the French and Spanish fleets joined forces to challenge Britain's supremacy at sea. D. João's advisers were divided. António de Araujo, the Minister for Foreign Affairs, favoured a French alliance hoping that cooperation with Napoleon's European project would make Portugal secure as a French satellite state and he was backed by a growing body of Francophile opinion among the country's elite. It seems that D. João even hoped for a dynastic marriage that would see his heir, the infante Pedro, marry Napoleon's niece.[8] Another court faction led by the Sousa Coutinho brothers favoured an alliance with Britain, which would, at least, secure the empire.

D. João, meanwhile, tried to find some room to manoeuvre between the stark choices represented by the two factions, but Araujo persuaded him that it would still be possible for Portugal to remain neutral, a neutrality that would be guaranteed by regular payments to France. Historians have concluded that D. João's policy of neutrality was doomed to failure from the start. It was in essence a policy of doing nothing and trying to appease the French – sitting still in the cage while fierce animals fought each other around and outside. It was a policy that suited the regent's temperament, allowing him to avoid making hard choices, and it might have succeeded had Napoleon been able to force a peace on Britain after his overwhelming military successes in central Europe in 1805 and 1806. Nor was D. João quite so supine as is sometimes suggested. Reform of the army went ahead, while plans began to be drawn up as early as 1803 for the removal of the government to Brazil as a last resort, which, of course, D. João wanted to avoid at all costs.[9]

In July 1807 events elsewhere in Europe meant that Portugal's neutrality was becoming impossible to maintain. At the Treaty of Tilsit Napoleon and Russia had made peace, a peace that was followed by the Berlin Decrees, which closed all the European ports to British commerce. Napoleon now demanded that Portugal also should close its ports. D. João hesitated as he knew that this would be followed by Britain taking action against Portugal's overseas territories. Napoleon now lost patience. On 13 October the Paris newspaper *Moniteur* published a declaration by the emperor that the House of Braganza had ceased to reign and on 27 October a secret treaty was signed with Spain for the partition of Portugal.

A French invasion force had been assembled on the Spanish frontier under the command of the former French ambassador in Lisbon,

Jean-Andoche Junot. With Araujo's encouragement D. João at last agreed to close his ports and authorized the confiscation of British property. General Junot's army, however, was already on its way, having crossed the frontier on 12 October 1807. A British fleet meanwhile patrolled off the mouth of the Tagus, threatening action against Lisbon and the capture of the Portuguese fleet, which it was known the French were eager to seize.

At first D. João toyed with the idea of remaining to face the French, while sending his son Pedro to Brazil,[10] but he realized that this would result not only in the loss of his throne and his own imprisonment but possibly the dismemberment of his country. At last, on 24 November, he gave the orders to embark the whole royal family and the government amid scenes of great confusion and disorder. Just four days were allotted for assembling and bringing on board the government archives and the royal library as well as the effects of the royal family and of the 15,000 people who were to travel with them. When the fleet, with the royal family on board, was finally ready to depart, it was detained for 26 hours by contrary winds. At last, with the French army already in the Lisbon suburbs, the wind changed and the armada left the Tagus for the safety of Sir Sydney Smith's escorting squadron. As Marcus Cheke described it, 'There is a Portuguese proverb to say that no good comes of a Spanish wind or a Spanish marriage, but in this case the east wind was an exception to the rule.'[11]

D. João and Carlota Joaquina travelled aboard separate ships.

An 1813 engraving of the embarcation of D. João VI to Brazil by Francesco Bartolozzi.

The Political Implications of D. João's Arrival in Brazil

The journey of the royal family and the country's elites to Brazil was a true exodus, an epic of misery as ill-prepared vessels, some with half-rotten timbers, struggled across the Atlantic through winter seas. On board the *Afonso de Albuquerque*, the Portuguese passengers became infested with lice.[12] To deal with the problem the ladies and Carlota herself had their heads shaved. The miseries of the voyage were not easily forgotten and are one reason why D. João for a long time resisted any suggestion that he should return to Portugal.

The king's arrival in Rio proved to be a turning point in the history of South America. History turns slowly, however, like the proverbial supertanker, and for long its new direction was not discernible – and D. João was certainly not a pilot with a course clearly marked on his charts. At first it seemed that the arrival of the Portuguese court in Rio had simply brought the archaic traditions of Portuguese royal government to Brazil. D. João, however, was accompanied not only by courtiers and officials but by large numbers of British because the price exacted by his allies for the security they offered him was the complete opening of Brazilian markets to British commerce. The arrival of a large number of people from Europe – Portuguese and British, but in time French, German, Swiss and others, even though they were mostly settled in and around the capital, was to lead to the growth of Brazil's own sense of its identity as separate from that of Portugal.

Once settled in Brazil, D. João and Carlota soon began to see the world from a wholly new perspective. The Portuguese monarchy was saved and instead of being confined to poor and backwards Portugal was installed in a large and wealthy country protected by the British navy from the wars and revolutions of Europe. Spain, meanwhile, was in a state of chaos and this chaos soon extended to the Spanish territories in America where independence movements were gathering strength. While D. João and his advisers saw the opportunity of reviving Brazil's long-standing ambitions to secure a port on the Rio de la Plata, which had been in abeyance since Colónia do Sacramento had been handed over to Spain in 1778, Carlota for her part aspired to act as regent for both Spain and her empire as the legitimate monarch, Carlos IV, was a prisoner in the hands of Napoleon.

Portugal, from having been a supine victim of the fluctuations of European politics, now became a major player in the rapidly changing political scene in the New World. However, as D. João eyed the possibility of annexing the Banda Oriental (modern Uruguay), and Carlota the possibility of installing herself as regent in Buenos Aires, the fate of both remained in the hands of Britain and its influential ambassadors, Lord Strangford and later Sir Edward Thornton. D. João and his wife lacked the resources and the political skills to have their own way and had been manoeuvred into signing two important treaties (those of 1808 and 1810), which superseded the famous treaties of 1654 and 1703 and opened the ports of Brazil to British trade, giving Britain a favoured nation status. Meanwhile a British army ousted the French from Portugal, becoming in its turn an army of occupation. A British general, Lord Beresford, took command of the armed forces and fortresses of Portugal. In Spain the fight against the French went on but the provisional government in Cádiz, far from welcoming Carlota with her well-known absolutist views, turned instead to liberal ideas and drew up the famous liberal constitution of 1812.

D. João, the King

D. João, meanwhile, began to enjoy life in Brazil. He introduced into the tropical environment the traditional court ceremonial of the Braganzas, including the weekly audiences with the people, the *beija mão* for ceremonial occasions, the religious processions, the lavish musical and operatic performances and the formal acclamation of the new king after the death of Queen Maria in 1816. Among the many traditional customs that D. João had brought with him was the right of all his vassals to bring their problems directly to him in person. The king allowed anyone to stop him and to address him personally when he was out in his coach or walking in the city. Their complaints or appeals were always heard and subsequently dealt with. Many foreigners bore witness to the fact that D. João was most amenable to a personal approach, which contributed in a major way to his growing popularity.[13]

The theatricality of the Braganza court was enriched by themes derived from the tropics and the New World, and lost nothing from an environment that included the celebrations of the black slave population and even the forest cults of the Indians. D. João also revived the conservatory at Santa Cruz, where slaves were taught to be musicians and singers. This highly accomplished slave orchestra performed at church services and public celebrations.

D. João himself was far from being a conventionally regal figure. Contemporaries commented on his dirty clothes, his lack of what today would be called personal hygiene, which led to skin complaints and sores, and to his strange habit of carrying around in his pockets cold roast chicken, on which he had a habit of snacking during the day. His awkward appearance on horseback to review his army in 1816 was an event so unusual, it might almost be described as unique in the annals of the monarchy.

In 1815 Lord Beresford, the commander of D. João's army in Portugal, paid a visit to Rio. When he returned in 1816 he wrote a detailed account of his experiences there to his friend the duke of Wellington. His assessment of the king is probably as accurate as any made at the time:

> He is extremely shrewd not a little bordering on cunning. He prides himself upon open dealing & sincerity, somewhat more than he practices it. He is very inquisitive upon all topics & reads every paper that comes to His ministers, indeed he always reads the dispatches of all kinds before they get them. His judgment is far from being bad, indeed I think it excellent on all subjects, but he never

Statue in Porto of
D. João VI on horseback.

abides by it, from timidity & a total want of resolution. He can not hold out in any instance against perseverance and then he is much more governed than he used to be by the interests & love of intrigues of His court & it is unfortunately too easy to get hold of him, as he is most susceptible to flattery & in particular to personal homage. He has many weaknesses but few if any personal vices. He is kind and good hearted & of a most forgiving disposition as he certainly bears little malice. He is most desirous of popularity and of being beloved by His people but I fear he loses their respect by His very kindness.[14]

While in Rio Beresford was assiduous in attending the Court, which he found bizarre and frustrating:

It is the most motley & threadbare concern you can imagine as everyone goes without discrimination, all colours & all characters. In short the Sal d'audience is a mixture as extraordinary & shows as much equality as the antichamber of Robertspierre [*sic*] could have produced. There is the Duke and the beggar, the general & the soldiers all pressed [?] together. It is a strange kind of monarchical republicanism.[15]

For the moment, the presence of so many Portuguese nobles and courtiers with their demands for precedence and position did not spoil the welcome the royal family received, though over a longer period a resentment against these Portuguese was to grow and begin to colour an emerging Brazilian nationalism.[16]

The Kingdom of Brazil

D. João's presence in Brazil was not all theatre and ceremonial. Safely installed in Rio, the king appeared to recover his ability to take initiatives and formulate policy. Moreover, once the wars in Europe were over he felt able to free himself to some extent from British tutelage. He resisted strong pressure from Britain to return to Europe and embarked on an ambitious policy in the south by sending his forces to occupy Montevideo, a policy Britain had firmly opposed. Explanations for the king's reluctance to return to Portugal have ranged from his inertia, the horrific memories of the last-minute flight from

Lisbon in November 1807 and his ill health. More significant was his realization that the wealth of the monarchy lay in Brazil rather than war-torn Portugal. He feared with some justification that, if he left Rio, Brazil would be lost to the Braganza monarchy. This last consideration, never given adequate weight by Britain, was nevertheless clear to a casual observer like the British naval officer James Prior, who wrote in 1813, 'there is no question among those who best know the country, that, but for the timely arrival of the government, Brazil would have followed, if not preceded, the efforts of the Spanish colonies for independence.'[17]

In December 1815 D. João issued a decree making Brazil a kingdom of the Braganza monarchy with status equal to Portugal. When the aged D. Maria died in February 1816, D. João was acclaimed as king of Brazil as well as of Portugal.

D. João's presence in Brazil coincided with many far-reaching changes that he oversaw and encouraged in a benevolent manner, which was surprising given the conservative, introspective and even reclusive traditions of the Braganza dynasty. The king brought with him a printing press and soon newspapers and books were being produced in Brazil for the first time. The Bank of Brazil was founded with the monopoly of issuing paper money and providing the king with a facility for financing his government. Academies were created for educating officers for the army and navy, and medical schools for the training of doctors. The first steam engines were employed, initially in the crushing of sugar cane. A Royal Academy of Fine Arts was another of D. João's creations to be placed alongside his patronage of theatre and opera. An innovation in which the king took particular interest was the creation of the Royal Botanical Gardens. These became a centre for experimentation and for the introduction of new plants, like tea, and are still among the notable institutions in Rio de Janeiro.

Reluctant to return to Europe, D. João entrusted the affairs of Portugal to a Regency Council, but he left Lord Beresford in command of the army as a counterweight to the regents and to provide him with an independent source of information about what was happening in Lisbon. He looked with some complacency on the tensions growing between Beresford and the Regency Council as a way of preventing power in Portugal from slipping from his grasp.[18] There were signs both in Brazil and in Portugal that liberal ideas were growing and leading to a demand for change. In 1817 there was a short-lived republican revolt in Pernambuco and a conspiracy among army officers in Lisbon. Both of these were suppressed, however, and for the moment allowed D. João to remain in Rio undisturbed.

D. João and the Liberal Revolution

In 1820 the structure of Braganza absolutism found itself under attack and threatened with collapse. Early that year an army mutiny and rebellion broke out in Spain, demanding the end of absolutism and the restoration of the liberal constitution of 1812. The movement spread to Portugal and soon found echoes in Brazil. D. João was not to know peace from this time until his death in 1826, but his naturally phlegmatic personality, and the natural dignity that he was able to display through his troubles, enabled him to survive the storms and to maintain some stability in both Portugal and in Brazil. He believed that playing for time was often a successful ploy when faced with revolutionary tumult and was prepared to play a long game, which was often more successful than the efforts of those who strove for short-term advantage in the turmoil that followed. This, at any rate, is a generous interpretation of the indecision and vacillation that so infuriated the foreign ambassadors in Rio and subsequently in Lisbon, who believed that decisive action was necessary for the situation to be brought under control.[19]

As revolutionary change gathered momentum, D. João relied a great deal on his son and heir, the infante Pedro, whose personal qualities complemented his own in so many ways. Pedro was popular and charismatic. He was prepared to be proactive, to take initiatives and to make decisions – all qualities that could not be used to describe his father. As Pedro was never happier than when taking vigorous action, he was left to deal with the growing tumult in Brazil. However, the situation in Portugal also needed to be addressed, and D. João reluctantly agreed to return to his European kingdom, leaving Pedro behind in Brazil as regent. This in effect split the united kingdom of Portugal and Brazil into two, each ruled by a member of the Braganza family, and it seems that D. João recognized as he left for Europe that Brazil's permanent separation from Portugal was now inevitable.[20]

The Final Phase

The last five years of D. João's life were tumultuous and frequently chaotic as revolution and counter-revolution unfolded in Portugal. The international community, especially Britain, France and the powers of the Holy Alliance, saw in Portugal a test case for their ideologies and a laboratory for a new European order. As Brazil rose in revolt and broke away from Portugal, D. João, infirm and prematurely aged, was tossed hither and thither in the stormy political waters and increasingly found his own family divided and pulling him in different directions. Nevertheless, the king clung to the few political assets he possessed. He was widely respected by the ordinary people in Portugal and his clear objective of preserving both Brazil and Portugal for the Braganza dynasty enabled him to give some direction to events.

On returning to Lisbon, D. João took up residence in the Bemposta palace, where remnants of the old court customs were reintroduced. He promised to accept the new constitution and submitted to the humiliations to which he was exposed as a constitutional monarch. His willingness to accept the constitution, which was eventually promulgated officially on 23 September 1822, helped to maintain his continued popularity. It is possible that he believed that events would soon bring about a change in the political direction and he was determined to occupy, as far as possible, the centre ground, especially as his wife, by refusing to take an oath to the Constitution, had placed herself uncompromisingly at the head of the ultra-conservatives, opposed to any change in a liberal direction.

In 1823 the situation created by the new Constitution was challenged when the king's younger son, Miguel, headed a movement, known as the Vila Francada, to restore the old absolutist order. The young prince, still only 21 years old, was certainly persuaded to lead this coup by his mother, Carlota Joaquina, but any move to have him replace his father was prevented when D. João himself agreed to join the popular movement against the Constitution. Shortly afterwards an army coup, known in Portuguese history as the Abrilada, led to demands that the Constitution be revoked and that Miguel be put in charge of the army. Behind this demand was Carlota Joaquina, once again, and a network of absolutist clerics and nobles. D. João, threatened with losing his throne, was saved by the intervention of the diplomatic corps and by the presence of Marshal Beresford, who happened to be in Lisbon angling to be appointed again to command the army. D. João was smuggled on board a British warship, the *Windsor Castle*, from which he issued decrees dismissing Miguel from the command of the army and sending him into exile.

His authority precariously restored, D. João came out from under the protection of British naval guns and retired to the solemn and antique glories of Mafra, but he remained terrified that Carlota would somehow find a way of having him declared insane and of bringing Miguel back to occupy his throne. 'Who is to defend me against my wife and son? They want to shut me up as mad. They say I must be mad, because my mother was mad,' he said to the British ambassador Sir William A'Court.[21]

D. João and his ministers now had to face the situation caused by Brazil's independence, which had been declared unilaterally by Pedro, who had been left behind as regent. The British Foreign Minister, George Canning, had written to Villa Real, the Portuguese Minister in London, that 'the King of Portugal has it yet in his hands to decide whether Brazil shall be independent by his act, or in spite of him.'[22] The negotiations, however, were largely out of D. João's control and in 1825 were entrusted to the mediation of a British envoy, Sir Charles Stuart. To gain D. João's assent to the settlement by which Portugal finally accepted Brazil's independence, it was agreed that the old king would remain as nominal sovereign of both Portugal and Brazil during his lifetime.

D. João was only 58, but in his lifetime he had witnessed a vast cultural revolution. His youth had been spent at his mother D. Maria's court, where monarchy was supported by the full panoply of processions, bullfights and antique court ceremonial, and he had witnessed the growing threat from Revolutionary France, experienced the flight to Brazil and the foundation of a tropical kingdom over which he had ruled. He had known the heady ambitions for territorial conquest and then the humiliations inflicted on him by the revolutionaries in Brazil and Portugal. Contemporaries had seen D. João as a weak, indecisive man who was blown around by events he could not understand, let alone control, but over these eventful years he had acquired not only patience but a canny ability to keep his eyes on essentials, and for him nothing was more essential than the preservation of the Braganza inheritance.

He died on 10 March 1826 during a lull in the political storm that was soon to overtake both his dominions, but with the knowledge that his dynasty was still enthroned on both sides of the Atlantic. And perhaps he also appreciated what should have been obvious to those who arranged the separation of Brazil from Portugal, that on his death Pedro, the emperor of independent Brazil, would inherit the Portuguese throne and would once again unite the two Braganza kingdoms in his person.

Queen Carlota Joaquina

No historian has a good word for Carlota Joaquina and most have seen in her rather bizarre appearance a reflection of her personality and morals. Among the crudest descriptions of her person is that of Laure Junot, Duchess d'Abrantès, who met the queen when she was in Lisbon with her husband, the French ambassador:

> Picture to yourself, reader, a woman four feet ten inches high at the very most, and crooked, or at least both her sides were not alike; her bust, arms, and legs, being in perfect union with her deformed shape. Still, all this might have passed off in a royal personage, had her face even been endurable; but, good Heavens! What a face it was! . . . She had two bloodshot eyes, which never looked one way . . . Then her skin, there was nothing human in it; it might be called a vegetable skin . . . Her nose descended upon her blue livid lips, which when open displayed the most extraordinary set of teeth that God ever created. Teeth, I suppose, they must be called, though they were in reality nothing but huge pieces of bone stuck in her large mouth, and rising and falling like reeds of a panspipe. This face was surmounted by a cranium covered with coarse, dry, frizzy hair which at first sight appeared to be of no colour.[23]

This grotesque depiction has been happily accepted by many writers. According to Sergio da Costa,

> The thick black hair that covered her arms and dried-up face bespoke her masculine, headstrong character. Her massive reddish nose, coarse pimply skin, her big sparkling eyes and narrow mouth that could not conceal her ill cared for teeth – all these traits justified the witty remark of the duchess of Abrantes who had spoken of her as 'one of nature's marvels'.[24]

These physical charms did not in any way prevent Carlota leading an active, eventful and increasingly promiscuous life, her succession of lovers giving rise to the sly comment, coming again from the incomparable pen of the duchess d'Abrantès, that 'the interesting thing about the royal family of Portugal is that one child never resembles a brother or sister.'

In her youth Carlota was, like so many royalty of the time, extremely keen on hunting. Laure Junot came across her when she was about to set off:

> She had a black horse, very small, like all the Portuguese horses, but sufficiently skittish to intimidate a good male equestrian. To my amazement, the princess mounted him *astride*, and giving him two or three smart cuts with the whip, she made him prance round the esplanade in front of the palace; and then she set off at full gallop, like a headlong youth of fifteen, just broke loose from college.[25]

In Brazil, Carlota, as the sister of Ferdinand VII of Spain, who since 1807 had been a prisoner in the hands of Napoleon, tried to establish her right to be the regent if not the sovereign of the Spanish territories, a policy that soon set her at odds once again with her husband. When Portuguese forces occupied Montevideo in pursuit of D. João's plan to annex the Banda Oriental, Carlota is said to have sold her jewels to finance the Spanish opposition in the city.

She maintained her own court separate from that of her husband and made herself notorious by insisting that everyone, including the representatives of foreign powers, should dismount and kneel when her coach passed them on the roads. Those who did not were forced by her outriders to comply, one of the victims being the British ambassador Lord Strangford. Carlota's extravagant behaviour in Brazil went beyond the humiliation of those she met on the roads. She not only took lovers, but was accused of arranging the murder of the wife of one of them.

Returning to a Lisbon in the throes of revolution, she insisted on maintaining the old traditions of the absolute monarchy. She installed herself in the palace at Queluz and Marianne Baillie recorded that ladies admitted to her presence had to remain kneeling, sometimes for hours since, according to ancient tradition, no one sat in the presence of Portuguese royalty.[26] Carlota had failed in her attempts to play a significant political role in South America but in 1822 the occasion presented itself to play a major part in Portuguese affairs. Her estranged husband, D. João VI, had taken an oath to uphold the new liberal constitution that had finally been agreed in 1822. Carlota refused to take the oath and with this public gesture rallied to herself the conservative forces of the kingdom that had been unable to act while D. João gave countenance to the activities of the Cortes. The Cortes, for its part, wanted her exiled but she refused to go and instead retired to her *quinta* at Ramalhão in Sintra, which became a centre for anti-liberal propaganda and conspiracy.

Carlota had considerable influence over her children. The infanta Teresa, who had been married to the Spanish prince Pedro Carlos, became a staunch defender of absolutist principles throughout her long life, but it was Miguel who fell most decisively under her influence. From her exile at Ramalhão, Carlota controlled the strings of conservative opposition, which ranged from some of the old nobility to units of the army and the Church. It was she who turned the supposed vision of Nossa Senhora da Barraca into a movement of political consequence that rallied swathes of the population to the conservative cause, and it was she who was behind the absolutist coups known as the Vila Francada and the Abrilada, which sought to make Miguel commander of the army (even though he was only 21 years old) and then the king. Carlota's plans were thwarted partly by D. João, who obtained the protection of the diplomatic corps in Lisbon, and then by the weakness of Miguel himself, who surrendered to his father and allowed himself to be sent into exile.

Carlota had already shown how she would use power once it fell into her hands. She was suspected of having been behind the mysterious murder of the marquês de Loulé, who was done to death in the royal palace of Salvaterra on 28 February 1824. When Miguel's forces occupied Lisbon and surrounded the king in his palace in April 1824, the queen moved from Queluz into the city, according to Marcus Cheke, 'like one of those vultures whose shadow is seen gliding over the sand where a man lies dying'.[27] During the few days when she and Miguel appeared to control events, large numbers of her personal enemies and supporters of the Constitution were seized and put in prison.

When D. João VI died early in 1826 a regency was established under his oldest daughter Isabel Maria, with Carlota excluded from having any part. But her turn soon came as Miguel was brought back from exile in the hope that three additional years of maturity would make him suitable to take over the regency and to marry his niece Maria da Gloria, who had been declared to be the legitimate heir of her grandfather (see Chapters Ten and Eleven). When Miguel arrived back in Lisbon in 1828, Carlota showed she still retained her influence over her son and it was she who persuaded him to make his bid for the Crown. Once installed as the acclaimed king of Portugal, Miguel, at Carlota's urging, proceeded to round up their opponents. The prisons were filled and estates were confiscated. The three years after 1828 have often been described as a reign of terror with Carlota undoubtedly the moving spirit.

She died on 7 January 1830, aged 54, without having lived long enough to witness the collapse of her ambitions with D. Miguel's defeat in the civil war that broke out in 1832. In 1833 José Barreto Feio anonymously published his *Dom Miguel, ses aventures scandaleuses, ses crimes et son usurpation*, which was soon widely circulated.[28] The black legend of Carlota and Miguel was born.

The Children of D. João VI and Carlota Joaquina

Most of the children of D. João and Carlota Joaquina were important in the history of their time.

Maria Teresa

The eldest daughter, Maria Teresa, was born in 1793.[29] In May 1810 she was married to her first cousin, Pedro Carlos, with whom she had been brought up at court. The couple conceived a son, Sebastião, before Pedro Carlos became ill with tuberculosis. He died on 26 May 1812, according to court gossip because of 'excessive conjugal activity'.[30] Left a widow at the age of nineteen, Maria Teresa remained with her son at court and acted as private secretary to her father, attending the Council of State, and returning with him to Portugal in 1821. Uncomfortable in the Portugal dominated by the revolutionary Cortes, Maria Teresa took her son to Madrid and settled at the Spanish court. There too a liberal revolution was underway and she found herself a hostage of the liberal forces when the French invaded in 1823. In Spain she formed a close alliance with her sister Maria Francisca, who had married Carlos, the brother of the Spanish king Ferdinand VII.

When Ferdinand died in 1833 she, her sister and Carlos were expelled by the Spanish Regent and retreated back to Portugal, where they sought the support of D. Miguel and launched the Carlist challenge for the Spanish Crown. With the defeat of D. Miguel in the Portuguese civil war, the two sisters and Carlos went into exile in Britain, where Maria Francisca died. Maria Teresa then travelled to Austria. In 1838 she married Carlos and joined him in northern Spain after heroic adventures avoiding capture by French and Spanish police.

The defeat of the Carlists forced Maria Teresa and Carlos to take refuge in France, where they lived for six years under police supervision. In 1845 Carlos passed his claim to be legitimate king of Spain to his son and lived the rest of his life in retirement in Trieste. After his death in 1855 Maria Teresa took over the leadership of the Carlist exiles. She was instrumental in the revival of Carlism in the 1870s when Carlos's great-grandson assumed the mantle of legitimacy. Maria Teresa died in 1874 at the age of 81, a great age for a member of a family that had never been known for its longevity.

António

Born March 1795. Died June 1801.

Maria Isabel

She was the third child and was born in May 1797. She married Ferdinand VII of Spain in 1816. Maria Isabel died at the end of 1818 after a caesarean section was performed to remove her dead unborn child.

Pedro

Became king in 1826 as Pedro IV of Portugal. He was also Pedro I, Emperor of Brazil.

Maria Francisca

Maria Francisca, born April 1800, was the fifth child. She was sent to Madrid in 1815 to marry Don Carlos, the brother of Ferdinand VII of Spain, who was newly restored to his throne. She had three sons, from whom are descended the Carlist pretenders to the throne of Spain. She died in 1834, after which Don Carlos married her sister Maria Teresa.

All three of these princesses married their Spanish uncles, carrying into the next generation the practice of royal incest that had begun when their grandmother D. Maria had married her uncle D. Pedro III.

Isabel Maria

She was born in 1801 and was the sixth child. She was the daughter closest to her father who, before his death, nominated her to be regent in Portugal on behalf of his heir D. Pedro. When she became regent she was 25 years old. She was epileptic and suffered from nervous complaints that sometimes threatened to follow the course of madness that overtook her grandmother. She remained regent for two years, eventually handing over the government to D. Miguel. During this time she is supposed to have given birth to an illegitimate child fathered by the son of her principal adviser.[31] Another rumour circulated that she had had a child by a British naval officer and for that reason a proposed marriage to the French prince of Condé had fallen through.[32] She remained unmarried and lived until 1876.

Miguel

Miguel was declared king of Portugal in 1828 and reigned until 1834. He died in 1866. Twenty-first century claimants to the Portuguese throne are descended from him.

Maria de Assunção

Born in 1805, she died unmarried in 1834.

Ana de Jesus Maria

The last child of Carlota Joaquina was born in October 1806. In 1827 she became pregnant by the marquês de Loulé and married him shortly before the birth of the child. The couple went into exile during the reign of D. Miguel, returning in 1834. Loulé subsequently served as prime minister and was raised to a dukedom. In all the couple had five children and the current duke de Loulé is considered by some royalists to be the legitimate heir to the throne.

With the exception of Isabel Maria, who as regent published the new constitution, the so-called Charter, in 1826 and remained committed to implementing it, the other sisters were all more or less aligned with the absolutist cause. When they returned with the king from Vila Franca after the coup that overthrew the constitutional government in 1823, they are described by Marianne Baillie as wearing the uniforms of colonels of their regiments with golden epaulettes, cocked hats and plumes of white feathers: 'It is astonishing how well the dress became these lovely creatures, who were perfectly wild with spirits, smiling and receiving the homage of a thousand flatterers with an air of proud delight, and nearly deafened by the noisier admiration of their humbler subjects.'[33]

D. Pedro IV, *c.* 1835, oil on canvas.

10

D. Pedro and D. Miguel

For better or for worse the Braganza rulers from the days of D. João IV had been dull and uninspiring individuals whose rather pedestrian talents had been compensated only by the pomp and ceremony with which they surrounded themselves. However, the two sons of D. João VI and Carlota Joaquina were strikingly different and, for a brief period of thirteen years, not only dominated the political scene but created the political waves that they rode with passion and bravado. D. Pedro was to 'flash across the sky of history like a turbulent meteor', as one biographer put it, and D. Miguel was not far behind him.[1]

Behind the story of the two brothers lies the conflict between post-revolutionary liberals and unrepentant and unreformed absolutists, with traditional religion attacked and resolutely defended, deep splits within the military, political and social elites, and a Portugal suffering the traumas of decolonization and constant interference and threats of interference by the European powers. It was a drama played out by a family whose members were divided by bitter hatreds and personal rivalries. As the events unfolded, the two princes, Pedro and Miguel, emerged as the symbolic representatives of rival ideologies, leaders of factions with conflicting visions of the nation's future in a changing international order.

D. Pedro

D. Pedro 'sat not on a throne, but on a rocking chair'[2]
– Harold Temperley

In April 1821 D. João VI returned to Portugal, leaving the 23-year-old infante Pedro in Rio as his regent. Any attempt to describe the role that the young prince was to play in Brazil or to understand the personality behind the public figure needs to be supported by an account of the main developments that marked the ten years he held power. After his father's departure D. Pedro found himself under pressure from the Portuguese Cortes to return, but in January 1822 he staged his first act of defiance by declaring that he would stay in Brazil (*fico*, 'I remain'). As the Portuguese liberal Cortes proceeded to try to return Brazil to full colonial status, D. Pedro threw in his lot with the Brazilian radicals and on 7 September 1822 declared Brazil's independence. On 12 October he was proclaimed emperor and on 1 December he was crowned.

During 1823 he was preoccupied with removing Portuguese military garrisons and with bringing all parts of the country under his control. In this he was assisted by the British adventurer Lord Cochrane, who was appointed to command the Brazilian navy. In 1824 D. Pedro became involved in debates over a new constitution for Brazil and, in the end, himself appointed a Council to devise a constitution according to his ideas. This centralized vision of the new Brazil caused rebellion in the north, which was suppressed. In 1825 negotiations with Portugal, carried out through the mediation of Sir Charles Stuart, led to Portugal finally recognizing Brazil's independence. A parallel treaty with Britain made provision for the end of the slave trade by 1830. In 1826 D. João VI died and D. Pedro succeeded as king of Portugal, briefly reuniting Portugal and Brazil under a single sovereign. Two months later he abdicated his Portuguese throne in favour of his daughter, Maria da Gloria. The same year his first wife, Leopoldina, died. Between 1825 and 1828 D. Pedro involved Brazil in a war to try to secure the Banda Oriental, the left bank of the Rio de la Plata. The war ended with the recognition of the independence of the region, which became Uruguay. In 1829 D. Pedro married for a second time and in 7 April 1831, after prolonged conflict with the Assembly, he decided to abdicate his Brazilian throne in favour of his son Pedro.

It is no exaggeration to say that during these ten years D. Pedro was responsible for most of the decisions that led to the creation of the modern state of Brazil. His was an extraordinary and decisive influence during a revolutionary period when the future shape and direction of the country was still to be determined. How had a young man still in his twenties been able to exert such influence?

D. Pedro grows up

D. Pedro was born on 12 October 1798 and was nine years old when he accompanied his father and the royal family to Brazil. He grew up in Rio and was profoundly influenced by the life he lived there. Unlike many of the Braganzas, he was strong, handsome and energetic, but was epileptic and suffered a number of grand mal seizures. It also seems probable that, as a boy, he suffered from what the twenty-first century would call ADHD.[3] Like earlier members of his family, he was passionately fond of riding and horsemanship and as a teenager spent much time with his brother Miguel at the royal ranch at Santa Cruz, where they broke in wild horses and where D. Pedro learned to be an expert farrier. Throughout his time in Brazil there were numerous occasions when he performed extraordinary feats of horsemanship, covering remarkable distances in short periods of time, leaving his retinue far behind.

Jean-Baptiste Debret, *Coronation of D. Pedro I in Rio de Janeiro*, 1822.

Like so many of the Braganza family, D. Pedro took instinctively to music, becoming an accomplished performer on a number of instruments. He composed pieces for public occasions and for the royal chapel and, according to one story, he composed the tune and the words for the national anthem of Brazil while riding from Ipiranga, where he had declared Brazil's independence, to São Paulo, where the anthem was performed in the theatre the same evening.[4] It is now known that this was not true, but it is significant that for so long it was believed that it was. Later an overture he had composed was included in a concert organized by Rossini in Paris. Unlike many of his ancestors, who had not been known for their literary tastes or skills, D. Pedro often turned his hand to poetry, composing lyrics that he set to music, and even to journalism, writing newspaper articles and pamphlets when he felt the occasion demanded it. He also became skilled in woodwork and carved a figurehead of himself for one of the new Brazilian warships.

D. Pedro's marriage and sexual liaisons

Like his ancestors D. Pedro II and D. Afonso VI, D. Pedro delighted in rowdy behaviour and made companions far below him in social status. He indulged recklessly in sexual adventures and, in the process, fathered a number of children. However, as heir to the throne it was essential he should marry and, after prolonged negotiations, a bride was found for him from the Austrian Habsburg family. On 13 May 1817 he was married by proxy to Archduchess Leopoldina, sister of Napoleon's wife Marie Louise. The marriage was successful and Leopoldina gave birth to seven children in all. However, marriage did not interfere for long with D. Pedro's sexual adventures and in 1822 he began the most notorious of his liaisons with Domitila de Castro. Without much concern to hide his infidelity from his wife or the public, he had Domitila housed in Rio where she bore him a number of children – a situation that, not surprisingly, caused acute distress to Leopoldina, especially when Domitila was introduced to the court as a lady-in-waiting. (Inevitably one recalls Queen Catarina's distress in similar circumstances at the court of Charles II.) D. Pedro's insensitive behaviour became extreme when, in 1825, he went north on board his flagship, taking with him both his wife and his mistress. In 1826 D. Pedro formally recognized his illegitimate children by Domitila and conferred titles on them and on their mother and her family. While seeing Domitila on

*Archduchess Maria
Leopoldina* by
Domenico Failutti,
1921, oil on canvas.

a regular basis, D. Pedro also had sexual relations with her sister, whom he made pregnant.[5]

The archduchess Leopoldina brought to the Braganza family not only teutonic genes, but an intellectual culture that had previously between lacking. She was well educated and had a genuine interest in natural science, pursuing her own studies in the intervals between bearing children. She was devoted to her husband and for some time was ignorant of the affairs he was conducting with other women. When she found out the real state of affairs there was little she could do; it was widely believed at the time that her distress at this situation contributed to her rapid decline in health and to her death in 1826 at the early age of 29.

D. Pedro was said to have been overcome with remorse at her death but by 1829 he was looking to marry again and eventually found a bride in the person of the seventeen-year-old Amélia of Leuchtenberg, granddaughter of Napoleon's first empress, Josephine. The connection with the Bonaparte family, as might be expected, appealed greatly to D. Pedro's vision of himself as an emperor. The couple were married by proxy in August 1829, Amélia having decided to give the large sum of money sent for the ceremony to an orphanage in Munich. D. Pedro's new wife became a mother to his orphaned children, but when her husband decided impulsively to abdicate and leave for Portugal she had little choice but to accompany him. The couple had one daughter, Princess Maria Amélia of Brazil.

The public face of D. Pedro

Although his sexual activity caused scandal in what was a conservative and religious society, D. Pedro showed that he was otherwise in tune with the intellectual and romantic culture of the age. He accepted many of the ideals of the liberals who were pressing for change not only in Portugal but also in Brazil and, as regent for his father in 1821, he abolished censorship and secret trials and set about a reform of education. He also embarked on a series of journeys to different parts of Brazil, dealing with regional discontent and rebellions, often by simply appearing and riding through the streets of interior towns. D. Pedro adopted aspects of the Brazilian way of life that helped to make him popular. He often dressed in the informal style common in Brazil. According to his biographer Neill Macaulay, 'except on official occasions, he dressed simply, often in white cotton trousers and a striped cotton jacket, with a bandana looped casually around his neck and a broad-brimmed straw hat on his head. Silver spurs would be attached to his boots.'[6] These qualities enabled him to provide effective leadership when the Braganza inheritance on both sides of the Atlantic was threatened by a wave of revolutionary activity in the early 1820s.

Unlike most of his forebears, D. Pedro took an active interest in military affairs and maintained the closest possible links with the armed forces. As a result, in the difficult years that followed the departure of his father, he was usually able to call on the support of the local militias and the regiments garrisoning Rio. This was seen to great effect when in April 1821 he was able to rally the military in Rio to suppress the radical assembly and allow his father and family a safe passage to Europe. D. Pedro took an active part in training the Brazilian army and in 1826, when the war in the Banda Oriental was going badly, he actually went south to take command himself and to reorganize the Brazilian forces. Later, during the civil war in Portugal, he not only fought alongside his troops in the most hotly contested engagements but took command of the army himself on at least two occasions. It was his loss of the support of the army in Brazil that was decisive in bringing him to the point of abdication in 1831.

In spite of the radical image that D. Pedro wanted to give to the newly declared empire, he adopted many of the trappings and practices of the traditional Braganza monarchy: the *beija mão*, the weekly public audiences, the celebration of royal birthdays with full court galas, and the religious observance. He not only continued the historic orders of chivalry but added three more – the Orders of Cruzeiro, Pedro 1 and Rosa – the last to honour his new bride Amélia. D. Pedro also continued to award titles of count and marquis, although these were not hereditary. He maintained two royal palaces, São Cristovão and the Paço da Cidade (City Palace), and had a rural retreat at Santa Cruz 50 miles from Rio. The palaces had a full complement of ceremonial court appointments.

The liberal emperor

D. Pedro shared with his father a strong desire to maintain the Braganza inheritance, but instead of defying the liberal trends of the time he placed himself at their head. He realized that at the root of the revolutionary nationalism that was breaking out in Brazil were growing tensions between Brazilians and Portuguese. When the newly summoned Cortes in Portugal tried to restore Brazil to its former colonial status and ordered D. Pedro himself to return to Portugal, he took the lead in defending Brazil's interests and refused to obey the summons. As Brazil moved inexorably towards independence, he was determined that this would not be a republican independence of the kind that was dividing Spain's former colonies in South America. History, however, is never quite as heroic as official narratives would have it. When, on 7 September 1822 on the banks of the river Ipiranga, D. Pedro received the dispatches from Lisbon summoning him to return, the occasion on which he made his dramatic decision to declare Brazil's independence, with himself as its emperor, he was squatting by the roadside with a severe attack of dysentery.[7]

D. Pedro had always been an admirer of his brother-in-law Napoleon. He saw himself in many ways as the Napoleon of the New World and adopted the title of emperor, which made a break with the old ideas of Portuguese kingship and emphasized the unity of the vast territory that stretched from the Amazon to the Rio de la Plata. As Sergio Correa da Costa put it, 'if the kingdom stood for heredity, tradition and divine right, the empire signified revolutionary conquest and popular acclamation. A paradoxical revolution from above.'[8] D. Pedro's idea was that an emperor should be the leading liberal revolutionary, bringing enlightened change to his country, rather than the upholder of ancient tradition. Although he did follow the ancient tradition of the Braganzas and was 'acclaimed' by the people, like Napoleon he also had himself crowned, with a crown made of six pounds of solid gold and diamonds.[9]

D. Pedro's liberalism has often been called into question as there were many occasions when he acted in an authoritarian and even violent manner in order to suppress dissent. However, his desire to separate himself from the old values of the aristocratic monarchy was clear throughout his short life. When, in the summer of 1823, he fell out with José Bonifácio and his brother, who had been among his principal supporters, the reason was his determination to end the repression of alleged dissidents that José Bonifácio had initiated.[10] D. Pedro's attitude towards slavery and the slave trade is critical in this respect. Although he was not in a position to take any unilateral steps towards the abolition of slavery, he is on record as saying, 'I know that my blood is the same colour as the negroes,' and in May 1823 he published, under a thinly disguised pseudonym, a long article in a Rio newspaper on slavery, in which he stated that 'slavery is the cancer gnawing away at Brazil.'[11] It was his treaty with Britain in 1825 that ostensibly made provision for the ending of the slave trade in 1830. This became one of the principal reasons why D. Pedro and the Assembly, which had been elected under the Constitution that he himself had drawn up, parted company. If many of his actions with regard to human rights and the economy would have pleased even the most radical of liberals, he was also prone to making rapid decisions and sweeping changes in the most authoritarian manner. When in 1821 there were rumours of dissent in Minas Gerais, D. Pedro set off with only a few companions and by his dramatic arrival on the scene not only overcame local dissent but made appointments and carried out sweeping changes in the province, in every way resembling Napoleon in the rapidity of his actions and radical nature of his reforms. However, again like Napoleon, these were carried out with little consultation and no compromise.[12]

D. Pedro's flirtations with liberalism came near to landing him in deep trouble when he allowed himself to be initiated into the Masonic Lodge of the Grand Orient. There he took an oath to accept the constitution that was being developed in the Constituent Assembly before its terms had been decided. When he became aware that he was being manipulated by this secret society, he quickly changed his attitude, deported some its leaders and threatened others with arrest.[13] This episode was in many ways typical of D. Pedro's approach to the politics of the day. Aware that the Masons were influential in the revolutionary manoeuvres of the time, he decided initially to join them rather than oppose them. As always, controlling the revolution meant placing himself at its head.

The events of January and February 1822, days when there was a tense stand-off between the Portuguese soldiers in Rio and the local inhabitants, again showed D. Pedro at his most decisive, organizing a Brazilian military force to isolate the Portuguese and eventually achieving their departure for Portugal. All through this crisis, which ended without a single casualty, D. Pedro was in charge of events, making sure of the support of the population with his famous statement that he would remain (*fico*) in Brazil in opposition to the demands of the Lisbon Cortes that he should return. Maria Graham, who witnessed the events in the capital, concluded that 'The coolness and presence of mind of the prince, no doubt preserved the city from much confusion and misery.'[14]

Although D. Pedro drew up constitutions for both Brazil and Portugal, he was, like Napoleon, very authoritarian and never hesitated to overrule elected assemblies or to use the military to overawe his opponents. In Portugal D. João VI had accepted, apparently without demur, the radical reduction of his powers contained in the 1822 constitution. In Brazil D. Pedro reacted to a similar proposal by the Constituent Assembly by assembling a military and naval force, dismissing the Assembly and himself constituting a council to produce a constitution that left considerable executive powers in the hands of the emperor. In the constitution that he finally promulgated for Brazil in 1824, there was incorporated, alongside the three-pronged division of powers dear to the hearts of liberal reformers, a moderating power (*poder moderador*) that the emperor could use to ensure the functioning of the government in case there was political deadlock. This power was used often and with effect both by D. Pedro himself and his successor D. Pedro II, but it was undeniably a further 'Napoleonic' element in Brazil's democracy.

D. Pedro's actions both in Brazil, when he declared the empire, and later in Portugal, when he introduced the Charter, continually wrong-footed the leading powers of Europe, which were intent on preserving the idea of the legitimacy of hereditary monarchy against the demands of revolutionary nationalists and liberals for constitutional government. D. Pedro's authority was undeniably that of a legitimate sovereign but, equally undeniably, it was he who declared the national independence of Brazil and introduced constitutional government in the countries where he reigned.

Why the Brazilian revolution did not replace Portuguese rule with a republic, like the thirteen colonies that made the U.S. and like the former Spanish colonies when they broke with Spain, is an interesting question. Two factors, apart from D. Pedro's active and largely successful manoeuvres to control the revolutionary situation, need to be considered. One was the consciousness among the conservative elite that republics, controlled by revolutionary assemblies, could adopt extreme measures and be infused with an unpredictable populist radicalism, as had happened in France. Moreover, there was at the back of everyone's minds the fear of a Haitian-style revolution involving the slave and free black population. Fearful of these outcomes, the land-owning elite of Brazil were prepared to establish a strong executive authority to counter the influence of an elected assembly. In this D. Pedro and José Bonifácio, his principal adviser, were agreed and this consideration formed the substance of D. Pedro's speech to the Constituent Assembly on 3 May 1823.[15] The other factor that worked against republicanism was the threat that Brazil would fragment as the Spanish empire had done. In the event, there was a succession of provincial secessionist movements that all tended to be republican in character. The constitution that was adopted was, therefore, a deliberate attempt to make the monarchy the focus for a national sentiment that would hold the country together, though in the short term what held the country together was less monarchical sentiment than the appointment in March 1823 of the brilliant, but rather sinister, Lord Cochrane to command the Brazilian navy and assert the control of D. Pedro's government over coastal Brazil.

Brazilian independence

D. Pedro had been extremely proactive in declaring Brazil's independence in 1822 and establishing a Brazilian constitution in 1824. His next objective was to achieve international recognition for the new state. Negotiations with Portugal were begun in 1824 but made no progress. The following year D. Pedro was helped by Britain, who wanted to negotiate a new commercial treaty with an independent Brazil. A British diplomat, Sir Charles Stuart, who had been a member of the Council of Regency in Lisbon during the Peninsular War, was appointed as Portugal's negotiator and went to Rio. The treaty recognizing Brazilian independence was eventually signed in August 1825 and was ratified by D. João in Lisbon in November. It was a remarkable document achieving an amicable separation of Portugal and Brazil by what can almost be called a sleight of hand. D. João was to be recognized as emperor of Brazil and king of Portugal; he was to retain the imperial title but was to grant his son the right to rule the independent Brazilian empire. This meant, in effect, that Brazil, nominally, had two emperors. Brazil was also to pay Portugal a 'divorce settlement' of two million pounds, while a commercial treaty provided for Portugal and Brazil to grant each other most favoured nation status. The treaty was couched in such a way that the Braganza king was seen to be granting his Brazilian kingdom independence under a Braganza monarch. The unspoken issue that the treaty did not cover was the status of D. Pedro as legitimate heir to his father's throne in Portugal. This subject had been too sensitive to resolve and it seems that D. João had deliberately left open the possibility of the two Braganza kingdoms once again being united under a single monarch.

Brazil's independence from Portugal was a largely peaceful decoupling, a decolonization without significant conflict, an experience that was to be unique in the history of European empires.

The affairs of Portugal

D. Pedro, unlike his father who was notoriously indecisive, made rapid and often impetuous decisions. His life was punctuated with emotional outbursts and decisive actions, often preceded by little thought as to consequences. He was determined to control events rather than be controlled by them, and again and again he rode his luck in situations where his opponents were disorganized and divided. When he heard of his father's death in March 1826, D. Pedro immediately had himself declared king of Portugal, in spite of the fact that the treaty separating Brazil from Portugal was only a few months old. As his father's eldest son his claim to the throne appeared to follow the canons of legitimacy and prevented the European powers from rejecting him or recognizing his brother as king. From his position in Brazil, a two-month voyage away, D. Pedro then began to plot the future for Portugal in a way that was to lead to confusion and ultimately civil war.

At first there was no challenge to his right to succeed to the throne of his father, as he was the eldest son. His accession was declared in Portugal and recognized throughout Europe. Later doubts were to be thrown on his legitimacy on the grounds that he had assumed Brazilian citizenship and therefore could not inherit the Portuguese throne. However, these arguments were advanced at a later date, not at the moment of his accession.[16] Miguel himself, living in exile in Vienna, also accepted his brother's legitimacy.

On D. João's death the infanta Isabel Maria had been declared regent for her absent brother, significantly excluding Queen Carlota Joaquina. The somewhat high-handed actions that D. Pedro now took once again wrong-footed not only the European powers but the leading figures in Portugal as well. He announced that he would bestow a Constitutional Charter on his country, a constitution which he apparently drew up himself on the model of the Brazilian constitution, and declared that he would abdicate his throne in favour of his daughter, Maria da Gloria, once the Charter had been accepted. He also made it a condition that his exiled brother, Miguel, should accept the Charter and be betrothed to Maria. D. Pedro entrusted to Sir Charles Stuart the task of carrying the Charter to Lisbon, giving the impression that this move was fully supported by Great Britain.[17] In this way D. Pedro hoped to heal the deep divisions in Portuguese society, reconciling legitimists and conservatives with the liberals. On paper his ideas made sense but he was too remote from events in Portugal to control them as he had controlled events in Brazil.

Abdication and the final struggle

D. Pedro's involvement in the affairs of Portugal severely damaged his standing in Brazil, where he was suspected of wanting to undermine Brazil's independence by linking it once again to Portugal. Although these suspicions were unfounded, they gradually grew into a populist movement that led inexorably to the emperor's abdication in 1831. His decision to abdicate was another of the impulsive moves that had punctuated his life. The decision was suddenly announced on 7 April 1831 and six days later he, his wife and Maria da Gloria sailed away on board an English warship, which had first been loaded with much of the furniture and silver from the royal palace. Apparently his infant son and his two daughters, Januária and Francisca, awoke on 14 April to find their father gone. His abdication of the Portuguese Crown and the grant of the Charter in 1826 had been a well-intentioned attempt to direct the future of the country but had resulted in civil war, usurpation and chaos. His abdication of his Brazilian crown had been a similar attempt to dispose of the future. He had appointed a guardian for his heir and had left the country in charge of a regency made up of three persons. The result fell short of civil war but led to a decade of power struggles and faction fighting that paralysed the life of the country. There was even a movement to call D. Pedro back to act as regent for his son, but this he wisely refused to consider.

After his abdication and the recognition of Maria da Gloria as Queen Maria II of Portugal, D. Pedro found he had to lead a military campaign to secure the throne for his daughter. In 1831, having abdicated two thrones, he was reduced to the status of duke of Braganza and came to Europe to conduct a diplomatic campaign in France and Britain to gain support for a reconquest of Portugal to wrest it from the control of his brother. During the next three years D. Pedro exerted himself to raise the money and men for an invasion. In 1832, from a base in the Azores, Porto was seized, but D. Pedro's forces then endured a prolonged six-month siege by the Miguelist army. Although he found fortune turn in his favour when the July Revolution of 1830 brought the liberal Louis-Philippe to the throne of France, and although he had the support of the key military figures who later became the dukes of Terceira and Saldanha, it was D. Pedro's own tireless leadership that turned a forlorn hope into a triumph. Lisbon was captured in 1833 and D. Maria II was acclaimed. In 1834 Portugal joined the newly negotiated

Quadruple Alliance of liberal regimes. Having triumphed in the civil war and placed his daughter on her throne, D. Pedro died in the room in the Queluz palace where he had been born. He was only 36. It is difficult to think of any European monarch, let alone any Braganza, who so emphatically imposed himself on the events of his age.

Dom Miguel: The Absolute King

D. Miguel is the arch-villain of Portuguese history. His story is perhaps the clearest example of the adage that history is almost always written by the victors. Having finally lost his struggle for the throne in 1834, he was forced into exile while history was written by the victorious liberals. There is a rival narrative maintained by some royalists who continue to recognize D. Miguel and his descendants as the legitimate sovereigns of Portugal, even bestowing on him some of the aura of Sebastianism. However, by the time D. Miguel was forced to accept defeat, the black legend had already been born. An anonymous memoir, *Dom Miguel, ses aventures scandaleuses, ses crimes et son usurpation par un Portugais* (Dom Miguel, his Scandalous Adventures, his Crimes and his Usurpation, by a Portuguese), appeared in 1833 and it soon became apparent that this was written by José Barreto Feio, who had known D. Miguel in Brazil, and incorporated material already published by Wilhelm Ludwig Eschwege, who was to become famous as the architect of the Pena palace in Sintra.[18] The same year appeared the first two volumes of *História do cativeiro dos presos de Estado na Torre de S. Julião da Barra* (The History of the Captivity of the State Prisoners in the Tower of St Julião da Barra), which recorded in great detail the experiences of the 618 prisoners who had suffered arbitrary imprisonment in the São Julião fortress during D. Miguel's regime. This book (volumes three and four appeared the following year) had been compiled by João Batista da Silva Lopes, who had been imprisoned there for three years. D. Miguel had other enemies as well and the reports of R. B. Hoppner, the British Consul General in Portugal, were particularly influential in cultivating the black legend.[19]

D. Miguel, born on 26 October 1802, was only five years old when the royal family escaped to Rio. He was named Miguel, after the Archangel who had expelled the rebel angels from Paradise, and the name later came to be considered highly symbolic.[20] In Rio he lived with his mother and was brought up in her court. As a young man his boisterous activities, often in the company of his elder brother, his violent behaviour and his consorting with bullfighters and cowboys remind one irresistibly of the seventeenth-century princes D. Afonso VI and D. Pedro II. Here was a prince free of the social constraints that govern the behaviour of ordinary citizens and able to indulge in riotous, testosterone-fuelled, masculine irresponsibility. Such behaviour made him hugely popular among the common people, who saw a prince who seemed to be one of themselves. But D. Miguel's riotous behaviour soon earned him a reputation for violence and cruelty. Even if one discounts the list of juvenile atrocities listed by Barreto Feio and allegations that, already at the age of seven, he used to fire his miniature cannon at the legs of courtiers, there are more sinister stories. For instance it was alleged that he had used hounds to hunt down and kill Chinese labourers employed in a tea plantation that D. João had tried to establish.[21] Barreto Feio records some incidents of which he appears to have been an eyewitness:

> I have myself often seen him, at the age of ten or twelve, wearing the uniform of a general decorated with a star and other decorations, running with other rascals from the neighbourhood, entering unexpectedly now into one house, now into another, sometimes also into mine, breaking the plates and glasses, smashing the furniture and tearing the upholstery. Then he would smear luxury objects and precious vases with excrement and meeting people he would give them blows or else present his hand to be kissed, according to how his humour and fancy struck him.[22]

Other stories were told in private letters from 'a lady of the court', including one occasion when one of the infantas was playing with a pretty little dog:

> The Infante [Miguel] said that he also had a pretty dog and went to get the biggest dog you ever saw. You then saw all the ladies trembling with fear and fleeing. He then offered the dog to the Viscondessa de Lourinhã and she, with reason, more dead than alive, pleaded for mercy.[23]

It is not clear that these stories tell anything except that D. Miguel was a young man who loved to behave in an outrageous manner, to frighten his sisters and conduct himself as badly as he dared. D. Pedro grew out of such behaviour and acquired more civilized qualities, playing and composing music, writing poetry and acquiring skills as a sculptor and farrier. There is no indication that D. Miguel followed him in this respect or that he ever demonstrated any degree of education. Although he acquired the good manners acceptable in the royal courts of Europe, he remained subject to violent emotional outbursts that he was not always able to control.

As young men D. Pedro and D. Miguel spent much time in each other's company and, certainly on D. Pedro's side, there was much affection. When D. João VI and his family returned to Lisbon in 1821, leaving D. Pedro behind as regent in Brazil, he tried to persuade his brother to join him in Rio and for the first time mentioned the idea of a marriage between his daughter Maria da Gloria and his brother.

D. Miguel's initiation into politics

D. Miguel did not return to Brazil but remained in Lisbon very much under the influence of his mother, who maintained a sort of self-imposed exile at Ramalhão where she gathered around her those who refused recognition to the new constitutional order brought about by the revolution of 1820. Marianne Baillie, who saw D. Miguel when he attended a ball with his family in January 1822, described him as 'a thin slight youth, with pale and rather elegant features, from which, however, every ray of intelligence seemed banished; solemn, upright, and immovable; when once seated, he had the air of a statue or an automaton.'[24]

D. Miguel first occupied the political stage as a major player in 1823 when he appeared as the leader of the Vila Francada, a counter-revolutionary movement organized by Carlota Joaquina and her associates. D. Miguel made a fine figure on horseback surrounded by a gang of like-minded bravos. It is probable that Carlota hoped to force her husband to abdicate and to install D. Miguel on the throne. D. João did not abdicate but he did agree to make D. Miguel, aged only 21, commander of the army. D. Miguel appears at this time as rather weak minded and was described by the duke of Palmela as 'a good man when among good men, and when among the bad worse than they'.[25] A second counter-revolutionary movement was organized by Carlota in April 1824 with D. Miguel once more playing a key role, leading troops loyal to him to occupy the streets and placing his father under what amounted to house arrest in his palace. Once again, his nerve failed him. When his father, who had taken refuge on board a British warship, summoned him to attend, D. Miguel obeyed and, on his knees, begged his father's forgiveness. Detained on board ship, D. Miguel was then sent abroad into exile at the Austrian court. This attempted coup, the so-called Abrilada, had failed but for nine heady days D. Miguel had in effect been king in Lisbon. On his orders numerous liberals and supporters of D. João were arrested and it was rumoured that D. Miguel had even ordered wholesale executions. However, these were never carried out after he had surrendered to his father.

D. Miguel in Vienna

D. Miguel stayed at the Austrian court for the best part of three years. His time in Vienna is memorable, first for the painting of the portrait that now hangs in the ducal palace of Vila Viçosa and which has become a kind of icon for those who cling to the memory of D. Miguel as the

D. Miguel by Johann Ender, 1827, oil.

legitimate sovereign. The portrait shows him in uniform, tall, slim and elegant with a handsome youthful face, apparently every inch the king in waiting – but look more closely and the image is cold, aloof and unbending, with little sign of human feeling.

D. Miguel's time in Vienna is also remembered for the party he gave to some young Austrian officers shortly before he left to return to Portugal in 1827. The story appeared in Barreto Feio's book and for that reason may be suspect, but it was repeated by Virgílio Arruda in his book *Dom Pedro e Dom Miguel do Brasil ao Ribatejo.* The party was held at the lodgings of one of the officers. The prince arrived at midnight and took his place at the table between two prostitutes who had been taken up from the street. Wine flowed and drunken debauches followed. However, as dawn approached they had to leave:

> The Infante proposed to make a French punch. A bowl was filled with eau de vie and sugar and was set alight. After having extinguished the lights, all those present, in a state of nature, formed a chain and danced around the bluish flame . . . a scene from the dance of demons, one of those dances that would have pleased Nero or Tiberius and which also imitated the debauches of Louis xv. In the middle of all the leaping and dancing the table was upset. The burning punch flowed through cracks in the floor onto some hay in the room below and in an instant the whole house was in flames. Two of the wretched girls and one of the officers, who was too drunk to save himself, perished. D. Miguel himself escaped being a victim but his clothing was seriously damaged by the flames.[26]

This story is significant because, if true, it shows that D. Miguel was not exactly the reformed character that D. João and D. Pedro, and even the wily Austrian chancellor Metternich, appeared to believe.

D. Miguel had a number of affairs, always with low-class women (again reminding one of D. Pedro ii and his amours) and he was alleged to have had two daughters with a certain Maria Evarista, but his affairs were never as public or as scandalous as those of his brother.[27]

D. Miguel is restored to favour

When D. João vi died, the emperor Pedro in Brazil was declared to be his heir and this was accepted by Miguel who, in a letter to his brother, recognized him as 'my legitimate sovereign' and 'the heir and successor to the crown of our glorious ancestors'. He also signed a letter to his sister accepting her regency until 'the intentions of the legitimate heir, who is our much loved brother and Lord the Emperor of Brazil, should be made known'.[28] D. Pedro's plan was to bring together absolutists and constitutional liberals by arranging a marriage between D. Miguel and D. Maria da Gloria, his daughter, another incestuous uncle/niece marriage of the kind that had resolved problems within the Braganza family before. If this marriage was agreed, and if Miguel would accept the constitution that D. Pedro had bestowed on Portugal, then the emperor stated he would abdicate in favour of his daughter.

D. Pedro's solution to the growing instability in Portugal that had followed the death of his father was, on paper, very ingenious and was widely accepted by all the countries of Europe with the exception of Portugal's nearest neighbour Spain, which declared that D. Miguel should be recognized as the absolute king. This encouraged Carlota Joaquina and her associates to reject the arrangement and to rally the conservative forces inside Portugal to armed opposition. Although the British Foreign Secretary, George Canning, had preached the doctrine of non-interference, it was widely assumed at the time that Britain favoured D. Pedro's constitutional settlement. The Spanish intervention in the small-scale civil conflict that broke out in 1826 persuaded Britain to send a small force of 5,000 men under Sir William Clinton to protect the integrity of the country and the person of the regent. Joan, 1st Viscountess Canning, who wrote a spirited defence of her late husband, George Canning, commented,

> when, therefore he [George Canning] encouraged the establishment of the constitution, he did so as well because he felt convinced that its rejection would entail the greatest evil upon Portugal, as because he knew that the party which was friendly to free institutions were, for the most part, likewise friendly to connection with England; while the party which was attached to absolute monarchy were hostile to that connection. The treaties which bind us to Portugal are of so onerous a nature, that it is of the utmost consequence to this country that we should have established there an amicable Government.[29]

However, there was a major flaw in D. Pedro's plan. It was entirely based on the assumption that D. Miguel had changed from the young hothead who had led the counter-revolution of the Abrilada and that he was now prepared not only to accept the constitutional Charter but the role allotted to him as a consort to the queen who would unite the nation.

D. Miguel took the oath to uphold the constitution on 4 October 1826 while still in Vienna, but a whole year passed while the first civil war was fought and while Britain and Austria worked out an agreement with D. Pedro that D. Miguel would take over the regency from Isabel Maria on the terms specified in the Charter and would rule as regent until D. Maria was old enough to marry. D. Miguel's return to Portugal was punctuated by a stay in London, which he reached on 30 December 1827. There he was feted by high society and by the Portuguese residents in Britain, but a significant incident took place when D. Miguel went to stay at Stratfield Saye, the country residence of the duke of Wellington, on 22 January 1828, shortly after Wellington had become prime minister. What happened was related some years later to Charles Greville:

D. Miguel by João Baptista Ribeiro, *c.* 1828.

He was at Stratfieldsaye with [the marquis de] Palmella [*sic*], where in the library they were settling the oath that Miguel should take, Miguel would pay no attention, and instead of going into the business and saying what oath he would consent to take (the question was whether he should swear fidelity to Pedro or Maria) he sat flirting with the Princess Thérèse Esterhazy. The Duke said to Palmella, 'This will never do. He must settle the terms of the oath and if he is so careless in an affair of such moment he will never do his duty.'[30]

This incident was a warning to the British government of the shaky foundations on which their Portuguese policy was based, for it showed how unwilling D. Miguel was to have his future conduct dictated to him by the British or anyone else. D. Miguel's stay in London had involved negotiations other than that over the oath. A loan had been raised and agreement reached for the withdrawal of Sir William Clinton's forces once D. Miguel should arrive.[31] D. Miguel proceeded to Lisbon on a Portuguese ship and his arrival on 22 February 1828 led to the most dramatic events of his life when at last he broke free from the bonds with which his brother and the international community had tried to tie him.

Lord Carnarvon's account of D. Miguel's seizure of the throne

Lord Porchester, the future 3rd Earl of Carnarvon, had been travelling in Portugal and was present in Lisbon when D. Miguel returned from exile. After his return to Britain he wrote a detailed and dramatic account of the events that unfolded. His book *Portugal and Galicia* was originally published in 1836 and went through three revisions up to 1848 after he had succeeded to the earldom. In it he reflected on the causes of the conflict that D. Miguel's usurpation had brought to Portugal:

> About two o'clock in the afternoon [of 22 February] the royal flag was seen flying from all the signal posts, and thundering salutes from the various shipping, answered by cannon at the castle, proclaimed the Infant's arrival . . . As he landed the soldiers cried out, 'long live the Infant!' the people replied with 'vivas' for the Absolute King. At the palace of Ajuda he was welcomed by his mother. Falling upon one knee, he imprinted the most fervent

kisses on her hand, and said, taking from his bosom an image of
the Virgin of the Rock [Nossa Senhora da Barraca], 'Behold this
relic, your parting gift. Mother, you see before you the same child
you lost in 1824.' From that moment the royal attendants knew
that his political tendencies were unaltered, her influence over his
mind unimpaired, and the fate of the Charter sealed.[32]

Over the following days there were demonstrations and riots in the street
with more 'vivas' for the Absolute King. On 26 February D. Miguel
was supposed to take a public oath at the Ajuda palace to uphold the
constitution and to replace his sister as regent:

At one o'clock Dom Miguel entered the saloon, accompanied by
his sisters. The Infanta Regent seated herself on the throne: the
Prince at first stood by her side under the Royal canopy; but, taking
him familiarly by the arm, she forced him to occupy part of her seat
during the delivery of the speech. She expressed her sincere desire
for the welfare of the Charter, and assured her hearers of the upright
intentions which had uniformly actuated her conduct in the administration of the Government, and of the pleasure with which she
now resigned it into her brother's hands . . . Dom Miguel's flashing
eyes gave indications of that impatient temper which has characterized him from his earliest years . . . The written oath of adherence
to the Charter was then presented to the Infant, who regarded it
with apparent confusion, and seemed unable or unwilling to read
it; at the same time the Duke de Cadoval drew near with a missal
to administer the oath; but his Excellency's wide-spreading mantle

Gold piece
with effigy
of D. Miguel I
of Portugal,
1830.

so effectually concealed the Infant from the general observation, that it was impossible to see him kiss the Sacred Book or hear him pronounce the solemn words. I was not far from the royal party, but cannot give any decided opinion upon that much-debated point, whether Dom Miguel really went through, or evaded, the forms prescribed.[33]

Lord Carnavon then describes the appointment of an 'absolutist' ministry, the beginnings of the purge of the army and the closure of the Cortes elected under the terms of the Constitution, all to the background of popular demonstrations in D. Miguel's favour. He tells the story, which later became famous, that when Sir William Clinton, in charge of the British troops, was injured by the kick of a mule, 'the Queen-Mother had purchased the recalcitrant brute, as a signal proof of the hate she bore the English'.[34] By the end of March, the counter-revolution had been carried through and, recognizing that D. Miguel was now firmly in control and any threat from Spain had disappeared, Clinton's army was withdrawn early in April.

Lord Porchester described the occasion when, before he left Lisbon, he was formally presented to D. Miguel: 'He said little, but his manner was gentle, and the gloom which darkened his countenance on that inauspicious morning when he vowed – a fruitless vow! – to defend the Charter, was replaced by a placid and good humoured expression.'[35]

D. Miguel the king

The dismissal of the constitutional Cortes on 13 March 1828 and the departure of the British army was swiftly followed by D. Miguel summoning the traditional Cortes of three estates. The traditional Cortes had not met since 1697 and there was some vagueness about the necessary procedures, but it assembled on 23 June and duly chose D. Miguel as king, which was followed by his acclamation. On 7 July D. Miguel took his oath before the three estates. For those who wanted then, and still want, to consider D. Miguel the legitimate king, these traditional procedures were all important.[36] Whether D. Pedro or D. Miguel was the legitimate heir of D. João VI soon became a complicated issue to be argued through abstruse and sometimes convoluted arguments about exactly what constituted real legitimacy. The supporters of

D. Miguel not only argued for his recognition but extended their arguments to where legitimacy would lie in the event of his death. The claims of Maria Teresa, the eldest daughter of D. João VI, were advanced and after her the claims of her son Sebastião, but here legitimacy ran into problems as Sebastião was a Spanish citizen and as such a foreign prince, like the emperor D. Pedro, who could not inherit.[37]

From as far back as his first appearance on the political stage in the Vila Francada in 1823, D. Miguel had stood for the traditions of the absolute monarchy and its close alliance with the Church. He had always been happy mixing with the ordinary people of Portugal, who repaid him with loyalty and admiration. At the same time, he had been uneasy moving in the higher ranks of society and clearly did not have the education that would have made that easy. Once he was acclaimed as king, he and his advisers promoted the cause of traditional absolutism both through his proclamations but also through his frequent public appearances and easy relations with the common people. In August 1830 he made a tour through the places around Lisbon that were most associated with Portuguese history and the history of his own family, visiting Batalha, Alcobaça, Aljubarrota and Óbidos, but also Mafra and Caldas da Rainha and Marinha Grande, associated with his grandmother. Everywhere he was greeted by, and mixed with, enthusiastic crowds. It is not difficult to see why the people of Portugal preferred him to Maria da Gloria, a queen whom no one had ever seen, who was a child and who had never set foot in Portugal.[38]

With absolute government restored, D. Miguel, urged on by his mother, proceeded to a massive purge of all liberal influence. Thousands of people associated with the constitutional regime now fled abroad or, if they were unable to do so, were imprisoned and had their property confiscated. Few trials were held: it was arbitrary government run amok. D. Miguel also signed the death warrants of a number of his opponents, though modern research has decided that only 115 people were actually executed. However, there were many informal killings and hundreds of those arrested were deported to the African colonies, which was, for many of them, the same as a death penalty.

British accounts of D. Miguel's regime

Although Britain had withdrawn its ambassador, R. B. Hoppner had been appointed Consul-General and kept Lord Palmerston abreast of events in Portugal by means of a series of colourful despatches. Palmerston was certainly experienced enough to discount Hoppner's obvious bias against D. Miguel and all his works, but there is little doubt that these dispatches contributed materially to the extremely negative view of D. Miguel's regime that became current in Britain.

In July 1831 two Frenchmen had been arrested and beaten by D. Miguel's police. The French government demanded an apology and compensation and a fleet was sent to threaten Lisbon. Hoppner's dispatches provided a commentary on the crisis as it unfolded. On 9 July he reported that D. Miguel had gone to Cascais to supervise defensive works against a French attack. Lisbon, meanwhile, remained quiet,

> except that the Police guard has been strengthened as well as the gangs of bludgeon men I have already had occasion to mention . . . the employment of whom as well as the conduct they pursue is most disgraceful to a civilised Government . . . The people [show] that state of degrading apathy induced by oppression.[39]

A week later he reports that

> business of every description was at a stand and the town was left at the mercy of an exasperated military police, and a lawless set of ruffians who under the pretence of attachment to their Government conducted themselves with a disgraceful and unheard of barbarity. During the last few days several lives have been sacrificed from the wanton cruelty of these men.[40]

He expressed fears that once the French had gone, vengeance would be taken on those suspected of being their sympathizers:

> Dn Miguel is even said to have at one time prepared every thing for his flight and to have had all his valuables already packed up for that purpose. This information was indeed communicated to me by the Infanta Dna Maria Isabella who at the same time requested my opinion whether if required she should accompany her brother on

his flight, when I by all means recommended her to stay at Queluz, as the surest chance of preventing a state of anarchy in the country.[41]

A week later he was reporting that 'between eight and nine hundred persons have been thrown into prison, of whom a great number are in the infirmary in consequence of previous ill treatment', and on 6 August that some prisoners were being placed in the arsenal: 'the convicts and criminals have been removed from their dungeons to make room for such as are guilty perhaps of no other crime than having expressed an opinion as to the legitimacy of Dn Pedro's rights.'[42]

Hoppner reported in detail on the attempt in August by some military units to overthrow the regime and on the executions that followed. He also reported on the dire state of Portuguese finances and on D. Miguel's efforts to raise forced loans from anyone who was deemed able to pay. Hoppner explained the role of the clergy in supporting D. Miguel:

> All the periodical papers which have appeared in favour of the usurpation of D. Miguel are written by the clergy & friars, and are all directed by the Apostolical Junta. All these writers are at the same time preachers & Confessors who preach from the pulpit and teach in the confessionaries the abominable doctrines of those periodicals which are read by the priests to their parishioners during divine service.[43]

Hoppner kept telling Palmerston that public opinion, although cowed, was hostile to D. Miguel and only awaited the opportunity to greet his overthrow. In this he was certainly wrong and this mistaken judgement throws some doubt on his more general interpretation of events.

In June 1832 Lord William Russell (brother of the future prime minister, Lord John Russell) was sent to Lisbon as an unofficial envoy to report on Spanish activities in Portugal. Russell was not an experienced diplomat but his letters and reports largely substantiated Hoppner's picture of D. Miguel's regime. Russell kept a diary as well as writing official dispatches. Shortly after his arrival he wrote, 'met at Mrs Hoppner's Donna Anna Camara, threatened with arrest . . . she gives a most deplorable account of Lisbon, never did I hear of such an atrocious Government'. And he adds 'Miguel is in his quinta & amuses himself by making the batteries fire.' Three days later – 'Miguel came twice towards the town to look at a new battery, he was huzzaed & caressed by the soldiers. He has two grooms behind him with long sticks to beat the people who don't salute him.'[44] When Russell first saw Miguel, it was near the palace of Queluz: 'he is a small pale man, covered with hair, & rides well.'[45] A week later Russell was told a bizarre story about 'Don Miguel having pursued us from Queluz with a blunderbuss to shoot us'. He reported this to Lord Palmerston, adding that the story 'I have since traced to come direct from Donna Isabella the Regent, so it is true.'[46] It is clear that D. Miguel, who had been such a tearaway in his youth, had not changed very much now that he was king, a judgement that is confirmed by the story that he once drove a coach containing two of his sisters so fast on bad roads that it overturned. He himself was pinned under the coach and broke his thigh.

It is difficult to know why D. Miguel acted with such violence instead of trying to unite the country behind a traditional monarchical regime that would gain international recognition. Apart from Spain, no country in Europe recognized D. Miguel as king. Diplomats were withdrawn and D. Maria da Gloria continued to be formally acknowledged as Queen of Portugal. The explanation favoured by liberal constitutionalists was to blame defects in D. Miguel's character that made him take pleasure in cruelty for its own sake, to which was added the weakness that allowed the aged and fanatical Carlota Joaquina to exert control over his actions. Russell also seems to have come to the conclusion that D. Miguel was a man who was weak as well as cruel and was being manipulated by others. In 1832 he wrote to Lord Palmerston, 'The power is in the hands of a faction, whose tool (and from the apathy He shows in his cause I might say whose unwilling tool) Dom Miguel is; His Royal Highness appears to have no distinctive quality besides cruelty, and that of the vilest kind.'[47]

However, there are other considerations. From the outset D. Miguel was extremely popular and there was no sign, during the period of his purges, that these damaged his popularity in any way. Part of his popularity can be put down to his hostility towards the British and his assertion of Portugal's independence from both British and French influence. Furthermore, there appeared to be no ill consequences following from his hostility towards the British. During the first premiership of the duke of Wellington (1828–30), British policy was distinctly favourable and it was widely believed that, had Wellington survived in office, D. Miguel would have been formally recognized by Britain.

D. Miguel's project comes to grief

Although D. Miguel was very popular in Portugal and had the strong backing of the Church and the conservative nobility, there was one part of Portugal he never managed to control. The small island of Terceira in the Azores refused to accept him and held out against forces he sent against it. It provided the liberal exiles and their queen, D. Maria da Gloria, with a toehold on Portuguese soil.

This might not have been very significant but in July 1830 the conservative Bourbon regime in France was replaced by the liberal Orléanist king, Louis-Philippe, and the same year in Britain the equally conservative duke of Wellington was replaced by Lord Grey and the Whigs. The international scene, which, if not supportive, had tolerated D. Miguel, now became much more hostile. Although neither France nor Britain envisaged a direct intervention in Portugal, the arbitrary arrests and confiscations of British and French property led to pressure backed by naval force to make D. Miguel give way. The French sent a fleet that seized two of D. Miguel's ships and demanded that prisoners be released, the judges involved and the intendant of police be dismissed and compensation be paid. The full demands of the French and their acceptance by D. Miguel's ministers were to be published in the *Gazeta de Lisboa*.

Meanwhile, in January 1830 Carlota Joaquina died. D. Miguel lost his strongest supporter but also the person who had constantly driven him to adopt extreme measures.

In 1831 D. Miguel's brother, Emperor Pedro, abdicated his Brazilian throne and came to Europe to organize support for D. Maria da Gloria. At first he made little progress and may even have contemplated making some kind of compromise deal with his brother, but by the end of 1831 he had raised enough funds to send a military expedition to the Azores and to contemplate an invasion of Portugal itself. European governments remained sceptical and D. Pedro and D. Maria received no overt help. However, Lord Palmerston, the British Foreign Secretary, turned a deliberately blind eye to the army and navy personnel enlisting in D. Pedro's forces. In July 1832 D. Pedro's small army of 7,500 men, which had assembled and trained in the Azores, seized Porto, which was abandoned by D. Miguel's forces without a fight. From that time Portugal was torn by civil war. Although D. Miguel's forces were far more numerous than those of D. Pedro, the liberal army took the initiative in June 1833 by invading the Algarve, defeating D. Miguel's fleet at sea and seizing Lisbon. In spite of these victories, D. Miguel's forces still controlled most of Portugal and the war dragged on for another twelve months. Weakened by a severe outbreak of cholera and confronted by the formation of the Quadruple Alliance of Spain, Portugal, France and Britain, signed on 22 April 1834, D. Miguel was driven back to his last stronghold in Évora. There, after suffering a final disastrous defeat, he agreed to the Convention, which was signed in the remote hill town of Évoramonte on 26 May.

By this agreement D. Miguel agreed to leave Portugal and never to return to the Iberian Peninsula nor to interfere in political matters in the future. As a gesture of peace and goodwill he handed over the Crown Jewels of Portugal to the victor.

There are unanswered questions about D. Miguel's failure to establish absolutism. There is no doubt that he was hugely popular in Portugal and had substantial support among the nobility and the Church as well as among the ordinary people. Why was he not able to turn these huge advantages into security for his regime? The conventional answer is that the major states of Europe refused to recognize him and gave sanctuary and hope to his exiled opponents. But a closer look at events suggests this is too simple. Although at first only Spain and the United States recognized his regime, it soon became clear that others could be won over. Eventually the Pope and also Russia offered their support and it seemed as though Wellington's government was also prepared to do so. Moreover, after D. Pedro came to Europe, there seemed to be the possibility of some deal. However, instead of courting international support, D. Miguel and his followers adopted policies towards foreign nationals and towards his regime's opponents that soon earned him a reputation as a 'murderer' and 'tyrant'.

Lord Carnarvon reflected at length on D. Miguel's failure: 'The best chance of preserving the old institutions of the country, was to be found in an honest recognition of the Charter.' D. Miguel 'might, at that period, have affixed his own limits to every measure of change', for 'relying for support exclusively on the Absolute party, could hardly have ventured to introduce reforms prejudicial to the interests of many of his partisans'. By working with the Charter, 'he would have acquired a more real authority and a more effective command over the resources of his country than had ever fallen to the lot of any Prince of the House of Braganza under the old despotic rule.' Had he sought to conciliate he would have united the country and, 'many, who became determined enemies, would have quietly acquiesced in his authority, if the impolitic measures of his Government had not rendered submission more perilous than resistance'.[48]

Epilogue

D. Miguel was only 32 when he lost his throne. Once safely out of Portugal and in exile in Italy he tried to retrieve something from the disaster. He protested against the Évoramonte Convention, claiming it had been imposed by force, and he reasserted his claim to the throne. He repeated this on a number of occasions, importantly in 1852 when, after his marriage, his first child was born. D. Miguel and his descendants maintained their claim to the Portuguese throne: during the breakdown of the political order in Portugal in the 1840s there were insurrections in his name. In 1846 he was actually acclaimed in Braga and the apparent collapse of constitutional government, coming at the time of the Carlist wars in Spain, seemed for a time to promise a revival of the absolutist cause.

D. Miguel lived in Rome until 1847, receiving a small pension from the Pope. He then moved to London and in 1851 married Princess Adelaide of Löwenstein. Over the next ten years the couple had a son and six daughters, all allegedly born over a container filled with earth brought from Portugal. They continued to live in Germany, first at Langensbold and then at Bronnbach.[49] By this time D. Miguel had ceased to be the *enfant terrible* of European politics and had settled down to the lifestyle of a country gentleman. Like all his family, he found his principal leisure activity in hunting and he died in the hunting field at the age of 64 on 14 November 1866. His widow, Princess Adelaide, became a nun and died in 1895 in the convent of St Cecilia on the Isle of Wight.

D. Miguel's remains were brought back to Portugal in 1967, as part of a general reconciliation between the conservative Estado Novo and the monarchists, and were buried in the Braganza family mausoleum in São Vicente da Fora in Lisbon.[50]

Eça de Queiroz and Oliveira Martins reflect on Miguelism and Sebastianism

After the fall of his regime D. Miguel became, for many people in Portugal, a figure of almost mystical significance, the king who disappeared but was waiting, like D. Sebastião, to return to save his country.

Eça de Queiroz's novel *A Cidade e a Serra* (*The City and the Mountains*) was published posthumously in 1901. It is the story of a wealthy young man, Jacinto, living in the decadent world of 1890s Paris, who is gradually overtaken by despair as the lures of civilization fail him one by one. From this he is rescued by a friend who persuades him to return to his ancestral home in the mountains of northern Portugal. Jacinto's wealth came to him from his grandfather, nicknamed the 'Galleon' because of his size and riches. One day 'Galleon' was out walking when he slipped on some orange peel and fell:

> From the little doorway in the garden wall, at that very moment, emerged a dark, clean-shaven man in a thick green baize coat, with jack-boots like a picador, who playfully and with easy strength lifted the enormous Jacinto to his feet and even picked up his gold-handled walking-stick . . . Jacinto was dumbfounded and dazzled to recognize no less a person than the Prince of the Realm, Dom Miguel.

From this time 'Galleon' became a devotee of the prince. When Miguel returned from exile in Vienna to claim his throne in 1828, 'Galleon'

> festooned the manor of Pampulha with flowers and raised a monument of cardboard and canvas, on which Dom Miguel, represented as his namesake, Saint Michael, all in white, complete with aureole and archangel's wings, was seen to pierce with his lance, from the saddle of a rearing horse, the Dragon of Liberalism, which, in its contorted agonies, was vomiting the Constitutional Charter.

When D. Miguel was driven a second time into exile, 'Galleon' vowed he 'did not wish to remain in the perverse country from which that good King of Portugal, who picked up fallen "Galleon" in the street, had been forced to depart' and retired to live 'a life of idleness and good food' in Paris.[51] That this is a commentary on the shallow realities of Miguelism, little more substantial than cardboard and canvas, hardly needs saying.

But there is more. As Jacinto becomes absorbed in rural life and spends his money helping to relieve the poverty of his tenants and workers, so the rumour spreads that he is an emissary of Prince Miguel (the son of D. Miguel), plotting the return of the legitimate king, and that Prince Miguel himself has actually returned and is living incognito as Jacinto's servant. When this topic emerges at a dinner party, one of the company exclaims, 'I hope that at least here, in Guiaes, we won't have the gallows raised.'[52] This rumour is confirmed by a meeting with a local seer who seizes Jacinto's hand and exclaims, 'Royal hand, giver's hand, hand that is sent from above, hand now seldom seen . . . May our Blessed Lord Jesus Christ be praised, who brought me here that I might see this man with my own eyes.' After further obscure sayings, the seer ends with "'Blessed be the Father of the poor" . . . Jacinto was amazed that there should still exist in the kingdom a Sebastianist. "But we all are, Jacinto, here in Portugal. Whether in the mountains or in the City each one awaits *his* Dom Sebastião . . .".'[53]

According to the historian Oliveira Martins, Miguelism became a manifestation of Sebastianism, a belief in a heroic figure who would return from exile to save his country: 'Bearing the name of Saint Michael, the Archangel, he flaunts the trappings of his role. He appears as the reincarnation of the king, Dom Sebastião, the "Desejado" (desired one), the guide of his people, just as, four centuries previously, the Mestre de Avis [D. João I] had been the great hope of the people of Lisbon.' Miguelism is

a spirit that takes over the body of the masses – another of the spectres that hovers over the future of Portugal . . . Disappearing to return in moments of national crisis . . . one can never be sure of the imminence of the spectral apparition, if the expectation which it creates anticipates the country's rescue or its perdition.[54]

11

The Constitutional Monarchs: D. Maria II, D. Fernando and their Sons, D. Pedro V and D. Luís

In July 1823 Maria Graham, the wife of an English naval captain and friend of Empress Leopoldina, had occasion to visit the palace in Rio to enquire after Emperor Pedro's health and to present the empress with a picture she had made. There she met the princesses, whom she described as being 'extremely fair, and like Her Majesty, especially the eldest, Dona Maria da Gloria, who has one of the most intelligent faces I have ever seen'.[1] The blonde princesses were a symbol, a portent for changes that were beginning in the Braganza family.

In 1817 the infante Pedro had married the Austrian archduchess Leopoldina. She not only produced princes and princesses on a yearly basis but introduced into the royal family a culture that was wholly new. The Braganzas up to that time had shown marked interest in music and the musical theatre, but their courts had never been centres of intellectual culture. With Leopoldina a new spirit was abroad. She was well educated and interested in studying scientific topics, encouraging the work of scientific research. Although she died prematurely in 1826, this serious interest in contemporary intellectual trends was carried on by D. Pedro, who took care over the education of his children, avoiding the carefree indulgence that had marked his own and D. Miguel's upbringing. This eventually showed impressive results in his son, Emperor Pedro II, whose whole character was shaped by intellectual and scientific interests.

The 'Germanification' of the Royal Family

The Germanic tradition that was introduced into the Braganza family by Leopoldina was reinforced when Maria da Gloria married Ferdinand (known in Portugal as Fernando) of Saxe-Coburg. Like all princes of that family, he was well educated, intelligent and, above all, in tune with contemporary culture. Their children were brought up under the supervision of a German tutor, Dietz.

The German influence was also seen in what was perhaps the most obvious monument surviving from the reign of D. Maria II and Ferdinand, the Pena Palace. This romantic concoction, a potpourri of styles, was designed by an amateur German architect and mining engineer, Wilhelm Ludwig von Eschwege, and was the forerunner of many romantic revival castles in Germany, culminating in the extravaganzas of Ludwig II of Bavaria.

If D. Maria II and Emperor Pedro II were half German, D. Maria's children were three-quarters German and her eldest son, D. Pedro V, married Stephanie, a Hohenzollern princess. Although both she and D. Pedro died young without having had any children, D. Pedro's successor, his younger brother, D. Luís, married the daughter of Victor Emmanuel of Savoy, whose mother had been Austrian. The German element in the royal family continued after the end of the monarchy when D. Manuel II married a Hohenzollern princess in 1913. D. Miguel's son, Miguel II, married Isabel von Thurn und Taxis. Duarte Nuno, who eventually united all the claims of the exiled Braganzas, was brought up in Germany and spoke German as his first language.

The Braganzas certainly benefited from the more diverse genes brought into the family. They even began to look like Germans, none more so than D. Carlos, Ferdinand of Saxe-Coburg's grandson, whose appearance was almost comically like that of a Prussian general. But more important was the fact that these marriages brought a family, famed for its traditional beliefs and antiquated customs, firmly into the modern world. With D. Fernando, D. Pedro V and D. Luís, Portugal had as heads of state men who were cultured and who looked to modernize the country and give it governments able to pursue progressive and liberal policies. However, George Young, writing in 1917, saw this change from a slightly different perspective: 'With Ferdinand the Braganza dynasty had undergone a change, which, while it produced rulers of far better quality than the Braganzas of the eighteenth century, had deprived the Crown of much of its Portuguese temperament, and consequently of its touch with the people.'[2]

The Braganza monarchs of the nineteenth century governed according to the Constitutional Charter drawn up for Portugal by

Emperor Pedro I (D. Pedro IV of Portugal) in 1826. Although ostensibly based on the British model – a chamber of elected deputies and a house of hereditary peers – it left considerable influence, if not exactly power, in the hands of the monarch. It was the monarch who could appoint ministers, dissolve the assembly and call elections, and who had the famous 'moderating power' (*poder moderador*) that gave him the responsibility to intervene to ensure that there was no political deadlock. The monarch was thus closely involved with politics without having power to direct the government or initiate reform. Inevitably this made the Crown the most visible target for public anger and resentment as Portugal descended into ever worse financial chaos and suffered successive humiliations abroad.

D. Maria II, 'the Educator'

Until Maria de Fátima Bonifácio published hers in 2007, there had never been a critical biography of D. Maria II. This probably reflects a neglect by historians (until recently) of the period of the 1830s and '40s, which were among the least glorious decades of Portugal's history.

D. Maria II was born on 4 April 1819 in Rio de Janeiro and as a small child was tutored by Maria Graham, who admired her intelligence and blonde good looks. In the bizarre family atmosphere that developed at the royal court, Maria was often in the company of her father's mistress, Domitila, and her children, rather than her own mother.[3]

In May 1826, following the death of her grandfather, D. João VI, and the abdication of his Portuguese throne by her father D. Pedro, she was declared Queen of Portugal. In July 1828 she left Rio bound for the Austrian court in Vienna, where she was to be betrothed to her uncle D. Miguel. En route she stopped in Britain, where a considerable gathering of exiles greeted her as their queen. Although only nine years old, she made a very good impression on the English as well as the Portuguese exiles she met: in April 1829 she held a reception in London at which she presented a banner to a loyal regiment in the Azores, which she had embroidered with her own hands.[4] She was received officially by George IV at Windsor and the diarist Charles Greville described a 'child's ball' at which she was present:

> It was pretty enough, and I saw for the first time the Queen of Portugal and our little Victoria. The Queen was finely dressed, with

a ribbon and order over her shoulder, and she sat by the King. She is
good-looking and has a sensible Austrian countenance. In dancing
she fell down and hurt her face, was frightened and bruised, and went
away. The King was very kind to her. Our little princess is a short
plain-looking child, and not near so good-looking as the Portuguese.[5]

D. Maria and Princess Victoria subsequently became friends and maintained a life-long correspondence, a friendship which deepened when
they married princes who were first cousins.

   Although her presence in London (and the time spent living at
Laleham House on the Thames, not far from Windsor), and the favour
of the British royal family, did not lead to any practical help, it at least
made it difficult for Wellington's government to make any moves towards
recognizing D. Miguel. Although D. Maria had charmed those she met
by her dignity and precocious ability to fulfil the ceremonial role of a
queen, her education had been neglected and this neglect persisted
when she was once again residing in Rio.[6]

   At this stage her father, D. Pedro, was not in any position to help
her win her throne as there was strong hostility in Brazil to any involvement with Portuguese affairs. British policy had been to support the
idea of a marriage between D. Maria and D. Miguel, which had been
the condition for D. Pedro abdicating the Portuguese throne. But with
the acclamation of D. Miguel as king in July 1828 this line of policy
looked increasingly improbable. As D. Pedro was unlikely to persuade
Brazil to support any attempt to place D. Maria on her throne, her
cause seemed early in 1829 to have reached its lowest point. Her only
asset was that she had been recognized as queen by all the European
powers who were reluctant to offer any recognition to D. Miguel. In
1829 D. Pedro gave orders for Maria to return to Brazil, and in August
she sailed for Rio in the company of her father's new wife, Amélia of
Leuchtenberg. This seemed to mark the end of any attempt to place her
on the Portuguese throne.

   In 1830 the international scene gradually become more favourable. Although D. Pedro seemed, at one stage, to have reached a point
where he might abandon D. Maria and the Charter if his brother would
grant an amnesty to all political prisoners and exiles, the July Revolution
in Paris and the fall of Wellington's Tory government in November
reawakened the possibility of a liberal consensus between two of the
three powers with the most direct interest in Portugal.[7]

D. Maria remained in Brazil until April 1831 when her father abdicated his Brazilian throne and set out for Europe with his family. Going first to Britain, D. Pedro met with little encouragement – he was annoyed that D. Maria was officially referred to as Her Majesty Queen Maria and not Her Majesty Queen of Portugal – and decided to accept Louis-Philippe's offer of a residence at the Château de Meudon.[8] While in France D. Pedro was able to negotiate a large loan and the French allowed him to use Belle-Île, off the coast of Brittany, as a base. From there, in February, he issued a declaration that he would once again assume the regency for his daughter. D. Maria spent two years in Paris, completing her education. She formed close connections with the family of Louis-Philippe and became attached to his son, the duc de Nemours.

At this stage D. Maria, recognized in Britain and France as queen, had never set foot in the country over which she aspired to reign, while her father, who had presumed to give Portugal a constitution that the people did not want, had not seen Portugal since he was ten years old. From early childhood she had been treated as royalty and from all this deference she seems to have learnt a rather authoritarian and arrogant outlook with no experience of the kind of humility and compromise, not to say guile, that would become necessary to fulfil the role of a constitutional and not an absolute monarch.

With the capture of Lisbon by the liberal forces in July 1833, it was considered appropriate for D. Maria to claim her kingdom. This she did, arriving in Lisbon on 22 September 1833. She was greeted with all the ceremonial that at one time had been bestowed on the absolute monarchs of Portugal: a Te Deum in the cathedral was followed by a formal *beija mão* in the Necessidades palace. The following year she paid a formal visit to Porto, but her life was then rapidly taken over by events. Her father became seriously ill and on 20 September the Cortes decided that, although she was only fifteen, she should be declared to be of age. Just four days later, on 24 September, her father died.

D. Maria's two marriages

Although D. Maria was barely of marriageable age, D. Pedro had already selected a husband for her. Augusto of Leuchtenberg was the brother of D. Pedro's second wife and, therefore, by marriage, Maria's uncle, the last such union in the history of incestuous marriages in the Braganza family. He was also related to Napoleon through his grandmother,

Joséphine, who had been Napoleon's first empress. This connection appealed strongly to D. Pedro's own Napoleonic tendencies and to his image of a modern, liberal royalty.

An early vote on the civil list indicated a strain of opposition to the institution of monarchy, even republicanism, but after considerable debate the sum of one *conto* per diem was allotted as the Crown's revenue, the equivalent of 12 per cent of national income.[9] The extravagance of the monarchy and of the ruling politicians who lavishly rewarded themselves and their followers soon became central to radical demands for a complete constitutional overhaul and were to pursue the Braganza monarchy to the very end.

Augusto arrived in Lisbon on 25 January 1835, but two months later became ill and died. It was alleged that the marriage had never been consummated and that D. Maria became a 'widow without ever having been a wife'.[10]

That D. Maria should marry again, and soon, seemed to be a matter of political urgency and preoccupied the diplomatic world as well as Lisbon political circles. It seems also to have preoccupied D. Maria herself, whose nature was described in British diplomatic correspondence as 'passionate' and who wanted to have a husband. One proposal, very much favoured by her stepmother Amélia, was that D. Maria should marry Augusto's brother Maximilian. However, she is alleged to have rejected this proposal on the grounds that he had a face like a fried potato (*cara de batata frita*).[11] The queen herself wanted to marry Louis-Philippe's son, the duc de Nemours, or, if he refused, his brother François, Prince de Joinville, but this raised huge diplomatic problems as a marriage to a French prince would have been strongly opposed by Britain and might even have threatened the survival of the Quadruple Alliance, which was so important to the post-civil war settlement in Portugal. A choice that was neutral in the eyes of the international community was Ferdinand of Saxe-Coburg, who arrived to claim his bride in April 1836. He was only nineteen years old and his queen just eighteen. D. Maria, it was reported, was more than anxious for the marriage to be consummated and a year later their first child, Pedro, was born. Fernando was then granted the title of king.

The duke of Loulé, who had married Ana de Jesus Maria, one of the sisters of D. Pedro, was, according to the Chancellor of the Duchy of Lancaster, Lord Holland, opposed to the Coburg marriage due to 'a secret and absurd hope that his Wife may ultimately be raised to the throne, he become King Consort, and his children succeed to the throne.'[12]

D. Maria and D. Fernando made a handsome couple. D. Fernando was described at the time as 'a fine figure of a man . . . with features that were prominent, correct and expressive'. Maria

> without being beautiful was a gracious model for a princess of her race, with her elegant stature, proud head and fine complexion, and skin fair and smooth as satin. Her eyes were light brown and sparkling; her bottom lip full like that of the Braganzas; her mouth gracious but firm like her character.[13]

She and her young husband had a happy and successful marriage, not least because the couple enjoyed the physical side of their married life. As the numbers of their children grew, the royal family were often seen together in public as a family. Like his cousin Albert in Britain, D. Fernando cultivated a bourgeois lifestyle, although D. Maria retained the old Braganza custom of the *beija mão*, which was only finally discontinued during the reign of her son D. Pedro v.[14] As the political scene in Portugal became ever more chaotic, they were, in the words of Francis Gribble, 'a royal party encamped on the edge of a volcano, eating freely of rice and dumplings, in an interval between the eruptions – the Queen bearing children, and the King playing billiards, as calmly as if cataclysms were unheard of things'.[15]

Victoria and D. Maria: two adolescent queens

D. Fernando was first cousin to both Queen Victoria and Prince Albert, whose marriage took place in 1840. The two royal families remained in constant touch, letters were exchanged and they all kept the head of the Coburg family, Leopold of the Belgians, informed of what was happening in their respective countries; he in turn readily responded with advice. But even before the marriage, Victoria and D. Maria had established a close personal relationship.

Their early lives are so remarkably similar, and run parallel to each other in so many ways, that they bring into sharp relief the difficulties any young woman had to face dealing with the political problems of the time. Victoria and D. Maria da Gloria were born within two months of each other in 1819. Both had German-speaking mothers and at the time of their births neither was in line for the throne. Both succeeded to their respective thrones when still teenagers: D. Maria was fifteen and Victoria was eighteen. Both queens then married Coburg princes who in many respects were similar in their tastes and in the way they envisaged the role of the royal family, deliberately adopting a bourgeois lifestyle and trying to reinvent the monarchy after the sleazy, not to say debauched, image that royalty had acquired during the reigns of George IV, D. Miguel and D. Pedro. The Coburg princes also indulged their not-so-bourgeois taste in building exotic palaces reflecting the architectural style of nineteenth-century romanticism, Albert building Osborne House and Balmoral, and D. Fernando the Pena Palace in Sintra.

Both queens had large numbers of children and the state of being pregnant was an important, possibly dominant, influence on their lives. D. Maria had eleven pregnancies (with seven of her children surviving) and Victoria nine. Both queens ran into trouble over the constitution

Princess Victoria of Kent, sketch portrait of D. Maria, queen of Portugal, 1833.

of their households and over their partisanship in the political turmoil of their early years: D. Maria dismissed the government of Palmela, and Victoria, in effect, made Peel's premiership impossible. Both faced physical dangers, with D. Maria besieged by mutinous soldiers in her palace at Belém in 1836 and Victoria experiencing assassination attempts. Both eventually found political father-figures, Victoria in Lord Melbourne and D. Maria in the count of Tomar, in whom they placed their trust and with whom they had a close personal rapport.

The coincidental similarity of their experience, coupled with the fact that the two had met in childhood, meant that Victoria considered D. Maria a close friend. The two exchanged letters. In 1838 D. Maria sent Victoria a 'bracelet with the portrait of little Pedro in it.' Victoria, for her part, hung in her closet a picture of D. Maria painted by Sir Thomas Lawrence in 1829.[16] On 4 April 1838 Victoria made a long entry in her diary, covering a wide variety of personal and political topics. At the very end, she records simply, 'It was the Queen of Portugal's 19th birthday.'[17]

Victoria followed intently what was happening in Portugal and her letters and diary entries provide a vivid commentary on these events and on how D. Maria was managing her role as constitutional monarch during the early years of her reign. On hearing of the marriage by proxy of D. Maria with Ferdinand of Saxe-Coburg, Victoria recorded:

> I cannot say how happy I am to become thus related to the Queen of Portugal, who has always been so kind to me and for whom I have always had a great affection. She is warm-hearted, honest and affectionate, and when she talks, is very pleasing. We have known each other since our 8th year (for there is only a month's difference in age between us). She is far from plain too; she has an exquisite complexion, a good nose and fine hair. I hear that Ferdinand is full of good and excellent qualities, has a pure and unsophisticated mind and is very good looking.[18]

In November 1835 a *pronunciamento* in Lisbon had forced the queen to appoint a ministry supported by radical politicians, and in September 1836 a revolution broke out in Lisbon demanding that the Charter be replaced by the 1822 Constitution. On 18 September Victoria wrote in her diary:

Baron Moncorvo brought yesterday the distressing news, the same unfortunate revolution which took place in Spain, has likewise taken place in Portugal, & that the Queen was forced to proclaim the constitution of 1820, similar to the one of 1812 [in Spain] . . . I do *so* feel for poor *dear* Ferdinand in this trying moment, as also for the poor good Queen. The difference between *this* & the one in *Spain* was: that in Portugal, they behaved respectfully towards dear Ferdinand & Donna Maria & in *Spain* they almost insulted the Queen Regent. In Portugal, thank God! No blood has been shed.[19]

Victoria wrote to her uncle Leopold on 21 November 1836:

I cannot tell you how distressed I was by the late unfortunate *con-tre-révolution manquée* at Lisbon . . . Mamma received a letter from Lord Palmerston . . . He speaks in the highest terms of our beloved Ferdinand, which proves that he becomes daily more and more worthy of his arduous situation, and says that the queen's situation 'is better than it was', less bad than it might have been 'after such an affair', and not so good as it would have been had poor Donna Maria waited patiently until all was ripe for action. Dietz wrote Mamma a most desponding letter, so much so, that had we not got Lord Palmerston's letter we must have thought all, all was over.[20]

Earlier in the month the British ambassador, Lord Howard de Walden, had written in a quite different vein to Palmerston:

The Queen has appeared mighty indifferent to all that has passed. Her personal feelings were very decided against Sa Bandiera [*sic*] and Passos and the men of the revolution, but it appeared to me that she was bored at Belem and that she really was glad to return to the Necessidades [palace] and go to the theatre. Not so the Prince, who has throughout behaved admirably.[21]

In January 1837, having met Sylvain Van de Weyer, the Belgian minister in London, Victoria wrote in her diary:

He gave us most interesting and most valuable information about Portugal; praised our dearest Ferdinand to the skies, said he showed cleverness, firmness and character which no other young man of his age hardly ever showed; said the poor queen was *totally indifferent* to whatever *happened* but was extremely *obedient* to Ferdinand who had great power over her; that the intrigues and villainy of the higher classes is incredible . . . What he told us about the nobility and higher classes is most distressing, as also about the Camarilla [clique] who surround the poor Queen.[22]

To King Leopold she wrote six days later, 'as for the Queen [D. Maria] what he told us does not redound much to her credit; one good quality, however, she has which is her excessive fondness for and real *obedience* to Ferdinand.'[23] In February 1837 Victoria recorded in her diary: 'Ferdinand is clearly gaining popularity, that both he and the Queen had been *very well* received at the theatre; and that the man who threw a stone at dearest Ferdinand . . . was a Frenchman an inferior officer, and whom Ferdinand had relieved in money several times.'[24]

Forced initially to accept this revolution, D. Maria soon listened to the advice of the 'marshals', the dukes of Terceira and Saldanha, and tried to dismiss the newly appointed ministers. Angry crowds in Lisbon forced her to retreat and two hundred British marines were landed to protect her, holed up in the Belém palace. It was Lord Holland's belief that the Septembrists wanted to 'drive the Queen to take refuge in our Ships', which would have effectively meant that she had given up the throne.[25] In July 1837 Terceira and Saldanha tried a military insurrection in the provinces. After this failed, Victoria commented to Leopold, 'the Civil War is ended, and the Chartists have been completely defeated; this is sad enough, but I was fearful of it; a counter-revolution never does well.'[26]

Victoria's deep and personal interest in the affairs of Portugal and in the problems that beset D. Maria seems almost as if she was measuring D. Maria's problems and her reaction to them against her own experience of politics in Britain. The diary shows that she constantly discussed Portuguese affairs with her ministers, but with a growing realization that D. Maria was not always making wise decisions and was failing to manage her role as constitutional monarch. On 16 February 1838 Victoria records 'being shocked at her [D. Maria] giving up her authority so tamely', and one can sense the loyalty and relief when she writes on 21 March 1838 after hearing of the defeat of the revolt of the *arsenalistas* in Lisbon, 'The Queen had behaved uncommonly well and had shown even more courage than Ferdinand . . . Lord Melbourne was very much pleased with the good news, and with the Queen's conduct; I said I knew she had more in her than people thought.'[27]

Later she delights to record D. Maria gaining in confidence in her dealings with Sá da Bandeira, the leader of the Septembrists, 'the only Minister the Queen has ever liked, or has been confidential with; she always bullies him though . . . She tells him, Lord Melbourne said, that he is a traitor, and then he answers "not quite so bad as that"; and she taps him familiarly with her fan.'[28]

Queen Victoria continued a staunch friend of D. Maria. In a letter to Lord Palmerston written in November 1846, when Portugal was torn by the civil war of the *patuleia*, she wrote: 'This state of affairs is the more distressing as Portugal has perhaps never had more really good and virtuous sovereigns than the present Queen and King; whoever is intimate with the Queen knows how really honest, good, well-meaning and courageous she is.'[29]

Political instability as democracy tries to find its feet

In 1831 D. Pedro had written to his daughter that he wanted to spare her the 'briars and thorns' (*abrolhos e espinhos*) of Portuguese politics,[30] but he died leaving his young daughter an almost impenetrable tangle of political confrontations. A summary of the main developments of the reign provides a context for the problems the queen and her husband faced. The first two years of D. Maria's reign saw three ministries dismissed and the state in dire financial trouble. This led in September 1836 to a radical coup, backed by the National Guard in Lisbon. The royal family took refuge in Belém and some British marines even landed as a guard. The radicals, known as Septembrists, summoned a Constituent Assembly and in 1838 issued a new constitution, which abolished inherited peers, replaced them with an elected Senate and removed the 'moderating' power of the Crown.

In July 1837 the dukes of Terceira and Saldanha combined to attempt a countercoup but their forces were defeated by another general of the civil war, Sá da Bandeira. He now had to suppress a radical uprising in Lisbon. The radical National Guardsmen, the *arsenalistas*, were said to have used bears 'in order to cause greater terror in the defenceless population of the capital'.[31] The end came in a shoot-out in the Rossio square in the city centre. A succession of ministries brought many of the old politicians back into power. In 1842 a coup

D. Maria II by João
Zephaniah Bell
(1819–53).

masterminded by António da Costa Cabral, a former radical who was
actually a minister in the government, and with the connivance and
encouragement of the queen, formally restored the Charter. With the
cooperation of the duke of Terceira, Costa Cabral carried through a
raft of reforms to taxation, public accounts and local administration,
which he brought under closer central control. His measures included
a land registry and, famously, the attempt on health grounds to prevent
burials inside churches.

Costa Cabral was, according to the Portuguese historian José
Saraiva, 'the first representative of political realism',[32] but he soon became
very unpopular. A man of humble origin, he had changed sides after the
defeat of the *arsenalistas* with what was seen as unforgiveable cynicism,
and he was deeply suspect as a favourite of the queen, who made him
the count of Tomar.

In April 1846 a popular revolt broke out in the north, known as the rebellion of Maria da Fonte, a mysterious and probably mythical female peasant leader. In the widespread rural disturbances that followed, the family vault at Vidigueira where Vasco da Gama was buried was plundered and the tombs damaged. Meanwhile a movement to restore D. Miguel gathered momentum and Randal McDonnell, one of D. Miguel's generals, appeared to lead the guerrillas, though Miguelism had, by this time, less to do with the claims of D. Miguel than a protest against poverty and economic misery. The spread of the revolt led to the dismissal of Costa Cabral.

A very unstable situation followed with growing confrontation between the old supporters of the Charter and Sá da Bandeira and the Septembrists. A civil war now broke out between the duke of Saldanha, backed by the queen, and Sá da Bandeira, supported by a Septembrist Junta in Porto. This war, known as the *patuleia*, at first went the way of the Junta but, as neither side gained the upper hand, the queen appealed for Spanish help through Costa Cabral in exile in Madrid. Prince Albert in England now sent an emissary, Colonel Wilde, to mediate. This failed and the powers of the Quadruple Alliance decided to intervene. A British naval contingent blockaded Porto and Spanish troops entered Portugal. In June the Septembrist Junta capitulated. Saldanha, once again in power, recalled Costa Cabral but the two fell out and Costa Cabral continued to hold office until 1851. Early in that year Saldanha staged another coup, backed by the Porto garrison and probably with the connivance of D. Fernando, who was commander-in-chief of the troops stationed in Lisbon. Costa Cabral and his government resigned and Saldanha once again formed a government that established a rapprochement with Sá da Bandeira and the remnants of the Junta of the *patuleia* war.

The year 1851 is usually considered to be the end of this period of instability and low-level civil war. The 1850s and '60s, coinciding with a decided upturn in the economy, were to be much more peaceful.

D. Maria and D. Fernando at sea in a political storm

D. Maria's first two years were, in more ways than one, a honeymoon period, which may have created the impression that the victory of D. Pedro in the civil war had resolved political differences and created a national consensus. This was far from being the case and Portugal was to experience fifteen years of political turmoil that flared up on three or four occasions into armed conflict.

The reasons for this chronic instability have their roots in the experience of the country since 1807, when the royal family had moved to Brazil. The struggle between Britain and France for dominance in the Iberian peninsula was not ended by the expulsion of Napoleon's armies from Spain in 1813. In 1823 the French invaded again and Britain had to confront the French to prevent a new invasion of Portugal itself. In 1827 the British found it necessary to send a military force to Portugal to prevent a French-backed Spanish invasion. In 1831, with Britain standing by, a French fleet entered the Tagus, presented D. Miguel with an ultimatum and sailed away with two of his ships. During the Civil War a senior French general, Comte Bourmont, was sent to command D. Miguel's armies, while Charles Napier, a British naval officer, disguised under the rather unconvincing pseudonym of Carlo Ponza, took command of D. Pedro's fleet. The rivalry continued even after the Quadruple Alliance of 1834 came into effect and provided an Anglo-French guarantee for the liberal regimes in Spain and Portugal. Britain intervened diplomatically to prevent D. Maria marrying a French prince and sent marines to defend the Belém palace when revolution broke out once again in Lisbon in September 1836. For the next fifteen years the British and French hovered in the wings ready to intervene, or threaten to intervene, in Portuguese politics, a threat that became reality in 1847.

The victory of D. Pedro and his supporters in the civil war had been followed by a schism in the Church caused in part by the drastic measures taken by the victorious liberals in abolishing the religious houses and nationalising Church lands. The schism was not remedied until formal agreement with Rome was reached in 1842.

Meanwhile, political ideology in Portugal became increasingly polarized between supporters of the Charter, a British-style constitution that had been gifted to Portugal by the absentee D. Pedro in 1826, and the supporters of the democratic constitution of 1822. The royal family was profoundly affected by these disputes as the Charter gave the monarch considerable powers in the political life of the country, while the 1822 constitution, although still monarchical in form, made of the monarch little more than a figurehead and recognized that all political power derived from and rested with the people. The rivalry of these two factions among the civil war's victors was intensified by the widespread poverty and unemployment among the soldiers demobilized

D. Maria II, Queen of Portugal by John Simpson, *c.* 1840, oil on canvas.

after 1834 and by the blatant corruption and manipulation of the
elections by the supporters of the Charter, who had been put in power
by D. Pedro.[33] This struggle for power, at first waged largely within the
capital but subsequently spreading to Porto as well, took place against
a background of considerable sympathy and support for the deposed
D. Miguel. His supporters, not well organized nor represented in the
official state institutions, were nevertheless active in the rural areas and
had the backing of the Church. A low-level rural unrest erupted frequently into guerrilla warfare, and found encouragement from the Carlist
movement in Spain. Don Carlos, who had been a refugee in Portugal
during the reign of D. Miguel and had left the country when D. Miguel

went into exile, was married to the Braganza princess Maria Teresa, who was one of the sisters of D. Miguel and D. Pedro.

These competing visions of Portugal's political future might have resolved themselves through constitutional means had it not been for the ambitions and rivalries of the victorious generals: Saldanha, Terceira and Sá da Bandeira. These grand military personalities repeatedly called out the regiments loyal to them to intervene in politics, while in Lisbon the National Guard, which elected its own officers and was nominally answerable to the Ministry of the Interior (Ministério do Reino), also became a player in the military confrontations.

To this chaotic mixture should be added the growing rivalry of the cities of Lisbon and Porto. Political movements based in one city were frequently opposed by the citizens of the other. On numerous occasions, it was in Porto that opposition to the government in Lisbon was organized. It was Porto that backed Costa Cabral in 1842; it was in Porto that the Septembrist Junta was formed in October 1846 and it was with soldiers from Porto that Saldanha carried out his coup in 1851. Porto had gained a reputation, going back to the revolution of 1820, of being the home of liberalism, but as the nineteenth century unfolded it was just as often Lisbon where radical politics were ignited and it was in Lisbon that republicanism eventually took root and where the monarchy was finally overthrown.

The political dramas of D. Maria's reign were played against a background of extreme economic distress felt by many parts of the country, especially during the 'hungry forties', which proved to be so politically disruptive throughout Europe.

In theory the monarch could have played a mediating role, as provided for in the Charter, reconciling, cajoling, building coalitions, uniting the country behind the symbolism of the monarchy, as D. Maria's brother, Emperor Pedro II, was able to do in Brazil. However, the English historian Francis Gribble wrote, rather unkindly, 'Dona Maria at sixteen or seventeen, could not be expected to have any more authority than a school girl who stamps her foot, and says "Shan't"'.[34] Lord Holland, commenting on the queen's power under the Constitution to dismiss ministers, reflected how bad it was for 'an inexperienced, wayward girl of 16 to have such a power [to dismiss ministers] and to exert it so peremptorily, suddenly and unexpectedly'.[35] Maria Bonifácio makes much the same point, adding that D. Maria could not depend, as her father had been able to do, 'on the loyalty of the army, indispensable for conferring a solid base for her authority'.[36] Moreover, early in her reign the queen surrounded herself with courtiers who were believed to form a closely related *camarilha* of corrupt aristocrats, the 'Ficalhos'. But there was more to it than that. She and D. Fernando became too committed to one faction and, in the count of Tomar, to one single politician. Like her grandson D. Carlos, she tried to resolve the political confusion in Portugal by placing her trust in a strongman who was prepared, if necessary, to suspend the constitution. This resort to the rule of a dictatorial figure was to prove fatal to D. Carlos; D. Maria was fortunate to survive.

The ascendancy of the Costa Cabral brothers marked the period between 1842 and 1846. These four years saw the restoration of the Charter and a government with a firm sense of direction. Costa Cabral, however, courted unpopularity, which finally found expression in the uprising that led to the war known as the *patuleia*. António Pereira dos Reis, later president of the Chamber of Deputies in the Cortes, wrote a long pamphlet, under the pseudonym of 'An Anglo-Lusitanian', in which he took the British government and its Consuls to task for misrepresenting the issues and for misunderstanding the politics of the war, which was being seen in Britain as a war of democracy against the corrupt administration backed by the queen. However, he did offer an explanation for the unpopularity of Costa Cabral.

> The Cabral administration fell because it was too domineering, too prone to vindictive persecution, and especially through the frightful unpopularity of the elder brother, José Cabral. It fell, nevertheless, in the midst of a career of national amelioration, betrayed by its own folly in maintaining an absurdly inefficient army, and by intrigues where they were least expected.[37]

This view is echoed in one of Lord Palmerston's letters to Prince Albert on Portuguese matters:

> The Cabrals are 'much dreaded' in Portugal because the general opinion in that country seems to be, that they are unscrupulous and unprincipled men, who, having come into office as needy adventurers, have grown rich by plundering the country, and who have formed around themselves a party of adherents, by allowing their followers to imitate their example in this respect.[38]

Palmerston clearly thought that D. Maria was 'in secret understanding with the Cabrals', a phrase to which Queen Victoria objected.[39] According to Charles Greville, 'Our Court continues to take the same interest in the Lisbon Coburgs and would willingly interfere in their favour with more vigour if the Ministers would consent to do so.'[40]

Britain's support was eventually given to the defence of the monarchy and the constitution but, although this was intended to be a stabilizing influence, it became increasingly problematic as the queen found herself caricatured as a puppet of the British. This intensified after the British naval blockade of Porto in 1847 helped to bring a swift end to the Septembrist Junta and the war of the *patuleia*. From being part of a solution, the royal family with its British family connections increasingly became part of the problem, and by the end of her reign D. Maria was faced by a rising tide of republican sentiment.

D. Maria II and D. Fernando survived the political turmoil, while her grandson and great-grandson did not and brought the monarchy crashing down. The historian Vasco Pulido Valente offers a sort of explanation:

> D. Miguel having been defeated, no one in the new regime seriously disputed the dynastic rights of D. Maria and her sons. During difficult periods there were certain discussions about an eventual abdication of the Queen and a regency (during the minority of the prince D. Pedro) of Palmela, the infanta Isabel Maria, the Duke of Loulé [who was married to D. Maria's aunt Ana] and even of Saldanha. But these never passed beyond frivolous speculations that no responsible person took seriously. If the Queen was not able to resist the national chaos, no regent would resist it for her . . . But if the dynasty was secure, the institutions existed in a vacuum. The monarchs of the 'old regime' had on their side tradition, the Church, the titled nobility, the provincial *fidalgos* and a vast magistrature that owed its existence to the Crown. Liberalism broke with tradition expropriated and antagonized the Church and the titled nobility, reduced the incomes, privileges and influence of the provincial *fidalgos* . . . and swept from the stage the magistrature. What remained? A middle class dispersed and weak, except in Lisbon and Porto, and an urban plebs that had been brought to the surface by the war under the designation of 'national battalions' and which later were partially organized into a National Guard.[41]

Yet during this period changes of huge long-term significance were legislated and the queen and her consort were clearly identified with modernization of the economy, the education system and the country's infrastructure. The queen herself was accorded the epithet of 'A Educadora' (the Educator).

D. Maria: the end

Maria had in many ways resembled her mother. She was blonde and handsome in a Germanic way. Like her mother she had no difficulty in becoming pregnant and her reign of nearly twenty years saw eleven pregnancies. She gradually put on weight and lost her girlish appearance. Like her mother she was to die in childbirth, having rejected the advice of her doctors not to venture on another pregnancy. 'If I die, I will die at my post,' she is alleged to have said.[42] She passed away on 15 November 1853, aged 34.

Although D. Maria often appeared to be blown off course by the violent political storms of the 1830s and '40s, she was a determined woman who saw it as her duty to try to make the Charter, which she had inherited from her father, work. She had to endure a great deal of abuse from a hostile radical press in the capital but was fortunate that none of the leading politicians of the day embraced republicanism. The French historian Labourdette commented that by the time of her death she was 'unanimously respected for her qualities as wife and mother, for her sense of duty and for her dignity as a queen'.[43] The Portuguese writer Vicente de Bragança Cunha commented that she had 'undergone twenty years of unparalleled humiliation at the hands of her politicians, whose unchivalrous treatment must have sunk deep into the heart of that woman'.[44]

D. Fernando

D. Fernando, who arrived to marry D. Maria II at the age of just nineteen, came to play a part in Portugal remarkably similar to the part played by his cousin Prince Albert in Britain. In many ways the two cousins were very similar, from their tall and handsome physique and their undoubted prowess in the marriage bed to their meticulous care over the education of their children and their active patronage of the arts and sciences. D. Fernando had stood by his wife throughout her turbulent reign and had helped and guided her in the succession of political crises that threatened the constitutional monarchy. In this his role was similar to that of Albert towards Victoria. There were differences. Fernando lived to provide support and advice for his two sons as well as his wife. He was given the title of King and eventually accepted the appointment as commander-in-chief of the army, which embroiled him deeply in the political affairs of Portugal, whereas Prince Albert, denied the royal title, wisely turned down the duke of Wellington's suggestion that he should succeed him in command of the British army. D. Fernando also long outlived his cousin. Albert's life was tragically cut short in 1861 (the same year as D. Pedro v and his brothers in Portugal, and possibly from the same cause, typhoid fever). D. Fernando lived on, dying in 1885 at the age of 68.

D. João v will always be associated with the building of Mafra, as will D. Maria I and her husband with the palace of Queluz. D. Fernando, the German king of Portugal, also built a palace that reflected his personality, his Germanic inheritance and the age in which he lived. In 1838 D. Fernando purchased land in Sintra that contained the ruins of an old monastery. The Pena palace was begun in 1844 when Portugal

William Ross,
Ferdinand II,
King Consort
of Portugal, 1852,
watercolour on
ivory laid on card.

had enjoyed a few years of relative stability under the autocratic government of Costa Cabral, and when the political disintegration and chaos of the late 1840s was yet to come. With the country economically weak, politically divided and falling far behind the development of the rest of western Europe, building an exotic palace seems an extraordinarily frivolous and pointless waste of the nation's limited resources. But such is and ever was the nature of monarchy. The architect was Baron von Eschwege, who had been one of the informants who contributed to Barreto Feio's *Aventures scandaleuses*. The building was a potpourri of styles, bringing together the Gothic, Manueline and Moorish traditions in Portuguese architecture and adding Germanic elements. The result looked unmistakably like one of the romantic castles along the Rhine and the palace was surrounded by a park planted with exotic trees.[45]

D. Fernando was an early enthusiast for preserving the Manueline architecture of sixteenth-century Portugal. He was a talented artist and musician and tried to promote the arts and sciences in many different ways, being involved in the foundation of the National Theatre. His cousin, Ernst, commented after a visit in 1839, 'Lisbon may thank Ferdinand for two things of the greatest importance. Firstly, the cleaning of the City and the improvement of the police. Secondly the improvement and support of agriculture.'[46] In 1866 the Danish writer Hans Christian Andersen described being introduced to D. Fernando in his town house in Lisbon:

Pena National Palace, 2010.

Halberdiers in old-fashioned uniforms, not unlike the Papal guards in the Vatican so far as costume is concerned, lined the main stair-case. A court attendant conducted me to an upper part of the castle, where I was received . . . in a vast room hung with pictures, and decorated with weapons and armour, including a knight on horseback. King Fernando, a tall good-looking man, greeted me kindly, talked of my writings and my visit to Portugal and . . . took me round the beautiful gardens himself . . . Thanks to the King's care and good taste the whole of the neglected and overgrown park had been turned into a fresh and delightful garden with lawns, flowers and great glasshouses where rare tropical plants now grew. When we parted the King shook me by the hand and said, 'I shall not say farewell, we shall meet again.' There was something so pleasant, albeit regal, in his manner, which made this audience very precious to me and unforgettable.[47]

On D. Maria's death D. Fernando acted as regent for two years until D. Pedro v 'came of age'. It was his long experience of managing politics during a very difficult period of Portugal's history that resulted in his being offered the throne first of Greece and then of Spain, following the crisis of 1869. However, D. Fernando had no desire to lie on any fresh bed of nails and in his middle years was determined to enjoy his cultural pursuits, his romantic palace and his relationship with an opera singer, Elise Hensler, which began soon after his son's death. At first he had no intention of marrying her but, after his relationship became public and he was rebuked by the Papal Nuncio, he married Elise. She was given a Saxe-Coburg title as Countess of Edla. On D. Fernando's death in 1885, she inherited the Pena Palace where she and her husband had also built an elegant Gothicized Swiss chalet. She died in 1929.

D. Pedro V

D. Pedro, the eldest son of D. Maria and D. Fernando, was born on 16 September 1837 and lived the first ten years of his life surrounded by unprecedented political turmoil and civil war. As with his predecessor, the infante José, whole sectors of the country came to pin their hopes on the young prince who, it was believed, would usher in a more stable, if not exactly a golden, age. When his mother died he was only sixteen and for the next two years his father, D. Fernando, acted as regent. Portugal found itself in the unique position of having two kings.

In marked contrast to earlier Braganza princes who had received only a sketchy formal education, D. Pedro's education was meticulously planned by his German tutor and included a tour of Portugal, which took place between April and June 1852, when he was fourteen. This is notable as there is little record of any previous member of his family trying to become acquainted with the country over which they ruled.[48] He also made two visits abroad, one in 1854 when he was already king but still a minor. He spent a month in England and then visited the Netherlands, Belgium, Germany and Austria. Afterwards he wrote a long account of his travels, which was eventually published long after his death. He was the first Braganza to leave any literary memorial.[49]

D. Pedro was intellectually precocious and allegedly already spoke French, German and Portuguese before he was two. He took readily to study but, as is common with intellectually gifted young men, this

Pedro v of Portugal by William Corden, *c.* 1854, oil.

was at the expense of social development. D. Pedro had few companions apart from his family and despised frivolous occupations. He openly expressed disapproval of his brother Luís's way of life and was also critical of his father. He became increasingly puritanical in his tastes and, in his letters, sounds the most appalling prig. In April 1857 he wrote in a letter, 'I lead the life of a hermit with my books – the best and most loyal friends in the whole country; my father amuses himself in a manner which I cannot approve nor imitate because it is so opposed to my principles.'[50] He showed no interest in women or in the social life of the court. In order to avoid the company of women he would on occasion leave the family at Sintra and take solitary refuge at Mafra.

Queen Victoria wanted to arrange a marriage between D. Pedro and Princess Charlotte. In a letter to the king of the Belgians in 1856, she wrote enthusiastically that, 'Pedro is full of resource – fond of music, fond of drawing, of languages, of natural history, and literature in all of which Charlotte would suit him and would be a real benefit to the country'.[51]

On his travels in Europe D. Pedro had met a young German princess, Stephanie von Hohenzollern-Sigmaringen, and she became for him an idealized female figure. He wrote about her in terms that leave little doubt that he had placed her on a pedestal as an ideal of womanhood, 'who understands how to subordinate the material side of the relations between man and woman to the sublime and Christian principle of companionship in marriage'.[52] Eventually a marriage was arranged and was celebrated in Lisbon on 18 May 1858. Prince Albert approved the choice of a 'princess who was a Catholic but coming from a family that was Protestant and liberal and with blood completely new and not corrupted with mixtures of Bourbon or Habsburg'.[53] However, it seems that, before Queen Stephanie's tragic death from diphtheria only fourteen months after the wedding, the couple had not had any sexual relations.[54] It is not difficult to see evidence that D. Pedro may have been a repressed homosexual.

Yet to the outside world D. Pedro appeared as a kind of ideal prince, exceptionally handsome, intellectually gifted, sober in his habits – apparently the perfect type of sovereign to nurse Portugal out of its twenty years of turmoil and civil war. He had the impressive example of his uncle, Emperor D. Pedro in Brazil, and he may have deliberately tried to adopt a similar style of kingship. From the moment he came of age in 1855 he was determined to be a conscientious monarch who would be closely in touch with the work of his government and read all the papers given to him to sign. One by one the practices of the old absolute monarchy that had survived the constitutional revolution were altered or discontinued. The *beija mão* was discontinued – D. Fernando was the last monarch to expect to have his hand kissed – and the old custom of petitioning the king in person at any time that the petitioner met him, a custom still observed by D. João VI, was replaced by two boxes being placed outside the Necessidades palace (the so-called *caixas verdes*), one for requests for alms and the other for other matters, including complaints against ministers or officials. D. Pedro showed he was no cipher when in 1856 he refused to create new peers in order for the government to get its legislative programme through. On the other hand, he was a keen supporter of the ambitious project to build railways and the administrative changes that led to the creation of an office of statistics, the publication of colonial government bulletins and the first steps towards the abolition of slavery in the colonies. Although D. Pedro was deeply interested in the plans to modernize the country over which he reigned, he did not have a happy relationship with the leading politicians who were trying to implement this policy. Almost without exception he held a low opinion of the political leaders and came to believe that they were all 'corrupt, inefficient and immoral'.[55]

D. Pedro had been warned by his father and by his cousin Prince Albert that his position as king meant that he reigned but did not rule. However, it is clear from his writings that he never fully accepted this role and believed that he had a duty to take an active part in the reform

Leopold Wiener (1823–1891), bronze medal for the marriage of Pedro V, king of Portugal, and Stephanie, queen of Portugal, 1858.

of the country, even if this meant just the writing of lengthy memoranda to ministers on key topics under discussion. D. Pedro maintained a regular correspondence with Prince Albert, whom he referred to as 'uncle' and whose advice he sought. Some of these letters are extremely long and set out in detail the king's thoughts and the details of political events in the country. D. Pedro had first met Albert in London in 1854. They immediately found they shared many political, social and intellectual opinions and D. Pedro became dependent on Albert's advice and approval. Their correspondence continued until D. Pedro's sudden death in 1861.

In general Pedro's short reign was a prosperous one for Portugal and the king gained high respect for his diligence, hard work and bravery when he refused to leave Lisbon when the capital was in the grip of cholera and yellow fever epidemics in 1856 and 1857. Had he lived, however, it is highly likely that his desire to be proactive in the national affairs would have made his position as a constitutional monarch difficult to sustain and, like his grandfather in not dissimilar circumstances, he would have been driven to abdicate on some point of principle. This at any rate was the opinion of D. Pedro's first biographer, Julio de Vilhena.[56]

However, this showdown never occurred. In the autumn of 1861 the king and two of his brothers, Fernando and Augusto, went to Vila Viçosa to hunt. There they contracted typhoid fever and Fernando died on 6 November. Five days later, on 11 November, D. Pedro died in the Palace of Necessidades where he had been born: he was 24 years old. Prince Augusto eventually recovered.

The shock of Pedro's death, coming so soon after that of his brother, caused Victoria to write a heartfelt letter to the king of the Belgians on 12 November 1861:

My Beloved Uncle, I hardly know *how* to *write*, for my head reels and swims, and my heart is very sore. *What* an awful misfortune is this! How the hand of death seems bent on pursuing that poor, dear family! Once so prosperous. Poor Ferdinand so proud of his children – of his five sons - now the eldest and *most* distinguished, the head of the family, gone, and also another of fifteen, and the youngest *still* ill! The two others at sea, and will land tomorrow in utter ignorance of everything . . . It is an almost incredible event! A terrible calamity for Portugal and a good *real* European loss! Dear

> Pedro was so good, so clever, so distinguished! He was so attached to my beloved Albert, and the characters and tastes suited so well, and he had such confidence in Albert! *All, all gone!* He is happy now, united again to dear Stephanie whose loss he never recovered . . .[57]

Worse was to follow. By a tragic coincidence, Prince Albert died, also of typhoid fever, on 14 December 1861 and the infante João was another victim of typhoid, dying on 27 December 1861.

It was widely believed that the death of D. Pedro and his brothers could not have been a coincidence. There followed a month of rioting and mass hysteria. Rumours of poisoning spread and popular anger was vented indiscriminately on the doctors, personnel of the court and on government ministers. He was the third successive Braganza monarch to have died at a young age, a tale of disaster that seemed destined to destroy the dynasty.

D. Luís

D. Luís lived for exactly 51 years – another relatively short Braganza life. He was born in October 1838, the second son of D. Maria II and D. Fernando. Like his great-grandfather D. João VI, D. Luís was not brought up with any expectation of succeeding to the throne. However, as he was only a year younger than D. Pedro, he came to share much of his brother's early life. They had the same tutors, moved together between the palaces of Mafra, Sintra and Vila Viçosa, and travelled together in Portugal and abroad between 1852 and 1854. They were the first Braganza princes to have visited countries outside Portugal or Brazil and they met the leading political figures in Europe at the time. Between 1851 (when he was thirteen years old) and the year of his accession in 1861 D. Luís served as a naval officer, rising to the rank of captain. This gave him considerable professional experience, which no previous Braganza monarch had had, and accounts for the close interest that he showed in scientific and technical matters during his reign.[58] His brother, however, was somewhat sceptical and maintained that D. Luís should have tried to get experience of active service in the British navy.

D. Luís was at sea when his brother died on 11 November and only heard the news when his ship reached Lisbon. On hearing of D. Pedro's death, he is alleged to have said, 'I have lost my brother and with him my liberty'.[59]

When D. Luís succeeded his brother as king, his father D. Fernando was still very much alive, so Portugal once again had two kings. His father lived until 1885 and remained an important influence in D. Luís's life almost to the end. D. Luís, in fact, survived his father by less than four years.

When he became king, D. Luís was 23 years old and unmarried. A priority for the king, as so often in the past, was to find a wife and produce an heir. Unlike some of his predecessors, he quickly found a suitable royal bride in Maria Pia, daughter of Victor Emanuel, newly crowned King of Italy. At fifteen years old, she was nine years his junior. The marriage was solemnized in Lisbon on 6 October 1862 and their first child, Carlos, was born less than a year later – a birth of more than usual significance as D. Miguel, in exile, still threatened to reclaim the Braganza throne if D. Luís, like his brother, should die without an heir.

Queen Maria Pia made a considerable impact in Portugal. She was a courageous woman of striking appearance and was prominent in patronizing many charitable causes. This to some extent ameliorated her reputation for adopting an extravagant life style. The historian Francis Gribble rather wickedly said of her that she 'cared little for any of the arts, save that of living magnificently and reigning proudly and devoutly . . . She longed with an equal longing for more monks and more foot-men.'[60] It was unfortunate for her reputation that she is alleged to have

D. Luís I,
19th century.

said on one occasion that 'those that want queens should pay'. By the 1870s the queen's extravagance had built into a level of debt she could no longer sustain – grist to the republican mill that was by then busy grinding away at loyalty to the monarchy.

As Portugal went through difficult times economically, the royal family became progressively out of touch with the realities of the country where they reigned. Maria Pia's extravagance was only part of the problem. After the first close and successful years of marriage, the couple became increasingly estranged and D. Luís returned to the promiscuous ways he had learnt in the navy and perhaps inherited from his grandfather. He had at least one illegitimate son, Pedro Luís António, whom he recognized in a will written in 1869. The royal marriage moved from a fairly commonplace situation of a husband having affairs and a wife suffering more or less in silence at home, to one much more scandalous that rapidly undermined public respect for the monarchy as a whole. While D. Luís took up with an actress from the Lisbon theatre called Rosa Damasceno, Maria Pia in 1887 (at the age of forty) began an affair with a lover called Rosa. The scandal grew. D. Luís threatened to abdicate, the queen declared she would separate and remove to Italy. Eventually Rosa was excluded from the court. Maria Pia reacted hysterically, refusing to eat. However, the couple did not separate and the reason was probably that in 1887 D. Luís began to show signs of the illness that would kill him two years later. In the event Maria Pia was at his bedside at the last.[61]

The king and queen travelled abroad in 1866 and planned another journey in 1867. It is said that D. Fernando intervened at this stage to persuade his son to abandon the idea of being absent at such a difficult time.[62] In all D. Luís made four journeys abroad. Aided by the new network of railways that connected European cities, he visited the major European capitals, met the reigning monarchs and acted very successfully as an unofficial ambassador for Portugal. Travelling abroad was a way that monarchs, whose powers were limited by their countries' constitutions, could exert significant influence. D. Luís's mother and grandfather had also travelled extensively, particularly to England and France, but these were the travels of exiles not of reigning monarchs.

Unlike Maria Pia, who was statuesque and dignified, D. Luís, like his great grandfather D. João VI, did not cut a very regal figure. Gribble describes him rather unkindly:

He developed with the years, into a blonde and podgy little man, who looked rather odd in the Admiral's uniform which he always wore – a comic opera Admiral, one would have said, if one did not know, rather than an actual mariner of the House of Henry the Navigator.[63]

In one respect, however, he resembled closely his Braganza ancestors. His mother had made sure that he was carefully educated in music and he became an accomplished cellist and also played the piano. In the palace he held musical soirées in which he would play alongside professional musicians, occasions which sometimes involved his father, D. Fernando, the other king, who had a good singing voice.[64] Like the first Braganza King D. João IV and his grandfather D. Pedro IV, he also composed.

Perhaps more remarkable was D. Luís's literary work. He found time to devote to the lengthy and time-consuming work of translating and during his life he published translations into Portuguese of *Hamlet*, *The Merchant of Venice*, *Othello* and *Richard III*, sometimes in limited editions and sometimes with dedications to charities. These translations were all republished in 1956. He also translated works from the French.

D. Luís also spent much money and effort on building up collections ranging from clocks to swords and coins. This kind of dilletantism in part reflected his education and in part the similar cultural dilletantism of his father, but arose also from the frustrations of being a largely powerless constitutional monarch.

As the nature of the Braganza monarchy changed from the absolutism of the eighteenth century, where the king dispensed justice and mercy, appointed his ministers and decreed new laws, to the constitutional monarchy where, to use the current phrase, the king reigned but did not rule, so the ceremonial and etiquette of old Braganza gradually fell into decay. The *beija mão* had been discontinued in the previous reign and although the Corpus Christi processions continued, they were a shadow of what they had once been. In 1866 the Danish writer Hans Christian Andersen witnessed D. Luís leading the procession. It was a sad occasion:

the proceedings were spoilt by heavy rain. The Queen did not take part in the ceremonies, only the King appeared. The procession started to come out of the church but immediately was brought

F. Machado,
Maria Pia, 1871,
oil on canvas.

to a standstill by a cloudburst. When it cleared a little the cortege started again, the clergy at the head. Then St George himself on horseback, a great wooden figure in armour with a spear in his hand, which wobbled backwards and forwards with the movement of the horse . . . After these came the Host, borne under a handsome canopy. The King himself was one of the foremost bearers. He was a young, good-looking man, very fair, with a particularly gentle expression. He was in velvet and silk. It began to pour with rain again before the whole procession was out of the church. I had a place on the balcony of a house near the church. The cortege had just got there and now turned round and went back inside, leaving only the clergy and St George with his attendants and page to continue their progress through the streets where, because of the bad weather, there were very few people.[65]

A constitutional monarch

When Bragança Cunha published his epitaph on the Braganza monarchy in 1911, he said of D. Luís that he was 'a king who possessed, in an eminent degree, all the virtues of the best Constitutional monarchs'.[66] Certainly he tried his best to abide by and defend the Constitution that had been reconfigured during the reign of his brother and tried not to interfere in political decisions as his brother had done. Although he became a close friend of Fontes Pereira de Melo, who gave his name to the progressive, development policies of the mid-century that historians still refer to as 'Fontismo', he tried to distance himself from the political parties and was firm in refusing to accept proposals that he considered contravened the Constitution.

His reign began with disorders in the capital and in the north of Portugal that were very reminiscent of the events of the 1840s, but the king took a firm approach and had the good fortune for the disorders rapidly to die down.

Towards the end of the 1860s he faced some difficult situations that he handled with some skill and success. A crisis for the monarchy of an unusual nature was averted in 1869. Following a revolution in Spain, approaches were made to both Portugal's kings, D. Fernando and D. Luís, to take the Spanish throne. Behind these proposals was a pan-Iberian movement that had the clear intention of uniting the two Iberian nations, following the example of Victor Emanuel in uniting Italy. Both Ferdinand and his son rejected these approaches, very conscious of the history of Portugal and the role of the Braganzas in establishing Portugal's independence. D. Luís is supposed to have said, 'that he meant to die as he lived – a Portuguese'.[67] The proposals finally died when D. Fernando married his mistress, Elise Hensler, which was considered to have disqualified him from further regal appointments.

In May 1870 the duke of Saldanha, at the grand age of eighty, tried to stage one last coup backed by the army. Artillery surrounded the palace, which was defended by loyal units. D. Luís defused the situation by calling on the octogenarian to head a ministry. But this final splutter of the civil wars of the 1830s and '40s was strongly opposed by most of the political class and by the queen, who made clear her hostility to the duke, telling him she would have had him shot if she had had the power to do so. Saldanha departed in August and went as ambassador to London, where he died in 1876 at the age of 86. With him also died away the last faint echoes of the age of Pombal, who had been his grandfather.

D. Luís had skilfully navigated these difficulties and continued to preside over the *rotativismo*, which saw political factions rotate in office. However, by the 1880s there were unmistakable signs that the relative stability that Portugal enjoyed during his reign was coming to an end. The Republican Party, established in 1870, had been the inspiration behind the national celebrations in 1880 that marked the three hundredth anniversary of the death of Luís de Camões. The government was also having to deal with a rapidly evolving situation in Africa. Urged on by the Lisbon Geographical Society, which had been founded in 1876 as a pressure group advocating a 'forward' policy in Africa, the Portuguese government now began to advance extensive claims to African territory. These culminated in the publication of the famous 'Rose Coloured Map', by which Portugal claimed a swathe of territory linking its coastal settlements in Angola and Mozambique. Not since the partition treaties with Castile in the sixteenth century had Portugal aspired to exert such influence on European and world affairs. Events in Africa made Portugal a significant player in the international diplomacy of the 1880s, but it was playing in a league beyond its resources to maintain for long and neither D. Luís nor his ministers saw the rocks ahead on which the monarchy was eventually to be shipwrecked.

D. Fernando died in 1885 and D. Luís, overtaken by the rapid deterioration of his own health, followed him on 19 October 1889. He was aged only 51.

The Failure of Constitutional Portugal

It is easy to see in the 55 years between the accession of D. Maria II in 1834 and the death of D. Luís in 1889 the long drawn-out failure of liberalism, a period punctuated by civil conflict, *coups d'état*, ever-rising debt and financial instability, which left Portugal weak and vulnerable in a Europe dominated by states that were increasingly industrialized and militarized. It is true that the largely liberal consensus of the ruling elites was unable to resolve the fundamental problems that left Portugal poor and underdeveloped relative to most of the rest of Europe, but there were considerable achievements along the way.

Among these should be included the abolition of the slave trade and of slavery in the colonies (though in both cases they continued in the form of contract labour). The abolition of capital punishment and universal suffrage for men were enacted in Portugal before they were in Britain. The abolition of the religious orders, the closure of most convents and monasteries, the sale of Crown lands and the abolition of entails and feudal burdens on land meant that Portugal took giant steps towards an economy based on capital investment and market forces. Significant investment took place in railways and urban infrastructure, while the cultural activity of the country was strengthened with the foundation of theatres, academies and institutes of all kinds. In all these developments the royal family took an active part and Portugal was in many ways fortunate in having, in D. Fernando, D. Pedro and D. Luís, monarchs who were educated and cultured.

However, none of these achievements seemed to provide remedies for the deep-seated sense of crisis in national identity and the perception of national decline off which the Republican movement was able to feed. The expansion in Africa and the acquisition of the colonies of Mozambique and Angola, far from providing a unifying sense of national pride, deepened the feelings of national inadequacy as Portugal struggled to finance, control and administer these vast acquisitions and was shown to be weak and ineffective in comparison with the aggressive colonial powers of France, Britain and Germany. In the end there was little that the Braganza monarchs, well-meaning though they may have been, could do to stem the tide of national failure, which saw tens of thousands of emigrants abandoning Portugal and sailing to seek a better life in Brazil or the United States.

Carlos and D. Luís Filipe Hunting at Vila Viçosa by Amadeu Ferrari, before 1908.

12

The Twilight of the Gods: D. Carlos and D. Manuel

The birth of D. Carlos on 28 September 1863 seemed to offer some hope for the continuation of the Braganza dynasty after the disasters that had overtaken the family between 1859 and 1861, when first the queen and then the king and two of his brothers had died, all in their prime of life.

D. Carlos, the Diplomat[1]

D. Carlos was carefully educated alongside his younger brother Afonso. Like his uncle, D. Pedro v, he went on a European tour and, when only twenty, acted as regent when D. Luís, his father, travelled abroad. D. Carlos was a gifted linguist and spoke Italian, French, German and English fluently. He and his younger brother Afonso were also very athletic. D. Carlos was an excellent shot, allegedly being able to shatter a plate thrown into the air and then to hit some of the pieces as they fell, and both young men, like previous princes of their house, took part in bullfights. Apparently, on one occasion, taunted by a lady of the court who observed that the bulls all had their horns covered, D. Carlos jumped into the bullring and made a number of passes with a bull whose horns were uncovered. He later recalled that 'no prince has ever run faster than I did during that prank'.[2]

His immaturity, however, nearly led him into trouble when in 1884 his name was associated with a conspiracy that was concocted in some of the cavalry regiments to place him on the throne in place of his father. He was sent to spend time away from the capital in Vila Viçosa, where he indulged in the traditional Braganza pursuit of hunting.[3] D. Carlos became fascinated by the people and landscape of the Alentejo. He interested himself in the agricultural potential of the country and in 1885 he helped promote a national agricultural exhibition.

D. Carlos was a highly gifted painter and his work was exhibited and won medals not only in Portugal but in Paris. He painted in both watercolour and oil and his subject matter was usually the nature, life and landscape of the Alentejo region. A selection of his work can be seen in the ducal palace of Vila Viçosa. It is alleged that the sculptor Rodin said of him, 'if he had not been king, he would have been a great painter', a compliment that is perhaps slightly two-edged.[4]

D. Carlos, limited in his governing role, used the prestige of the Crown to sponsor scientific work, particularly in the realm of ocean-ography and ornithology. The king's interest in birds began with his prowess in shooting them, but soon took a scientific turn. At the age of 24 he wrote a book on the ornithology of Portugal, which he revised over the next ten years and eventually published in 1893 under the title *Catálogo illustrado das aves de Portugal*. In 1896 he began his scientific investigations into marine life off the coast of Portugal, an interest that he linked to the need to help the fishing industry. He made the royal yacht available for scientific expeditions and in 1899 published *Resultados das investigações scientificas feitas a bordo do yacht 'Amélia' . . . em 1898*. Further publications covered subsequent expeditions undertaken up to 1903. D. Carlos was not content with purely scientific work but sponsored public exhibitions and the foundation of the Sociedade Portuguesa de Ciências Naturais (Portuguese Society for the Natural Sciences). The first meeting was held in 1907 and plans were laid for the creation of a marine biology station. In all his scientific work the king used his ducal title, calling himself D. Carlos de Bragança.[5]

D. Carlos's marriage

As he came of age, the marriage of the infante Carlos became a matter of political as well as dynastic importance. Various attempts were made to find a bride among the most prestigious royal houses, but by the 1880s marrying into the Portuguese royal dynasty did not appear particularly attractive to European princesses. In the end D. Luís and Queen Maria Pia had to settle for a princess from the deposed French royal house of Orléans, which must have been considered decidedly second best as a marriage for their son.

Marie Amélie was the daughter of the Comte de Paris. She had been born in 1865 in London, where her family lived in exile, but at the age of six had returned with her father to France where the family lived at the Château d'Eu. She was brought up in very restricted aristocratic circles and when she was twenty travelled to Vienna, where she met Emperor Franz Joseph. The life of a deposed family, which still tried to maintain some pretensions to royalty, was particularly empty and futile. However, although the Orléans family never regained the French throne, they did marry into other royal families, notably with the marriage of the Comte d'Eu to Isabel, the heiress to the Imperial throne in Brazil. In this way they remained part of the network of monarchical families.

D. Carlos and Marie Amélie were married on 22 May 1886. The marriage soon produced two princes, Luís Filipe (born 21 March 1887) and Manuel (born 15 November 1889). Marie Amélie became an important personality in the dying days of the Portuguese monarchy and her

The duke and duchess of Braganza, Crown Prince and Princess of Portugal, with their infant son D. Luís Filipe, 1888.

Marie Amélie, 1900s.

image was romantically portrayed in Lucien Corpechot's *Souvenirs sur la Reine Amélie de Portugal*, published 1914 and in English translation in 1915. This memoir, written by a French journalist while its subject was still very much alive, reads almost like a work of fiction that bathes the last days of the Portuguese monarchy in a soft glow of regret. The queen is portrayed as a woman whose courage was tested in many dramatic ways. Corpechot recounts stories of her rescuing the infant Luís Filipe from a cradle that had somehow caught fire, and plunging into the sea to help save a fisherman who had got himself into trouble. Less dramatic were her visits to hospitals during typhoid fever and smallpox epidemics in Lisbon. She became the active patron of numerous charitable institutions that Corpechot lists. A record of these gives a good impression of the way the royal family, deprived of real political power, tried to use its prestige to support projects to improve social care, a tradition that links back to Queen Leonor and the foundation of the Misericórdias. Corpechot's list includes the Children's Hospital at Rego; paying for free meals for the unemployed at the Refuge for Vagrants; the Great Royal Dispensary at Alcântara, which ministered to children, providing free meals and inoculation against smallpox; the Royal Bacteriological Institute; the National Society for the Relief of the Tuberculous; the Institute for Helping the Shipwrecked; and the Institut d'Outre-Mer to provide relief for the families of those who had served in the colonies.[6]

Yet, in spite of these royal projects, and Queen Amélie's readiness to mix with ordinary people (she apparently played tennis in the public parks), she became increasingly unpopular, the target for Republican accusations of extravagance and, Corpechot hints, jealousies and intrigues within her own household. He hints that the problem may have rested with the close female friendships that she cultivated. The Portuguese historian Filipe Ribeiro de Meneses attributed her unpopularity to 'religiosity and support for the Jesuit Order' and then, rather bizarrely, adds that her 'uncommon height did not help matters; around 1.8 metres [6 feet] tall, she towered over contemporaries'.[7]

The rising tide of political crises

Less than two months after becoming king, D. Carlos had to face the first of a succession of political crises that destabilized the country and called into question the whole future of the monarchy.

On 11 January 1890 Great Britain sent an ultimatum to Portugal threatening war if Portuguese forces did not halt their advances in Africa. The origins of this crisis went back at least fifteen years when, in 1875, an international arbitration, the MacMahon Award, gave possession of Delagoa Bay in southern Africa to Portugal. From that date Britain and Portugal became involved in prolonged negotiations over the building of a railway from Delagoa Bay to the Transvaal mines, over navigation on the Zambesi and ultimately over where the frontiers between their spheres of influence lay. In 1876 the Lisbon Geographical Society had been founded as a pressure group advocating a forward policy, seeing economic opportunities in Africa that would help lift Portugal from its chronic economic backwardness and financial straits. Spurred on and supported by the Society, Portuguese explorers crossed and recrossed the central African interior and large territorial and mining concessions were made to would-be entrepreneurs. In 1886 Portugal published the famous 'Rose Coloured Map', establishing its claim to a band of territory that stretched from Angola on the west coast to Mozambique on the east. Treaties were signed with France and Germany, and Portugal pushed ahead with measures to secure the effective occupation of the territory outlined in the map.

The British ultimatum was seen in Portugal as an outrageous display of force by an old ally with whom Portugal had been carrying on peaceful negotiations ever since the 1875 award. When the Portuguese government inevitably submitted to Britain's demands, public anger exploded, forcing the ministers to resign. The administration that took over tried to reach a settlement with Britain but its efforts were defeated in the Portuguese parliament and it too resigned. D. Carlos now faced a crisis where none of the leading politicians was able to form a government. After a month in which Portugal was without any government at all, an administration was formed by a retired general. As D. Carlos tried to find a viable political way forward, the Crown itself became the target of public resentment. D. Carlos, related through his grandfather to Queen Victoria, was accused of betraying the country to Britain. In the autumn of 1890 a military revolt occurred in Porto in support of the Republican movement. When the territorial dispute with Britain was finally resolved in August 1891, the broad band of territory outlined in the Rose-Coloured Map had been reduced to the two colonies of Angola and Mozambique, separated by a swathe of British territory. Queen Victoria marked the occasion with the award of the Order of the Garter to D. Carlos. Although intended as a signal honour, this was not well received in Portugal and seemed to point to an element of collusion between the Portuguese king and Britain.[8] Throughout Europe the crisis was seen as one in which not only the future of southern Africa but the future of the monarchy in Portugal was at stake.

The ultimatum was followed by a financial crisis that inexorably led to the partial repudiation of Portugal's foreign debt in 1892. The origins of this go back to the European-wide recession that began after the banking crisis of 1873. Portugal had been badly affected by the economic downturn, as explained by William Clarence Smith:

> Agriculture was faced with a flood of cheap foodstuffs in both foreign markets and the home market, infant industries wavered in the face of cut-throat competition, and the merchant navy was on the point of being swept off the high seas altogether. Public revenues fell, the deficit on the balance of payments grew alarmingly, gold reserves dwindled, and the country could no longer service its foreign debt. By the 1890s bankruptcy loomed . . .

In 1892 Portugal effectively came off the gold standard, let the currency float, unilaterally reduced interest rates and rescheduled repayments for foreign holders of government bonds.[9]

The king tried to respond positively to this burgeoning crisis. While he contributed to the voluntary subscriptions that followed the British ultimatum, he also agreed to give up 20 per cent of his Civil List allocation.[10] To try to restore some sense of normality, the royal family made a tour of the north in 1891 before the official acclamation that marked the beginning of the new reign.

In spite of the ultimatum, D. Carlos firmly believed that Portugal should try to re-establish the closest possible alliance with Britain. He also did his best to strengthen ties with Spain and made a visit to Alfonso XIII in 1892. He went to Britain in 1895, again in 1901 for the funeral of Victoria and the following year for Edward's coronation. In 1904 he visited Britain yet again. In 1903 Edward VII came on an official visit to Portugal, a visit commemorated with the naming of Parque Eduardo VII in Lisbon. There were official visits also by the Kaiser and the president of France. D. Carlos certainly worked hard and with some success to place Portugal on the diplomatic circuit.

The atmosphere of crisis continued through the 1890s with growing unrest in the cities, Republican agitation and unresolved financial issues. The security of Portugal and its African empire remained in doubt. Approaches were made to Portugal to get rid of its empire in return for a financial settlement with Britain and Germany, while these two powers signed a secret treaty in 1898 making provision for the future partition of the Portuguese colonies.

Meanwhile successive Portuguese governments took steps to try to put the empire on a more secure basis. Successful military campaigns in Mozambique led to the whole south of the territory coming securely under Portuguese control, victories which boosted morale back home, while agreements were reached first with the Transvaal Republic and then, during the Boer War, with the occupying British forces that secured a lucrative arrangement for the recruitment of Mozambican labour for the South African mines and for traffic on the Delagoa Bay railway, which had finally opened for business in 1895. Re-exports of colonial produce began to form a major part of Portuguese overseas trade and contributed substantially to the balance of payments. Portugal also benefited from remittances from the growing number of emigrants in

Brazil and the United States, while the coaling station at Porto Grande in the Cape Verde Islands made this one of the most important ports in oceanic commerce. All was not gloom for Portugal, except for the chronic failure to form stable and lasting governments able to find a long-term solution to the country's financial problems.

Rise of Republican sentiment

Calls for a republic had occasionally been heard during the political confusion of D. Maria II's reign, particularly after the 1848 revolution in France had replaced the Orléanist monarchy with a republic. However, these made little impact while the leading political figures, like the dukes of Saldanha and Terceira, were strongly monarchist. However, in 1870 a Republican party was formed with branches in the major Portuguese cities. The deep sense of national decline, which is reflected in the novels of Eça de Queiroz, provided the cultural context in which Republicanism emerged in Portugal. This was seen as essentially a moral decline and was manifested most obviously in Portugal's military and economic weakness. As tens of thousands of Portuguese emigrated to find a new life abroad, Portugal itself seemed once again threatened by a unification of the Iberian peninsula. The message of the Republicans was one of national renewal, 'to replace traditional religious worship with the cult of the nation',[11] and it was a leading Republican, Teófilo Braga, who in 1880 masterminded the national celebrations to mark the three-hundredth anniversary of the death of Luís Vaz de Camões. The grand procession that was designed to mark the homage of the nation to the great poet featured allegorical representations of industry and agriculture, the great discoveries, the African empire and the medieval knights who had won Portugal's independence. The occasion was also marked by the reburial of his bones, together with those of Vasco da Gama, in the Jerónimos monastery at Belém, like the relics of medieval saints. The message of these celebrations was vividly nationalistic and in 1881 the Republicans were successful in getting three deputies elected.

In 1898 national celebrations were organized to mark the four-hundredth anniversary of Vasco da Gama's discovery of the sea route to India. Since the Republican celebrations in 1880 it had been revealed that the bones that were thought to have been those of Vasco da Gama in fact belonged to other members of his family. Now, the central event

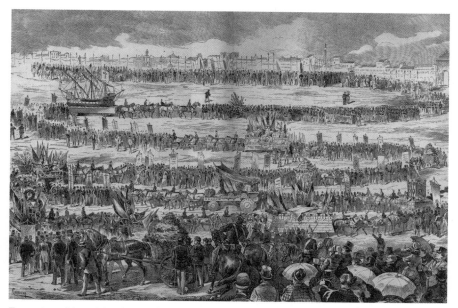

Engraving of the celebrations in Lisbon of the tricentennial of Luís de Camões, 1880.

of the celebrations was to be the transfer of the 'real' body of Vasco da Gama from the family vaults in Vidigueira to be buried alongside Camões in the Jerónimos monastery.[12]

Republicanism was fed by anticlericalism, which once again became focused, as it had been in the 1830s, on the religious orders, which had been allowed to re-establish themselves in Portugal.[13] Republicanism was both anti-monarchical and anti-clerical, attacking in a two-pronged intellectual assault the alliance of the altar and the throne, which was seen as the ideological basis of the monarchy. However, the Republican movement had little support until in 1889 news came of the replacement of Emperor Pedro II in Brazil by a republic, an event that was closely followed by the British ultimatum. George Young later wrote of these events:

> The effect of the ultimatum in weakening the monarchy was combined with a strengthening of the Republican movement by the fall of the Emperor of Brazil, and this from no personal fault or political defeat of the constitutional monarchy, but from a preference for the republican principle . . . The establishment of republicanism in this vastly more prosperous and populous Portuguese community overseas – a community that had no

such cause for complaint against the results of its constitutional monarchy as had the mother country, made Portuguese republicanism at once a practical possibility.[14]

In the elections of 1900 three Republicans were returned by the voters in Porto. D. Carlos now became personally involved in a struggle with Republicanism, which led him inexorably into acting unconstitutionally. Declaring the Porto election null had little effect as a rerun of the vote returned the three Republicans again and D. Carlos had to silence Republican opposition in the Cortes by closing the parliamentary session. In the 1904 local elections Republican candidates won twelve of the districts in Lisbon. The following year there were disturbances in the fleet also linked to Republican sentiment. Portugal was becoming increasingly ungovernable. The Republicans did not campaign on any programme of reform and were certainly not socialists. For them, only a change of regime could save the nation. This was succinctly expressed in 1905 by Basílio Teles: 'With what right do they demand whether the Republican Party has a programme? The Portuguese monarchy is this [programme]: incompetence, lack of shame, oppression.' The Republican programme was simply the 'summary demolition of the regime'.[15] However Republicanism, although well established in the two major cities, had not become a viable national movement. What made it so was the 'dictatorship' of João Franco, which briefly brought together a widespread national coalition in opposition to the Crown.

The failure of constitutional government

By the early twentieth century there was a widespread realization that constitutional government, as it had operated since 1851, was failing. Splits occurred in the two main parties, the Regeneradores and Progressistas, and the king himself was on record as expressing his own sense of the failure:

> I can change nothing in this condition of things, for no responsible Minister and no parliament . . . would lend itself to the measures required to put an end to the scandal. If only I could find an honest man – a patriot who would put the honour and interest of Portugal before his personal interests and those of his

adherents! How gladly and gratefully I would support such a man with all the power at my command! How willingly would I delegate to him all the authority which I have in order that he might introduce the era of reform which I and the Portuguese people equally desire.[16]

As Douglas Wheeler explained, the deep-rooted cause of this political impasse was to be found in 'the cleavage between rural provincial interests and the coastal, commercial middle-class interests; or, to put it in another way, between two Portugals, the rural and the urban, the apolitical and the political; finally the relationship with Spain which, especially in the educated elite, fomented fear, hostility, and conflict.'[17] Or, as Miguel Torga wrote, the 'lack of harmony between the conscience of the country and of the capital'.[18]

Rotativismo had worked after a fashion during the fifty years after 1851. Incoming governments, appointed by the king, had manipulated elections to give themselves a majority. Between 1834 and 1910 there had been 43 elections and the powers bestowed on the king by the constitution to dismiss the Cortes had been employed thirty times. During D. Luís's reign of 28 years, the parliament had been dissolved eleven times.[19] But this system was now failing as the parties splintered into factions. There was no organized political party that any longer unequivocally supported the constitution or the monarchy, and D. Carlos famously commented that Portugal was now 'a monarchy without monarchists'.[20]

Declining respect for the king

As political instability increased in the early years of the century and the old *rotativismo*, which D. Carlos saw as his duty to try to operate, failed to provide viable administrations, the king's own prestige went into steep decline. It had always been part of Republican propaganda to find fault with the monarchy on a personal level. Scurrilous rumours had circulated about D. Maria II during the height of the disorders in the 1840s and D. Carlos received the same treatment. Although in many respects an intelligent and accomplished man, his private life left him vulnerable, as his frequent affairs became the subject of ribald speculation. The king was unwise enough to pursue his love life rather too publicly in the resorts of Estoril and Cascais and to write love letters

Carlos in Paris, 1905.

and verses to his amours that found their way into the public domain. As the king put on weight, he became almost comically Germanic in appearance, his corpulent figure giving rise to the nickname of the *balão cativo* (captive balloon) 'because he was fat and remained always tied to a place where there were beautiful women'.[21] Queen Amélie suffered in the same way. In January 1908 a novel by António de Albuquerque appeared entitled *O Marquês da Bacalhoa*. 'In this book was put into writing all the rumours that circulated in Lisbon and which completely denigrated the royal family . . . the great scandal of the book lay in the constant insinuations of a lesbian relationship, and above all in explicit scenes of lesbianism.'[22]

The king and João Franco

In 1901 a member of the Regeneradores, João Franco Castelo Branco, broke away from the main body of the party and founded the Regenerador-Liberal movement, which was strongly pro-monarchy and wanted to give the king greater constitutional powers. In May 1906 the government of Ernesto Hintze Ribeiro resigned but instead of calling elections, as would normally have happened according to the traditions of *rotativismo*, D. Carlos called on João Franco to form a government. Franco had already made his position clear. He wanted to broaden the base of political support from the narrow elites who had traditionally formed the Progressistas and Regeneradores. He stated that he wanted to 'hunt in the game reserves of the Republicans'.[23] His was to be a royalist and increasingly authoritarian populism. Throwing the traditions of constitutional monarchy to the winds, D. Carlos gave his support unequivocally to Franco and his mission to transform Portuguese politics and with it the fortunes of the country.

Franco began to carry out major reforms, at first with widespread support in the political community. However, it soon appeared that reform could only be carried out at the expense of rights guaranteed under the constitution. Franco became increasingly dictatorial, controlling the press and eventually issuing a decree exiling those found guilty of political offences. D. Carlos became correspondingly open

DOM CARLOS Ier, ROI DU PORTUGAL
Assassiné le 1er Février 1908

D. Carlos, from a contemporary postcard.

in his support. In April 1907 he dissolved the assembly at the request of Franco, who then carried out a widespread programme of censorship of the press that saw the closure of numerous newspapers and periodicals. This was followed by the dissolution of local government organizations and their replacement by appointed commissions. Opponents were imprisoned without trial. To try to address some of the social issues, the government raised salaries for public servants and instituted pensions. Public works were begun to provide employment.

It was the attempt to settle the debts of the Crown that gave Franco's opponents, and in particular the Republicans, a perfect cause around which to rally public opinion. Franco and D. Carlos came to an agreement whereby the Crown's debts would be cancelled through transferring to the state certain Crown properties, including the Coach Museum and the royal yacht. This was little more than a sleight of hand as the royal yacht had originally been paid for by the taxpayer. Franco then increased the civil list. This was in August 1907 and came after the assembly had been dissolved and Franco was ruling by decree. The complicity of the king with Franco's authoritarian and unconstitutional government seemed to have paid off in the crudest possible way.

Opposition now grew in all directions, not only from the increasingly vocal Republicans but also from the divided and weakened remnants of the two traditional parties. To deflect calls for D. Carlos to abdicate in favour of his son, Luís Filipe was sent on a major tour of the colonies, the first time that a member of the royal family had visited Africa. In November 1907 D. Carlos gave an interview with the French newspaper *Le Temps*, in which he explicitly defended Franco, declaring that 'I am very satisfied with him' and that this new regime had to last for the good of the country.[24] This interview apparently convinced Republicans of the need for an armed insurrection. In January 1908 Franco ordered the temporary closure of the main opposition newspapers. This was followed on 28 January by a failed Republican attempt to seize the Ministry of the Interior, after which 93 Republicans and some other politicians were imprisoned. The government responded with a draconian new law empowering it to exile anyone convicted of crimes against the state 'when the interests of the state demanded it'. D. Carlos, staying at Vila Viçosa for the hunting, signed it into law on 31 January.

The murder of D. Carlos and Luís Filipe

Following the decree of 31 January, a semi-secret organization linked to the Republicans, known as the Carbonária, planned to assassinate Franco. When unable to locate him at his home (it was rumoured that Franco changed where he slept every night) the murderers made their way to the Terreiro do Paço where the king and the royal family were disembarking from the steamer that had carried them across the river after their return from Vila Viçosa. The king and queen were met by the king's uncle, Afonso, and by his younger son, Manuel, who intended to ride with them in an open landau to the Necessidades palace. The queen's biographer, Lucien Corpechot, described the scene:

> As [the queen] stepped on to the quay of Lisbon, flowers were presented to her as she was greeted. The king received the congratulations of the official personages and had a long talk with João Franco. No sinister omen; nothing to give warning that so tragic a moment is about to be born of this present one – so calm, so peaceful, so exactly like moments of the past; the usual actions, after the usual formula, some cheering, some salutes. The king and queen get into the same open carriage.[25]

Without warning, a number of shots were fired, killing the king and wounding the Crown Prince. One of the murderers stepped up onto the coach and the Crown Prince, Luís Filipe, although wounded, drew his own revolver and fired four shots. The queen, armed only with a bouquet of flowers, thrust it into the face of the killer. The second assassin now mounted the step of the coach and fired into the face of Luís Filipe, mortally wounding him. Further shots wounded the infante Manuel. The two who had fired were killed by the police at the scene and the coach was driven rapidly to the Arsenal building in case there were other gunmen lying in wait. With the king and Luís Filipe dead and Manuel wounded, it was Queen Amélie who assumed control of the situation.

The two men who had fired at the royal family were Alfredo Costa, a salesman, and Manuel Buiça, a teacher and skilled marksman known personally by the king, who had presented him with his gun as a prize in a shooting competition. It seems that at least one other unidentified gunman, and possibly as many as three others, made their escape.

The murder of D. Carlos and Luís Filipe, *Le Petit Journal*, 16 February 1908.

The fact that the king had no armed escort when he and the royal family prepared to drive through the crowded streets, in spite of the fact that there had been a failed Republican uprising only days earlier, seems to point, at the very least, to criminal negligence on the part of the authorities.

Lucien Corpechot, in his memoir on the life of Queen Amélie, commented on the night spent by D. Carlos at Vila Viçosa before his return to Lisbon: 'some dark destiny brought Dom Carlos back to the cradle of his race before making him a mark for the bullets of his assassins.'[26] A week after the murders, the king and his son received a state funeral with all the magnificent but antique ceremonial that for centuries had marked the key moments in the lives of the Braganza monarchs. Contemporaries, however, remarked that there was no great concern expressed in Lisbon after the initial shock. Monarchs around the world expressed horror and outrage, but this was not reflected in the reaction inside Portugal. A formal inquiry was set up to discover the details of the plot. After two years it produced a report but this was never published. Subsequent research has acquitted the Republican party of any involvement, although it seems that at least one of its members, Afonso Costa, was implicated as was José de Alpoim, a politician from the Progressistas.[27]

Meanwhile a public subscription had been opened for the families of the murderers and later, once the Republic had been declared, they were treated as national heroes and, according to Aubrey Bell, a notable scholar of Portuguese literature, writing in 1915, 'the procession to their graves has been continued on each anniversary of this cowardly deed.'[28]

D. Manuel II, the Patriot

There were few at the time who doubted that the murder of D. Carlos marked the end of the monarchy. King Edward VII of Great Britain is supposed to have said to the Portuguese ambassador, the marquês de Soveral, 'What a country is this where they kill the king and a prince and the first measure which is taken is to dismiss the ministry? The revolution triumphed, is that not the case?'[29] João Franco had hoped to hold on to power but the day after the murders, he had a most uncomfortable meeting with both Queen Amélie and the dowager queen, Maria Pia, a ghost from a now distant past. She is reported to have said to him, 'Franco, you promised to save the monarchy but you have ended by digging its grave.'[30] He offered his resignation two days later and his ministry was dismissed. The 'dictator', who had so recently been assured of royal favour and the permanence of his regime, fled to Spain. Only a few days before he had decreed exile for opponents of the regime: it was ironic that he himself was the first to be exiled.

The murder of D. Carlos and Luís Filipe might have resulted in a surge of sympathetic support for the royal family, but this did not happen. It seemed that royalty had no bank of credit or loyalty on which to draw. The leading Republicans, taken by surprise by the murders, merely redoubled their attacks. When D. Manuel ventured out of his palace to attend a formal Mass for the dead in the magnificent Jerónimos monastery, he travelled in a closed carriage flanked by cavalry, almost invisible to the crowds who lined the route.[31]

The prolonged death throes of the Braganza monarchy

D. Manuel, who now became king, was the second son of D. Carlos and Queen Amélie. He had been destined for the navy, like his grandfather, and began his training in the Escola Naval in 1907. Like so many of his family he was interested in music and was on record early in life as saying his ambition was to conduct an orchestra.[32] Aged only eighteen at the time of the murders, he was very much under the influence

D. Manuel II in uniform, 1909.

of Queen Amélie and Queen Maria Pia, two foreign dowager queens. Still a teenager feeling his way, he had called on Admiral Francisco Ferreira do Amaral to form a government. The admiral was a very experienced man who had been governor both in India and Angola and was not too closely associated with either of the two historic parties. Immediate steps were taken to try to calm the situation in the country and to undo the political disasters of the previous year. Political prisoners were released, the censorship of the press lifted, the municipal commissions wound up and the increase in the royal civil list cancelled. Elections were held in April, but when it came to counting the votes violence broke out in Lisbon and its suburbs. When the trouble died down fourteen people had been killed and a hundred injured. Extreme Republicans naturally blamed the violence on the king and threatened revenge. The new reign had started badly.

On 6 May, for the last time, a Braganza king was 'acclaimed' with all the ancient ceremonial that had surrounded that event for centuries and, riding in a state coach back to his palace, he was loudly cheered by the crowds.[33] This was followed by a carefully programmed royal progress in the north of the country.[34] Once these formalities were over, the politicians returned to their business and the Republicans launched a series of attacks directed not so much at the youthful D. Manuel himself, but at the old issues, the British ultimatum, the debts of the royal family and the dictatorship of João Franco. The debates continued into the summer to the exclusion of all other business. In an attempt to settle the issue of the royal debt, it was decided that a number of the royal residences would be transferred to the state, which undertook their maintenance: these included Belém, Caxias, Queluz, Sintra, Ajuda and Necessidades. Mafra and Pena, as well as the Ducal Palace of Vila Viçosa, were apparently omitted from this arrangement. It must have seemed absurd to contemporaries that there should have been so many palaces maintained by the king of such a small country. In retrospect, one can see in this transfer a major step towards the dismantling of the monarchy itself.

Briefly the policy of 'calming' seemed to have worked in 1909. *Rotativismo* had been restored and it was 'business as usual' for Progressistas and Regeneradores. However, if it was hoped that this comprehensive settlement of the issue of the royal debt would finally put this vexatious question to sleep, it soon became clear that the Republicans were not seeking reforms or a resolution of individual issues but a change of regime. Between December 1908 and May 1909 four governments rose and fell, and two more by June 1910. The last government of the monarchy took office under Teixeira de Sousa at the end of June 1910. When the new parliamentary session opened in September Manuel read from the throne a wide-ranging government programme of reforms but these were, as Aubrey Bell was later to write,

> Mere words? But it only depended on the opponents of the Government to translate some of them at least into reality. The Government was only too willing . . . [but] the Republicans did not want reform – they wanted a revolution. Had angels from Heaven drawn up a programme of reforms the Republicans would still have cried for a revolution.[35]

The king had, from the beginning, been assiduous in performing public duties, receiving delegations, attending military functions and greeting representatives of foreign countries, receiving heads of state, dining aboard visiting warships and royal yachts, and signing cultural and economic protocols. In November 1909 he made a formal visit to

D. Manuel II on his state visit to England, 1909.

Spain and a more private one to Britain, where he discussed African questions and made tentative overtures for a marriage to a princess of the British royal family.[36] In his absence his uncle Afonso, who had served as viceroy in Goa, acted as regent. D. Manuel also attended the funeral of Edward VII and the coronation of George V. It seems that, young as he was, he made a very favourable impression in a world tense with the strains that were soon to lead to the First World War.

During a visit to Paris in 1909 D. Manuel met the actress Gaby Deslys, famous already for her beauty and her dance routines. The king apparently fell in love and an affair began that was soon all over the European newspapers. In 1910 D. Manuel visited her in Paris and invited her to spend holidays with him in Portugal. The Republican newspapers made much of the affair, asserting that D. Manuel was following in his father's footsteps, wasting the royal civil list on buying jewels for a music hall star. When D. Manuel went into exile he remained in touch with Gaby until his marriage in 1913. It is believed that, probably as a legacy of this affair, D. Manuel became afflicted with syphilis, which prevented him from having children. A passionate relationship between a twenty-year-old man and an actress ten years older than him

Gaby Deslys, *c.* 1910.

would hardly be surprising but for the extraordinary back story that ran through Gaby's life and continued even after her premature death. After she died in 1920, a family from a village in the Olomouc region of what was then Czechoslovakia tried to claim her inheritance. Their story was that their daughter Hedwig had met Gaby Deslys, whom she closely resembled. The two young women swapped identities. While Gaby entered the world of espionage using Hedwig's name, Hedwig assumed Gaby's identity, made a successful stage career and won the heart of the youthful D. Manuel. This extraordinary story, which made D. Manuel the lover of the daughter of a Czech-speaking hotel cleaner, rather than a French courtesan, is a romantic tale that will probably never die.[37]

The Republican coup

The Republicans had briefly been thrown off balance by the assassination but soon resumed their active campaign against the Monarchy. In retrospect, the municipal elections held on 1 November 1908 were of decisive importance. The monarchist parties failed to come together or organize a single list, with the result that in Lisbon there was an overwhelming victory for the Republicans and one of their number, Braamcamp Freire, became president of the Municipal Council, which became a sort of government in waiting. The Republicans were well aware of the role played by disaffected military units in the republican coup in Brazil in 1889, and realized that any plan to overthrow the monarchy depended on gaining support within the army and the navy, and with ensuring as far as possible that there would be no outside intervention. In May 1910 a group of Republicans went to London to make sure that it was understood that any change of regime was a purely internal matter. By October the plans were laid, but had to be brought forward when a leading Republican was assassinated, an event that provided the perfect opportunity.

In spite of all the preparations the coup nearly failed. There was some resistance from loyal troops, which apparently led the leading Republican naval officer, Admiral Candido dos Reis, to commit suicide fearing that the coup had failed. There was some confused fighting in the Lisbon streets but most of the army units stood by and maintained a kind of neutrality. Decisive action came from popular elements on the street and from the Carbonária secret organizations. On 5 October two warships began firing on the Necessidades palace and D. Manuel agreed to move to Mafra with the two queens. From there he boarded the royal yacht, which his uncle had brought to the coastal town of Ericeira. D. Manuel apparently wanted to sail to Porto and rally support in the north of Portugal, which was believed to be strongly royalist, but once at sea an impromptu royal council advised leaving Portuguese waters and sailing to Gibraltar.

Douglas Wheeler, who made a detailed study of the Revolution, pointed out that the Republicans had repeatedly failed with their attempts to overthrow the monarchy by force. Attempts at revolution in 1891, 1896, 1906, 1908 and early 1910 had all been snuffed out. In October 1910 'the Republican leadership and their allies took advantage of a favourable movement of public opinion, the unwillingness of the army to defend the monarchy and a discredited government'.[38] The idea of a change of regime was widely supported and the Republic was declared throughout Portugal with little opposition. For many people, the declaration of the Republic was thought to be a solution, in itself, to national decline and all the ills confronting the country – a sort of Republican version of 'Sebastianism'. The Republic found its main support among the middle classes, including even liberal monarchists, fearful of the rise of street violence and the threats to order and property. Earlier popular revolutions in Portugal had brought about regime change and overthrown governments – in 1820, 1836 and 1846–7 – but on these occasions the monarchy, although threatened, had had powerful defenders. In 1910 there was no figure comparable to the dukes of Terceira and Saldanha to defend D. Manuel's throne, and it largely fell by default.

D. Manuel II's namesake D. Manuel I had been called 'the Fortunate'. It was suggested that D. Manuel II might appropriately be called 'Manuel, the Unfortunate'.

Epitaph

It is tempting to attribute the fall of the monarchy to failings in the monarchs themselves. The disasters that overtook the royal family from the death of D. João VI in 1826 seemed to indicate some fatal flaw in the dynasty's political as well as physical DNA: D. Pedro IV dying at the age of 36, his daughter D. Maria II at 34, D. Pedro V and his brothers dying in 1861, all in their twenties, the murders of D. Carlos and his son and the final accession of the last king Manuel at the age of eighteen, who was forced into exile and who never had children. The physical death of the ruling house of Braganza was stalked by its failure to breathe life into the institutions of constitutional monarchy.

Most commentators at the time and since have found D. Carlos's espousal of the 'dictatorship' of João Franco to be the final mistake that fatally holed the ship of monarchy below the waterline. However, the same commentators have agreed that some radical reform of the constitution was needed, a radical reform that could only be carried out by a strong political figure. The problem lay with D. Carlos, whose personal reputation would not sustain his decision to defy the constitution. He was 'a prince whose record gave him no right to represent the nation', as George Young put it, while João Franco was described by the same author as a 'somewhat sinister personality, of no public or private standing . . . whose reputation had not even earned for him public respect'.[39] Instead of rallying monarchist sentiment to the cause of reform, Franco and D. Carlos between them alienated almost all the constituencies they might have called upon for support.

As Portugal grappled unsuccessfully with national debt, while poverty stalked the streets of the cities and tens of thousands emigrated to find a future in the New World, the monarchs of Portugal pursued their empty rituals, moving from one vast and useless palace to another and consorting with foreign royalties in an endless round of state visits, carried out in the name of diplomacy but increasingly irrelevant to the needs of the country.

However, it was not just the monarchy of Portugal that was doomed, although it was the first to go. The First World War swept away the monarchies of Russia, Germany and Austria-Hungary. The public grandeur that was supposed to reinforce monarchical power and authority served in the end only to make it the perfect target for the politically discontented.

The Twilight of the Gods: Life after Death for the Braganzas

After their flight from Portugal, the royal family split up. D. Manuel sought refuge in Britain with his mother and uncle, while his aged grandmother Maria Pia returned to the land of her birth in Italy. D. Manuel was brought to Britain on George v's royal yacht. He was granted a pension of £1,120 a month (equivalent to approximately £100,000 in

2019) by the Republican government and was able to draw on the income of the Casa da Bragança. On George v's intervention many of the private possessions, furniture and so on belonging to the Crown were sent to England.

The exiled family made no serious attempt to stage a comeback. Life in exile was far too comfortable and there was a recognition that the days of the monarchy were over. In Portugal, however, monarchism took a longer time to die. Shortly after the Republican coup, the royalist former governor of Angola, Henrique Paiva Couceiro, had demanded that a referendum be held, which the Republicans refused. A year later he led a force of dissidents that had gathered beyond the frontier in Galicia on an invasion of Portugal and celebrated the restoration of the monarchy on the very day when the rest of Portugal was celebrating the first anniversary of the Republic. D. Manuel hesitated to give this movement any support, possibly because of the active participation of members of D. Miguel's family and because he was deeply suspicious of the devious game being played by Spain in harbouring royalist exiles. Instead he encouraged the British government to recognize the Republic.

In July 1912 Paiva Couceiro led a second invasion of the north. By this time the political events in Portugal were becoming entangled with the power blocs facing up to each other in Europe. The Portuguese monarchists received tacit support from Germany and Austria-Hungary, as well as Spain, with Britain and republican France lending support to the Portuguese Republic. After the failure of this incursion waves of arrests were carried out and the Republic reached an agreement with Spain and Brazil for exiled monarchists to leave Spain and settle in the New World.

On 4 September 1913 D. Manuel married Auguste Victoria of Hohenzollern, but the marriage produced no children. Meanwhile, the long unmarried Afonso, D. Carlos's brother and former viceroy of India, contracted a marriage with a thrice-divorced American heiress. This caused a rift in the royal family and Afonso was excluded from D. Manuel's will. During the First World War D. Manuel worked for the Red Cross. The war, however, divided the exiled Braganzas as the descendants of D. Miguel joined the Austrian army. This threatened to be highly embarrassing when Portugal entered the war on the side of Britain and France in 1916. Miguel II then resigned his commission and worked instead for the Order of Malta in the care of the wounded.[40]

In 1914 the foundation of the Integralismo Lusitano movement was, to start with, strongly pro-monarchist and helped to move monarchists in Portugal away from the liberal constitutional position that the Braganzas had always supported since 1834. After an election in 1918, in which monarchists had won a third of the seats, Paiva Couceiro launched his third invasion of the north in January 1919. This time the monarchy was formally declared in Porto and the monarchist flag flew from town halls, but the movement received no support from D. Manuel, or this time from Spain. Once again the Republic gained control and rounded up monarchist sympathizers.[41] Integralists now broke with the monarchists and pursued a course that was to lead eventually to fascism. This was the last serious attempt to restore the monarchy in Portugal and from that time the monarchical cause drifted into the realms inhabited largely by right-wing fantasists.

Meanwhile Portuguese monarchism was in the process of being taken over by the descendants of D. Miguel, who had acquired a prestige and importance among European royalty far greater than D. Miguel himself had ever enjoyed.

D. Miguel may have lost his throne in 1834 but his children married royalty and occupied thrones around Europe. Of his six daughters, Maria das Neves married the younger brother of the Carlist claimant to the Spanish throne. Her great-aunt had married the first Don Carlos. Maria Theresa became the third wife of the Archduke Karl Ludwig and hence the stepmother of Franz Ferdinand of Sarajevo fame. Maria José married a Bavarian prince and her daughter married Albert, heir to the throne of Belgium, becoming queen of Belgium in 1909. Maria Ana married the heir to the Grand Duchy of Luxembourg and became Grand Duchess in 1905.

In exile in Germany, D. Miguel had had one son, also called Miguel (known as Miguel II). Miguel II led an adventurous life, travelling widely in Europe and India, and even visited Portugal incognito. In 1877 he married Isabel von Thurn und Taxis, a clear indication that Miguel's family, like the French Orléanists, still retained their caste among European royalty. He and Isabel had three children. He married a second time in 1893 to his cousin Princess Maria Teresa von Löwenstein, and they had seven daughters and one son, Duarte Nuno, who was born on 23 September 1907 at Seebenstein in Austria and was baptised with water brought from the birthplace of the Braganza family in Guimarães. Miguel II established very close relations with Emperor

Franz Joseph, who gave his residence extraterritorial status, like an embassy. After the murder of D. Carlos, Miguel II contacted D. Manuel to offer his support, even though he never renounced his own family's claim to the throne. He hoped that D. Manuel would rescind the law that banished D. Miguel and his descendants from Portugal. Unfortunately the press got hold of this letter and the correspondence caused D. Manuel some embarrassment.[42] Miguel II and D. Manuel met for the first and only time on 30 January 1912 in Dover.

Miguel II's eldest son by his first wife, always known as Prince Miguel, dabbled in monarchical politics after the Republic was declared and was an associate of Paiva Couceiro. He joined with his father in transferring the 'Miguelist' legitimacy to Duarte Nuno in 1920 and died before his father on 21 February 1923.[43] Prince Miguel married an American heiress, Anita Stewart, in 1909. She was obligingly raised to the rank of princess by Emperor Franz Joseph. Although Miguel II had resigned his Austrian commission when Portugal entered the war, his son Prince Miguel had fought in the Austrian army and this became an issue in the early 1920s when Portuguese monarchists sought to bring the two branches of the family together. In 1920 Miguel II went through a phantom abdication (if this is possible for someone who had never occupied a throne). His rights were then transferred to his youngest son, Duarte Nuno. In 1922, by the Pact of Paris, D. Manuel recognized Duarte Nuno as the heir to the phantom monarchy, although the validity of this 'pact' has been disputed.[44] Miguel II died on 11 October 1927.

When the Republic was overthrown by a military coup in 1926, it was widely anticipated that a monarchical regime would be restored in Portugal and many monarchists were now appointed to important positions in the state. However, political infighting and manoeuvring eventually brought António de Oliveira Salazar to undisputed power in 1930. Salazar was well aware of how unstable Portugal had been under the monarchy but was ready to meet many monarchist expectations, especially with regard to the Church and religion. This helped to reconcile members of the pro-monarchist Integralismo movement to the new regime, the Estado Novo, which was formally inaugurated in 1933.

However, D. Manuel himself was not summoned back. The ex-king had now largely abandoned any expectation of a restoration. He had become a great book collector and devoted himself to the catalogue of his library, two volumes of which were published in his lifetime and a third after his death. D. Manuel died unexpectedly on 2 July 1932 from an inflammation of the throat that was not treated in time. He was 42, another Braganza to die young. By this time monarchists were in favour in Portugal and the body of the ex-king was returned on board a British cruiser for a state funeral and burial in the royal pantheon, attended by Óscar Carmona, the president of Portugal; Salazar, the prime minister; and the Cardinal Patriarch of Lisbon, Manuel Cerejeira.

After D. Manuel's death a final settlement was reached between the family and the state, the Fundação da Casa de Bragança being founded as a trust to manage the palace and collections of Vila Viçosa and the income from other Braganza properties.

On 19 October 1932 the various monarchist factions came together to declare Duarte Nuno King Duarte II of Portugal. Duarte Nuno had been brought up in Germany and spoke German as his first language. During and after the war he lived in Switzerland. In 1942 he married Maria Francisca, great-granddaughter of Emperor Pedro II of Brazil. This was a deliberate move to bring together all the fragmented fractions of the exiled Braganzas. The marriage took place in Petrópolis in Brazil, where the emperor and Isabel, the Princess Imperial, were buried. [45]

After the laws banishing the members of the royal family had been revoked in 1950, Duarte Nuno returned to live in Portugal. He became an outspoken supporter of Salazar and hoped that the ageing dictator would secure the return of the monarchy as the best way of securing the future of the Estado Novo and its values. In this he was deceived and it is now clear that Salazar never had any intention of restoring the monarchy. There was a brief flicker of a monarchist revival after the 1974 democratic revolution in Portugal, when a monarchist party, the PPM, won six seats and joined a conservative coalition. Duarte Nuno died deeply disillusioned in 1976, shortly after the democratic revolution had finally confined the Estado Novo to the dustbin of history.

Duarte Nuno's son, Duarte Pio, was born in Switzerland in 1945. He returned with his parents to Portugal in 1952 and was educated in Portugal, eventually becoming an air force helicopter pilot and serving in Angola. In 1995 Duarte Pio married, but not into ci-devant royalty.

In general, the modern Braganzas have employed themselves in farming and in patronizing good causes. They have largely realized the ambitions of Ferdinand, the Saxe-Coburg king, to become a bourgeois, even if upper-class bourgeois, family. But the past seemingly never dies entirely. In 2014 there was a bizarre incident when a dispute arose over the right to make awards in the Order of Saint Michael of the Wing, a supposed medieval order that had been revived by D. Miguel after his exile. The right to make these awards was, after a number of court cases, secured by Duarte Pio.

The Braganzas maintain their network of family ties among the former royal dynasties. These once royal families have formed a kind of exclusive club that holds meetings, celebrates marriages within their hallowed circles and indulges in the luxury of using titles and making awards in phantom orders of chivalry. Their pretensions are supported by a crowd of sycophantic hangers-on, often more royalist than the royals themselves, and perhaps by dreams that one day the political wheel of fortune may bring them back to their thrones, as indeed happened to the Spanish royal family, which lost its throne in 1931 but was restored in 1975 after the death of General Franco.

13

D. Pedro II, Emperor of Brazil

O n the whole, the Braganzas had been no better and no worse
than other ruling dynasties. They had had their share of fail-
ures, illiterates, the physically weak and mentally unstable. They had
had rulers who suffered from absurdly grandiose pretensions, who
were vengeful, who neglected public affairs, who were philanderers
and epileptics. They had maintained extravagant courts but had tried
to support attempts to reform and invigorate their country, mostly
with limited success. They had suffered more than their fair share of
ill health, infant mortality and premature senility and death. In general, they had tried to remain in touch with the prevailing popular
sentiment, conscious that when the dynasty failed to do this, it would
inevitably cease to reign. In the chequered story of this monarchy, it is
rare to come across any outstanding individual who has been generally
admired, who was able to rule effectively and embrace all the essential
qualities of kingship – but this was the case with D. Pedro II, emperor
of Brazil, who was one of the last of the dynasty to occupy a throne.[1]

The Legacy of Brazil's First Emperor

D. Pedro IV (D. Pedro I, emperor of Brazil), the eldest son of D. João
VI and Carlota Joaquina, had died young but had left an extraordinary
legacy to the two countries over which he had reigned, however briefly.
In the turmoil of the 1820s he had granted a constitutional Charter to
Portugal in an attempt to settle the deep divisions among the population, but this only had the effect of causing the country to spiral down
into civil war. He had abdicated his Portuguese throne in favour of his
seven-year-old daughter, Maria da Gloria, who had been born in Brazil

and had never visited Portugal and was unknown there. Five years later, in 1831, he abdicated the throne of the Brazilian empire that he had founded like some New World Napoleon, and passed it to his son Pedro, a five-year-old child. In the three years of life left to him D. Pedro devoted his energies to placing his daughter on her Portuguese throne, leaving the child emperor to fend for himself in a new and half-formed nation that threatened any moment to disintegrate into warning factions and breakaway provinces.

Brazil in 1831 was one of the largest states in the world but had only been a single entity since 1816 and independent of Portugal since 1822. The events of the previous fifteen years had constituted the first tentative moves towards creating a united nation from this vast territory, which occupied half of the South American continent. Most of the population still inhabited the coastal regions where there was a scattering of coastal towns dating back to the early days of settlement in the seventeenth century. The eighteenth-century mining boom in the interior had died down and the economy remained overwhelmingly based on plantation agriculture, which employed slave labour. This economy, which at one time had been almost a sugar monoculture, had now diversified and produced tobacco, cotton and, above all, coffee. The growth of coffee production had increased the demand for slaves, which were being imported in large numbers. Brazil had little industry and the retail and commercial sector of the economy was in the hands of foreigners, Portuguese and English. Brazil had very poor communications and the distant provinces were largely autonomous, ruled by local landowning elites with little interference from the government in Rio. The largest part of the population was made up of African slaves, native Amerindians and those of mixed race. Rates of illiteracy were very high and public affairs were administered by small elite groups, many of European origin or who had been educated in Europe. In short, a Brazilian nation barely existed and the vast territory had little or no unity except that provided by its history. It was surrounded in South America by the former colonies of Spain, which had fragmented into warring republics, while in North America the newly independent United States had adopted a Federal Constitution that had created divisions, which were soon to lead to a devastating civil war. Only Canada, far to the north and outside Brazil's range of vision, was a relatively peaceful country – still under the British Crown – that would become a united country at the very time that the United States colapsed into chaos.

In 1831, when Emperor Pedro I abruptly abdicated and left, it seemed that Brazil might fragment either into a loose federation of autonomous provinces or more likely into a mosaic of independent republics. There were federalist revolts in the extreme south, the northeast and in Minas Gerais in the interior, while in Rio the small group of experienced politicians and administrators were deeply divided by personality and by the long-standing resentments that existed between native Brazilians and those born or educated in Portugal.

The Brazilian politicians who had forced D. Pedro I to abdicate had not wanted to get rid of the monarchy. The Constitution that had been promulgated in 1824 had already acquired the status of a fundamental law that guaranteed the unity of the state and the security of property. It was easy to assume that the new emperor, who was only five years old, would become simply a figurehead who would unite the country but who would never aspire to rule it. The use that the first emperor, D. Pedro I, had made of the *poder moderador* was forgotten or at least set aside in the public memory.

The Child Emperor

Within days of his abdication on 7 April 1831, D. Pedro I sailed away taking with him Maria da Gloria, the young queen of Portugal, and his new wife Amélia of Leuchtenberg. He did not even say goodbye to his son, who woke to find his father gone. The little emperor was left with his two elder sisters, Francisca and Januária, but otherwise with no family. Even before his father had departed, the traditional ceremony of acclamation had been performed before the citizens of Rio. The scene was described by Mary Williams in her biography of the emperor:

> On the second story balcony of the palace was their sovereign, surrounded by his sisters and his ministers of state, who were likewise splendid in the imperial green and gold. The tiny emperor, little more than five years old, was standing on a chair, that the people might more easily see him. He was a delicate looking child, with light golden hair, fair skin, and German blue eyes, and with a slightly projecting lower lip that betokened his Habsburg ancestry. In almost gay wonder, he gazed on his cheering subjects and responded to their vivas by waving a handkerchief.[2]

Before he left, his father had appointed an official guardian for the boy and an *aio*, a tutor, who was responsible for his person and his education. He had also established a regency consisting of three persons. This arrangement was to lead to nearly a decade of bitter disputes as the guardian and the regents struggled for control of the palace and the person of the emperor. In this situation, the monarchy might have been rapidly swept away to be replaced by a republic, but this did not happen. It was the very fact that the government of the country, and the country itself, threatened to break down into chaos that not only saved the little emperor's throne but even strengthened the institution of monarchy. As the politicians who were left in control proved increasingly incapable of settling their differences and governing the country effectively, so growing numbers of people began to see in the person of the emperor a solution to these problems: someone who would have undisputed legitimacy and whose authority would override factions and personalities. The emperor, even while still a child, became the

Portrait of Emperor Pedro II as a boy by Félix Taunay, 1837, oil on canvas.

hope for the future, a symbol of national unity and of law, order and authority.

Meanwhile the little boy grew up without the emotional support of father or stepmother, aware that he was different and that people treated him in some special way. This might have produced an emotionally disturbed and spoilt young man, like his uncle D. Miguel, who would indulge in undisciplined, self-willed behaviour and who would prove to be unable to exercise the constitutional authority he would inherit. Instead D. Pedro developed as a silent, introspective, studious child who learnt his lessons, and early showed an unusual degree of self-control. His sisters provided him with some intimate family connections, but they never became close and later were to marry and leave Brazil. D. Pedro remained deeply attached to the memory of his father, whom he never accused of having deserted him. This steady, if reserved, child impressed those who came in contact with him and encouraged the idea that he should be declared 'of age' before he reached his fifteenth birthday. After months of bitter wrangling among the members of the assembly, D. Pedro was declared to have reached his majority on 23 July 1840. A year later, on 18 July 1841, he was crowned in a ceremony heavy with every kind of symbolism designed to place the new monarchy of Brazil firmly within the traditions of European royal families, but with a Brazilian character to make it seem relevant to the New World. The young emperor had a sword engraved with the arms of Portugal and an armillary sphere, the symbol adopted by the Avis kings of Portugal, appeared on printed copies of the Constitution, but the emperor himself was draped in a poncho of feathers, allegedly a gift from an Amerindian chief. D. Pedro apparently accepted all this ceremonial in relative silence and with as good a grace as possible.

The Emperor Grows to Fill his Shoes

Not surprisingly D. Pedro began by following the advice of those nearest to him, but it was not long before his very existence as the ultimate source of authority began to have a stabilizing effect on Brazilian affairs and the personalized political factions gave way to more stable party structures. While his sister D. Maria II had to contend with rival military grandees in Portugal who were liable at any moment to come forward with a *pronunciamento*, Pedro was fortunate to be able to rely on a very able military commander in the marquês (later duque) de

Caxias, who taught the young emperor how to ride and use a sword and who was always unassailably loyal – until, that is, he unilaterally threw up his command of the army in the Paraguayan War.

D. Pedro inherited the traditions of the Braganza court. He regularly held a *beija mão* and weekly audiences when anyone could approach the throne with a petition. He was also punctilious in attendance at Mass and on celebrating religious festivals. It soon became clear that he was not inclined to do away with tradition and this helped to rally the conservative classes to his support. D. Pedro had been an emperor in waiting while still in the womb and a national institution from the moment he was born. His image was carefully managed and stories about him were discreetly edited. According to Lilia Schwarcz, 'in the scarce iconography of the period, we can see how the image of an eternally old king began to be moulded'.[3] From his early youth he was in many respects already an old man.

D. Pedro assumed the throne at an age when he was growing fast. He eventually reached the unusual height of 6 foot 3 inches (190 cm), far taller than most Brazilians. His features were not particularly handsome, as his inheritance from his grandparents D. João VI and Carlota Joaquina on one side and the notoriously ungainly Habsburgs on the other did not augur well. His large head and pronounced jaw, however, were offset by his height and before he was twenty he began to grow the beard that would be the hallmark of his imperial personality. In a short study of the character of the emperor, published after the return of his body to Brazil in 1922, the poet and diplomat Carlos Magalhães de Azeredo wrote that 'the striking physical aspect of the man who was the incarnation of the fatherland contributed without any doubt to accentuate the reverence in which he was held.' He records the impression that was made on one observer when the emperor visited Athens during his European tour of 1876–7: 'He was the *grand seigneur par excellence*. Anyone who entered that vast salon full of people who were all authentically aristocratic would instinctively realize who among all those noblemen was the emperor.'[4]

Like his Braganza forebears, D. Pedro was committed at an early age to marriage in order to secure a male heir for the throne. He appears to have had little say in the matter and when a willing bride was found in the person of Teresa Cristina, daughter of Francesco, king of the Two Sicilies, the marriage was arranged with little delay. A proxy wedding took place in Europe and the couple were eventually married in

Rio on 4 September 1843. Many young men find their first sexual experiences marked with awkwardness and embarrassment and it appears that D. Pedro at first reacted against a bride with whom he could not easily converse and who lacked obvious female attractions. Eventually a young man's libido, or perhaps a young emperor's sense of duty, allowed the marriage to be consummated and in February 1845 Teresa Cristina gave birth to their first child. Three children were to follow at yearly intervals and D. Pedro and Teresa Cristina became, if not a loving couple, at least good and constant friends. Then, in 1848, for reasons that are not known, the couple ceased their sexual relations and there were no more children.

D. Pedro gradually freed himself from the supervision of the courtiers who surrounded him. In 1845–6 he went on a prolonged tour in the southern provinces, enjoying the freedom from court etiquette. He was away six months and returned a grown man who now began to take charge of affairs. The Brazilian Constitution, which had been drawn up by his father, gave a major role to the Crown. The emperor had the famous *poder moderador* (moderating power) that conferred on him the right to nominate ministers and to dismiss or summon the

Emperor D. Pedro II
of Brazil, *c.* 1851,
daguerreotype.

Engraving of Emperor
Pedro II, the moderating
power, 1865, by
Henrique Fleiuss.

Assembly. In addition, he enjoyed a vast array of patronage powers, which allowed him to grant petitions, award titles and honours and make appointments to a wide range of offices and positions. D. Pedro now began to exercise these powers and to draw all the strings of influence into his hands. It was to be the quiet way he used this influence that was to be so effective, in contrast to the impulsive and sometimes erratic decision-making that had characterized his father.

The Citizen Emperor

Sober, respectable and conservative, D. Pedro did nothing rash and showed no brilliance or genius. However, he took pleasure in learning languages (as well as the major European languages, he studied Hebrew, Arabic, Sanskrit and at least one native Brazilian language, Tupi-Guarani): 'Until the end of his life he considered study to be both an obligation and nourishment for the intellect.'[5]

D. Pedro believed that Brazil should develop as a European country and enjoy European standards of civilization, and he made a conscious attempt to keep abreast with intellectual developments in Europe, particularly in France. He built up a large private library that eventually numbered 20,000 volumes and carried on a wide correspondence with family members, scientists and writers in Europe. He soon acquired a reputation, unusual among European royalty, of being learned and an intellectual. D. Pedro was not just indulging in his own taste for literary culture, he was deliberately trying to become a model of citizenship for Brazilians to follow. He used his wide powers of patronage to promote people who conformed to his own standards of honesty and impartiality and to his concepts of European civilized values.

Meanwhile D. Pedro became a full-time professional ruler. His daily routine was entirely taken up with ceremonial duties, tours of inspection, interviews with ministers and the weekly *despachos* in which the whole cabinet had to assemble and discuss their programmes in the emperor's presence. In addition, he held weekly public and private audiences for ambassadors and visiting dignitaries. A French ambassador recalled that when the emperor disagreed with a view that was being expressed 'he gives me a sideways look, which is of a truly Castilian pride . . . At such moments he has an astonishing resemblance to Philip III as painted by Velázquez.'[26] Into this busy schedule he fitted time to read, as well as to attend the opera and to write his own letters. He never employed a secretary and himself noted or retained in his memory an immense range of detail about personalities and public affairs.

To help him manage this vast range of activity, his youthful reserve and taciturnity gradually evolved into a studied politeness and courtesy, which was shown to all with whom he came into contact. As Roderick Barman wrote, 'His conduct, his culture, and his concern for the public good made Pedro II everything that a simple citizen should be. Pedro II's exemplary behaviour, his learning, and his personal dignity [caused] everyone to esteem and respect him as their ruler.'[27] By the mid-1850s, when he was barely thirty years old, he had established an extraordinary hold over public affairs and over decision-making at all levels.

As other successful monarchs have found, however, the respect and ultimately devotion with which he was held depended to a considerable extent on the conservatism and respectability with which he surrounded himself. D. Pedro never espoused ideas that were in the least controversial and appeared content, for all his admiration of French culture, to live in a slave-owning society. He was always concerned to respect popular opinion and not to move ahead of an established consensus on any controversial question. Capital punishment was an example. The emperor wanted to see it abolished but, rather than take on such a controversial issue, he preferred to use his right under the Constitution to grant clemency and to commute death sentences, to allow the practice to wither away.

With regard to the treatment of children and the role of women in society, he was the very image of the benevolent patriarch. This was not always an attractive trait. Although he was always loyal to members of his family and to those who served him and whom he had known since childhood, he dominated the lives of his children and his wife, leaving them little opportunity for self-expression or for dissent. Teresa Cristina, in particular, was never allowed to travel anywhere without the emperor: when his daughter, Leopoldina, was in Petrópolis expecting her second child, the empress was not allowed to go alone to visit her daughter. Not surprisingly, D. Pedro found relations with the men who entered his family through marriage very difficult to manage. His relations with Luigi, count of Áquila, who married his sister Januária, were so bad that eventually the couple left Brazil and never returned. He also had problems with the comte d'Eu, who married his daughter Isabel, but eventually appointed the comte to command his armies in the south, which had the effect of removing him from close proximity.

It seems that quite early on D. Pedro came to believe that the monarchy in Brazil would die with him. The emperor's sons both died in infancy, Afonso in June 1845 and Pedro in January 1850. This left his daughter Isabel as heir to the throne. Although eventually he entrusted her to take over as regent while he travelled abroad, he never educated her to succeed him and kept her and her husband as far removed from affairs of state as possible. D. Pedro saw himself very much as a 'life-president' who had the immense task of welding a vast and ethnically diverse country into a united nation, but he believed that only he could do this and that after him a republic was inevitable.

D. Pedro had no interest in the trappings of royalty. Elaborate ceremonial was part of his duties as ruler, not something that he himself enjoyed. As Roderick Barman expressed it, 'Pedro II saw himself as the center of the world, he also appreciated how transitory, foolish, and unreal that world was. He was simultaneously committed to and yet sceptical of the role assigned to him in life.'[8]

He gave away a large part of his civil list to support individual petitioners or causes in which he was interested. He did not care about what he ate or drank and his table became notorious for poor food and indifferent hospitality. He apparently seldom spent more than twenty minutes at table. His only concession to the Braganza tradition of extravagance was his plan to build a new summer palace in the mountains 80 kilometres from Rio. Work on Petrópolis began in 1843 when he was only eighteen, but this was no Mafra or Pena. Instead he built a relatively small and conservative country house that would have been considered modest even for a Brazilian landowner. Its interior was dark and cool and hung with sober portraits, as would befit a president's residence. Around it grew up a town peopled by German immigrants. According to the great Brazilian sociologist Gilberto Freyre, D. Pedro 'recognized the value which the German presence represented for Brazil for the growth of a Brazilian population which was more "biblico" in the sense of being more literate than the latins and with education superior to any other, equally European, settlers'.[9]

The city of Petrópolis soon became characterized by the interesting and experimental architecture commissioned by the courtiers who followed the emperor to his summer retreat and remains a fascinating monument to the culture of the Brazilian empire. In contrast the royal palaces in Rio de Janeiro, São Cristóvão and the City Palace, as well as the royal *fazenda* at Santa Cruz, were increasingly neglected.

The Project to Create a Civilized Brazilian Nation

D. Pedro came to see that his mission as emperor was to bring Brazil into the community of civilized nations. This was a project that had an international political dimension, distancing a peaceful, united Brazil from the turmoil of the neighbouring Spanish-American republics, but it also had cultural implications. The emperor wanted to support the idea of a Brazilian nation that would draw on its own past history and would assimilate themes from the tropical environment, including native American culture. For this reason he actively supported the 'Indianist' writers and artists who tried to construct a romantic version of Brazil's past. However, for D. Pedro the real model for a civilized society was undoubtedly France and he wanted to do everything he could to bring the education and cultural world of Brazil into line with what he saw as the French model of European civilization. Although he may never have used the phrase, he undoubtedly thought of Brazil as being a 'white man's country' and Brazilian culture as being essentially European.

To fulfil this cultural mission, D. Pedro was very conscious that, as emperor, he needed to shine in the galaxy of European royalty and this he certainly achieved through his interest in, and patronage of, the arts and sciences. He was seen by contemporaries, and certainly saw himself, as emulating the great monarchs of the past who had been patrons of literature and the arts. Early in his reign he gave strong encouragement to the Brazilian Historical and Geographical Institute as a centre of literate culture in Rio. He also used funds at his disposal directly to support a wide range of historical, literary and scientific projects, associating his name with any endeavour that sought to underpin the idea of a unique Brazilian nation with its own individual character and history.

Political Events

During D. Pedro's long reign the internal affairs of Brazil moved from a situation of chronic unrest, where the country was threatened with social upheaval and disintegration, to a state of prosperity and political stability. In the 1840s there were revolts in the provinces, notably in the southern province of Rio Grande do Sul. There were also slave revolts and outbreaks of violence against Portuguese immigrants. By the 1850s these had been overcome and for two decades Brazil enjoyed internal stability, and an expanding economy, while the telegraph and the construction of railways and roads brought a degree of modernization.

In 1864 D. Pedro was confronted with an issue that forced him to take decisive action. The Paraguayan invasion of Argentina and southern Brazil produced a situation that could not be managed by conciliation and negotiation. The emperor decided that the problem should be met head on. The army and navy were sent south to join the forces of Uruguay and Argentina, and he himself followed with his son-in-law, threatening to abdicate and enlist as a volunteer if his government objected.

At first the war went well and the emperor appeared at a victory parade at which the Paraguayan troops who had been forced to surrender at Uruguaiana in September 1865 were made to march past the heads of state of Brazil, Argentina and Uruguay. Soon, however, the war reached a stalemate. The emperor had now, uncharacteristically, started to see the issue as a personal dispute between himself and the Paraguayan president, Francisco Solano López, and he threw all his political weight behind the need for victory. Not until January 1869 did the war turn once again in Brazil's favour with the capture of Asunción. By this time its prosecution had caused deep divisions among Brazil's political elite and had begun to call into question the emperor's judgement.

In 1869 the Brazilian commander, the marquês de Caxias, resigned his post by the simple expedient of returning to Rio. D. Pedro was left without a competent commander-in-chief and decided to appoint his son-in-law, the Comte d'Eu, to the post. Once this had been approved by the Council of State, the Comte took up his appointment and in the course of the next year definitively defeated the last Paraguayan army and killed the fugitive Solano López. In a gesture significant for the future of Brazil as well as Paraguay, the Comte used his occupation of Asunción to get the provisional government to free all slaves in the country and abolish slavery.

The Paraguayan War had proved a triumph for the determination of the emperor and greatly enhanced his and his country's standing in South America, but it had led to the loss of thousands of lives and had exhausted the treasury. Indirectly it had resulted in the growth of opposition to the very concept of imperial government and in December 1870 the first Republican Manifesto was published.

While the Paraguayan War was still in progress, there were also battles to fight at home. The Law of Free Birth, a first cautious step towards the emancipation of the slaves, was passed and the electoral reform that introduced direct elections was finally enacted in 1871, just after the war came to an end.

Slavery

Brazilian society was permeated at every level by slavery. During the early part of D. Pedro's reign, in spite of a treaty signed with Britain that declared the slave trade illegal, an additional 700,000 slaves were imported to meet the soaring demand for labour on the plantations.

As emperor, D. Pedro owned slaves. The *fazenda* at Santa Cruz was run by slaves and some of these were sent to help in the construction of the new imperial city of Petrópolis, where a slave market was one of the first public institutions to be established. D. Pedro, however, disapproved of slavery, not least because it did not form part of his image of the European civilization to which he believed Brazil should aspire. In 1851 Brazil was confronted by the possibility of an armed ultimatum from Britain over the continuation of the slave trade and D. Pedro persuaded the government to take the initiative and definitively close Brazil's ports to slave imports.

The continued existence of slavery remained an unresolved problem. Characteristically, rather than tackle the problem, he believed that it could be made to wither away once the labour market had been transformed by immigration from Europe.

The Civil War in the United States and Lincoln's decision to declare the emancipation of the slaves in 1863 brought the issue to the fore in Brazil. With the emperor's encouragement, laws were drafted to declare the children of slaves free and to bring the institution itself to an end in thirty years' time, laws reminiscent of those adopted by Portugal for its African colonies. But in this, as in so much else, the emperor only acted when he believed that public opinion itself was changing.

The first tentative measure to abolish slavery, the Law of Free Birth, was only passed in 1871 after a long drawn-out struggle in which D. Pedro used all his guile and perseverance against determined conservative opposition. Although the law eventually reached the statute book, it did little immediately to advance the cause of emancipation. It did, however, stimulate opposition among the diehard slave owners who began to see the emperor not as a neutral force in politics, but as their enemy.

At the same time as the Law of Free Birth was introduced, a movement began for the voluntary emancipation of the slaves, a movement which had the active support of the emperor. D. Pedro used the honours system to promote the cause of emancipation and charitable organizations were formed for buying slaves their freedom, while slaves willing to enlist in the armed forces were automatically freed. To coincide with this, organizations were created to encourage and even to subsidise immigration from Europe.

D. Pedro and his daughter believed that Brazilian society should emulate that of France, a vision in which there was little room for the slaves and their descendants. When he was a boy D. Pedro had once had his portrait painted with a black nursemaid and later in her life Princess Isabel formed a close friendship with a violinist of mixed race who accompanied her on the piano. But otherwise there are few examples of the Imperial family concerning itself with the vast black population of Brazil, a blindness that may be understandable but did not bode well for the future of Brazil. Gilberto Freyre described D. Pedro as

> in his early years of rule a pedantic child presiding with a certain air of superiority over cabinets of old men, some having Indian blood and even African, often profoundly sensible countrymen but lacking French culture . . . For there was no greater academician in our country than Pedro II. Nor anyone less native and more European.[10]

D. Pedro's Travels Abroad

In 1871, although the Paraguayan war had only recently been brought to an end, D. Pedro took what was, in effect, a holiday. He was motivated in part by the death of his daughter Leopoldina, who had died in Europe on 7 February 1871 at the young age of 23. She had married Ludwig August of Saxe-Coburg, whose father had been first cousin of Queen Victoria and of King Ferdinand of Portugal. Although she had died very young, she had already given birth to four sons. Pedro set out with the empress for Europe in May 1871, leaving Isabel as regent in his place. His departure coincided with the climax of the campaign to implement the Law of Free Birth and it seems that the emperor deliberately absented himself to prevent the political turmoil from damaging the monarchy itself. D. Pedro travelled in an unofficial capacity as Pedro d'Alcântara and at his own expense. The boat on which he embarked called at Bahia and Recife, allowing D. Pedro to see something of the northern part of his empire, albeit in an unofficial capacity. The visit to Europe gave him, briefly, the freedom of an ordinary citizen to do what he liked, when he liked. Although he visited Queen Victoria and Emperor Franz Joseph, he was primarily concerned to meet educated Europeans and to see the 'sights' of Europe. He returned to Brazil in March 1872.

In 1876 he determined to go on his travels again, perhaps thinking that his absence would deflate some of the criticism being levelled at him for his constant interference in political affairs. Once again Isabel was to stand in for him as regent. D. Pedro had decided to attend the centenary celebrations of the American Declaration of Independence and was the first head of state formally to visit the United States. This time he did not travel incognito and seems to have deliberately used his visit to gain favourable publicity for Brazil and also for himself. He spent the months of April to July in the United States and made a short visit to Canada. Free from the affairs of state, he once again recovered his physical and mental vigour and tirelessly explored every aspect of a country that he considered both enlightened and modern. His intellectual curiosity extended to religion and he attended one of Moody and Sankey's revivalist meetings as well as a Mormon service in Salt Lake City.

D. Pedro then set off for Europe and the Middle East, indulging a determination to see and experience everything the Old World had to offer. As well as the major European cities, his travels took him to Finland, Moscow, Istanbul, Odessa, Athens, Jerusalem and Egypt. It was a breathtaking tour, made all the more exhausting as this time he was travelling as the emperor and was, to some degree, the whole time on a public stage. Whereas in Brazil he had to be an aloof figure, neutral, impartial and with no friends outside the court circle and the family, in Europe he could indulge in much greater freedom and allow his desire for female company and that of scientists and intellectuals to blossom. He had cut himself off from the affairs of Brazil and, it seems, was very reluctant to return to resume his duties.

The emperor's third absence in Europe followed a serious illness – complications that arose from his increasingly serious diabetes and possibly from a mild stroke. He was persuaded to go once again to Europe and left in June 1887. This was supposed to be a convalescent visit, but once in Europe he ignored his doctor's advice and tried to recapture the freedom and intellectual excitement of his previous visits. The result was a serious relapse that brought him close to death. Although he recovered somewhat, he returned in August 1888, ill and increasingly frail. Inevitably all eyes were turned to the question of the succession.

Princess Isabel, the Redemptress

D. Pedro's eldest daughter, Isabel, was born in 1846. After the death of her brother in 1850, she became heir to the throne and was known as the Princess Imperial. At the age of fourteen she took the oath to the Constitution. She and her sister Leopoldina (born in 1848) were fortunate enough to have chosen as their *aia* (personal tutor) the

Comtesse de Barral, a French-educated woman of great charm and culture, who not only won the hearts of the two girls but captivated that of their austere father as well. The letters exchanged between the members of the royal family and the Comtesse are one of the main sources for the internal history of the Brazilian empire.

Isabel grew up in a patriarchal family and turned into a serious and strongly religious person, somewhat isolated from the everyday world, as her father had been, and with little interest in politics. At the age of eighteen a husband was found for her in the Comte d'Eu, a grandson of Louis-Phillipe, and the couple were married in October 1854. Isabel's biographer, Roderick Barman, explained how Isabel, by all accounts an intelligent woman with a strong character, was so constrained by the male-dominated society of Brazil and by the relationship with her patriarchal father that she was unable to free herself to play a wider role in society or in public affairs: 'She was trapped and confined within an assigned role that, as her father shaped it, was devoid of any autonomy or agency. Like Henrik Ibsen's Nora, she lived in a doll's house.'[11]

Isabel, although heir to the throne, took little interest in public affairs, which she was more than happy to leave to her father. Her

Princess Isabel photographed by Abram-Louis Buvelot, c. 1851.

French husband, however, wanted a more active role but was not allowed by the emperor to play any significant part until in 1869, almost out of the blue, he was offered command of the Brazilian army in the closing stages of the Paraguayan War. This was seen by the emperor as a way to resolve a severe difficulty brought about by the sudden resignation of the previous commander-in-chief, the marquês de Caxias. It would also meet the Comte d'Eu's persistent requests to be allowed to join the army. Although the war was brought to a successful conclusion, the Comte d'Eu suffered a nervous collapse that brought on a permanent state of depression and ill health. In August 1870 he and Isabel went to Europe where they stayed until April 1871, when Isabel had to return to take up the regency. Once the emperor had returned from his own furlough in Europe, the couple went abroad again and stayed in Europe from April 1873 to June 1874. These prolonged absences, which Isabel welcomed and enjoyed, removed them from the public eye in Brazil and made it difficult for her to be viewed as a possible alternative or successor to her father.

Isabel had not become pregnant during the first six years of her marriage, while her sister Leopoldina gave birth to four sons before her death from typhoid at the age of 23. Between 1872 and 1874, however, Isabel suffered two miscarriages and a stillbirth. The effects of these tragedies intensified her religious devotion and removed her still further from playing any significant role in public life. On 15 October 1875 she eventually gave birth to a son who was, naturally enough, christened Pedro after his grandfather and great-grandfather.

Isabel became regent again during her father's absence in 1876–7, a time when she once again became pregnant. She performed her duties without any enthusiasm and with a marked failure to project her personality onto the public consciousness. When her father returned she retreated into private life to await the birth of her second child, Luís. Isabel's third child, another son, António, was born in 1881. The birth of three sons seemed to promise a secure future for the dynasty and caring for them and their education became her main preoccupation.

In her early life Isabel was very much under the influence of her father. Later she became devoutly religious and, if she had any public reputation it was that of a *beata*, a religious enthusiast. For the most part, she lived a private life with her family. Her husband, after his brief career commanding the army, became increasingly a hypochondriac and suffered from deafness. Neither she nor her father did anything to make the royal family a centre of social life in the capital or to attract a wider circle of acquaintances beyond a few old friends. Apart from a visit to Minas Gerais in 1868 to see if the hot springs there would assist her attempts to become pregnant, and an official visit to the southern provinces in 1885, she saw little of Brazil and its people and they saw little of her.

Isabel spent much of her time in Europe where her husband's family had been restored to their property by the newly installed French Republic in 1871. She was in France in 1887 when she heard of the emperor's illness and once again she hastened back to become regent. During her previous regencies she had not had to deal with serious political issues and her activities had largely been of a formal kind. Now she was faced with a problem that was threatening to tear Brazil apart in a replay of the devastation that had overtaken the United States in 1861. The crisis over slavery was reaching boiling point. Violence was occurring in many parts of the country as abolitionists confronted the determination of slave owners to prevent emancipation, and slaves increasingly deserted the plantations. Faced with a situation that she felt was getting out of control, Isabel became convinced that the *poder moderador*, which she exercised as regent, no longer required her to remain neutral and impartial.

In a memorandum on the issue of ending slavery, drafted in December 1888, Isabel wrote: 'The concept, already innate within me was intrinsically humanitarian, more, generous, great and supported by the Church . . . It was out of conviction that it would be best for the nation which I had a duty to watch over.'[12] She determined to cut the apparently tangled 'Gordian Knot' of slavery, dismissed her Conservative government and appointed a government made up of those who would support immediate emancipation. The emancipation law, the so-called Golden Law, was signed by Isabel on 13 May 1888 in one of the most dramatic and truly heroic episodes in not only Brazilian history but the whole story of the Braganza dynasty. It is one of the ironies of history that a woman who had been kept away from public affairs by her patriarchal father, and who had apparently been absorbed in the private affairs of her family, should have shown the strength and determination to take on the power of the plantation owners and to make such a dramatic change in the course of Brazil's history. This heroic act is still remembered and respected in Brazil: in Petrópolis it is possible to buy a replica of the pen that Isabel used to sign the emancipation decree. However, although emancipation was widely approved throughout the country, it was the hatred of the conservative slave owners, who lost their 'property' without any compensation, that within less than a year led to the end of the monarchy and her exile from Brazil. Summarily thrown out of Brazil, Isabel is reported to have said to her friend Amandinha Dória, 'If abolition is the cause for this, I don't regret it; I consider it worth losing the throne for.'[13]

Ill Health, Premature Ageing and Exile

When D. Pedro II returned from Europe in 1872 he found it less easy to manage national affairs in the way to which he had been accustomed. The complexity of affairs in a country whose economy was rapidly growing, and which was now connected by telegraph to its outlying parts, made it impossible for the emperor to retain a personal grip on all aspects of government. Yet he continued to try to operate the system that had worked well for him for thirty years. Increasingly his interest in every aspect of the government came to be seen as meddling interference and his unwillingness to delegate, even to a private secretary, made it impossible for him any longer to keep abreast of national affairs.

Criticism and opposition grew from both conservatives and liberals, while the overriding importance of the monarchy in securing national unity receded in importance. D. Pedro himself was aware that the position of the emperor was changing in the public perception but he considered it his duty to persist with his role as emperor. When he returned from his second expedition abroad, the excitement and activity he had shown while touring Europe and receiving the plaudits of the press and the intellectual world was rapidly replaced by a depression, which took the form of aloofness towards his family and silence.

As D. Pedro's grip on public affairs grew weaker, he suffered many signs of premature ageing. His health began to deteriorate through diabetes and he suffered a minor stroke. Although only in his late fifties he appeared an old man, with a long white beard, increasingly set in his ways, wearing antiquated clothes, shunning all the pomp and ceremony of monarchy that he had espoused in his youth. Yet he was unwilling to delegate any of his authority to his daughter or even to trusted ministers. No attempt was made to manage the succession that now seemed imminent and Isabel and her husband, out of respect for the emperor, did not try to reinvent the monarchy for a new, younger generation.

In 1887 D. Pedro's health collapsed and he went to Europe to convalesce. He returned in August 1888, still revered by many but increasingly irrelevant to the future of the country in the opinion of the younger generation of educated Brazilians. Much of his time was now spent away in Petrópolis, the world of Rio moving ahead now without the emperor in control.

The end came suddenly and unexpectedly. Although Republican rhetoric was widespread in the press, Republicans were not tightly organized and were unable to win seats in the Assembly. In November 1889, however, a grievance that affected army officers flared up. The emperor, away in Petrópolis, dismissed the affair as of little significance and his ministers were wholly unprepared when a section of the army declared the Republic and appointed General Deodoro da Fonseca as interim president. (Inevitably one is reminded of the coup in Lisbon in 1974, which had its origin in the grievances of regular army officers.) The emperor was informed of the changes in a letter handed to him by a junior officer. He and his family were summarily put on board a ship and sent to Europe without any money and with little luggage. It was a cruel end to an illustrious episode in Brazil's history and, perhaps not surprisingly, it soon resulted in political chaos and civil war.

D. Pedro, Isabel and their family settled in Europe. Teresa Cristina died shortly after reaching Europe on 28 December 1889. After some uncertainty, the emperor resided in Cannes while his daughter and her husband went to the Comte's family property in Normandy. D. Pedro tried to resume the life he had previously enjoyed in Europe, but he

D. Pedro II of Brazil and Princess Isabel of Brazil, 1889.

was now too old, tired and ill to accomplish much. Queen Victoria noted in her diary seeing the old emperor in April 1891:

> Afterwards we went down to receive the poor old Emperor of Brazil, who was accompanied by his daughter Isabelle, and his grandson young Pedro Coburg. We took him into the drawing room. He was very talkative but his memory is rather confused and he speaks very indistinctly. Otherwise he looks much better than when I saw him last at Florence in 88.[14]

D. Pedro died in a hotel in Paris on 5 December 1891, aged 66.

The Empire in the Making of Brazil

In 1890 D. Pedro, now in exile, decided to donate his private collection of pictures to Brazil. As a memorial to his wife, the collection was entitled the Teresa Cristina Maria Collection. The anthropologist Lilia Schwarcz described this as 'an effort to construct and perpetuate a certain national memory . . . a suitable model to oppose to the image of the South American republics, with their civil wars and anarchy, a model for the imposition of a civilized "European" image.'[15] Among its thousands of items, the collection contained 600 images of the emperor himself.

Most monarchs, particularly those who lose their thrones and retreat into exile, fade rapidly from the public memory and, after their deaths, cease to have any influence in the countries where they once reigned. Perhaps only Louis XIV of France and Queen Victoria still command the public imagination in their respective countries in a way that carries meaning. However, to these two should be added Emperor D. Pedro II, whose commanding personality can still exert a decisive influence on Brazilian culture and identity. However critical some writers were over aspects of his reign, the reputation of the emperor emerged after his death unscathed and even enhanced.

A recent book about the emperor, admittedly written by a descendant, describes the man whose legend shows no sign of dying:

> A hundred and twenty years have passed since, in a very modest Parisian hotel, D. Pedro II, one of the most illustrious Brazilians, died. Notable for how much he achieved for his country, for the

great example he gave to the people and for the code of honour that
he preached to the politicians of his day, D. Pedro created a whole
civilization under the stimulus of his personal actions, and in all
the sectors of the life of the country he left the mark of his influence. Displaying a personality that was democratic and simple, no
one during his reign was exiled or condemned to death. The liberty
of the press was sacred to him . . . During his long reign on no
occasion did he ask for or accept an increase in his civil list, which
he employed in great part on works of charity and on patronizing
artistic talent . . . D. Pedro II desired to give the empire an image
of culture and progress that would stand out among the republics
that surrounded it. In this he was, without any doubt, victorious.
With a spirit profoundly linked to the thought of the nineteenth
century, he brought these ideals also to his own country.[16]

The exile of the emperor and the end of the monarchy was greeted
by a sense of embarrassment tinged with regret. He had dominated
the story of Brazil as it emerged as a strong, unified nation state and
only the very old could remember a time when Brazil had not been
ruled by the emperor. Why could the Republicans not have waited for
the old man to die? When the new self-proclaimed president, Deodoro
da Fonseca, visited the Historical and Geographical Institute, in many
ways the institution that most represented the vision that D. Pedro had
held for Brazil, he was told he could not sit in the emperor's chair. And
he did not try to.[17]

Reasons can be enumerated to explain the fall of the monarchy.
The emperor himself had long outgrown the youthful energy with
which he had adopted the theatrical manifestations of royalty. He had
become an old man, careless of his appearance, neglecting his palaces,
set in his ways, no longer able to manage the political life of the nation
but unwilling to delegate his powers. As he aged and became increasingly ill, it was clear that the monarchy was dying with him. His daughter
Isabel, who had acted so strong-mindedly to bring about the emancipation of the slaves, made little attempt to step into her father's shoes.
Her actions had been greatly resented by the slave-owning landowners
and her religious devotions were suspect to many people. Although
there was great affection for the old emperor among all classes and he
was seen very much as a much-loved aged grandfather, nobody could
any longer see him or his daughter as the people who would take Brazil

forward into the new century. In a careful analysis of the reasons for the fall of the monarchy, Emília Viotti da Costa discussed how the passing of the Golden Law emancipating the slaves may have contributed to the coup that ended the monarchy only a year later. Although there was no direct collaboration between the landowners and the military who carried out the coup, there is no doubt that the emancipation of the slaves undermined the solid base of support that the landowning class had hitherto provided for the monarchy. Although the monarchical constitution was soon replaced by a republican one, the events of 1889 should really be seen as a military coup d'état rather than a concerted republican movement:

> The movement of 15 November did not initially have any republican intent, it only envisaged the fall of the ministry. Beyond this intention . . . there were no plans to dethrone the emperor who was venerated by everyone. The republican sentiment only affected a minority in the army made up of a small erudite fraction who 'spent their bellicose ardour winning Napoleonic battles in the classroom and moving their armies energetically across the maps in the school library'.[18]

Whatever the causes, however, the way the regime change came about was seen as demeaning and even shameful. The Republicans took a long time to establish a viable political culture. In 1893 a federalist movement erupted into civil war and Princess Isabel, in Europe, was approached to lend her support. This she refused to do, unwilling for the memory of the empire to be associated with bloodshed.

Meanwhile, the memory of the tired old man who had died in exile in a Parisian hotel was being resurrected. Obituaries throughout Europe celebrated his life's work as though he were still a reigning monarch and as early as 1892 there were calls for his body to be brought back for burial in Brazil. The image of the emperor began to appear everywhere, an idealized figure, one of the great heroes of the nation and represented even by many Republicans as the greatest 'republican' of them all – the man who most clearly embodied the ideals and spirit of the new Republic. In the words of Lilia Moritz Schwarcz, 'The second emperor was immortalized by his own plans, by the interpretations of his historians, his painters' canvases, his composers' tunes, the projects for his scientific institutions, and even by his beautiful

Petrópolis, which went on being the favourite summer residence for the Republican elite.'[19]

As the centenary of Brazil's independence approached, the movement to have the emperor's body returned grew in strength and in 1920 the banishment of the imperial family was revoked. Princess Isabel was now too frail to attempt to return to Brazil and she died on 14 November 1921. In 1922 the Comte d'Eu embarked to return, but died on board the ship in which he was travelling.

In 1922 D. Pedro's coffin and that of his wife were brought back to Petrópolis with great ceremonial. Pedro, the emperor's eldest grandson, was able to attend the ceremonies. The centenary of D. Pedro's birth on 2 December 1925 was celebrated as a national holiday and in 1939 the family mausoleum in Petrópolis Cathedral was completed to further ceremonial, attended by the president of the Republic. For some Republicans, however, the return of D. Pedro's body had dark significance. It was a ghost returning to haunt the Republic: 'It is a gesture of Shakespearean terror, when faced by the ghost of the brother whose crown he has taken. It is, in fact, a gesture of fear and remorse.'[20]

The Most Serene House of Braganza

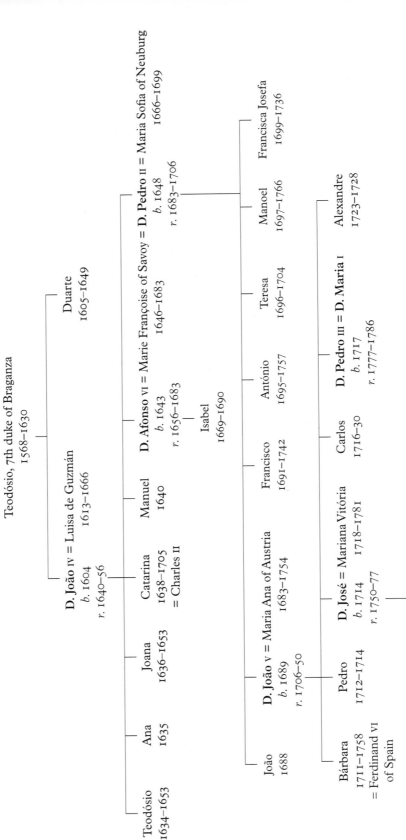

Teodósio, 7th duke of Braganza
1568–1630

Duarte
1605–1649

D. João IV = Luisa de Guzmán
b. 1604   1613–1666
r. 1640–56

D. Afonso VI = Marie Françoise of Savoy = **D. Pedro II** = Maria Sofia of Neuburg
b. 1643   1646–1683   b. 1648   1666–1699
r. 1656–1683   r. 1683–1706

Isabel
1669–1690

Manuel
1640

Catarina
1638–1705
= Charles II

Joana
1636–1653

Ana
1635

Teodósio
1634–1653

Francisca Josefa
1699–1736

Manoel
1697–1766

Teresa
1696–1704

António
1695–1757

Francisco
1691–1742

D. João V = Maria Ana of Austria
b. 1689   1683–1754
r. 1706–50

João
1688

Alexandre
1723–1728

Carlos
1716–30

D. Pedro III = **D. Maria I**
b. 1717   1777–1786
r. 1777–1786

Pedro
1712–1714

Bárbara
1711–1758
= Ferdinand VI
of Spain

D. José = Mariana Vitória
b. 1714   1718–1781
r. 1750–77

Maria Benedita = José
1746–1829

Maria Francisca
1739–1771

Maria Ana
1736–1813

D. Maria I = **D. Pedro III**
b. 1734
r. 1777–1816

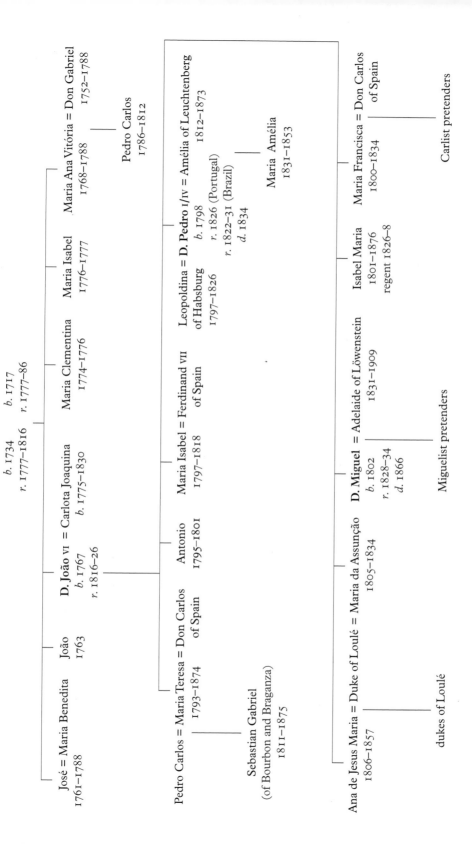

D. Maria I = **D. Pedro III**
b. 1734   *b.* 1717
r. 1777–1816   *r.* 1777–86

José = Maria Benedita
1761–1788

João
1763

Maria Ana Vitória = Don Gabriel
1768–1788   1752–1788

Pedro Carlos
1786–1812

Maria Isabel
1776–1777

Maria Clementina
1774–1776

D. João VI = Carlota Joaquina
b. 1767   *b.* 1775–1830
r. 1816–26

Antonio
1795–1801

Maria Isabel = Ferdinand VII
1797–1818   of Spain

Leopoldina = **D. Pedro I/IV** = Amélia of Leuchtenberg
of Habsburg   *b.* 1798   1812–1873
1797–1826   *r.* 1826 (Portugal)
  r. 1822–31 (Brazil)
  d. 1834

Maria Amélia
1831–1853

Maria Francisca = Don Carlos
1800–1834   of Spain

Carlist pretenders

Isabel Maria
1801–1876
regent 1826–8

Pedro Carlos = Maria Teresa = Don Carlos
1793–1874   of Spain

Sebastian Gabriel
(of Bourbon and Braganza)
1811–1875

D. Miguel = Adelaide of Löwenstein
b. 1802   1831–1909
r. 1828–34
d. 1866

Miguelist pretenders

Ana de Jesus Maria = Duke of Loulé = Maria da Assunção
1806–1857   1805–1834

dukes of Loulé

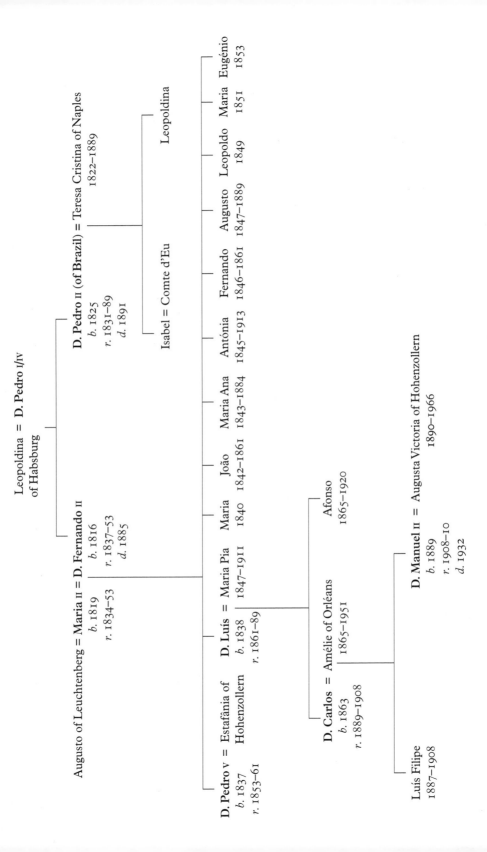

GLOSSARY

aio	valet, tutor, supervisor
alcaide-mor	castellan of a fortress
auto-da-fé	ceremony at which those condemned by the Inquisition were punished
azulejos	decorative ceramic tiles
barraca real	'royal shack': the wooden building where the royal family resided after the earthquake
beija mão	ceremony of the kissing of hands
caixas verdes	green boxes in which those wanting to petition the Crown had to place their petitions
Casa da Braganza	property of the Braganza family
Casa do Infantado	endowment for the younger branch of the royal family
casa real	royal household
cavaleiros	knights
cruzado	Portuguese silver coin
despachos	meetings between Emperor Pedro II and his cabinet
encoberto	'the hidden one': referring to the anticipated return of King Sebastião
falcoaria	falconry at Salvaterra dos Magos
fazenda	plantation in Brazil
fidalgos	noblemen or gentlemen
graças	word used to describe the prerogative of the Crown to grant remission of sentences
homens ricos	noblemen
infante/infanta	title of Portuguese prince or princess
liga formal	alliance between Portugal and France
meninos de Palhavã	half-brothers of D. João V
padroado real	the ecclesiastical rights of the Portuguese Crown over the church in Africa and the East
patuleia	name given to the civil war in Portugal of 1846–7
poder moderador	moderating power
povo	common people
pronunciamento	coup or attempted coup staged by a general

rotativismo	process by which the two major political parties in Portugal in turn succeeded each other in forming an administration
Santa Casa da Misericórdia	charitable institution for the care of the sick, the destitute and so on
talha dourada	carved, gilded wood
tapada	hunting reserve
tenças	retainers paid to noblemen for attending court

REFERENCES

1 The Idea of Monarchy and the Rise and Fall of the Dynastic State

1 Alan Freeland, 'Imagined Endings: National Catastrophe in the Fiction of Eça de Queiroz', *Portuguese Studies*, XV (1999), p. 105.
2 Lilia Moritz Schwarcz, *The Emperor's Beard* (New York, 1998), p. xxii.
3 See discussion in Luís de Sousa Rebelo, 'The Idea of Kingship in the Chronicles of Fernão Lopes', in *Medieval and Renaissance Studies on Spain and Portugal in Honour of P. E. Russell*, ed. F. W. Hodcroft et al. (Oxford, 1981), pp. 167–79, esp. p. 169.
4 John Adamson, 'Introduction: The Making of the Ancien-Régime Court, 1500–1700', in *The Princely Courts of Europe*, ed. John Adamson (London, 1999), p. 17.
5 Ana Cristina Duarte Pereira, *Princesas e Infantas de Portugal (1640–1736)* (Lisbon, 2008), p. 31.
6 Amy Jenkins, 'Royal Variety Show: Markle joins the biggest soap of all time', *The Guardian*, 19 May 2018.

2 The Early History of the Portuguese Monarchy

1 Mário Domingues, *D. Maria I e a sua época* (Lisbon, 1972), p. 185.
2 Ana Maria Alves, *Iconologia do poder real no período Manuelino* (Lisbon, 1985), p. 21.
3 Ibid., pp. 57–9.
4 Ibid., p. 21.
5 John Adamson, ed., *The Princely Courts of Europe* (London, 1999), p. 17.
6 Ana Isabel Buescu, *Dom João III* (Lisbon, 2005), p. 156.
7 Ana Cristina Duarte Pereira, *Princesas e Infantas de Portugal (1640–1736)* (Lisbon, 2008), pp. 14–16.
8 Jean-François Labourdette, *Histoire du Portugal* (Paris, 2000), p. 130.
9 António Baños-Garcia, *D. Sebastião Rei de Portugal* (Lisbon, 2004), p. 15.
10 Labourdette, *Histoire du Portugal*, p. 314.
11 Baños-Garcia, *D. Sebastião Rei de Portugal*, pp. 16–17.
12 Labourdette, *Histoire du Portugal*, p. 315.
13 From Francisco Bethencourt, 'The Unstable Status of Sebastianism', in *Utopia in Portugal, Brazil and Lusophone African Countries*, ed. Francisco Bethencourt (Bern, 2015), pp. 53, 68–9.

3 Overview of the Braganza Dynasty and the Culture of Royalty

1 Caetano Beirão, *D. Maria I, 1777–1792* (Lisbon, 1934), p. 40.
2 Caetano Beirão, ed., *Cartas da Rainha D. Mariana Vitória para a sua família de Espanha* (Lisbon, 1936).
3 Beirão, *D. Maria I*, p. 47.

4 William Beckford, *Italy with Sketches of Spain and Portugal*, 2 vols (London, 1834).

5 Nathaniel Wraxall, *Historical Memoirs of My Own Time*, 3rd edn (London, 1818).

6 Duc de Châtelet [Baron Dezoteux de Cormatin], *Voyage du ci-devant duc de Châtelet, en Portugal*, ed. Jean-François, baron de Bourgoing (Paris, 1798).

7 Laure Junot, *Memoirs of the Duchess D'Abrantès (Madame Junot)*, 8 vols (London, 1831–5).

8 *Elogio académico da Senhora D. Maria primeira, recitado por José Bonifácio de Andrada e Silva* . . . (Rio de Janeiro, 1857).

9 Rose Macaulay, *They Went to Portugal* (London, 1946).

10 Translated as *The Portugal History; or, A Relation of the Troubles that happened in the Court of Portugal in the years 1667 and 1668 . . . by S.P., Esq.* (London, 1677).

11 Translated into English as *The History of the Revolutions of Portugal* (London, 1735).

12 Charles Dellon, *Account of the Inquisition at Goa* (London, 1815).

13 Anon., *Description de la ville de Lisbonne où l'on traite de la cour, de Portugal, de la langue Portuguaise, & ses moeurs, des habitans* (Paris, 1730); Portuguese trans. in Castelo Branco Chaves, *O Portugal de D. Joao v: visto por tres forasteiros* (Lisbon, 1989).

14 Joseph François Lafitau SJ, *Histoire des découvertes et conquestes des Portugais dans le Nouveau Monde*, 2 vols (Paris, 1733); Nicolas de La Clède, *Histoire Générale de Portugal*, 2 vols (Paris, 1735).

15 Charles François Dumouriez, *Etat présent du Royaume de Portugal en l'année 1766* (Hamburg, 1797).

16 Marquis de Bombelles, *Journal d'un Ambassadeur de France au Portugal, 1786–1788* (Paris, 1979).

17 Abbé Guillaume-Thomas Raynal, *Histoire philosophique et politique des établissemens et du commerce des Européens dans les deux Indes* (Amsterdam and The Hague, 1773–4).

18 Mário Domingues, *D. Maria I e a sua época* (Lisbon, 1972), pp. 160–61.

19 Beirão, *D. Maria I*, p. 53.

20 Jean-François Labourdette, *Histoire du Portugal* (Paris, 2000), p. 434.

21 Ibid., p. 435.

22 Jenifer Roberts, *The Madness of Queen Maria* (Chippenham, 2009), p. 60.

23 Ana Cristina Duarte Pereira, *Princesas e Infantas de Portugal (1640–1736)* (Lisbon, 2008), p. 25.

24 Diogo Ramada Curto, 'Ritos e ceremónias da monarquia em Portugal (séculos XVI a XVIII)', in Francisco Bethencourt and Diogo Ramada Curto, *A memória da Nação* (Lisbon, 1991), pp. 201–65 (p. 263); quotation from Malcolm Howe, *The Braganza Story* (Lisbon, 1999), p. 179.

25 Beirão, *D. Maria I*, p. 57 and frontispiece.

26 Roberts, *The Madness of Queen Maria*, p. 45.

27 Châtelet, *Voyage du ci-devant duc de Châtelet*, p. 129.

28 Harold Temperley, *The Foreign Policy of Canning, 1822–1827* (London, 1925), p. 191.

29 Marleide da Mota Gomes and Miguel Chalub, 'Dom Pedro I of Brazil and IV of Portugal: Epilepsy and Peculiar Behavior', *Arquivos de Neuro-Psiquiatria*, LXV (2007), pp. 710–15.

30 For the scandal caused by this marriage, see Domingues, *D. Maria I e a sua época*, pp. 175–7; Junot, *Memoirs of the Duchess D'Abrantès*, IV, p. 252.

31 Bombelles, *Journal d'un Ambassadeur de France au Portugal*, p. 40.

32 Roderick Barman, *Citizen Emperor: Pedro II and the Making of Brazil, 1825–91* (Stanford, CA, 1999), p. 7.

33 Pereira, *Princesas e Infantas de Portugal*, p. 37.

34 Domingues, *D. Maria I e a sua época*, p. 10.

35 Pereira, *Princesas e Infantas de Portugal*, p. 51.

36 Roberts, *The Madness of Queen Maria*, p. 39.

37 Sergio Correa da Costa, *Every Inch a King* (London, 1950), p. 34.

38 Pereira, *Princesas e Infantas de Portugal*, p. 51.

39 Agnes Strickland, *Lives of the Queens of England*, 6 vols (London, revd edn 1896), vol. IV, p. 440.

40 For example, Beirão, ed., *Cartas da Rainha D. Mariana Vitória*, pp. 35, 42.

41 Quoted in Kirsten Schultz, *Tropical Versailles* (London, 2001), p. 155.

42 Ibid., p. 156.

43 Pereira, *Princesas e Infantas de Portugal*, pp. 39–40.

44 Domingues, *D. Maria I e a sua época*, p. 154.

45 Caetano Beirão, quoted ibid., p. 155.

46 Bombelles, *Journal d'un Ambassadeur de France au Portugal*, p. 70.

47 Beckford, *Italy with Sketches of Spain and Portugal*, p. 123.

48 Philadelphia Stephens, 'Account of the Royal Visit to Marinha Grande', in Roberts, *The Madness of Queen Maria*, pp. 145–58 (p. 154). This detailed and fascinating account of the royal visit was little known before it was published by Jenifer Roberts in 2009.

49 Marcus Cheke, *Carlota Joaquina, Queen of Portugal* (London, 1947), p. 39.

50 Bombelles, *Journal d'un Ambassadeur de France au Portugal*, p. 62.

51 Cheke, *Carlota Joaquina, Queen of Portugal*, p. 94.

52 Francis Gribble, *The Royal House of Portugal* (London, 1915), pp. 242–3.

53 Letter dated 26 March 1745, in Beirão, ed., *Cartas das Rainha D. Mariana Vitória*, p. 245.

54 Stephens, 'Account of the Royal Visit to Marinha Grande', in Roberts, *The Madness of Queen Maria*, p. 57.

55 Châtelet, *Voyage du ci-devant duc de Châtelet*, pp. 118–19.

56 Junot, *Memoirs of the Duchess D'Abrantès*, IV, p. 234.

57 Beirão, ed., *Cartas das Rainha D. Mariana Vitória*, p. 217.

58 For example, Domingues, *D. Maria I e a sua época*, pp. 187–8.

59 Pereira, *Princesas e Infantas de Portugal*, p. 39.

60 Cheke, *Carlota Joaquina, Queen of Portugal*, pp. 77–8, 92–3.

4 The Rise of the Braganza Ducal Family and the Reign of D. João IV

1 J. H. Elliott, *Richelieu and Olivares* (Cambridge, 1984), p. 64.

2 This section is based on 'The Portuguese Restoration and the General Crisis of the Seventeenth Century', Chapter 6 in Malyn Newitt, *Portugal in European and World History* (London, 2009), pp. 97–112.

3 Hipólito Raposo, *Dona Luisa de Gusmão* (Lisbon, 1947), p. 143.

4 Christian Hermann and Jacques Marcadé, *Les royaumes ibériques au XVIIe siècle* (Liège, 2000), p. 142.

5 António de Oliveira, 'Levantamentos populares do Algarve em 1637–1638', *Revista Portuguesa de História*, XX (1983), p. 33.

6 Anon., *O Sebastianismo: breve panorama dum mito português* (Lisbon, 1978), p. 10.

7 Abbé Vertot, *The History of the Revolutions of Portugal*, 5th edn (London, 1754), p. 26.

8 Quoted in I. S. Révah, *Le Cardinal de Richelieu et la Restauration du Portugal* (Lisbon, 1950), p. 8.

9 Vertot, *The History of the Revolutions of Portugal*, p. 16.

10 Quoted in Raposo, *Dona Luisa de Gusmão*, p. 156.

11 See discussion in Francisco Ribeiro da Silva, 'D. João IV, O Restaurador', in *História dos Reis de Portugal*, ed. Manuela Mendonça (Vila do Conde, 2011), II, pp. 163–209 (pp. 174–6).

12 See letters from the Crown to the duke printed in Révah, *Le Cardinal de Richelieu et la Restauration du Portugal*, pp. 55–97.

13 Raposo, *Dona Luisa de Gusmão*, p. 149.

14 Thomas Carte, *The History of the Revolutions of Portugal, from the foundation of that kingdom to the year MDCLXVII. With letters of Sir Robert Southwell during his embassy there to the Duke of Ormond* (London, 1740), p. 143.

15 Vertot, *The History of the Revolutions of Portugal*, p. 46.

16 Fernando Dores Costa, *A Guerra da Restauração, 1641–1668* (Lisbon, 2004), p. 15.

17 Carte, *The History of the Revolutions of Portugal*, p. 153.

18 Robert Jephson, *Braganza: A Tragedy, Performed at the Theatre Royal in Drury-Lane* (London, 1775).

19 Fernando Castelo Branco, *Lisboa Seiscentista* (Lisbon, 1969), p. 50.

20 Pedro de Mariz, *Dialogos de Varia Historia em que se referem as vidas dos Reyes de Portugal* (Lisbon, 1806), vol. II, p. 166.

21 Letter of François Lanier, Lisbon, 27 July 1643, printed in Edgar Prestage, *Informes de Francisco Lanier sobre Francisco de Lucena e a corte de D. João IV* (Coimbra, 1931), p. 13.

22 Rose Macaulay, 'Mac-Flecknoe's Father', in *They Went to Portugal* (London, 1946), p. 82.

23 For the trial of Lucena, see Prestage, *Informes de Francisco Lanier sobre Francisco de Lucena*.

24 Ana Maria Homem Leal de Faria, 'D. Pedro II, O Pacífico', in *História dos Reis de Portugal*, ed. Mendonça, II, p. 272; Joaquim Verissimo Serrão, *História de Portugal*, V (Lisbon, 1996), pp. 34–6.

25 Ribeiro da Silva, 'D. João IV, O Restaurador', p. 196.

26 Ibid.
27 Ana Cristina Duarte Pereira, *Princesas e Infantas de Portugal (1640–1736)* (Lisbon, 2008), pp. 62–5.
28 Conde de Ericeira, *História de Portugal restaurado*, ed. António Doria, 4 vols (Porto, 1945), vol. II, p. 418.
29 Pereira, *Princesas e Infantas de Portugal*, pp. 42–3.
30 Ribeiro da Silva, 'D. João IV, O Restaurador', p. 208.

5 The Children of D. João IV

1 Quoted in Lillias Campbell Davidson, *Catherine of Bragança, Infanta of Portugal and Queen-consort of England* (London, 1908), p. 64.
2 Quoted in Maria da Conceição Emiliano Castelo-Branco, 'The Stormy Passage to England of "A queen coming from Far"', *Revista de Estudos Anglo-Portugueses*, XXIII (2014), pp. 129–49 (p. 133). This article also contains a very useful bibliography of writings on Caterina.
3 Davidson, *Catherine of Bragança*, p. 73.
4 John Evelyn, *The Diary of John Evelyn*, ed. William Bray (London, 1907), vol. I, p. 370; diary entry for 30 May 1662.
5 Frances Parthenope Verney and Margaret M. Verney, eds, *Memoirs of the Verney Family during the Seventeenth Century*, 3rd edn (London, 1925), vol. II, p. 173.
6 Earl of Clarendon, *Clarendon: Selections from The History of the Rebellion and the Life by Himself*, ed. G. Huehns (Oxford, 1978), p. 397.
7 Ibid., p. 398.
8 Gilbert Burnet, *History of His Own Time* (London 1724), vol. I, p. 174.
9 Verney, *Memoirs of the Verney Family*, vol. II, p. 316.
10 Burnet, *History of His Own Time*, vol. I, p. 262.
11 Samuel Pepys, *The Diaries of Samuel Pepys*, ed. Robert Latham and William Matthews, 11 vols (London, 1970–83), vol. V, p. 188; diary entry for 24 June 1664.
12 Burnet, *History of His Own Time*, vol. I, p. 262.
13 Verney, *Memoirs of the Verney Family*, vol. II, p. 332.
14 Burnet, *History of His Own Time*, vol. I, p. 238.
15 John Dryden, *The Second Part of Absalom and Achitophel: A Poem* (London, 1682)
16 Agnes Strickland, *Lives of the Queens of England*, 6 vols (London, revd edn 1896), vol. IV, p. 404.
17 Gertrude Z. Thomas, *Richer than Spices* (New York, 1965), p. 31.
18 Edward Corp, 'Catherine of Braganza and Cultural Politics', in *Queenship in Britain, 1660–1837*, ed. Clarissa Campbell Orr (Manchester, 2002), p. 65.
19 Ibid., pp. 53–73.
20 Ibid.
21 Davidson, *Catherine of Bragança*, p. 462.
22 'Sir Robert Southwell to Lord Arlington', in Thomas Carte, *The History of the Revolutions of Portugal, from the foundation of that kingdom to the year MDCLXVII. With letters of Sir Robert Southwell during his embassy there to the Duke of Ormond* (London, 1740), p. 199.

23 For a long time this was carelessly attributed to the authorship of Samuel Pepys as its author was given as 'S.P.' and a copy was found in Pepys's own library. It is still catalogued in the British Library as by Samuel Pepys. However, in 1979 Helen Butz investigated the authorship and demonstrated that this was in fact an English translation of a French work entitled *Relation des troubles arrivez dans la cour de Portugal en l'année 1667 et en l'année 1668* (Amsterdam, 1674) by Michel Blouin, Sieur des Piquetièrres (hence S.P.). Blouin had been interpreter to the French ambassador in Madrid. See Helen Butz, 'The Authorship of *The Portugal History Made Plain*', *Papers of the Bibliographical Society of America*, LXXIII/4 (1979), pp. 459–62. It is significant that the first part of the conde de Ericeira's *História de Portugal restaurado* was published during the same decade, in 1678.

24 *The Portugal History; or, A relation of the Troubles that happened in the Court of Portugal in the years 1667 and 1668 . . . by S.P., Esq.* (London, 1677), p. 38.

25 John Colbatch, *An Account of the Court of Portugal under the Reign of the Present King Dom Pedro II. With some discourses on the interests of Portugal, with regard to other sovereigns; containing a relation of the most considerable transactions that have passed of late between the court, and those of Rome, Spain, France, Vienna, England etc.* (London, 1700), p. 44.

26 Ibid.

27 Pepys, *The Diaries of Samuel Pepys*, II, p.197; diary entry for 17 October 1661.

28 *The Portugal History*, pp. 55–6.

29 Maria Paula Marçal Lourenço, 'D. Afonso VI, O Vitorioso', in *História dos Reis de Portugal*, ed. Manuela Mendonça (Vilo do Conde, 2011), vol. II, pp. 211–63 (p. 219).

30 Conde de Ericeira, *História de Portugal restaurado*, ed. António Doria, 4 vols (Porto, 1945), vol. III, p. 11.

31 Pedro de Mariz, *Dialogos de Varia Historia em que se referem as vidas dos Reyes de Portugal*, 2 vols (Lisbon, 1806), vol. II, p. 187.

32 Joaquim Verissimo Serrão, *História de Portugal*, vol. V (Lisbon, 1996), pp. 47–8.

33 Lady Fanshawe, *Memoirs of Lady Fanshawe*, ed. Beatrice Marshall (London, 1905), p. 134.

34 Ibid., p. 136.

35 Lourenço, 'D. Afonso VI, O Vitorioso', p. 250.

36 Colbatch, *An Account of the Court of Portugal*, pp. 43–4.

37 Lourenço, 'D. Afonso VI, O Vitorioso', p. 251.

38 Ibid., pp. 253–6.

39 Ericeira, *História de Portugal restaurado*, vol. III, p. 12.

40 Carte, *The History of the Revolutions of Portugal*, pp. 201–2.

41 António Baião, ed., *Causa de Nulidade de Matrimónio entre a Rainha D. Maria Francisca de Saboya e o Rei Afonso VI* (Coimbra, 1925). Details summarized in Paula Lourenço, Ana Cristina Pereira and Joana Troni, *Amantes dos Reis de Portugal* (Lisbon, 2008), pp. 166–70.

42 Avelino de Freitas de Meneses, ed., *Portugal da Paz da Restauração ao Ouro do Brasil, Nova Historia de Portugal*, vol. VII (Lisbon, 2001), p. 193.

43 Serrão, *História de Portugal*, vol. v, pp. 197–8, 208.

44 Lourenço, 'D. Afonso vi, O Vitorioso', pp. 213–14.

45 Discussed ibid., pp. 233–6.

46 Serrão, *História de Portugal*, vol. v, p. 204.

47 Ana Cristina Duarte Pereira, *Princesas e Infantas de Portugal (1640–1736)* (Lisbon, 2008), p. 43.

48 Colbatch, *An Account of the Court of Portugal*, p. 6.

49 Ibid., p. 3.

50 Anon., *Mémoire touchant le Portugal*. A translation of an excerpt from this *mémoire*, which is located in the British Library, Sloane MS 2294, fols 14–16, is given in A. D. Francis, *The Methuens and Portugal* (Cambridge, 1966), pp. 26–8.

51 Anon., *Description de la ville de Lisbonne où l'on traite de la cour, de Portugal, de la langue Portuguaise, et ses moeurs, des habitans* (Paris, 1730); Portuguese trans. in Castelo Branco Chaves, *O Portugal de D. Joao v: visto por tres forasteiros* (Lisbon, 1989), p. 55.

52 Anon., *Mémoire touchant le Portugal*, trans. in Francis, *The Methuens and Portugal*, p. 27.

53 Colbatch, *An Account of the Court of Portugal*, p. 4.

54 Ana Maria Homem Leal de Faria, 'D. Pedro ii, O Pacífico', in *História dos Reis de Portugal*, ed. Mendonça, vol. ii, pp. 265–313 (pp. 268–9).

55 Serrão, *História de Portugal*, vol. v, p. 194.

6 D. João V: The Golden Age

1 José Saramago, *Baltasar and Blimunda*, trans. Giovanni Pontiero (London, 1998), p. 274.

2 Ibid., p. 75.

3 Ibid., p. 317.

4 Ibid., p. 176.

5 Ibid., pp. 298–9.

6 Ibid., pp. 268–9.

7 Ibid., p. 249.

8 Ibid., p. 248.

9 Ibid., pp. 20, 40.

10 Pedro Cardim, *Cortes e cultura política em Portugal do antigo regime* (Lisbon, 1998), p. 105.

11 Stephen Fisher, *The Portugal Trade* (London, 1971), p. 31.

12 Anon., *Description de la ville de Lisbonne où l'on traite de la cour, de Portugal, de la langue Portuguaise, & ses moeurs, des habitans* (Paris, 1730); Portuguese trans. in Castelo Branco Chaves, *O Portugal de D. Joao v: visto por tres forasteiros* (Lisbon, 1989), p. 51.

13 Avelino de Freitas de Meneses, ed., *Portugal da Paz da Restauração ao Ouro do Brasil*, Nova Historia de Portugal, vii (Lisbon, 2001), p. 203.

14 Joaquim Verissimo Serrão, *História de Portugal*, vol. v (Lisbon, 1996), p. 236.

15 David Erskine, ed., *Augustus Hervey's Journal: The Adventures Afloat and Ashore of a Naval Casanova* (London, 2002), p. 75.

16 Ibid., p. 122.
17 Rómulo de Carvalho, *Relações entre Portugal e a Russia no século XVIII* (Lisbon, 1979), p. 16.
18 For details of the marriage negotiations and journey to Lisbon, see Eduardo Brazão, *O Casamento de D. João V* (Lisbon, 1937).
19 Quoted in Paula Lourenço, Ana Cristina Pereira and Joana Troni, *Amantes dos Reis de Portugal* (Lisbon, 2008), p. 187.
20 Ana Cristina Duarte Pereira, *Princesas e Infantas de Portugal (1640–1736)* (Lisbon, 2008), p. 53.
21 Ibid., pp. 53–9, 234–48.
22 Ibid., pp. 183–4.
23 Charles Frédéric de Merveilleux, 'Memórias instrutivas sobre Portugal', in *O Portugal de João V visto por três forasteiros*, trans. Castelo Branco Chaves (Lisbon, 1983), pp. 129–30 (p. 144).
24 Erskine, ed., *Augustus Hervey's Journal*, p. 75.
25 Merveilleux, 'Memórias instrutivas sobre Portugal', p. 142.
26 Lourenço, Pereira and Troni, *Amantes dos Reis de Portugal*, p. 191.
27 Richard Twiss, *Travels through Portugal and Spain in 1772 and 1773* (London, 1775), p. 36.
28 [Gabriel-Joseph de La Vergne, Comte de Guilleragues], *Lettres Portugaises* (Paris, 1669); trans. W. R. Bowles as *Letters from a Portuguese Nun to an Officer in the French Army* (London, 1808).
29 Lourenço, Pereira and Troni, *Amantes dos Reis de Portugal*, p. 192.
30 Anon., *Description de la ville de Lisbonne*, p. 50.
31 Quoted in Jean-François Labourdette, *Histoire du Portugal* (Paris, 2000), pp. 375–6.
32 Merveilleux, 'Memórias instrutivas sobre Portugal', pp. 150–51.
33 Ibid., p. 181.
34 Anon., *Description de la ville de Lisbonne*, pp. 71–2.
35 Merveilleux, 'Memórias instrutivas sobre Portugal', p. 147.
36 Vincent Barletta, 'Introduction: The Baroque as Conversation-starter', *Journal of Lusophone Studies*, XII (2014), pp. 13–21.
37 Carvalho, *Relações entre Portugal e a Russia no século XVIII*, p. 4.
38 Angela Delaforce, 'Lisbon, "This New Rome": Dom João V of Portugal and Relations between Rome and Lisbon', in *The Age of the Baroque in Portugal*, ed. Jay A. Levenson (New Haven, CT, 1993), p. 52.
39 A clear and detailed statement of this view of D. João V is in Timothy Walker, *Doctors, Folk Medicine and the Inquisition* (Leiden, 2005), pp. 155–65.
40 Delaforce, 'Lisbon, "This New Rome"', p. 62.
41 Labourdette, *Histoire du Portugal*, p. 381.
42 Serrão, *História de Portugal*, vol. V, p. 262.
43 A. Ayres de Carvalho, 'Dom João V and the Artists of Papal Rome', in *The Age of the Baroque in Portugal*, ed. Jay A. Levenson (New Haven, CT, 1993), p. 35.
44 Delaforce, 'Lisbon, "This New Rome"', p. 63.
45 William Dalrymple, *Travels through Spain and Portugal in 1774; with a short account of the Spanish Expedition against Algiers in 1775* (London, 1777), p. 135.

46 William Beckford, *The Journal of William Beckford in Portugal and Spain,
    1797–1788*, ed. Boyd Alexander (London, 1954), p. 129.
47 Ibid., pp. 180–81.
48 Saramago, *Baltasar and Blimunda*, p. 77.
49 Labourdette, *Histoire du Portugal*, pp. 375–6.
50 This is the thesis of Timothy Walker's detailed study *Doctors, Folk
    Medicine and the Inquisition.*
51 Serrão, *História de Portugal*, vol. v, p. 236.
52 Caetano Beirão, ed., *Cartas das Rainha D. Mariana Vitória para a sua
    família de Espanha* (Lisbon, 1936), p. 243.

7 D. José: The Reformer

 1 Jean-François Labourdette, *Histoire du Portugal* (Paris, 2000), p. 402.
 2 Nathaniel Wraxall, *Historical Memoirs of My Own Time*, 3rd edn
    (London, 1818), pp. 11–12.
 3 David Erskine, ed., *Augustus Hervey's Journal: The Adventures Afloat and
    Ashore of a Naval Casanova* (London, 2002), pp. 125–6.
 4 Suzanne Chantal, *La vie quotidienne au Portugal après le tremblement de
    terre de Lisbonne de 1755* (Paris, 1965). All quotations are taken from
    the Portuguese translation, *A vida quotidiana em Portugal ao tempo do
    terramoto* (Lisbon, 1965), p. 70.
 5 Improbable as this may sound, it was recorded and illustrated by
    Paulo Dardini. See Aline Gallasch-Hall de Beuvink, *O Real Teatro de
    Salvaterra de Magos* (Casal de Cambra, 2016), p. 18.
 6 Chantal, *A vida quotidiana em Portugal ao tempo do terramoto*, p. 71.
 7 Wraxall, *Historical Memoirs of My Own Time*, p. 23.
 8 Ibid., p. 235.
 9 For an account of the theatre at Salvaterra de Magos, see Gallasch-Hall
    de Beuvink, *O Real Teatro de Salvaterra de Magos*; extracts from *Notícia
    de uma viagem a Portugal, 1765–1766*, quoted pp. 24–7.
10 Charles François Dumouriez, *Etat présent du Royaume de Portugal en
    l'année 1766* (Hamburg, 1797), p. 236.
11 Caetano Beirão, ed., *Cartas das Rainha D. Mariana Vitória para a sua
    família de Espanha* (Lisbon, 1936), pp. 53, 56.
12 Dumouriez, *Etat présent du Royaume de Portugal*, p. 238.
13 Quoted in Jenifer Roberts, *The Madness of Queen Maria* (Chippenham,
    2009), p. 8.
14 Wraxall, *Historical Memoirs of My Own Time*, pp. 14–15.
15 William Beckford, *Italy, with Sketches of Spain and Portugal*, 2nd edn
    (London, 1834), vol. II, p. 72. It is only fair to record that a Frenchman
    who described the theatre at Salvaterra in 1766 thought that the male
    actors were excellent.
16 Wraxall, *Historical Memoirs of My Own Time*, pp. 15–16.
17 Chantal, *A vida quotidiana em Portugal ao tempo do terramoto*, p. 69.
18 Dumouriez, *Etat présent du Royaume de Portugal*, p. 236.
19 Quoted in A. D. Francis, *Portugal, 1715–1808* (London, 1985), p. 104.
20 Marcus Cheke, *Dictator of Portugal, Marquis of Pombal* (London, 1938),
    p. 10.

21 Chantal, *A vida quotidiana em Portugal ao tempo do terramoto*, p. 67.

22 Mário Domingues, *D. Maria I e a sua época* (Lisbon, 1972), p. 59;
    Kenneth Maxwell, *Pombal, Paradox of the Enlightenment* (Cambridge,
    1995), p. 152.

23 Cheke, *Dictator of Portugal*, p. 208.

24 Ibid., p. 184.

25 Erskine, ed., *Augustus Hervey's Journal*, p. 164.

26 Cheke, *Dictator of Portugal*, p. 205.

27 Beckford, *Italy, with Sketches of Spain and Portugal*, vol. II, p. 44.

28 Caetano Beirão, *D. Maria I (1777–1792)* (Lisbon, 1934), p. 72.

29 John Smith [Athelstane], *Memoirs of the Marquis of Pombal with Extracts
    from his Writings*, 2 vols (London, 1843), vol. I, p. 289.

30 Duc de Châtelet [Baron Dezoteux de Cormatin], *Voyage du ci-devant
    duc de Châtelet, en Portugal*, ed. Jean-François, baron de Bourgoing
    (Paris, 1798), pp. 131–2.

31 William Beckford, *The Journal of William Beckford in Portugal and
    Spain, 1787–1788*, ed. Boyd Alexander (London, 1954), pp. 50–51. These
    passages were repeated almost word for word in *Italy, with Sketches of
    Spain and Portugal*, vol. II, pp. 25–7.

32 Wraxall, *Historical Memoirs of My Own Time*, pp. 17, 19–20.

33 Giuseppe Gorani, *Mémoires pour servir à l'histoire de ma vie (1806–7)*
    (Milan, 1936); quotation from Portuguese trans. as *Portugal: A Corte e
    o Pais nos anos 1765 a 1767* (Lisbon, 1989), pp. 118–19; Chantal, *A vida
    quotidiana em Portugal ao tempo do terramoto*, p. 68.

34 Ibid., p. 17.

35 Beckford, *The Journal of William Beckford in Portugal and Spain*, p. 262.

36 Ibid., p. 103 n. 1.

37 F. A. Dutra, 'The Wounding of King José: Accident or Assassination
    Attempt?', *Mediterranean Studies*, VII (1998), pp. 221–9.

38 Erskine, ed., *Augustus Hervey's Journal*, pp. 153, 179.

39 Chantal, *A vida quotidiana em Portugal ao tempo do terramoto*, p. 77. This
    anecdote, like many others, was first recorded by the Duc de Châtelet,
    Voyage du ci-devant duc de Châtelet, p. 126.

40 Marquis de Bombelles, *Journal d'un Ambassadeur de France au Portugal,
    1786–1788* (Paris, 1979), p. 64.

41 Maxwell, *Pombal, Paradox of the Enlightenment*, p. 150.

42 A.P.F., *Parallelo de Augusto Cesar e de Dom Jose o Magnanimo Rey do
    Portugal* (Lisbon, 1775).

8 D. Maria I and D. Pedro III

1 For these accounts of her childhood, see Caetano Beirão, *D. Maria I
   (1777–1792)* (Lisbon, 1934), pp. 32–4.

2 Luís de Oliveira Ramos, *D. Maria I* (Lisbon, 2010), pp. 41–2.

3 Beirão, *D. Maria I*, p. 47.

4 Arthur William Costigan, *Sketches of Society and Manners in Portugal*,
   2 vols (London, 1787), vol. II, p. 357. Doubt has been cast on the real
   authorship of the letters supposed to be by Costigan. See Beirão,
   D. Maria I, pp. 81–2.

5 Duc de Châtelet [Baron Dezoteux de Cormatin], *Voyage du ci-devant duc de Châtelet, en Portugal,* ed. Jean-François, baron de Bourgoing (Paris, 1798), p. 120.

6 Marquis de Bombelles, *Journal d'un Ambassadeur de France au Portugal, 1786–1788* (Paris, 1979), p. 99.

7 Jenifer Roberts, *The Madness of Queen Maria* (Chippenham, 2009), p. 15.

8 William Beckford, *The Journal of William Beckford in Portugal and Spain, 1787–1788,* ed. Boyd Alexander (London, 1954), p. 262.

9 This is the interpretation of events given in Beirão, *D. Maria I,* p. 62.

10 Ibid., pp. 72–3.

11 Quoted ibid., p. 37.

12 Beckford, *The Journal of William Beckford in Portugal and Spain,* p. 277.

13 Costigan, *Sketches of Society and Manners in Portugal,* vol. II, p. 119.

14 Roberts, *The Madness of Queen Maria,* p. 35.

15 Mário Domingues, *D. Maria I e a sua época* (Lisbon, 1972), p. 48.

16 Roberts, *The Madness of Queen Maria,* p. 69.

17 Domingues, *D. Maria I e a sua época,* p. 45.

18 Ibid., p. 79.

19 Bombelles, *Journal d'un Ambassadeur de France au Portugal,* p. 103.

20 William Beckford, *Italy, with Sketches of Spain and Portugal,* 2 vols (London, 1834), vol. II, pp. 196–7.

21 Kenneth Maxwell, *Pombal, Paradox of the Enlightenment* (Cambridge, 1995), p. 137.

22 Quotations are all from the 'Account of the Royal Visit to Marinha Grande' by Philadelphia Stephens in Roberts, *The Madness of Queen Maria,* pp. 145–58.

23 Oliveira Ramos, *D. Maria I,* p. 237.

24 Châtelet, *Voyage du ci-devant duc de Châtelet,* p. 29.

25 Ibid., pp. 31–2.

26 Costigan, *Sketches of Society and Manners in Portugal,* vol. II, p. 132.

27 Maxwell, *Pombal, Paradox of the Enlightenment,* p. 157.

28 Beirão, *D. Maria I,* pp. 95–6.

29 Domingues, *D. Maria I e a sua época,* p. 74; Beirão, *D. Maria I,* pp. 98–100.

30 Charles François Dumouriez, *Etat présent du Royaume de Portugal en l'année 1766* (Hamburg, 1797), p. 237.

31 Châtelet, *Voyage du ci-devant duc de Châtelet,* p. 126.

32 In Ana Maria Rodrigues, ed., *D. João VI e o seu tempo,* Commissão Nacional para a Comemorações dos Descobrimentos Portugueses (Lisbon, 1999), p. 23, it is said that the Portuguese princess married the future Ferdinand VII. This is a mistake. Ferdinand VII did indeed marry a Portuguese infanta as his second wife, but this was Maria Isabel, daughter of D. João VI and Carlota Joaquina, and the marriage took place in 1816.

33 Domingues, *D. Maria I e a sua época,* p. 194.

34 Ibid., pp. 195–6.

35 Bombelles, *Journal d'un Ambassadeur de France au Portugal,* p. 103.

36 Beckford, *The Journal of William Beckford in Portugal and Spain,* p. 242; diary entry for 22 October 1787.

37 Ibid., p. 235.

38 Beirão, *D. Maria I*, p. 45.

39 Laure Junot, *Memoirs of the Duchess D'Abrantès (Madame Junot)*, vol. IV (London, 1831), pp. 295–6.

40 Roberts, *The Madness of Queen Maria*, p. 135.

41 Beirão, *D. Maria I*, pp. 66–8.

42 Bombelles, *Journal d'un Ambassadeur de France au Portugal*, p. 103.

43 Discussed by Boyd Alexander in Beckford, *The Journal of William Beckford in Portugal and Spain*, p. 28.

44 Ibid., p. 233.

45 Maria Ines Ferro, *Queluz: The Palace and Gardens* (London, 1997), pp. 14–17.

9 D. João VI: The Merciful

1 Maria Ines Ferro, *Queluz: The Palace and Gardens* (London, 1997), p. 38.

2 Marquis de Bombelles, *Journal d'un Ambassadeur de France au Portugal, 1786–1788* (Paris, 1979), p. 94.

3 Ibid., p. 69.

4 Marcus Cheke, *Carlota Joaquina, Queen of Portugal* (London, 1947), p. 110.

5 Sergio Correa da Costa, *Every Inch a King* (London, 1950), p. 29.

6 Oliveira Marques in Ana Maria Rodrigues, ed., *D. João VI e o seu tempo* (Lisbon, 1999), p. 30.

7 Paula Lourenço, Ana Cristina Pereira and Joana Troni, *Amantes dos Reis de Portugal* (Lisbon, 2008), pp. 217–19.

8 He did eventually marry Napoleon's sister-in-law. Neill Macaulay, *Dom Pedro: The Struggle for Liberty in Brazil and Portugal, 1798–1834* (Durham, NC, 1986), p. 54.

9 For an up-to-date assessment of these plans, see A. R. Disney, *A History of Portugal and the Portuguese Empire*, vol. I (Cambridge, 2009), p. 330.

10 Jean-François Labourdette, *Histoire du Portugal* (Paris, 2000), p. 483.

11 Cheke, *Carlota Joaquina*, p. 23.

12 Patrick Wilcken, *Empire Adrift: The Portuguese Court in Rio de Janeiro, 1808–1821* (London, 2004).

13 See estimate of D. João's personal qualities in Oliveira Lima, *Dom João VI no Brazil, 1808–1821* (Rio de Janeiro, 1908), pp. 939–43. For the custom of petitioning the king, see Kirsten Schultz, *Tropical Versailles* (London, 2001), pp. 152–5.

14 Wellington Papers, Southampton University, WP 1/519 Beresford to Wellington, 22 Sept 1816.

15 Ibid.

16 These events are brilliantly, if differently, described in Wilcken, *Empire Adrift* and Schultz, *Tropical Versailles*.

17 James Prior, *Voyage along the Eastern Coast of Africa . . . in the Nisus Frigate* (London, 1819), p. 99.

18 For the relations of Beresford with D. João and the Council of Regency. see Malyn Newitt and Martin Robson, eds, *Lord Beresford and the British Intervention in Portugal, 1807–1820* (Lisbon, 2004).

19 Cheke, *Carlota Joaquina*, pp. 66–8.
20 Macaulay, *Dom Pedro: The Struggle for Liberty*, p. 86.
21 Quoted in Cheke, *Carlota Joaquina*, p. 149.
22 Harold Temperley, *The Foreign Policy of Canning, 1822–1827* (London, 1925), p. 219.
23 Laure Junot, *Memoirs of the Duchess D'Abrantès (Madame Junot)*, vol. IV (London, 1831), p. 230.
24 Costa, *Every Inch a King*, p. 21.
25 Junot, *Memoirs of the Duchess D'Abrantès*, vol. IV, p. 232.
26 Cheke, *Carlota Joaquina*, p. 85.
27 Ibid., p. 135.
28 José Victorino Barreto Feio, *Dom Miguel, ses aventures scandaleuses, ses crimes et son usurpation par un portugais de distinction*, trans. J. B. Mesnard (Paris, 1833).
29 Alexandra Wilhelmsen, 'Maria Teresa of Braganza: Portuguese Princess of Beira, Spanish Infanta, Wife of the Pretender Carlos V', *Mediterranean Studies*, VI (1996), pp. 79–106.
30 Macaulay, *Dom Pedro: The Struggle for Liberty*, p. 40.
31 Julia Nery, *Infantas de Portugal* (Lisbon, 1998), p. 31.
32 Malcolm Howe, *The Braganza Story* (Lisbon, 1999), p. 45.
33 Quoted in Cheke, *Carlota Joaquina*, p. 117.

10 D. Pedro and D. Miguel

 1 Sergio Correa da Costa, *Every Inch a King* (London, 1950), p. 63.
 2 Harold Temperley, *The Foreign Policy of Canning, 1822–1827* (London, 1925), p. 212.
 3 Marleide da Mota Gomes and Miguel Chalub, 'Dom Pedro I of Brazil and IV of Portugal: Epilepsy and Peculiar Behavior', *Arquivos de Neuro-Psiquiatria*, LXV (2007), pp. 710–15.
 4 Neill Macaulay, *Dom Pedro: The Struggle for Liberty in Brazil and Portugal, 1798–1834* (Durham, NC, 1986), p. 125. The persistence of the belief in D. Pedro's authorship of the national anthem is symbolic of the importance that many Brazilians still attach to the monarchy. In fact the music of the anthem was composed after he had left Brazil in 1831 by Francisco Manuel da Sylva to words by Ovídio de Carvalho e Silva.
 5 Paula Lourenço, Ana Cristina Pereira and Joana Troni, *Amantes dos Reis de Portugal* (Lisbon, 2008), p. 233.
 6 Macaulay, *Dom Pedro: The Struggle for Liberty*, p. 175.
 7 Marcus Cheke, *Carlota Joaquina, Queen of Portugal* (London, 1947), p. 103; Macaulay, *Dom Pedro: The Struggle for Liberty*, p. 123.
 8 Costa, *Every Inch a King*, p. 86.
 9 Ibid.
10 Macaulay, *Dom Pedro: The Struggle for Liberty*, p. 152.
11 Ibid., p. 147.
12 Ibid., pp. 119–20.
13 Costa, *Every Inch a King*, pp. 93–6.
14 Elizabeth Mavor, ed., *The Captain's Wife: The South American Journals of Maria Graham 1821–1823* (London, 1993), p. 57.

15 Macaulay, *Dom Pedro: The Struggle for Liberty*, p. 146.

16 Maria de Fátima Bonifácio, *D. Maria II* (Lisbon, 2011), p. 15.

17 See discussion of Sir Charles Stuart's role in [Lady Canning], *An Authentic Account of Mr Canning's Policy with Respect to the Constitutional Charter* (London, 1830).

18 Virgílio Arruda, *Dom Pedro e Dom Miguel do Brasil ao Ribatejo* (Santarém, 1972), p. 40.

19 Charles Webster, *The Foreign Policy of Palmerston*, vol. I (London, 1951), pp. 241, 250; José Victorino Barreto Feio, *Dom Miguel, ses aventures scandaleuses, ses crimes et son usurpation par un portugais de distinction*, trans. J. B. Mesnard (Paris, 1833); João Batista da Silva Lopes, *História do cativeiro dos prezos d'Estado na Torre de S. Julião da Barra de Lisboa*, 4 vols (Lisbon, 1833–4); R. B. Hoppner, 'Observations on the true state of Portugal and views of the Faction who now govern it, with respect to England and Spain', National Archives (NA), Kew, FO 63/389, Hoppner to Palmerston, 26 December 1832; C. S. Buckland, 'Richard Belgrave Hoppner', *English Historical Review*, XXXIX (1924), pp. 373–85.

20 Arruda, *Dom Pedro e Dom Miguel do Brasil ao Ribatejo*, p. 38.

21 Macaulay, *Dom Pedro: The Struggle for Liberty*, p. 68.

22 Barreto Feio, *Dom Miguel, ses aventures scandaleuses, ses crimes et son usurpation*, p. 13.

23 Arruda, *Dom Pedro e Dom Miguel do Brasil ao Ribatejo*, p. 42.

24 Marianne Baillie, *Lisbon in the Years 1821, 1822, and 1823*, 2 vols (London, 1824); reprinted in *Women's Travel Writings in Iberia*, ed. José Ruíz Mas (London, 2013), vol. II, pp. 38–9.

25 Quoted in Cheke, *Carlota Joaquina*, p. 120.

26 Barreto Feio, *Dom Miguel, ses aventures scandaleuses, ses crimes et son usurpation*, p. 20; Arruda, *Dom Pedro e Dom Miguel do Brasil ao Ribatejo*, p. 43.

27 Arruda, *Dom Pedro e Dom Miguel do Brasil ao Ribatejo*, p. 46.

28 Quoted in Cheke, *Carlota Joaquina*, p. 159.

29 [Canning] *An Authentic Account of Mr Canning's Policy*, p. 31.

30 Charles Greville, *A Journal of the Reigns of King George IV, King William IV and Queen Victoria*, 8 vols (London, 1888), vol. III, p. 27.

31 Maria da Graça Vicente, 'D. Miguel, O Rei Absoluto', in *História dos Reis de Portugal*, ed. Manuela Mendonça (Vila do Conde, 2011), vol. II, pp. 541–87 (p. 560).

32 Earl of Carnarvon, *Portugal and Galicia*, 3rd edn (London, 1848), p. 196.

33 Ibid., p. 198.

34 Ibid., p. 210.

35 Ibid., p. 222.

36 Vicente, 'D. Miguel, O Rei Absoluto', p. 564.

37 Vasco Pulido Valente, *Os militares e a política (1820–1856)* (Lisbon, 1999), p. 82.

38 Vicente, 'D. Miguel, O Rei Absoluto', p. 567.

39 NA FO 63/371, Hoppner to Palmerston, 9 July 1831.

40 Ibid., Lisbon, 16 July 1831.

41 Ibid.

42 Ibid., 30 July and 6 August 1831.
43 NA FO 63/373, Hoppner to Sir George Shee, 12 November 1831.
44 Georgiana Blakiston, *Lord William Russell and his Wife* (London, 1972), p. 249.
45 Ibid., p. 250.
46 Ibid., pp. 251, 253.
47 Quoted in Buckland, 'Richard Belgrave Hoppner', p. 380.
48 Carnarvon, *Portugal and Galicia*, pp. 204–6.
49 Malcolm Howe, *The Braganza Story* (Lisbon, 1999), p. 113.
50 Vicente, 'D. Miguel, O Rei Absoluto', pp. 585–7.
51 José Maria de Eça de Queiroz, *The City and the Mountains*, trans. Roy Campbell (London, 1955), pp. 5–7.
52 Ibid., p. 189.
53 Ibid., pp. 196–8.
54 Luís de Sousa Rebelo, 'Oliveira Martins: The Spectres in his Historiography', *Portuguese Studies*, XX (2004), pp. 108–22 (pp. 119, 121).

11 The Constitutional Monarchs: D. Maria II, D. Fernando and their Sons, D. Pedro V and D. Luís

 1 Elizabeth Mavor, ed., *The Captain's Wife: The South American Journals of Maria Graham, 1821–1823* (London, 1993), p. 160.
 2 George Young, *Portugal Old and New* (Oxford, 1917), p. 248.
 3 Neill Macaulay, *Dom Pedro: The Struggle for Liberty in Brazil and Portugal, 1798–1834* (Durham, NC, 1986), p. 190.
 4 Maria da Fátima Bonifacio, *D. Maria II* (Lisbon, 2011), p. 48.
 5 Charles Greville, *A Journal of the Reigns of King George IV, King William IV and Queen Victoria*, 8 vols (London, 1888), vol. I, p. 214.
 6 For Maria's stay in Britain, see Bonifácio, *D. Maria II*, pp. 46–55.
 7 For Maria's prospects during the years 1828–31, see ibid., pp. 21–32.
 8 Abraham Kriegel, ed., *The Holland House Diaries, 1831–1840* (London, 1977), p. 8.
 9 Bonifácio, *D. Maria II*, p. 78.
10 Paula Lourenço, Ana Cristina Pereira and Joana Troni, *Amantes dos Reis de Portugal* (Lisbon, 2008), pp. 252–3; Bonifácio, *D. Maria II*, p. 85.
11 Bonifácio, *D. Maria II*, p. 88.
12 Kriegel, ed., *The Holland House Diaries*, p. 336.
13 From the *Memórias* of Bulhão Pato, quoted in Bonifácio, *D. Maria II*, p. 95.
14 Fernando Policarpo, 'D. Maria II, A Educadora', in *História dos Reis de Portugal*, ed. Manuela Mendonça (Vila do Conde, 2011), vol. II, p. 633.
15 Francis Gribble, *The Royal House of Portugal* (London, 1915), pp. 221–2.
16 Royal Archives, Windsor (RA) VIC/MAIN/QVJ (W), 1 June 1838, 15 September 1838, available at www.queenvictoriasjournals.org.
17 Ibid., 4 April 1838.
18 Ibid., 6 February 1836.
19 Ibid., 18 September 1836.
20 Victoria to Leopold, 21 November 1836, in *The Letters of Queen Victoria*, ed. A. C. Benson and Viscount Esher, 3 vols (London, 1908), vol. I, p. 54;

for the so-called 'Belemzada', see Vasco Pulido Valente, *Os militares e a política (1820–1856)* (Lisbon, 1999), p. 117.

21 Charles Webster, *The Foreign Policy of Palmerston*, vol. I (London, 1951), p. 486.

22 RA VIC/MAIN/QVJ (W), 10 January 1837.

23 Victoria to Leopold, 16 January 1837, in *The Letters of Queen Victoria*, ed. Benson and Esher, vol. I, p. 58.

24 RA VIC/MAIN/QVJ (W), 5 February 1837.

25 Kriegel, ed., *The Holland House Diaries*, p. 352.

26 Victoria to Leopold, 3 October 1837, in *The Letters of Queen Victoria*, ed. Benson and Esher, vol. I, p. 92.

27 RA VIC/MAIN/QVJ (W), 21 March 1838.

28 Ibid., 28 July 1838.

29 Brian Connell, *Regina v Palmerston* (London, 1962), p. 49.

30 Bonifácio, *D. Maria II*, p. 113.

31 Quoted in José Hermano Saraiva, *História concisa de Portugal*, 19th edn (Lisbon, 1998), p. 301.

32 Ibid., p. 302.

33 Bonifácio, *D. Maria II*, pp. 102–4.

34 Gribble, *The Royal House of Portugal*, p. 215.

35 Kriegel, ed., *The Holland House Diaries*, p. 312.

36 Bonifácio, *D. Maria II*, pp. 85, 98.

37 Anon. [António Pereira dos Reis], *A Letter to Joseph Hume Esq MP upon the late Debate on Portugal in the British House of Commons by an Anglo-Lusitanian* (London, 1847), p. 108.

38 Connell, *Regina v Palmerston*, p. 60.

39 Ibid., p. 59.

40 Quoted in E. Feuchtwanger, *Albert and Victoria* (London, 2006), p. 72.

41 Valente, *Os militares e a política*, p. 37.

42 Quoted in Roderick Barman, *Princess Isabel of Brazil* (Wilmington, DE, 2002), p. 246.

43 Jean-François Labourdette, *Histoire du Portugal* (Paris, 2000), p. 537.

44 Vicente de Bragança Cunha, *Eight Centuries of Portuguese Monarchy* (London, 1911), p. 151.

45 Malcolm Jack, *Sintra: A Glorious Eden* (Manchester, 2002), pp. 147–50.

46 Quoted in Gribble, *The Royal House of Portugal*, p. 221.

47 Hans Christian Andersen, *A Visit to Portugal, 1866*, trans. Grace Thornton (London, 1972), pp. 32–3.

48 António Ventura, 'D. Pedro V, O Esperançoso', in *História dos Reis de Portugal*, ed. Manuela Mendonça (Vila do Conde, 2011), vol. II, p. 641.

49 Ibid., pp. 643–4.

50 Quoted in Lourenço, Pereira and Troni, *Amantes dos Reis de Portugal*, p. 261.

51 Victoria to Leopold, 13 October 1856, in *The Letters of Queen Victoria*, ed. Benson and Esher, vol. III, pp. 211–12.

52 Lourenço, Pereira and Troni, *Amantes dos Reis de Portugal*, p. 262.

53 Maria Filomena Mónica, ed., *Correspondência entre D. Pedro V e seu tio o príncipe Alberto* (Lisbon, 2000), p. 15.

54 The likelihood that this was the case is discussed ibid., pp. 16–17.

55 Ibid., p. 9.
56 Ventura, 'D. Pedro v, O Esperançoso', p. 681.
57 Victoria to Leopold, 12 November 1861, in *The Letters of Queen Victoria*, ed. Benson and Esher, vol. iii, pp. 465–6.
58 António Ventura, 'D. Luís, O Popular', in *História dos Reis de Portugal*, ed. Manuela Mendonça (Vila do Conde, 2011), vol. ii, pp. 685–9.
59 G. F. White, *A Century of Spain and Portugal, 1788–1898* (London, 1909), p. 332.
60 Gribble, *The Royal House of Portugal*, p. 248.
61 Lourenço, Pereira and Troni, *Amantes dos Reis de Portugal*, pp. 271–4.
62 Ventura, 'D. Luís, O Popular', p. 700.
63 Gribble, *The Royal House of Portugal*, p. 247.
64 Ventura, 'D. Luís, O Popular', p. 718.
65 Andersen, *A Visit to Portugal, 1866*, pp. 35–6.
66 Bragança Cunha, *Eight Centuries of Portuguese Monarchy*, p. 176.
67 Ibid., p. 177.

12 The Twilight of the Gods: D. Carlos and D. Manuel

1 The epithet usually given to D. Carlos is *O Diplomata* (the Diplomat) but Malcolm Howe has *O Martirazado* (the Martyr).
2 Joseph Joûbert, *Dom Carlos 1er, roi de Portugal* (Paris, 1908), p. 6.
3 Teresa Maria Sousa Nunes, 'D. Carlos, O Diplomata', in *História dos Reis de Portugal*, ed. Manuela Mendonça (Vila do Conde, 2011), vol. ii, pp. 737–8.
4 Joûbert, *Dom Carlos 1er, roi de Portugal*, p. 7.
5 For D. Carlos's scientific work, see Mário Ruivo, 'D. Carlos de Bragança, naturalista e oceanógrafo', *Oceanos* (April 1992), pp. 102–11.
6 Lucien Corpechot, *Memories of Queen Amélie of Portugal* (London, 1915), pp. 266–80.
7 Filipe Ribeiro de Menseses, *Afonso Costa* (London, 2010), p. 6.
8 Vicente de Bragança Cunha, *Eight Centuries of Portuguese Monarchy* (London, 1911), p. 222.
9 Gervase Clarence-Smith, *The Third Portuguese Empire, 1825–1975* (Manchester, 1985), pp. 81, 85.
10 Nunes, 'D. Carlos, O Diplomata', p. 749; G. F. White, *A Century of Spain and Portugal, 1788–1898* (London, 1909), p. 350.
11 Alan Freeland, 'Imagined Endings: National Catastrophe in the Fiction of Eça de Queiroz', *Portuguese Studies*, xv (1999), p. 126.
12 For the farce surrounding the discovery of the 'real' bones of Vasco da Gama, see Sanjay Subrahmanyam, *The Career and Legend of Vasco da Gama* (Cambridge, 1997).
13 Nunes, 'D. Carlos, O Diplomata', pp. 762–3.
14 George Young, *Portugal Old and New* (Oxford, 1917), p. 262.
15 Quoted in José Hermano Saraiva, *História concisa de Portugal*, 19th edn (Lisbon, 1998), p. 346.
16 Quoted in Malcolm Howe, *The Braganza Story* (Lisbon, 1999), p. 81.

17 Douglas Wheeler, *Republican Portugal: A Political History, 1910–1926* (Madison, WI, 1978), p. 10.
18 Quoted ibid., p. 19.
19 Ibid., p. 26.
20 Ibid., p. 31.
21 Paula Lourenço, Ana Cristina Pereira and Joana Troni, *Amantes dos Reis de Portugal* (Lisbon, 2008), p. 277.
22 Ibid., pp. 278–9.
23 Nunes, 'D. Carlos, O Diplomata', p. 768.
24 Ibid., p. 773; Bragança Cunha, *Eight Centuries of Portuguese Monarchy*, p. 230.
25 Corpechot, *Memories of Queen Amélie of Portugal*, p. 191.
26 Ibid., p. 187.
27 See discussion in Eurico Carlos Esteves Lage Cardoso, *D. Manuel II: O Rei Patriota* (Lisbon, 2003), pp. 31–2. This book is written by a prominent monarchist.
28 Aubrey Bell, *Portugal of the Portuguese* (London, 1915), p. 189.
29 Nunes, 'D. Carlos, O Diplomata', p. 778.
30 Cardoso, *D. Manuel II: O Rei Patriota*, p. 37.
31 Ibid., pp. 48–9.
32 Ibid., p. 22.
33 The ceremony is described in detail ibid., pp. 51–4.
34 Maria Odete Sequeira Martins, 'D. Manuel, O Patriota', in *História dos Reis de Portugal*, ed. Manuela Mendonça (Vila do Conde, 2011), vol. II, p. 797.
35 Bell, *Portugal of the Portuguese*, p. 193.
36 Martins, 'D. Manuel, O Patriota', p. 803.
37 Lourenço, Pereira and Troni, *Amantes dos Reis de Portugal*, pp. 285–7.
38 Douglas Wheeler, 'The Portuguese Revolution of 1910', *Journal of Modern History*, XLIV (1972), pp. 175–6, 194.
39 Young, *Portugal Old and New*, pp. 270–71.
40 Paulo Drummond Braga, *Nas Teias de Salazar: D. Duarte Nuno, entre a esperança e a desilusão* (Lisbon, 2017), p. 29.
41 Wheeler, *Republican Portugal*, pp. 194–8.
42 Braga, *Nas Teias de Salazar*, p. 42.
43 Virgílio Arruda, *Dom Pedro e Dom Miguel do Brasil ao Ribatejo* (Santarém, 1972), pp. 273–8.
44 For the detail of this story, see Malcolm Howe, *The Braganza Story* (Lisbon, 1999).
45 Braga, *Nas Teias de Salazar*, p. 17.

13 D. Pedro II, Emperor of Brazil

1 D. Pedro II has been known as 'the Magnanimous' and his daughter, Isabel, as 'the Redemptress'.
2 The quotation comes from Mary Wilhelmine Williams, *Dom Pedro the Magnanimous: Second Emperor of Brazil* (Chapel Hill, NC, 1937), quoted in Robert M. Levine and John J. Crocitti, eds, *The Brazil Reader* (Durham, NC, 1999), p. 104.

3 Lilia Moritz Schwarcz, *The Emperor's Beard* (New York, 1998), p. 40.

4 Carlos Magalhães de Azeredo, *Dom Pedro II: Traços da sua Physionomia Moral* (Rio de Janeiro, 1923), p. 12.

5 Carlos Tasso de Saxe-Coburgo e Bragança, *Dom Pedro II na Alemanha: Uma amizade tradicional* (São Paulo, 2014), p. 12.

6 Quoted in Roderick J. Barman, *Citizen Emperor: Pedro II and the Making of Brazil, 1825–91* (Stanford, CA, 1999), p. 176.

7 Ibid., p. 112.

8 Ibid., p. 82.

9 Quoted in Saxe-Coburgo e Bragança, *Dom Pedro II na Alemanha*, p. 12.

10 Gilberto Freyre, *The Mansions and the Shanties: The Making of Modern Brazil* (New York, 1963), p. 356.

11 Roderick J. Barman, *Princess Isabel of Brazil* (Wilmington, DE, 2002), p. 240.

12 Quoted ibid., pp. 183–4.

13 Quoted ibid., p. 249.

14 Royal Archives VIC/MAIN/QVJ (W), 2 April 1891.

15 Schwarcz, *The Emperor's Beard*, pp. 13, 14.

16 Saxe-Coburgo e Bragança, *Dom Pedro II na Alemanha*, p. 11.

17 Schwarcz, *The Emperor's Beard*, p. 354.

18 Emília Viotti da Costa, *Da monarquia à república*, 7th edn (São Paulo, 1998).

19 Schwarcz, *The Emperor's Beard*, p. 355.

20 From an article by Humberto de Campos in *A Semana* (September 1922), quoted in Schwarcz, *The Emperor's Beard*, p. 361. The reference is to Shakespeare's *Richard II* (King Henry IV was the first cousin, not the brother, of Richard).

BIBLIOGRAPHY

The works listed here are those that have been cited in the References.

A.P.F., *Parallelo de Augusto Cesar e de Dom José o Magnanimo Rey do Portugal* (Lisbon, 1775)

Adamson, John, ed., *The Princely Courts of Europe* (London, 1999)

Alexandre, Valentim, *Os Sentidos do Império: questão nacional e questão colonial na crise do antigo regime* (Porto, 1993)

Alves, Ana Maria, 'A etiqueta de corte no período Manuelino', *Nova História*, I (1984), pp. 5–26

——, *Iconologia do poder real no período Manuelino* (Lisbon, 1985)

Andersen, Hans Christian, *A Visit to Portugal, 1866*, trans. Grace Thornton (London, 1972)

Anon., *O Sebastianismo: breve panorama dum mito português* (Lisbon, 1978)

Anon., *Description de la ville de Lisbonne où l'on traite de la cour, de Portugal, de la langue Portuguaise, & ses moeurs, des habitans* (Paris, 1730); Portuguese trans. in Castelo Branco Chaves, *O Portugal de D. Joao V: visto por tres forasteiros* (Lisbon, 1989)

Arruda, Virgílio, *Dom Pedro e Dom Miguel do Brasil ao Ribatejo* (Santarém, 1972)

Baião, António, *Causa de Nulidade de Matrimónio entre a Rainha D. Maria Francisca de Saboya e o Rei Afonso VI* (Coimbra, 1925)

Baillie, Marianne, *Lisbon in the Years 1821, 1822, and 1823*, 2 vols (London, 1824); reprinted in *Women's Travel Writings in Iberia*, ed. José Ruíz Mas (London, 2013), vols. I and II

Baños-Garcia, António, *D. Sebastião Rei de Portugal* (Lisbon, 2004)

Baretti, Joseph, *A Journey from London to Genoa, through England, Portugal, Spain and France*, 2 vols (London, 1770)

Barletta, Vincent, 'Introduction: The Baroque as Conversation-starter', *Journal of Lusophone Studies*, XII (2014), pp. 13–21

Barman, Roderick, *Citizen Emperor: Pedro II and the Making of Brazil, 1825–91* (Stanford, CA, 1999)

——, *Princess Isabel of Brazil* (Wilmington, DE, 2002)

Barreto Feio, José Victorino, *Dom Miguel, ses aventures scandaleuses, ses crimes et son usurpation par un portugais de distinction*, trans. J. B. Mesnard (Paris, 1833)

Bebiano, Rui, *D. João V: poder e espectáculo* (Aveiro, 1987)

Beckford, William, *Italy, with Sketches of Spain and Portugal*, 2 vols (London, 1834)

——, *The Journal of William Beckford in Portugal and Spain, 1787–88*, ed. Boyd Alexander (London, 1954)

Beirão, Caetano, *D. Maria I, 1777–1792* (Lisbon, 1934)

——, ed., *Cartas da Rainha D. Mariana Vitória para a sua família de Espanha* (Lisbon, 1936)

Bell, Aubrey, *Portugal of the Portuguese* (London, 1915)

Benson, A. C., and Viscount Esher, eds, *The Letters of Queen Victoria*, 3 vols (London, 1908)

Bethencourt, Francisco, 'The Unstable Status of Sebastianism', in *Utopia in Portugal, Brazil and Lusophone African Countries*, ed. Francisco Bethencourt (Bern, 2015)

Blakiston, Georgiana, *Lord William Russell and his Wife* (London, 1972)

Blouin, Michel, Sieur des Piquetièrres, *Relation des troubles arrivez dans la cour de Portugal en l'année 1667 & en l'année 1668* (Amsterdam, 1674)

Bombelles, Marquis de, *Journal d'un Ambassadeur de France au Portugal, 1786–1788* (Paris, 1979)

Bonifácio, Maria de Fátima, *D. Maria II*, 2nd edn (Lisbon, 2011)

Braga, Paulo Drummond, *Dom João III* (Lisbon, 2002)

——, *Nas Teias de Salazar: D. Duarte Nuno, entre a esperança e a desilusão* (Lisbon, 2017)

Bragança Cunha, Vicente de, *Eight Centuries of Portuguese Monarchy* (London, 1911)

Brazão, Eduardo, *O Casamento de D. João V* (Lisbon, 1937)

Bromley, William, *Several Years Travel through Portugal, Spain, Italy, Germany, Prussia, Sweden, Denmark and the United Provinces* (London, 1702)

Buckland, C. S., 'Richard Belgrave Hoppner', *English Historical Review*, XXXIX (1924), pp. 373–85

Buescu, Ana Isabel, *Dom João III* (Lisbon, 2005)

Burnet, Gilbert, *History of His Own Time*, 2 vols (London, 1724)

Butz, Helen, 'The Authorship of *The Portugal History* Made Plain', *Papers of the Bibliographical Society of America*, LXXIII/4 (1979), pp. 459–62

[Canning, Lady], *An Authentic Account of Mr Canning's Policy with Respect to the Constitutional Charter* (London, 1830)

Cardim, Pedro, *Cortes e cultura política em Portugal do antigo regime* (Lisbon, 1998)

Cardoso, Eurico Carlos Esteves Lage, *D. Manuel II: O Rei Patriota* (Lisbon, 2003)

Carnarvon, Earl of, *Portugal and Galicia*, 3rd edn (London, 1848)

Carrere, J.B.F., *Voyage en Portugal, et particulièrement à Lisbonne* (Paris, 1798)

Carte, Thomas, *The History of the Revolutions of Portugal, from the foundation of that kingdom to the year MDCLXVII. With letters of Sir Robert Southwell during his embassy there to the Duke of Ormond* (London, 1740)

Carvalho, A. Ayres de, 'Dom João V and the Artists of Papal Rome', in *The Age of the Baroque in Portugal*, ed. Jay A. Levenson (New Haven, CT, 1993), pp. 31–48

Carvalho, Rómulo de, *Relações entre Portugal e a Russia no século XVIII* (Lisbon, 1979)

Castelo Branco, Fernando, *Lisboa Seiscentista* (Lisbon, 1969)

Castelo-Branco, Maria da Conceição Emiliano, 'The Stormy Passage to England of "A queen coming from Far"', *Revista de Estudos Anglo-Portugueses*, XXIII (2014), pp. 129–49

Chantal, Suzanne, *La vie quotidienne au Portugal après le tremblement de terre de Lisbonne de 1755* (Paris, 1965); Portuguese trans. as *A vida quotidiana em Portugal ao tempo do terramoto* (Lisbon, 1965)

Châtelet, Duc de [Pierre Dezoteux de Cormatin], *Voyage du ci-devant duc de Châtelet, en Portugal*, ed. Jean-François, baron de Bourgoing (Paris, 1798)

Chaves, Castelo Branco, *O Portugal de D. João V: visto por tres forasteiros* (Lisbon, 1989)

Cheke, Marcus, *Dictator of Portugal, Marquis of Pombal* (London, 1938)

——, *Carlota Joaquina, Queen of Portugal* (London, 1947)

Clarence-Smith, William, *The Third Portuguese Empire, 1825–1975* (Manchester, 1985)

Clarendon, Earl of, *Clarendon: Selections from The History of the Rebellion and the Life by Himself*, ed. G. Huehns (Oxford, 1978)

Colbatch, John, *An Account of the Court of Portugal under Pedro II* (London, 1700)

Connell, Brian, *Regina v Palmerston* (London, 1962)

Corp, Edward, 'Catherine of Braganza and Cultural Politics', in *Queenship in Britain, 1660–1837*, ed. Clarissa Campbell Orr (Manchester, 2002), pp. 53–73

Corpechot, Lucien, *Memories of Queen Amélie of Portugal* (London, 1915)

Costa, J. P., *D. Manuel, 1495–1521: Um Principe do Renascimento* (Lisbon, 2005)

Costa, Sergio Correa da, *Every Inch a King* (London, 1950)

Costigan, Arthur William, *Sketches of Society and Manners in Portugal*, 2 vols (London, 1787)

Croker, Richard, *Travels through Several Provinces of Spain and Portugal* (London, 1799)

Curto, Diogo Ramada, 'Ritos e ceremónias da monarquia em Portugal (séculos XVI a XVIII)', in Francisco Bethencourt and Diogo Ramada Curto, *A memória da Nação* (Lisbon, 1991), pp. 201–65

Dalrymple, William, *Travels through Spain and Portugal in 1774: with a short account of the Spanish Expedition against Algiers in 1775* (London, 1777)

Davidson, Lillias Campbell, *Catherine of Bragança, Infanta of Portugal and Queen-consort of England* (London, 1908)

Delaforce, Angela, 'Lisbon, "This New Rome": Dom João V of Portugal and Relations between Rome and Lisbon', in *The Age of the Baroque in Portugal*, ed. Jay A. Levenson (New Haven, CT, 1993), pp. 49–80

Disney, A. R., *A History of Portugal and the Portuguese Empire*, 2 vols (Cambridge, 2009)

Domingues, Mário, *D. Maria I e a sua época* (Lisbon, 1972)

——, *D. João V o homem e a sua época* (Lisbon, 1964)

——, *D. João V: conferencias e estudos comemorativos do segundo centenário da sua morte (1750–1950)* (Lisbon, 1952)

Dryden, John, *The Second Part of Absalom and Achitophel: A Poem* (London, 1682)

Dumouriez, Charles François, *Etat présent du Royaume de Portugal en l'année 1766* (Hamburg, 1797)

Dutra, F. A., 'The Wounding of King José: Accident or Assassination Attempt?' *Mediterranean Studies*, VII (1998), pp. 221–9

Eça de Queiroz, José Maria de, *The City and the Mountains*, trans. Roy Campbell (London, 1955)

Elliott, J. H., 'The Spanish Monarchy and the Kingdom of Portugal, 1580–1640', in *Conquest and Coalescence: The Shaping of the State in Early Modern Europe*, ed. Mark Greengrass (London, 1991), pp. 48–67

——, *Richelieu and Olivares* (Cambridge, 1984)

Elogio académico da Senhora D. Maria primeira, recitado por José Bonifácio de Andrada e Silva . . . (Rio de Janeiro, 1857)

Ericeira, Conde de, *História de Portugal restaurado*, ed. António Doria, 4 vols (Porto, 1945)

Erskine, David, ed., *Augustus Hervey's Journal: The Adventures Afloat and Ashore of a Naval Casanova* (London, 2002)

Evelyn, John, *The Diary of John Evelyn*, ed. William Bray (London, 1907)

Fanshawe, Lady, *Memoirs of Lady Fanshawe*, ed. Beatrice Marshall (London, 1905)

Fanshawe, Richard, *Original Letters during his Embassies in Spain and Portugal* (London, 1702)

Ferro, Maria Ines, *Queluz: The Palace and Gardens* (London, 1997)

Feuchtwanger, E., *Albert and Victoria* (London, 2006)

Fisher, Stephen, *The Portugal Trade* (London, 1971)

França, Eduardo d'Oliveira, *O poder real em Portugal e as origens do absolutismo* (São Paulo, 1946)

Francis, A. D., *The Methuens and Portugal* (Cambridge, 1966)

——, *Portugal, 1715–1808* (London, 1985)

Freeland, Alan, 'Imagined Endings: National Catastrophe in the Fiction of Eça de Queiroz', *Portuguese Studies*, xv (1999), pp. 105–18

Freyre, Gilberto, *The Mansions and the Shanties: The Making of Modern Brazil* (New York, 1963)

Gallasch-Hall de Beuvink, Aline, *O Real Teatro de Salvaterra de Magos* (Casal de Cambra, 2016)

Gomes, R. C., *A corte dos Reis de Portugal no final de Idade Media* (Linda-a-Velha, 1995)

Gorani, Giuseppe, *Mémoires pour servir à l'histoire de ma vie (1806–7)* (Milan, 1936); Portuguese trans. as *Portugal: A Corte e o Pais nos anos 1765 a 1767* (Lisbon, 1989)

Greville, Charles, *A Journal of the Reigns of King George IV, King William IV and Queen Victoria*, 8 vols (London, 1888)

Gribble, Francis, *The Royal House of Portugal* (London, 1915)

Guedes, Carmina Correia, *A educação dos príncipes no Paço da Ajuda, 1863–1884*, ed. Isabel Silveira Godinho (Lisbon, 2004)

[Guilleragues, Gabriel-Joseph de La Vergne, Comte de], *Lettres Portugaises* (Paris, 1669); trans. W. R. Bowles as *Letters from a Portuguese Nun to an Officer in the French Army* (London, 1808)

Hermann, Christian, and Jacques Marcadé, *Les royaumes ibériques au xviie siècle* (Liège, 2000)

Hoppner, R. B., Dispatches to Lord Palmerston and Sir George Shee, National Archives, Kew FO 63/371, 63/372, 63/373

Howe, Malcolm, *The Braganza Story* (Lisbon, 1999)

Iams, T. M., 'Braganza Diplomacy in the Crucible of the French Revolution', *Journal of the American Portuguese Society*, xi (1977), pp. 30–40

Jack, Malcolm, *Sintra: A Glorious Eden* (Manchester, 2002)

Jephson, Robert, *Braganza: A Tragedy, Performed at the Theatre Royal in Drury-Lane* (London, 1775)

Joûbert, Joseph, *Dom Carlos 1er, roi de Portugal* (Paris, 1908)

Junot, Laure, *Memoirs of the Duchess D'Abrantès (Madame Junot)*, 8 vols (London, 1831–5)

Kriegel, Abraham, ed., *The Holland House Diaries, 1831–1840* (London, 1977)

Labourdette, Jean-François, *Histoire du Portugal* (Paris, 2000)

La Clède, Nicolas de, *Histoire Générale de Portugal*, 2 vols (Paris, 1735)

Lafitau SJ, Joseph François, *Histoire des découvertes et conquestes des Portugais dans le Nouveau Monde*, 2 vols (Paris, 1733)

Leal de Faria, Ana Maria Homem, 'D. Pedro II, O Pacífico', in *História dos Reis de Portugal*, ed. Manuela Mendonça (Vila do Conde, 2011), vol. II, pp. 265–313

Lima, Oliveira, *Dom João VI no Brasil, 1808–1821* (Rio de Janeiro, 1908)

Link, Henry Frederick, *Travels in Portugal* (London, 1801)

Lodge, Sir Oliver, ed., *The Private Correspondence of Sir Benjamin Keene* (Cambridge, 1933)

Lourenço, Maria Paula Marçal, 'D. Afonso VI, O Vitorioso', in *História dos Reis de Portugal*, ed. Manuela Mendonça (Lisbon, 2011), vol. II, pp. 211–63

Lourenço, Paula, Ana Cristina Pereira and Joana Troni, *Amantes dos Reis de Portugal* (Lisbon, 2008)

Macaulay, Neill, *Dom Pedro: The Struggle for Liberty in Brazil and Portugal, 1798–1834* (Durham, NC, 1986)

Macaulay, Rose, 'Mac-Flecknoe's Father', in *They Went to Portugal* (London, 1946)

Magalhães de Azeredo, Carlos, *Dom Pedro II: Traços da sua Physionomia Moral* (Rio de Janeiro, 1923)

Manchester, A. K., 'The Transfer of the Portuguese Court to Rio de Janeiro', in *Conflict and Continuity in Brazilian Society*, ed. Henry H. Keith and S. F. Edwards (Columbia, SC, 1969), pp. 148–63

Mariz, Pedro de, *Dialogos de Varia Historia em que se referem as vidas dos Reyes de Portugal*, 2 vols (Lisbon, 1806)

Martins, Maria Odete Sequeira, 'D. Manuel, O Patriota', in *História dos Reis de Portugal*, ed. Manuela Mendonça (Vila do Conde, 2011), II, pp. 779–824

Mavor, Elizabeth, ed., *The Captain's Wife: The South American Journals of Maria Graham, 1821–1823* (London, 1993)

Maxwell, Kenneth, *Pombal, Paradox of the Enlightenment* (Cambridge, 1995)

Mélanges d'études portugaises offerts à M. Georges Le Gentil (Lisbon, 1949)

Memórias do Marques de Fronteira e d'Alorna, ed. Ernesto de Campos de Andrada, 5 vols (Coimbra, 1928–32)

Mendonça, Manuela, ed., *História dos Reis de Portugal*, 2 vols (Lisbon, 2011)

Meneses, Avelino de Freitas de, ed., *Portugal da Paz da Restauração ao Ouro do Brasil*, Nova Historia de Portugal, VII (Lisbon, 2001)

Merveilleux, Charles Frédéric de, 'Memórias instrutivas sobre Portugal', in *O Portugal de João V visto por três forasteiros*, trans. Castelo Branco Chaves (Lisbon, 1983), pp. 129–230

Miller, S. J., *Portugal and Rome: An Aspect of the Catholic Enlightenment* (Rome, 1978)

Mónica, Maria Filomena, ed., *Correspondência entre D. Pedro V e seu tio o príncipe Alberto* (Lisbon, 2000)

Monteiro, Nuno Gonçalo, 'Seventeenth- and Eighteenth-century Portuguese Nobilities in the European Context: A Historiographical Overview', *E-Journal of Portuguese History*, I (2003), pp. 1–17

Mota Gomes, Marleide da, and Miguel Chalub, 'Dom Pedro I of Brazil and IV of Portugal: Epilepsy and Peculiar Behavior', *Arquivos de Neuro-Psiquiatria*, LXV (2007), pp. 710–15

Murphy, James, *Travels in Portugal in 1789 and 1790* (London, 1795)

Nery, Julia, *Infantas de Portugal* (Lisbon, 1998)

Newitt, Malyn, *Portugal in European and World History* (London, 2009)

——, and Martin Robson, eds, *Lord Beresford and the British Intervention in Portugal, 1807–1820* (Lisbon, 2004)

Nunes, Teresa Maria Sousa, 'D. Carlos, O Diplomata', in *História dos Reis de Portugal*, ed. Manuela Mendonça (Vila do Conde, 2011), vol. II, pp. 731–78

Oliveira, António de, 'Levantamentos populares do Algarve em 1637–1638', *Revista Portuguesa de História*, XX (1983), pp. 1–98

Oliveira Ramos, Luís de, *D. Maria I* (Lisbon, 2010)

Pepys, Samuel, *The Diaries of Samuel Pepys*, ed. Robert Latham and William Matthews, 11 vols (London, 1970–83)

Pereira, Ana Cristina Duarte, *Princesas e Infantas de Portugal (1640–1736)* (Lisbon, 2008)

Pereira dos Reis, António, *A Letter to Joseph Hume Esq MP upon the late Debate on Portugal in the British House of Commons by an Anglo-Lusitanian* (London, 1847)

Personagens Portuguesas do seculo XVII (Lisbon, 1942)

Policarpo, Fernando, 'D. Maria II, A Educadora', in *História dos Reis de Portugal*, ed. Manuela Mendonça (Vila do Conde, 2011), vol. II, pp. 589–634

Prestage, Edgar, *Informes de Francisco Lanier sobre Francisco de Lucena e a corte de D. João IV* (Coimbra, 1931)

——, 'The Treaties of 1642, 1654, and 1661', in *Chapters in Anglo-Portuguese Relations*, ed. Edgar Prestage (Watford, 1935)

——, *Memórias sobre Portugal no reinado de D. Pedro II* (Lisbon, 1935)

Prior, James, *Voyage along the Eastern Coast of Africa . . . in the Nisus Frigate* (London, 1819)

Raposo, Hipólito, *Dona Luísa de Gusmão* (Lisbon, 1947)

Raynal, Abbé Guillaume-Thomas, *Histoire philosophique et politique des établissemens et du commerce des Européens dans les deux Indes* (Amsterdam and The Hague, 1773–4)

Révah, I. S., *Le Cardinal de Richelieu et la Restauration du Portugal* (Lisbon, 1950)

Ribeiro da Silva, Francisco, 'D. João IV, O Restaurador', in *História dos Reis de Portugal*, ed. Manuela Mendonça (Vila do Conde, 2011), vol. II, pp. 163–209

Ribeiro de Menseses, Filipe, *Afonso Costa* (London, 2010)

Roberts, Jenifer, *The Madness of Queen Maria* (Chippenham, 2009)

Rodrigues, Ana Maria, ed., *D. João VI e o seu tempo*, Comissão Nacional para a Comemorações dos Descobrimentos Portugueses (Lisbon, 1999)

Ruivo, Mário, 'D. Carlos de Bragança, naturalista e oceanógrafo', *Oceanos*
(April 1992), pp. 102–11
Saraiva, José Hermano, *História concisa de Portugal*, 19th edn (Lisbon, 1998)
Saramago, José, *Baltasar and Blimunda*, trans. Giovanni Pontiero (London, 1998)
Saxe-Coburgo e Bragança, Carlos Tasso de, *Dom Pedro II na Alemanha: Uma
amizade tradicional* (São Paulo, 2014)
Schultz, Kirsten, *Tropical Versailles* (London, 2001)
Schwarcz, Lilia Moritz, *The Emperor's Beard* (New York, 1998)
Serrão, Joaquim Verissimo, *História de Portugal*, 18 vols (Lisbon, 1977–2010)
Silva e Souza, Camillo Aureliano da, *A anti-catastrophe, história d'elrei
D. Affonso 6.º de Portugal* (Porto, 1845)
Silva Lopes, João Batista da, *História do cativeiro dos prezos d'Estado na Torre
de S. Julião da Barra de Lisboa*, 4 vols (Lisbon, 1833–4)
Smith [Athelstane], John, *Memoirs of the Marquis of Pombal with Extracts from
his Writings*, 2 vols (London, 1843)
Sousa Rebelo, Luís de, 'The Idea of Kingship in the Chronicles of Fernão
Lopes', in *Medieval and Renaissance Studies on Spain and Portugal in
Honour of P. E. Russell*, ed. F. W. Hodcroft et al. (Oxford, 1981),
pp. 167–79
——, 'Oliveira Martins: The Spectres in his Historiography', *Portuguese
Studies*, XX (2004), pp. 108–22
Stephens, Philadelphia, 'Account of the Royal Visit to Marinha Grande',
in Jenifer Roberts, *The Madness of Queen Maria* (Chippenham, 2009),
pp. 145–58
Subrahmanyam, Sanjay, *The Career and Legend of Vasco da Gama*
(Cambridge, 1997)
Temperley, Harold, *The Foreign Policy of Canning, 1822–1827* (London, 1925)
Thomas, Gertrude Z., *Richer than Spices* (New York, 1965)
Twiss, Richard, *Travels through Spain and Portugal in 1772 and 1773*
(London, 1775)
Valente, Vasco Pulido, *Os militares e a política (1820–1856)* (Lisbon, 1999)
Ventura, António, 'D. Pedro V, O Esperançoso', in *História dos Reis de
Portugal*, ed. Manuela Mendonça (Vila do Conde, 2011), vol. II, pp.
635–81
——, 'D. Luís, O Popular', in *História dos Reis de Portugal*, ed. Manuela
Mendonça (Lisbon, 2011), vol. II, pp. 683–729
Verney, Frances Parthenope, and Margaret M. Verney, eds, *Memoirs of the
Verney Family during the Seventeenth Century*, 3rd edn, 2 vols (London,
1925)
Vertot, Abbé, *The History of the Revolutions of Portugal*, 5th edn (London, 1754)
Vicente, Ana, 'A Rainha de D. Maria I e a Rainha de D. Maria II – na visão
de autores/historiadores ingleses', in *Actas do I Congresso Internacional de
Estudos Anglo-Portugueses* (Lisbon, 2001), pp. 77–86
Vicente, Maria da Graça, 'D. Miguel, O Rei Absoluto', in *História dos Reis de
Portugal*, ed. Manuela Mendonça (Vila do Conde, 2011), II, pp. 541–87
Victoria, Queen, *Diaries*, Royal Archives, Windsor VIC/MAIN/QVJ (W), available
online at www.queenvictoriasjournals.org
Viotti da Costa, Emília, *Da monarquia à república*, 7th edn (São Paulo, 1998)
Walker, Timothy, *Doctors, Folk Medicine and the Inquisition* (Leiden, 2005)

Webster, Charles, *The Foreign Policy of Palmerston*, 2 vols (London, 1951)

Wellington Papers, Southampton University, WP 1/519 Beresford to Wellington, 22 September 1816

Wheeler, Douglas, 'The Portuguese Revolution of 1910', *Journal of Modern History*, XLIV (1972), pp. 172–94

——, *Republican Portugal: A Political History, 1910–1926* (Madison, WI, 1978)

White, G. F., *A Century of Spain and Portugal, 1788–1898* (London, 1909)

Wilcken, Patrick, *Empire Adrift: The Portuguese Court in Rio de Janeiro, 1808–1821* (London, 2004)

Wilhelmsen, Alexandra, 'Maria Teresa of Braganza: Portuguese Princess of Beira, Spanish Infanta, Wife of the Pretender Carlos v', *Mediterranean Studies*, VI (1996), pp. 79–106

Williams, Mary Wilhelmine, *Dom Pedro the Magnanimous: Second Emperor of Brazil* (Chapel Hill, NC, 1937)

Wraxall, Nathaniel, *Historical Memoirs of My Own Time*, 3rd edn (London, 1818)

Young, George, *Portugal Old and New* (Oxford, 1917)

ACKNOWLEDGEMENTS

I would like to thank Marilla Macgregor, Elizabeth Mancke and Joan Newitt for reading and commenting on individual chapters in this book. I would also like to acknowledge the help and advice given to me by Maria Fernanda Allen, Richard Correll, Malcolm Howe and Abdoolkarim Vakil.

PHOTO ACKNOWLEDGEMENTS

The author and publishers wish to express their thanks to the following sources of illustrative material and/or permission to reproduce it. Some locations are also supplied here for reasons of brevity.

From Juan Alvarez de Colmenar, *Beschryving van Spanjen en Portugal* (Leiden, 1707): p. 134; photo Archivo Municipal de Lisboa: p. 268; from *L'Assiette au Beurre* (1905): p. 280; Biblioteca Nacional de Portugal, Lisbon: p. 157; Biblioteca da Universidade de Coimbra: p. 117; from William Bradford, *Sketches of the Country, Character, and Costume, in Portugal and Spain* (London, 1809): p. 129; Château de Versailles: p. 147; Government Art Collection, London: p. 93; from *Harper's Weekly* (1889): p. 318; from Nicolas de Larmessin, *Les Augustes Représentations de Tous les Rois de France* . . . (Paris, 1690): p. 101; photos Library of Congress, Washington, DC: pp. 289, 318; Metropolitan Museum of Art (Open Access): pp. 112, 258; Museo Nacional del Prado, Madrid: p. 264; Museu Imperial, Petrópolis: pp. 248, 301; Museu Militar, Lisbon: p. 75; Museu Municipal do Porto: pp. 220, 245; Museu Nacional de Arte Antiga, Lisbon: pp. 32, 154; photos Museu Nacional de Boas Artes, Rio de Janeiro: pp. 184, 203; Museu Nacional dos Coches, Lisbon: p. 44, 108 (top), 141, 165; Museu Paulista, University of São Paulo: p. 205; National Portrait Gallery, London: p. 88; photo New York Public Library: p. 134; photos Joan Newitt: pp. 56, 68, 132, 144, 187; from *O Ocidente: revista ilustrada de Portugal e do estrangeiro* (1880): p. 277; Palácio Nacional de Ajuda, Lisbon: pp. 128, 256; Palácio das Necessidades, Lisbon: p. 138; Palácio Pimenta, Lisbon: pp. 28, 139; Palácio de Queluz: pp. 160, 178; Paço de Vila Viçosa: pp. 78, 97, 217; Pinacoteca do Estado de São Paulo, São Paulo: p. 200; photo Rijksmuseum, Amsterdam, reproduced by kind permission: p. 105; Royal Collection: pp. 240, 253; from William Salmon, *Polygrafice* . . . (London, 1685): p. 91; photo Leiloeira São Domingos: p. 222; State Hermitage Museum, St Petersburg: pp. 150, 171.

them or their use of the work), and share alike: if readers alter, transform, or build upon this image, they may distribute the resulting work only under the same or similar license to this one.

INDEX

Page numbers in *italics* indicate illustrations